AMERICAN GODDESS

COLE JAMES

Dedication

I dedicate this book to my five children—my greatest pride and joy.

Throughout the development of this novel, I reached out to my adult children, asking for help with proofreading, feedback, and remarks. Unfortunately for me, those requests went unanswered. It seemed a stretch for them to picture their father as a fictional novelist, and so, despite their promises, real support never came.

Still, a heartfelt shout-out to all of them. Whether they believed in the story or not, they inspired me to finish it—on my own.

To my beloved sister who promised to read my manuscript a thousand times, I ask, please read the book.

Acknowledgments

I'd like to acknowledge my sleep disorder for keeping me wide awake almost every night, into the early hours of the morning and, in its own way, encouraged me to develop this story and finally put all those images into words.

Big shout-out to all my family. You were all part of this journey, whether you knew it or not

About the Author

As an avid reader and enthusiast of over a hundred fiction thrillers, Cole James was inspired to embark on a personal mission: to create, develop, and write his own fictional story. Twice divorced and a father of five—three adults and two minors—Cole balanced his life as a full-time financial advisor, devoted father, martial arts enthusiast, and personal fitness coach. His journey into writing began during a period of sleepless nights, which he transformed into self-storytelling sessions that eventually evolved into full-fledged book writing.

Chapter One
Abigail Rachel Jameson

At sixteen, Abigail Rachel Jameson was nearly fully grown. She stood at an impressive five feet eleven inches—and was still growing. Naturally slim, with deep sea-blue eyes, ash-blonde hair, thin blonde eyebrows, and high cheekbones, she had full lips and the most stunning, straight white teeth. Her smile didn't just light up her own face; it illuminated the person she was smiling at. To call her "drop-dead gorgeous" would be an understatement. She was simply perfect.

Abigail, or Abby as everyone called her, embodied both elegance and natural beauty. Knowing a girl like Abby—but feeling too intimidated to approach her—was torment. The dream was in the imagination, but the reality of seeing her, hearing her, and sitting behind her in class was the nightmare of every hopeful young boy in her school.

Beyond her beauty, Abby was intelligent, charming, and gifted with language skills. She was also athletic, playing as a key member of the school's varsity volleyball team. Born and raised in Texas, she was a true "Southern Gal," as her parents and family liked to call her. Her younger sister, Katherine, was just as stunning and would one day grow up to be as beautiful as Abby. The family lived on a cattle and horse ranch in southern Texas, roughly an hour's drive from the nearest city, where Abby and Katherine attended school.

Abby frequently traveled out of state for volleyball games, often drawing large crowds wherever her team played. With that came unwanted attention—macho wolf whistles, lame pickup lines, and immature antics—but she paid no mind to any of it. Abby was focused on her objective: winning. As team captain, she kept her teammates motivated, offering words of encouragement, pulling them into huddles, and leading their team chants.

One of the highlights of her young career came when her team played a match at Madison Square Garden, the legendary home of the New York Knicks. Playing there was a once-in-a-lifetime opportunity, especially at such a young age. Every time Abby touched the ball or served; the crowd erupted in cheers. The spotlight, the commentator, and the cameras were all on her, but she remained as cool as a snowman in the Antarctic. She delivered a flawless game and led her team to victory. By the time the final whistle blew, the entire stadium was on its feet in a standing ovation. Before the team could even leave the court, a long line had already formed for autographs. That night at the Garden would remain one of the most unforgettable moments of her life.

Back home in Texas, the peace of the family ranch was interrupted one weekend when a convoy of cars pulled up unexpectedly. Abby's father, uncle, and three of her older male cousins wasted no time in approaching the lead vehicle, ready to intercept any trespassers. This was a private family gathering, and uninvited guests weren't welcome. Lunch was nearly ready, but the girls were still at the stables. Abby, Katherine, and their two female cousins had been brushing the horses after a short ride when they noticed the cars. Curious, they quickly made their way toward the long outdoor table set up for the occasion.

Two men from the convoy stepped out cautiously and approached the family.

"Howdy!" greeted the man leading the group.

Silence.

The family stood shoulder to shoulder in a line-back formation, staring him down. One of Abby's cousins idly chewed on a hay strand while the rest stood with arms on their hips, scrutinizing the visitors.

The man stepped forward, extending his hand. "Howdy! My name is Robert Uttering, sir." He was addressing Rick, Abby's muscular, broad-shouldered cousin.

Rick stepped aside to reveal Frank, Abby's father, standing directly behind him.

"Not only are you trespassing on my property and scaring my horses," Frank said in his thick Southern drawl, "but you're also interrupting my family time. Both are sacred to me and mine. A man can get himself shot for less around these parts."

Robert raised his hands in a gesture of peace. "I mean no disrespect, sir. Not to you, your family, or your horses. I come on a mission. It took us over two days to find your ranch."

"State your case and be off with you," Frank ordered.

"If I may sit down for a few moments with you and your wife, sir, I'll state my case and then be on my way."

By this time, Abby's mother, Anne, had joined the group. She stood beside her husband as Robert continued.

"Well, absolutely, dear," Anne said warmly. "And you're all welcome to join us for lunch."

"Thank you, ma'am. I won't lie—I'm famished, and so is my team."

"Say no more, young man," Anne replied, gesturing toward the house. "Come, let's discuss the purpose of your visit."

Anne led the way into the lounge area, with Frank making up the tail and Robert in between.

As they sat down, Frank offered Robert a drink, and he politely accepted a glass of water. Robert explained the reason for his visit, admitting that his journey to the ranch was unusual. He confessed that he had come more out of desperation than professionalism.

After five minutes, Abby was called into the house.

"Abby, this is Mr. Robert Uttering from New York," Anne Jameson said.

"Please, call me Robert," he interjected. "There's no need to be formal," he added, smiling like a wiry fox that had just found the chicken coop.

Frank said nothing, just stood there, staring at the man.

"Robert, this is our daughter, Abby," Anne continued.

Robert turned his attention to the young girl. "Pleased to meet you, Abby. I have briefly explained my unexpected—but hopefully not unwelcome—visit to your parents. You see, I drove down from New York rather than flew because I wanted to discuss the possibility of hiring you.

"I run the biggest and most well-known modeling agency in the world—not just in the United States, but globally. We represent the highest-paid top models in the industry. One of our most reliable and talented scouts spotted you playing volleyball. They took pictures, sent them to me, and here I am.

"I rarely travel to meet potential models, but I was compelled to make this trip personally. And now, standing in front of you, I realize that the pictures, descriptions, and appraisals were all understated. I am completely overwhelmed and in total awe. In all my years in the modeling industry, working with girls from all over the world, I have never encountered anyone like you.

"My original plan was to evaluate you, return to New York, and consider whether I wanted to work with you. But that's out the window now. This has never happened before. My secretary is drafting a modeling contract as we speak—just for you. I want you to work with us. You can name your rate, decide how much you want to be paid per assignment. I am not leaving here, not leaving Texas, not leaving this ranch, without a positive answer from you and your parents."

Finally, Abby thought to herself. He stopped talking.

She looked at her mom, then her dad, then back at her mom. The two were very close, so she waited for her mother to speak first.

"Well, don't look at me, hon," Anne said. "What do you think of what Mr.—I mean, what Robert just said?"

Abby hesitated. "I never thought about it before. I want to graduate high school, go to college, and become a veterinarian. I want to take care of our horses and the neighbors' animals. I've never considered being a fashion model. I don't even know how much they get paid."

"Well, I don't know about this," Frank chimed in. "It's too much, too soon. We're just simple folks, minding our own business, running our ranch, looking after our horses. We don't know squat about this fashion business."

"Please, I understand this is a lot to process," Robert said. "It's sudden and overwhelming, and I don't expect you to decide right now. I have the contract here—please take a copy, review it, make any changes you want, and call me when you're ready. I'll be in town. If you'll allow me, I'll go to my car and get the typed contract—"

"Oh, of course, certainly," Anne said.

Abby just stood there, speechless. She turned to her mom, then her dad, then back to her mom again.

"Well, hon, this could pay your college tuition if you decide to take the offer," Anne said. "You wouldn't have to quit school. You could graduate at your own pace. And if you're successful, you could even pay for your sister's tuition. Wouldn't that be nice?"

"Are you saying I should become a fashion model, Mom?" Abby asked with an amused grin. "The new face of Victoria's Secret?"

"Oh, stop that!" Frank snapped. He stood up and stormed out of the room, muttering under his breath. "Seeing my daughter in all those skimpy clothes… she'll catch a cold wearing just that. The thought of everybody seeing her like that, half-naked… it's just plain stupid."

Robert re-entered the room, looking back at Frank as they crossed paths. He heard the muttering and raised an eyebrow.

"What was that all about?" Robert asked, puzzled.

"Oh, don't mind him," Anne said with a gentle smile. "This is all up to Abby. She needs time to think it over, to digest your offer, to imagine what it would mean for her… and for us. This isn't a decision we can make in a single conversation. I suggest you return to New York, and once we've had a chance to discuss it as a family, we'll be in touch. Or rather, Abby will."

"I'm staying at the San Antonio Marriott Rivercenter, and I'm not leaving until we sign a contract," Robert insisted. "I don't have anywhere urgent to be. Take your time—I'm not going anywhere."

"I ain't going anywhere," Abby corrected him. Then she sighed. "Oh, never mind. Robert, I'm deeply flattered by everything you've said. It hasn't fully sunk in yet, but I'm sure it will once you leave. I'd also like to talk it over with my sister and my cousins. It's a family thing with us Southerners."

"Like I said, take your time," Robert replied. "This is a big step, but I assure you, you won't regret saying yes. Here's the contract— please feel free to consult legal counsel. That's standard procedure."

"Thank you, Robert," Anne said.

"Thank you," Abby echoed.

"Robert, would you care for a drink?" Anne continued. "Please join us on the patio. This is close family time, but you won't be intruding. You're welcome to invite your colleagues in, too."

Robert politely declined the offer. "Oh, that is very kind of you, but we'd best be getting back to the city. The fashion world never sleeps. Take your eyes off the ball for one second, and you're history."

"Sounds like you played volleyball," Abby quipped. "That's exactly what happens in volleyball. Take your eyes off the ball, and wham! You're down! Well, I must go. Thank you again—I'm truly flattered."

Abby left her mom to show Robert out of the house and to his car, where his colleagues were waiting.

Did he really have to travel out here in a convoy of four cars? All SUVs, like the FBI or Secret Service? Jeez, she thought. Some people think they're so important.

"Bye, Robert," she said as his car backed up and made a U-turn.

He rolled down his window and called out, "I'm at the Marriott downtown. I'm not going anywhere."

The convoy pulled out and drove away.

Chapter Two
Abby

Abby ran out to the stables in search of her sister and cousins. She found them cleaning out the stalls, hauling buckets full of horse waste and unconsumed hay. One of the horses had already been led out to the field behind the stables to stretch its legs. Abby loved coming down to the stables—taking care of the horses, talking to them, and telling them she would be their doctor one day. She had made up her mind: she wanted to be a veterinarian.

"So, what did they want with you? You on the FBI's Most Wanted list?" joked her cousin Rebecca, who was a year older than Abby.

"I think she's involved in espionage, and now they've caught up with her," added her other cousin, Ashley, Rebecca's younger sister. Ashley was the same age as Katherine—fourteen.

"Come on, Abby, don't be so secretive," said Katherine impatiently, tugging at her sister's arm. "What did they want? Are you in trouble?"

Abby shook her head, moving toward the next stall and running a hand over the horse's head. "First of all, that was not the FBI, the Secret Service, or even the sheriff, for that matter. And second— aren't y'all just a little too curious? Ever heard the saying... curiosity killed the cat?"

"And satisfaction brought it back. Grab her arms, pull her down into the hay!" Rebecca ordered the younger girls. "She's not getting away with this. We'll bury her in the hay until she tells us."

The three girls lunged at Abby, grabbing her arms and dragging her toward the towering haystack in the corner of the barn.

"Okay, okay!" shrieked Abby. "Let go, and I'll tell y'all."

The girls let go, watching her with curious eyes.

Abby took a deep breath, then grinned. "That, my dear friends, was none other than Mr. Robert Uttering, director of the world's biggest and most famous modeling agency."

"Robert who?" uttered Rebecca. "Never heard of him. What's he doing driving around in a Secret Service car with all those agents if he doesn't work for the government or isn't a sheriff?"

"Those were not Secret Service cars... oh, never mind! Robert Uttering owns a fashion modeling agency and wants me to be his new recruit. How about that?" She pointed at Ashley. "You can do my hair." Then at Rebecca. "And you can do my makeup." Finally, she turned to Katherine, smirking. "And you, little sis, can be my manager. How about that? Huh? Am I gonna be world-famous or what?"

"So what did you say? I know Dad is just gonna freak," said Katherine.

"Well, I asked Mom what she thought. She encouraged me to go for it. I'm still a little hesitant but excited at the prospect. I think I'm gonna do it," replied Abby.

The four girls were thrilled at the idea of Abby becoming a fashion model—traveling the world, staying in plush hotels, meeting famous people. They joked about how many Instagram followers she would have and asked if she was seriously going to hire them. They tossed hay at each other, giddy with excitement at the thought of knowing someone famous, maybe even being invited to glamorous parties. Who knew? Maybe they'd even meet famous actors or date a celebrity.

But as much as her cousins were excited for her, Abby wasn't sure this was what she wanted. She had already mapped out her future—she was going to be a horse doctor, specializing in equine care. She didn't crave fame, extravagant parties, or a life in the spotlight.

That evening at dinner, Frank didn't wait long to react. As soon as everyone was seated, he exploded.

"You're not gonna be a Victoria's Secret model, wearing those secret things—those, those… whatever you call them! No daughter of mine is going on TV not wearing anything, showing off her body for those people!"

Frank was red in the face, banging his fist on the table as he shouted at Anne. "You tear up those papers! You hear me? Tear them up! And I don't want to see that Bobby Utterer—or whatever his name is—back here in my house again!" He stomped out of the dining room, walked to the patio, then down the steps and out into the field.

Anne smiled at the girls, mocking Frank's "Secret People, Secret Clothes" comment.

"Secret things, he called them," Katherine added, shaking her head.

The three girls giggled quietly, not wanting Frank to hear them.

"Well, at least he didn't wait till everyone forgot the story before freaking out," Abby said, completely unfazed by her father's reaction.

"I guess we'd better include 'no secret things' for you to model," Anne joked.

They all laughed.

After a moment, Abby turned to her mom, her voice more serious this time. "So, you think I should go, Mom? Be a fashion model? Quit school, travel around the world?"

"Well, honey, this is a once-in-a-lifetime opportunity. School isn't going anywhere. There's no age limit for graduating high school or getting a college degree. This… this right here is a chance to explore new horizons, to step into a world most people only dream of. And when you've had enough, you can come back with an encyclopedia of adventures and experiences."

"What if it doesn't work, Mom? What if I hate it? What if I'm lonely and get depressed? I've never been anywhere without you, Dad, and Katherine. I'm not sure I'll like all the attention, the fame, the intrusion into my life."

Anne reached across the table and squeezed Abby's hand. "Sleep on it, honey. Talk it over with your sister tonight. But I say go for it! This could be your fate, your destiny. I'm thrilled and excited for you. And no matter what happens, we'll always be here for you. You'll never know if this is right for you unless you try. And if you don't like it, you can quit. But at least try it first."

She stood up, pushing her chair back. "I'd better go look for your dad and reassure him. No 'Secret Things.'"

They all laughed.

The girls finished their dinner and went up to bed to chat. They talked late into the night, excitedly naming famous people they had seen on television and in magazines, wondering if Abby would cross paths with them during her travels and future modeling assignments. The more they discussed the fashion world—catwalk shows, Victoria's Secret's world-famous Fashion Show, and high-profile events—the more Abby warmed to the idea of becoming a model.

What once felt like unfamiliar, intimidating territory now seemed like an exciting adventure.

Still, she wanted more reassurance from her mother before making her final decision. She would sleep on it before accepting or rejecting Robert Uttering's offer.

Katherine, however, was already sold on the idea. She imagined herself as Abby's manager and caretaker, thrilled at the thought of being part of her sister's glamorous new life. Just wait until Abby told her friends—wait until she told the whole school!

The Next Morning

The next morning, Abby went downstairs to the kitchen and found Frank and Anne sitting at the table, sipping coffee. Anne looked up at her daughter, giving her a discreet smile and a wink.

Abby walked around to kiss her father on the cheek, then sat down without saying a word.

"Sleep well last night?" Frank asked softly, without lifting his head.

"Hmm, okay, I guess," Abby muttered as she poured cereal into her bowl and added a little milk. "Considering Katherine jumped into my bed and I was squashed all night."

Her father chuckled. "Well, your mom and I stayed up half the night talking about this modeling thing. As you know, I had—well, still have—some concerns about you quitting school so suddenly and moving all the way to New York, especially since you don't have any family there. But…" He paused, hesitating. "Your mother managed to convince me that this is a golden opportunity for you and that you should seize it—grab it with both hands—because it may never come around again."

He looked at Abby with a soft smile. "Okay, that's what we decided. It took some convincing, though. You know how stubborn I can be—sometimes. Not always, but sometimes. It wasn't easy. But we'll countersign the contract if you really want to go for it."

"Oh, Daddy, you're the best!" Abby shrieked. She rushed around the table, hugging him tightly and kissing his cheek a hundred times before moving to her mom and doing the same. "You're both the best! Thank you for letting me go. And if it doesn't work out, I can always come back."

Just then, Katherine walked into the kitchen, rubbing her tired eyes and looking confused. She sat down at the table, glancing between them.

"Did I miss something?" she asked, still half asleep. "What's all the excitement about? Somebody win the jackpot?"

"Yep, me! I did!" Abby grinned. "I'm going to New York! Mom convinced Dad to let me go! Isn't that awesome?"

"Wow! Dad, you're the best. Mom's just so hard to disagree with sometimes," Katherine added, looking directly at her mother with a knowing smirk. She offered the slightest wink and a half-grin.

"I'm not always the bad guy," Anne said with a playful smile.

They all laughed loudly.

Chapter Three
Abby

That afternoon, Robert and his troop of "Secret Service" agents arrived at the ranch to discuss certain reservations and modifications to the modeling contract on offer to Abby.

One of the key reservations insisted upon by Anne was a clause prohibiting Abby from participating in the Victoria's Secret Lingerie Show. Her father had insisted on that clause, as he didn't want the whole world to see his daughter in her underwear.

There were other clauses that included medical insurance coverage, accommodation, travel, and family tickets for any and all shows when requested. Access to their daughter at all times—no restrictions. Remuneration—how and when she would be paid. Modeling rates, legal recourse to be provided in all instances, and other minor additions to the contract.

Anne also insisted that this was a pre-contract and that the final contract would be signed upon review by the family attorney. Needless to say, Robert agreed to everything that was discussed. Anne signed, as Abby was still a minor and needed parental approval. Then Frank and Abby signed. Katherine wanted to sign but was politely told that her signature was not necessary.

Robert stood, shaking hands with both parents.

"Thank you for your trust in me and my agency. We'll take good care of your daughter. I'll make her the most sought-after, best-paid, most recognizable face, person, and model in the world."

Anne smiled, but Frank gave a serious look.

"Well, Robert, my wife here will first kill me, then she'll hunt you down to the furthest, tiniest asteroid in the entire universe, if anything happens to my daughter. You better take good care of my baby girl."

Robert chuckled, nodding in understanding. He turned to leave, heading straight for the door. He was off to the airport, back to New York, where his presence was desperately needed. His time in Texas had run past the scheduled time, and his absence had caused some serious chaos in the office.

But it had all been worth it.

Bingo! This was the jackpot!

In two weeks, Abby would pack her bags and head for New York, where Robert and his team would be waiting. She needed time to say goodbye to her friends, her cousins, and her family. She knew it would be hard, but once she made up her mind, there was no turning back—no matter what.

Chapter Four
Isabella Katherine Reyes

"Be good today, my darling," Javier, Isabella's father, had said while she ate her breakfast. "Today, you will have a new car with a new driver to accompany you."

A new car? What did she know or care about cars? A new driver? They all looked the same to her. Stiff, clumsy, boring, robot-like—wearing hand-me-down suits and non-matching ties, with big, off-color shoes that matched only their worn, tired, expressionless faces.

She didn't even look up or acknowledge this new "gift." She barely acknowledged her surroundings or any presence of any kind. It was the same every morning before she left and when she arrived home. Stoic, single-minded aloofness—yet driven by a steely willpower to command her own space. Nothing and nobody could or would determine her agenda and how to execute her tasks, irrespective of how mundane they were.

There was an aura around her that commanded total respect and compliance. The people around her knew better than to interject or act in an unsolicited manner. A simple "good morning" was often met with a cold silence—or sometimes, she would merely respond with, "Really? Good morning for what?"

It would be inaccurate to describe her as surly or bad-tempered. She was strong-minded with a well-defined personal objective, a clear sense of direction, and a level of intelligence that often astounded and embarrassed those in her entourage—embarrassed them, as she, on so many occasions, exposed their limited capacity to comprehend the most basic analogy.

Isabella Katherine Reyes was a very beautiful twelve-year-old girl. Stunningly beautiful, to be more precise. Her ash-blonde hair and cold, deep blue eyes that reflected no emotion and rejected even the slightest affability were her trademark looks. The expression "the eyes are the window to the soul" did not apply to Isabella.

Her eyes were a deep turquoise blue that concealed any emotional expression and left the onlooker bewildered. Her eyes, if anything to go by, dictated her assertiveness and command. For instance, a cold, hard stare was usually followed by a brisk, determined walk or an instant dismissal by ignoring all in her presence.

Isabella often displayed this attitude, as her world—as she so rightly determined—was surrounded by mere incompetent mortals without any sense of reasoning. It was in her character to take the higher ground with everybody. They were all pawns on her chessboard—indispensable and without value except when used to her benefit and in the strategic direction.

Isabella walked out to greet her new car and new driver, who was to accompany her to school, then extra-curricular activities that consumed her everyday schedule. The new car was a brand-new black European model with a white leather interior. She didn't know or care exactly what make or model it was. It was comfortable and functional; that's all she cared about.

The driver, however, caught her attention. Her cold blues flickered a little as she approached. He was new, just like the car. He was interesting—unlike the car. He was young, tall, and very well built, with short light brown hair and green, smiling eyes. *Ex-military,* she thought, but said nothing. It was a refreshing change from the "worn leather" type drivers she was used to. She gave nothing further away.

He opened the rear door for her without greeting her. She looked at him with disdain and entered the backseat opposite the driver. Nothing was said until they arrived at the morning destination—her school.

He exited the car and opened the door for Isabella to exit. She stepped out of the car without acknowledging him or saying anything. He escorted her to the entrance and watched her walk in. Eyes on her, yet aware of everything and everyone in the immediate vicinity. Darting left, right, and straight without really moving his head in any direction. He saw everything and everyone. The slightest movement caught his attention.

He situated himself in a way that enabled him to have a panoramic perspective of the topography while at the same time positioning himself to master the circumstance without too much of an effort.

Isabella walked into the building, and waiting inside the hallway was Carmen—the closest anyone could be called a best friend to Isabella. The two greeted each other with a customary kiss on each cheek before walking to their classroom, where class was about to begin.

Life in the seventh grade didn't impose much of a need for pre-class preparation and seldom, if ever, warranted thoughtful analysis of curricular subject matter. There were mostly girls in the class, even though it was a co-ed school. This was the most elite private school in the region—not just the city, but the entire region.

The parents of all the pupils were high-level politicians or insanely wealthy individuals in the billionaire or multimillionaire bracket. Carmen's father, for example, was the Regional Governor. Isabella's father, on the other hand, was the main campaign contributor for Carmen's father's political ambitions. Not that he did any campaigning, as the voting outcome was a preordained result. Still, elections were required by law, even if no one paid much attention to the rules of the regional or national constitution. So, the Governor called for elections, ran unopposed, and made victory speeches promising change and a better life for his constituents.

More often than not, these speeches were a repeat of the previous victory speech—a blatant copy, word for word. A speech promising an increase in quality of life: new and improved infrastructure, better education, more jobs, enhanced security, etc. None of which were ever carried out, even in the simplest of forms.

The people were not duped, of course, but any dissent was met with a swift, hard rebuke that reminded other potential dissenting voices to quietly resume their daily lives without fuss. The outcome of any clandestine resistance was often openly displayed from overhanging bridges and sometimes even in the town square—on spiked metal fences. To dissent was to commit murder-suicide: murdering one's own close family and relatives, with suicide being the result of one's actions.

The slogan "Be happy" was tied to the very fact of waking up each morning. This was a gift not to be taken for granted, as tomorrow was not promised to anyone. So, wake up, be grateful for what you have, thank God for your life, protect your family, and be happy.

This was the real message in the victory speeches of José Manuel Rodriguez de la Hoya, the Regional Governor of La Ciudad and father of Carmen de la Hoya.

The man had risen from obscurity to a prominent and powerful political position. He was beholden to Isabella's father, Javier. He was never to forget this. He never allowed himself even a second to neglect this factor in his political maneuverings and policy decisions. One slip-up—even if unintentional—led to severe, critical reminders that served as indefinite deterrents.

Nothing was "unintentional" for Javier Carlos Ozabel Reyes. Javier never entertained the concept of context and declared that one should always be the master of their own circumstances. A lapse in judgment, he said, was the renowned source of all wars. A war is declared when one party underestimates the other and embarks on a single-minded, self-gratifying endeavor, provoking a similar response from the opposing party.

To avoid the constant threat of war with every decision or venture, one must take control of their circumstances and carefully consider the consequences. Therefore, all weaknesses, lapses in judgment, absent-mindedness, or lack of thorough planning were met with swift, severe countermeasures.

Punishment.

Punishment, in the eyes of Javier, fit the bill for swift, severe countermeasures. He believed that these immediate reactions would deter laxness and absent-mindedness, whether under his employ or when conducting business with him. He held all accountable to this philosophy, and no one escaped his wrath—not even his immediate family, except maybe for one.

Nothing ever went unpunished. José de la Hoya knew this all too well and made sure he always paid tribute to Javier Reyes.

The two seventh graders walked unhurriedly to their classroom. Carmen chatted nonstop about what she had done over the weekend—shopping with her mom, disputing with her less fortunate cousins, driving across the border into McAllen to the Plaza Mall for ice cream, more shopping, and of course, her horse-jumping lessons on her own personal horse.

Isabella was totally bored with her friend's weekend activities but listened silently, occasionally nodding her head.

"Escoba is such a champion. He's ready—I think we're going to win the next competition," Carmen continued. "He is just so ready; I'm so lucky to have him. I love him. I don't know what I'd do without Escobar. Definitely the love of my life. I miss him. I miss him so much. I wish it was the weekend already so that I could ride him."

Wow, the girl must be brain-dead, thought Isabella.

Escobar! What a name to give a horse! "Dainty Feet" or "Lightning Streak." Hmm, okay, it wasn't a racehorse, but maybe "Jumpin' Jack Horse" or something close would be understandable—but "Escobar"?

Oh my God.

Isabella wanted to scream, but being the good friend she was, she simply mumbled, "Sounds like you two were made for each other. Match in heaven."

"You are so right! No brainer why you're my best friend. You must get your own horse so we can go out riding together on my dad's ranch. We could, you know, have the cook prepare us a picnic and . . . yeah, we could even have a short race."

Carmen chatted excitedly, happy and content that someone understood her love for her horse and that she was not being unreasonable about her horse-riding activities.

Isabella, on the other hand, was thankful that they had reached the classroom and walked in without further commentary.

Ms. Sarah, the English teacher, was writing something on the blackboard. Not only did she teach English literature, but she was from England. This was an international academic establishment— Monterrey International School.

It was an exclusive private school founded by the late Henry Montoya Monterrey and his English wife, Elizabeth-Ann, in the late 1970s. Their goal was to cater to the young children of expats who flocked to Mexico seeking employment in the Mexican oil fields. English was the first and formal language at MIS, with Spanish being a compulsory "elective," and a third language of choice for students from multilingual backgrounds.

When it was established, MIS counted a mere fifty pupils of all ages. Some were interns, with very few day scholars, as parents often worked late, long hours and needed the educational aspect for their offspring considered. Given the current political, cultural, and economic climate, the boarding school was closed indefinitely. Only day-school students were accepted. Furthermore, security arrangements were impossible to ensure, rendering potential boarders high-risk targets for felons.

The girls took their places at their pre-assigned desks located at the front of the class. There were four rows of desks, with four desks in each row. Isabella sat directly behind Carmen in the second row, being the first in the row. The classroom was fairly spacious, with a high five-meter ceiling.

Directly behind the rows of desks were the same number of language "centers," situated in a similar fashion. These language desks were also pre-assigned. It was a fairly large, spacious classroom, and the students didn't need to move through the halls during the day at all—except for science classes that were conducted in labs. For experiments and chemical testing, of course.

"Good morning, class," Ms. Sarah greeted as the students settled in, shuffling through their bags for books, pencils, writing pads—anything to keep them occupied for a few seconds.

"Today, we will start mathematics, so please bring out your textbooks and turn to the workbook exercises section," she said in a calm, distinctly pronounced English accent—London, middle class. "We are going to look at problem-solving, then you will all create your own problems and solve them."

She paused, glancing around the room.

"I will start. A man has four children who each have two children. He marries a woman with two children who each have four children. How many grandchildren do they have? This is a multiplication and addition problem, people."

Isabella, unlike Carmen, didn't need to take out her calculator to find the answer.

"Sixteen, Ms. Sarah," she said in a calm voice.

Ms. Sarah smiled. "Well done, Isabella! Does everybody understand how we get sixteen?" She looked around to see if any students seemed confused. "Now," she continued, "it's your turn. Create your own math problems, solve them, and write everything down. We'll go over them together."

Sitting in this class, surrounded by these clueless kids, was excruciatingly boring for Isabella. She needed to get out, get away from Carmen and Pablo—or whatever the horse's name was.

"Jeez," breathed out Isabella.

Time was going so slow today. She just couldn't wait for the final bell.

"Isabella, is everything alright?" Ms. Sarah asked.

"Yes, Miss Sarah. Could I be excused for a bathroom break, please?" Isabella replied.

"Oh, and me too, Miss! Please!" chimed in Carmen.

"Why not the whole class while we're at it," an exasperated Isabella said sarcastically.

Ms. Sarah, missing the tone entirely, clapped her hands together. "Oh! Good idea. Let's all take a five-minute break."

Isabella thought she was going to die.

After the bathroom break, when everybody had solved their respective mathematical problems, they moved to the back of the class for language studies. There were headphones at each station. They would all study Spanish together, then the third language of choice. They all spoke fluent Spanish, so they basically concentrated on grammar and literature.

Finally, the bell rang, and school was out for the day. This was when the day began for Isabella. Her afternoon was full. No time for jumping around on a horse called Pablo—or whatever its name was. She had real activities.

Isabella hurried out of the class, but not before Miss Sarah shouted out, "Please read Enid Blyton's *Five Go Off to Camp*, chapters one, two, and three, for discussion in class tomorrow."

As Isabella raced toward the entrance—well, technically, the exit, as she was already inside—she heard Carmen running to catch up with her.

"Isa, wait up! What's the hurry? Do you want to come for lunch? I'd like to introduce you to Escoba. I'm sure you'll love him. You'll just love him when you set eyes on him. Come on, Isa, it'll be fun."

"Can't, darlin'. You know my schedule. Kiss Pablo for me. I'll hook up with you and McHorseface another time."

Carmen groaned in frustration. "Escoba! His name's *Escoba*, not Pablo or McWhatever! Oh, Isa, you can be so mean sometimes!"

Isabella reached into her bag, pulled out an apple, and gave it to Carmen.

"Give this to the four-legged little man for me. Okay?" She walked out of the building and toward her waiting car.

New car. New driver. Well, let's see what this greenhorn has in him.

This morning, before leaving for school, he hadn't said anything to her. He looked mute—not saying a word, not opening his mouth, not even to say "Good morning," which was customary. Not only customary but obligatory—under driver protocols.

Isabella mentally ran through the rule list that she had established for all her drivers.

Rule Number One: Say *Good morning* to the Client!

And Isabella was the Client.

Well, it was too late for Rule Number One now; it was 1:45 p.m. School was out for the day.

What was Rule Number Two again? Hmm . . . Okay, well, we can improvise here.

Let's make Rule Number Two: Say *Good afternoon* to the Client!

Isabella smiled to herself—*inwardly*, never outwardly. At least not while she was being watched.

The new driver's eyes followed her as she stepped toward the car. Still—nothing. No greeting. No "Good morning, Miss." No "Good afternoon, Miss."

Not that she wanted to be addressed as *Miss* or anything that formal, but he didn't know that. He didn't know what she wanted. He was new. He *should* have been polite. Should have respected protocol—even if there wasn't an official one.

Isabella didn't offer anything in the way of conversation or acknowledgment of his presence. She didn't even look at him as he stood there with the rear door opened for her. He tried to take her school bag from her as she stepped into the car, but she held onto it.

He closed the door, walked around to the driver's side, got in, and started the car.

Behind them, in her flashy Mercedes-Benz, was Carmen and her driver. These were the only cars allowed to drive right up to the school's main entrance.

Isabella's car slowly pulled away from the curb and rolled down the driveway toward the main street.

"Stop the car!" Isabella ordered the driver. Curious more than anything, she spoke softly but harshly. "Can't you talk?"

He stopped the car in the middle of the driveway, just before reaching street level. He looked down, then slowly turned to face her and shook his head. No movement of the mouth. Sad eyes looked at Isabella as he picked up a small whiteboard and wrote with a felt-tip pen:

"No, I can't speak. I have a medical condition, lost the ability to talk. I'm sorry if that bothers you."

"What's your name anyway?" asked Isabella a little aggressively.

The driver took his whiteboard and wrote his name:

"Ryan."

"Ryan what?" she queried further. "Do you at least have a last name? Where are you from and who hired you?"

Ryan wiped the whiteboard clean and proceeded to answer Isabella's barrage of questions. His full name was Ryan O'Connor. He had no family that he cared about. He was from Cleveland, Ohio, and an ex-Marine. He continued writing, stating that he was honorably discharged from the Marine Corps and that he was recruited by one of his ex-Marine superiors as a favor.

As he continued writing, the car behind them honked impatiently. It was Carmen and her driver.

"Tell them to be patient!" Isabella shouted to her driver. Then, realizing what he had just told her, she got out of her car, walked to the waiting Mercedes behind, and tapped on the driver's window.

"If you ever honk at me again—*ever*—I'll rip out your Adam's apple with my bare hands and feed it to her stupid horse! You hear me?" She looked at Carmen and said calmly, "You and your undercover clown here need to learn patience and respect real fast! You got that?"

Not a word more was said as she walked back to her car. Her driver stood outside, scanning his surroundings—building tops, trees, passing cars, school kids pouring out of the building. His eyes were everywhere, watching attentively.

Isabella got back into the car, and they drove off.

Carmen was in tears, bawling her eyes out that her beloved best friend could treat her that way. She didn't love anybody more than Isabella, so why did she treat her like just one of the other girls? They were special, the two of them. The Elite.

Tears kept flowing as she sat back in her car, and her driver drove her home. She would confront Isabella tomorrow and demand more respect.

Still a little angry, Isabella looked at the driver via the rearview mirror and said, "Can you at least hear me? I don't need to speak in sign language to you, do I?"

Well, of course he could hear; he had demonstrated that already by answering her with his whiteboard and felt-tip pen.

"Of course you can. Silly of me! Okay, do you have a cell phone?"

He nodded.

"Well, write it down on your little speech board. I need to text you the address of where we are going."

He wrote down his number, and Isabella texted him the address via WhatsApp.

"It is a private parking lot downtown. Here's the remote control to enter." She handed him the small black device. "The same remote control will open the door of the private garage."

Isabella sat back in her seat, put her earphones on, and listened to her Russian lessons.

When they got to the parking lot, the driver pressed the remote, and the iron gates opened.

"Drive up to the third floor," she instructed him.

On the third floor, he pressed the remote again, and a garage door opened in the far right corner of the floor. It was a very wide garage that could easily fit three and a half cars.

Inside was an old, beat-up white Chrysler. Its tires were almost worn out, the tinted windows were peeling, and the right-side mirror was broken. The letters "H, S, L, E, R" from "Chrysler" were missing, leaving only "C, R, Y."

"Drive into the garage," she again ordered, but a little more gently this time.

They pulled in and parked her shiny new car next to the old, beat-up one. She looked at him and said, "Wait here until I call you."

She got out of the car, took her gym bag with her, and got into the front seat of the banger.

After what seemed like ages—but was not more than ten minutes—she called for him.

He walked over to the passenger side and stood there. Isabella looked at him with a mixture of amusement and bewilderment.

"Get in and drive, silly," she said.

It was his turn to be perplexed.

"Get in, I'll explain," she added.

He got into the driver's seat, and before he could start the car, she had already texted him the address of where they were going next. After backing out, he closed the garage door with the remote and followed the GPS instructions on his phone.

This was *not* part of the instructions he had received from Isabella's father. This was definitely not part of his driving duties, as outlined by the head of the drivers' pool. He had to decide— refuse and turn back or go along with it.

If he refused, he'd be fired on the spot. Better to play along and take it up with his superiors later.

When he approached Isabella at the passenger side of the banger before driving out, he noticed that she had changed her clothes. She was no longer wearing her school uniform but was now dressed in a black tracksuit with white sneakers. No visible or noticeable brand name on any of the clothes she was wearing.

Her hair was tied back in a ponytail, and she wore a baseball cap to cover her long, beautiful blonde hair.

As he drove, she braided her ponytail and tied the end with a simple brown elastic. She tried to look ordinary. Then she put on brown contact lenses to hide the most beautiful blue eyes he had ever seen.

Well, now that did the trick. She really did look—well, *almost* looked—ordinary.

They got to where the GPS system had directed them. It was on the other side of town from where they had picked up the banger—an inner-city, run-down neighborhood.

Kids with no shoes were running around in the middle of the street. Slightly older kids were trying to hit a baseball with pitiful frequency. Adult men were sitting on the sidewalk with cerveza bottles openly held, drinking away whatever they could in the hot sun.

Still, they drove through, albeit at a slow pace, for fear of running over the kids running around, until they came to what appeared to be a rundown but still-standing mall.

"This is the community center," explained Isabella. "Park over there in that free space," she said, pointing to what was not clearly defined as a parking space. It was a space, all right, but it was a space for anything that wanted to use it—dogs, cats, rats, birds, whatever had the need, whichever came first.

Being in this part of town, risking the safety of the client, having no backup, and not "calling it in" was not part of his job description.

He felt vulnerable—vulnerable to attack, to being outnumbered, outmaneuvered, outgunned—out *everything*. Still, he would defend the client with his life. That's the only way he knew how. Nothing would happen to her. Not on his watch.

"All you gotta do is drive the daughter to school and back. No stress. Easy job. Get you back on your feet," they had said.

"They" was an old friend of his who had introduced him to a friend, who knew somebody looking for an American driver living locally. He had fit the bill.

But this right here—this was something else entirely. This was taking a young, affluent schoolgirl out of her comfort zone and into the poorest neighborhood in the city. It was highly imprudent. In this neighborhood, people were treated with disdain and excluded from society. To the local authorities, the people here didn't even exist.

They didn't live in proper accommodations built to any standard construction codes. Many didn't have running water. The houses were made from brick and mud with corrugated metal roofs. Entire families lived in spaces no bigger than one hundred square feet. Cooking was done outside on open fires. The roads were barely paved, with massive potholes caused by years of rain and degradation. People moved around mostly on 125cc motorbikes—three or sometimes four to a bike. The children looked ragged, and in the green spaces, men lay sprawled out, oblivious to the world. God only knew what they were under the influence of.

Right in the middle of it all, like a magnet drawing the chaos toward it, sat a dilapidated mall. Years ago, someone had tried to bring civilization, modernization—*life*—to this struggling area.

The driver parked the car in the open space, and they walked toward the center. He felt deeply uncomfortable. To him, the people living here were operating below a subsistence level, and that made them unpredictable. In his mind, they could not be trusted not to attack.

Now was not the time to think about job descriptions. Now was the time to be vigilant, watchful, attentive, careful.

"Be alert to sounds. Watch for fast movement—anything coming fast. Listen for loud, distracting noises. When under attack, look for higher ground. Look for cover. Shield the client." He repeated the words to himself like a mantra.

He was sweating now, drenched, in unfamiliar territory and surrounded by potential hostiles. Abandoned cars with no wheels lined the street—possible IEDs, for all he knew.

Isabella, on the other hand, strolled calmly toward the building, singing with the children as they ran to her, calling her name and leaping into her arms. She was happy to be here—among *her people*, as she would later explain.

He understood the change of clothes now. He only wished she'd warned him about this part of the trip. In his crisp driver's uniform, he looked painfully out of place. But no one paid him any attention.

Inside the building was a sports center for kids. Directly in the middle was an open floor for activities. On the back wall to the left stood a climbing wall equipped with safety ropes for beginners and younger children. In front of it was a gymnastics area—parallel bars, a gym floor, a single bar, and padded flooring that actually worked.

To the right, in the far corner, was a mini skate park with small ramps and mounds for trying out skateboard tricks. Between the gym floor and the judo mat sat a boxing and wrestling ring. The judo area supported multiple martial arts disciplines: Aikido, Brazilian Jiu-Jitsu, Taekwondo, Chinese Kung Fu, and Karate.

Off the main floor were changing rooms—girls on the left, boys on the far right.

Isabella made her way to the girls' area to change for her activities. It was Monday, which meant two classes: first, Taekwondo for ninety minutes, then Jiu-Jitsu for another ninety.

On Tuesdays, it was Aikido for an hour, followed by Kung Fu. Wednesdays were gymnastics and then salsa dancing. Thursdays mirrored Mondays, and Fridays were like Tuesdays.

This was who she was—her world, her people, her passions. Her *hobbies*, if you could call them that.

Isabella loved martial arts—not just the physical techniques, but the spiritual control, the discipline, the mastery over the body and its impulses. Emotional control. Spiritual awareness. The precision of discipline, like the Buddhist monks. She worked to unify all those

39

elements—mind, body, spirit—into one seamless unit. She had learned to move fluidly from one discipline to the next, adapting without pause.

She knew what she wanted in life, what she dreamed of, who she was, and where she was going. At a very young age, Isabella was the master of her own destiny.

Martial arts allowed her to transition effortlessly—from school to home, to social life with her parents and their peers, to Carmen and the other girls at school, and finally, to *this* place—*her* place. It all became one fluid movement. Martial arts gave her that power.

There were about thirteen kids in the Taekwondo class, mostly girls. They ran laps around the dojo for the first ten minutes as a warm-up, then moved into stretching exercises. Taekwondo demanded loose limbs, as it involved a lot of kicking.

Isabella had been practicing for six years, having started at age six. She had begun with private lessons at home and later found out where her Sensei held group sessions. That's when she started coming to the center.

After ninety minutes of disciplined movement, sweat, and energy, she was thoroughly warmed up. But now came Jiu-Jitsu—her least favorite martial art. It felt too close to wrestling for her liking.

This class was mostly boys—fifteen in total, with just three girls. The girls were nine, ten, and twelve. Isabella, at twelve, was the oldest and largest of the girls, though two boys were still bigger than she was.

Sensei almost always paired her with a boy while the other two girls worked together.

"Okay, everybody on your backs!" Sensei called out. "Move across the floor. Wiggle your backs like snakes or worms and move across the floor and back. Come on, go! Keep your hands by your sides."

They all wiggled across the tatami from one end and back.

"Okay, Joachim, you pair up with Isa—on your back. Isa, you sit on top of him. Go!"

Isabella sat on Joachim's stomach.

"Combat!" Sensei shouted.

Isabella tried to neutralize his hands while controlling any movements he made. Joachim, on the other hand, had to get Isabella off of him and neutralize her. They went at it, each one grabbing the other, pulling at arms, using legs and feet to maneuver.

Finally, Isabella locked onto Joachim's arm, slid off him, and held it in a tight arm lock. Joachim tapped out.

"Yay, Isa… we won!" the girls cheered.

Isabella was sweating slightly—it was intense and very physical. Now it was her turn to be on the ground, with Joachim sitting on her, trying to control her.

He was all over her. They half rolled over, Joachim attempting the same arm lock she had used. She countered and tried a different move—a leg-over-the-shoulders lock. Lifting her hips off the ground, she swung her legs up and around his neck. Now he had to use one hand to control her hands and the other to try and unlock her feet from behind his neck.

She twisted to one side, feigning submission, then suddenly lifted herself upright. Her legs still wrapped tightly around his neck, she forced him to fall backward. She squeezed a little tighter, and he tapped out again.

"Good job, Isa. Go drink some water. Well done," said Sensei. "Joachim, you stay here on the floor. Javier, you're on top. Go. Fight!"

And it was on.

The rest of the class sat in a circle, watching the matches unfold. One by one, each student took their turn in the middle. Sometimes, it was Team A against Team B.

Isabella loved the fight, the technique, the ability to defeat an opponent bigger—and maybe stronger—than her. Each victory, even among friends, gave her a growing sense of self-confidence.

Chapter Five
Isabella

It was 5 p.m. when they left. They drove back to the parking lot in the city center to exchange cars and head home. The trip home seemed like it took ten minutes when, in reality, it was a thirty-minute drive. Isabella had dozed off in the back seat. When the car stopped and the engine shut down, she opened her eyes and looked around, half-dazed.

"We're home already," she said, stating the obvious. She gathered her belongings, including her school bag and gym bag, and went into the house.

"You're late! Why? Where have you been?" her father asked from the living room.

She walked upstairs to her room without answering. She had completely ignored him, as if he were invisible and she were deaf. She dropped her bags in her room and went looking for her mom.

"Mom! Mom, where are you?" she called out.

"I'm here, sweetheart! In my room, resting!" said Abby, Isabella's mom.

Her Abby was always resting. She didn't work, didn't cook, didn't do any housework or gardening for that matter, but she was always resting. Isabella always sympathized with her mom— unconditionally. Back in the day, her mom had been a top model, traveling the world on modeling assignments. She had met Javier on one of those assignments when she was eighteen, and they rekindled the courtship years later.

Isabella walked into her mom's room, jumped on the bed, and hugged and kissed her.

"Your eyes are brown again, sweetheart. Or are you an alien who only looks like my daughter?" Abby teased with a smile.

"I was at the sports center, Mom. I just want to fit in and not look like a privileged brat. So I put on these contacts that change the color of my eyes."

"I know, hon. How was your day? Got any homework that needs looking at? Have you seen your dad? What did he say?"

"No homework. I did it in class while the others were still figuring the problems out. Yes, I've seen Dad—still like a stuck CD: 'You're late, where were you, blah blah blah.'"

Her mom chuckled softly, though there was a hint of concern in her eyes. "Alright, sweetheart. I'm glad you're on top of things. Go on, get yourself ready for family dinner."

"Okay, I'm going to take a shower and get ready for dinner," Isabella said, leaning in to kiss her mom on the cheek again. "See you at dinner, Mom!"

With that, she hopped off the bed and skipped out of the room, smiling to herself and skipping as she walked to her room.

She showered, washed her hair, and scrubbed herself, wanting to get rid of the thought of Joachim—from Jiu-Jitsu—on top of her, sweating on her, breathing on her. Finally, she felt clean enough to get out of the shower and get herself ready for dinner with the family.

Dinner was always formal. In fact, there were two kinds of formal. First was the family formal: Mom, Dad, and Isabella. The family dining room consisted of a large dining table with eight chairs around it. Dad sat at the head, with Mom at the other end and Isabella in the middle. Always the same seating.

The second kind of formal was dinner in the ballroom. Here, seating was arranged according to the importance of the guests. The ballroom seated twenty but could quite easily accommodate twenty-four. Isabella never had dinner in the ballroom. No kids were allowed. Kids were considered a nuisance and should neither be heard nor seen. Dinners there required formal attire—evening gowns for the women, while the men were required to wear evening black-tie apparel. The only women allowed had to be accompanied.

Isabella never wanted to eat there anyway. They all looked so stuffy and boring. She could barely tolerate family dinner time—undeniably the most intolerable and unappetizing mealtime event she could think of.

Everything was served. There were three maids to serve the dinner—one for each person. They fetched the food from the kitchen in polished silverware, rolled it out on three trolleys, and covered it like it was meant to be a surprise. Each trolley carried the full menu and was rolled out to each individual. Then, simultaneously, they would open the tops, present the meal, and proceed to serve. Dad was always served first, then Mom, then Isabella.

Of course, this was Dad's moment. His moment of control over everyone and everything. His mood dictated whether you enjoyed your meal or not, whether the food tasted good or not. His taste mattered—no one else's did. His conversation, his topic of discussion, his world—he was king.

So, he spoke.

"So, Isabella, how was school today?"

"Hmm… like every other day," she retorted.

"So, how is school every other day?" he countered.

"Fine," she replied.

"What is fine? What does that mean? 'Fine' is vague!"

"Well, you answered your own question," she answered cheekily.

"What are you talking about? I'm trying to talk to you. I'm interested in your day. You answer me in riddles!" he bellowed.

"School is fine, Dad—vaguely fine. No ups, no downs… hmm, maybe one down. Carmen and her horse. But otherwise, fine."

He was not done with her, nor with responses that bordered on insubordination and disrespect.

"School finishes at 1:30 p.m., and you only come home at 5 p.m. Where were you?"

"Yes, and yes," Isabella said curtly.

"Yes, what? Yes, what? Fine, yes. Now, suddenly, you can say no more than one word at a time!"

"Hmmm, Dad, you ask questions or make statements to which you already know the answers. Yes, school finishes at 1:30 p.m. Yes, I came home at five. And I was in the shower until now," Isabella answered, looking straight and hard at her father. She didn't blink or turn away.

"Who is your driver? I want him here right now!"

Isabella turned to the maid standing behind her and said, "Better set another place. We have a guest for dinner."

"You don't decide… I decide. Me!"

"But Dad, you already decided. But you can change your mind if you want to." She turned to the maid. "Err, on second thought, don't bother. He can have my place. All this shouting has made me lose my appetite," said Isabella with a slight smirk on her face.

"No, you sit down! You stay here and finish your dinner!" Javier screamed at his daughter, red in the face and in an uncontrollable rage.

Isabella ignored him. She pushed her chair back and stood up. She walked around the table to her mother, who sat silently at the other end, her eyes downcast, clearly displeased with the tension between father and daughter. Isabella leaned down, kissed her mother on the cheek, and whispered, "Goodnight, Mom."

As she turned to leave, Javier's rage shifted to Abby.

"And you!" he shouted, pointing an accusatory finger at her. "You just sit there and say nothing. You encourage her, you push her, you mold her! I swear, I swear, this is a conspiracy against me... All your fault!" he shouted, tense with rage and ready to explode.

Isabella paused at the doorway, her back still turned, but Javier wasn't finished.

"You come back here and sit down!" he bellowed, his face flushed and contorted with anger. "Come back this minute, or I swear I'll..."

"Or you'll what?" Isabella turned around and faced her father. "You'll what? You'll shoot me? Go ahead, shoot me. But I'm not having dinner with you—not tonight, not tomorrow, not ever!" She walked out of the dining room and into the kitchen.

Javier turned to his wife. "You turned my daughter against me. You're both trying to kill me. She's fighting your battles for you, against me! You will never win! You hear me? Never! I will kick you both out of my house before I let you win! You gave birth to yourself. There are two of you! Two! Where is my son? You promised me a son! Where is he?"

Javier was hysterical now. Abby just sat there quietly, a slight smirk on her face, as if everything he said was all true. He had his way of controlling her, but he could—and would—never control Isabella.

Abby had her weapon.

But for how long?

Isabella went to the kitchen for a light snack, where Corella was waiting for her. Corella was the head chef and in charge of everything that went on in the kitchen. She had started out as Isabella's childminder, helping Abigail with all the baby duties— even feeding baby Isabella in the early hours of the morning when she cried for food.

Now that Isabella was an independent young woman, Corella had been moved to kitchen duties. This was the second most important job in the house: cooking and protecting Javier and his family from sabotage and possible food poisoning.

Corella had cared for Isabella since birth. She often slept in Isabella's room when her parents traveled abroad or entertained late into the night. She was like a second mother to Isabella. The two were inseparable, often discussing the competence of the hired help, planning dinner menus, and setting household rules together.

Isabella loved only her mother more than Corella. When her mother wasn't available, she sought comfort in Corella. Their bond was deeper than a typical surrogate mother-daughter relationship. Corella not only nurtured Isabella but also provided spiritual protection. She guided, shielded, and safeguarded Isabella's spirit from all forms of harm.

Corella was her protector.

Her guide.

Her shield.

Her weapon.

She looked up and smiled at Isabella as she walked into the kitchen.

"Aha, I know just what you're wishing for," Corella said, grinning and showing her not-so-white teeth.

"I guess you heard all the shouting," Isabella offered as a response.

"I think even the people across the border in Ruaz City heard everything."

"I feel sorry for Mom," said Isabella, not showing any outward signs of contempt or sadness. "Sometimes I just wish that she would fight back," she added.

"Here, come. Come help make your chicken Caesar salad. You can quickly fry the chicken breasts while I prepare the lettuce and the rest."

The two bustled around the kitchen, chatting and laughing about everything and nothing in particular. The dining room incident was forgotten; their minds were occupied by light-hearted topics.

When the salad was done, Corella prepared a lunch snack for Isabella for the next day.

Isabella left the kitchen and went straight to bed. She brushed her teeth thoroughly after enjoying two glasses of Corella's homemade iced tea. She didn't like to drink too many sugary or fizzy drinks, but Corella's iced tea was world-renowned—at least in Isabella's world.

Chapter Six
Abby

Anne and Katherine drove Abby to San Antonio International Airport. Frank stayed home, not wanting to break down in front of hundreds of strangers at the airport when it was time to literally let go. He had already said his goodbyes to Abby at home, tears running down his cheeks, sobbing uncontrollably. He had never, even in his worst nightmare, envisaged his family breaking up like this.

Okay, going off to college was to be expected, and in-state colleges were just as good as any across the country. So it really wasn't the same. But New York? That was another world. His baby girl was traveling across the country to a foreign place, with all those foreign people and no family close by. What would become of her?

He buried his head in Anne's shoulder, sobbing unashamedly. Abby wrapped her arms around her dad, hugging him tightly, promising to text and FaceTime every day.

"What's this FaceTiming thing?" he asked her, pulling back, drying his eyes, and blowing his nose.

"It's video calling. I can either voice call you or video call you, and we can see each other when we speak," Abby explained.

"Do we have one of those types of video recorders, sweetheart?" Frank asked, directing the question to his wife.

"Yes, love, on your cell phone," she replied patiently. "They have voice calling, video calling, texting, and emailing. You can do all that with your cell phone these days."

"Hmm. Well, honey, you face me every day. You hear? Face me, darling. I wanna see who you're with every day."

"Yes, Dad, I promise!"

They hugged again, reluctantly letting go—it was time to leave for the airport.

Anne had calculated roughly a one-hour and twenty-minute drive from George West to San Antonio, plus about fifteen minutes to cross town to the San Antonio International Airport.

The atmosphere in the car was heavy. Anne tried hard to break the sullenness and cheer the girls up. She joked about sending a packed lunch to Abby in New York if they starved her. Better still, she said she would move to New York and cook all her meals. She even tried singing silly songs, but nothing helped. The girls were being torn apart, and it hurt.

Katherine was trying her best to be brave, to accept the eventuality of it all and keep it together. The truth was, she wasn't doing a very good job—tears ran down her cheeks nonstop. She was at a complete breaking point, in total despair. She reached out her hand to the front seat. Abby turned in her seat, grabbed her sister's hand with both of hers, and the two just broke down sobbing.

Then it was Anne's turn—to literally howl like an owl during mating season. She pulled over at the first possible stopping place, turned in her seat, grabbed both her daughters, and just howled. They stayed there for a good twenty minutes. Drying her eyes, Anne pulled back onto I-35 toward San Antonio.

They arrived at the airport with time to spare. Anne parked in the short-term lot, and they rolled Abby's travel bag to the departure lounge. Anne took care of all the boarding formalities.

As they headed toward the departure gates, a woman holding a sign with Abby's name printed on it approached them.

"I thought that's supposed to happen at the destination, not the departure," said Anne. "This is my daughter Abby. Will you be traveling to New York with her?"

The woman smiled warmly and nodded. "Yes. Robert insisted that we receive Abby here in Texas already."

"Well, that's certainly reassuring, especially from a mother's point of view. Thank you. I feel much better already. It certainly helps—it does."

"Well, we don't usually proceed in this manner. This is not regular protocol, ma'am. However, Robert insisted, and well... as you know, Robert is the boss. The boss broke protocol, and here we are.

"Yes, I will be traveling with Abby, assisting her through the usual airport arrival procedures, and then taking her to the apartment where she'll be staying. We usually leave the girls free on the first day for unpacking and acclimatization. On the second day, we have orientation and introductions, and then the first classes begin.

"There are different classes, but the first class is all about walking. We teach the girls how to walk. It may seem basic and straightforward, but it is actually the foundation. If a girl can't walk properly—like a model—in different shoes, then we send her back home. But don't worry too much; we won't be sending Abby back home anytime soon."

"Well, that's just what I *am* worried about—y'all not sending my baby back home anytime soon," Anne chimed in.

The flight was called over the airport PA system. Abby hugged her mom, tears flowing freely like an open shower tap, though no sound came out. She then hugged her sister—her best friend, her other half. They had to be literally torn apart so Abby could catch her flight.

Sitting on the plane, waiting for takeoff, Abby created two group chats. In the first, she added her mom, her dad, and Katherine. In the second, she added Katherine and her two cousins. Phones had to be turned off for the entire flight, so Abby amused herself by reading through the in-flight entertainment guide and picking out movies to watch.

When they arrived in New York, a driver was waiting in the arrivals hall with their names on a card. He took Abby's travel bag and escorted them to a stretch limousine. He opened the door for the two women to get in and went around to the driver's side.

Once inside, he explained, "The rear refrigerators are filled with complimentary drinks. Please help yourself."

"Thank you," Abby replied.

"Do you know where to go?" asked Abby's escort.

"Yes, it's all taken care of. Please relax—we'll be there shortly."

Abby didn't feel like chatting in the car any more than she had on the plane. She sat silently, staring out the window, taking in the sights. It was a culture shock.

She took out her cell phone and group-texted her family: *We just arrived in New York. We're in this big extra-long limo. It feels so wrong being here without you guys. I miss you. I don't think I want to do this. I want to come home.*

She started crying again.

The apartment was on the Upper East Side of Manhattan. The driver carried Abby's bag into the apartment and left. Her travel companion showed Abby to her room, introduced her to her roommate, and then left.

"Welcome!" said the girl. "I understand that we will be roommates. My name is Radka. I am from the Czech Republic. I am seventeen years old. This is my second year here. Soon, I will be given modeling assignments. I'm ready to be out there. I'm sorry I talk too much. All the girls say this to me. Where are you from?"

Abby stared at Radka, moved to sit on her bed, and buried her face in her hands. She couldn't stop the tears.

What had she gotten herself into? No way was she going to get used to this.

To top it all off, she had to share a room with this talkative, wannabe airhead from God-knows-where.

Check-something.

She lay back on her bed, pulled the covers over her, and cried herself to sleep. Tomorrow, she would call Robert and tell him this was all a big mistake—that she wanted to go home to her family.

The next morning, Abby woke up totally disoriented. She opened her eyes and saw a strange person standing next to her bed. She sat up, startled, about to ask who she was and what she was doing in her room when she suddenly remembered where she was. New York!

Oh my God, she thought.

"You want to join us?" Radka asked.

"What?"

"You want to join us? We have a free day today. Some of the girls would like to see some of the New York sights, like the Emperor's Building and the Statue of Liberty. And maybe take a bus to Kharlim. Yes? It's good for you?"

"Emperor's Building? Kharlim? What are you talking about? Never mind, never mind," said Abby, still a little disoriented. "Look, it's called the Empire State Building, not the Emperor's Building. And Harlem, not Kharlim. I don't know—I just woke up," she added raspily.

"Fine, we wait if you come!" insisted Radka.

"Well, maybe I'll tag along—only because I don't want to sit here and cry all day. I miss my family. I wanna go home."

Abby looked around. All the girls came out of their rooms to greet her. There were eight girls in the apartment: four rooms, two girls per room, two showers, two toilets, one fully equipped kitchen with a dining table for six, and a fairly spacious lounge area with a large flat-screen television mounted on the wall. Fashion TV played all day when no one was watching anything specific. The program kept their mouths watering and inspired them. It kept them focused and pushed them individually to explore their limits. Their ultimate dream was to be recognized in the industry, to walk the greatest catwalks, and to be featured on Fashion TV.

It took Abby all of thirty minutes to get ready. The girls waited for her downstairs in the coffee shop. She walked in, her hair still damp, wearing blue jeans and all-white sneakers. Her hair was tied in a ponytail, pulled up behind her ears, exposing her geometrically perfect ears and earlobes, diamond stud earrings sparkling and lighting up her already radiant face.

The girls—all seven of them—just stared and said nothing. There was Anna, the youngest at fourteen; Helen, a biracial girl aged fifteen (Anna and Helen shared a room); Radka, Abby's roommate; Yulia from Ukraine, sixteen; Kristina, seventeen, from Germany; Amanda, eighteen, from Canada; and finally, Kelly, the oldest at twenty, from Australia. A truly international group.

They agreed the best way to sightsee was to board the hop-on, hop-off sightseeing bus. They bought their respective tickets and began their free day. They also decided to stick together and not wander off individually.

The first stop was the Empire State Building, where they spent close to two and a half hours. Then, the bus stopped at the quay, where they took a boat ride around Liberty Island to see the Statue of Liberty up close. In the past, when Abby was a little girl, tourists could disembark on Liberty Island and actually climb the big green statue. For security reasons, this was no longer allowed. They stayed on the boat and took pictures as they circled the island.

Despite the cultural diversity of the group, the girls had fun together, and Abby appreciated the distraction. She actually laughed a little, listening to the accents and pronunciations as the girls ordered hot dogs in Central Park. It really was a fun day. She liked all the girls a lot, but she felt especially drawn to Anna—fourteen years old and already five-foot-ten.

Anna was quiet, shy, and a little withdrawn. Abby liked her instantly. Later, she asked if she could switch roommates without hurting Radka's feelings.

As soon as they got back to the apartment, Abby FaceTimed her family. Then, she talked with her cousins, telling them who she was with, where they went, and how much fun they had.

Tomorrow, she would call Robert. Today, she was just too tired.

The next day, the girls were woken up early by Kelly—the "morning person"—who took it upon herself to awaken her cohabitants each morning. They ate an unsupervised breakfast and headed for the subway. The closest station was roughly half a mile away, up to the main road near the closest grocery stores. The Red Line took them all the way down to Union Street Station. After a brief stroll across Union Square, they arrived at the building—Fashion Academy, or FAC, as it was known to students and faculty alike.

The faculty were all ex-industry professionals—no longer earning as models, dancers, or makeup artists, but contributing in a more advisory capacity. They were known as "Walking Consultants," "Makeup Technicians," "Wardrobe Advisors," or "Designers." They weren't called teachers or professors or anything typically associated with formal education. That would require formal credentials, and it would imply a classic teacher-student dynamic.

This wasn't a school in the traditional sense. It was an academy. The difference was that at the academy, students didn't attend to earn a diploma based on memorized content. Instead, they came to hone their talents and skills to a level that would be universally recognized—marketable, even.

Hence, at the academy, there were no teachers—only instructors and advisors. No students—only potential performers.

Abby was swept up in the adrenaline of the morning: waking up, getting herself ready, eating breakfast, and rushing down to the subway with the other girls en route to the FAC. She had never experienced this kind of independence before. At home, her mom was always there, making breakfast and driving her to school. If she overslept, Katherine would wake her—sometimes with a practical joke like putting feathers in her ears. And if that didn't work, the feathers went up her nose. That always got her up instantly, rubbing her nose and grumbling in irritation.

"Good morning, girls," greeted the academy director. "My name is Dianna McDermott, and I am the director of the academy—or the FAC, as we like to call it. You can all call me Dee. I will be responsible for your training schedule and daily routines. I will also manage your eating regimes—both content and frequency. All the advisors and technicians report to me and work under my guidance and direction.

"As potential fashion artists, you are here because we have recognized something special in each and every one of you. That's why we've invited you here—to realize your potential and pursue your dream. If this is not the place for you, we will recognize it immediately, and you will be released."

"We are not the only academy, but we are the best—the Rolls Royce of all fashion academies in the world. Once you are released from here, with our approval, you will be recognized; you will receive mandates and assignments. You will go on to be the most recognized faces in the world, gracing the most important catwalks from London to Paris, Tokyo, Rome, Milan, Beijing, and other fashion centers. Which is why you are here. But if you are released prematurely, then you will be better advised to modify your ambitions modestly.

"Do not underestimate the program you are about to embark on. It is specifically designed to prepare you for the grueling schedule that awaits you once you are approved and receive your first assignment. Sacrifice, hard work, obedience, strict adherence to the recommended nutrition and wellness programs, and dedication objectives will push you to triumph and succeed in the world's hardest, most difficult job. We will take you to the top, but it is how you conduct yourself during the time that you are here that will keep you there.

"You are not yet ladies. You are not yet women. You are all still girls. Welcome. Day one is now! As of this moment, I will be your mother, your father, your brother, your sister, and your best friend. No time and no place for boyfriends. Remember that. We have a list of rules and regulations that will determine your behavior at all times! Failure to comply will result in immediate release! Study these rules, girls. Study them and know them by heart. You may have the talent, but if you choose to ignore and flout these rules, you will be released.

"I will now leave you in the capable hands of your advisors. My door is always open. Good luck, girls."

With that, Dee turned and left the girls to be led away by the advisors. They were split into two groups, which determined their schedules for the day. Group A, Abby's group, was led away to the catwalk room, while Group B was taken to the composure room to learn how to pose when being photographed.

Once inside, Andy took the girls under his command.

"Okay, first, you are all to take your shoes off and leave them outside the door. Now, space yourselves out at arm's length and walk across the room—nice and easy, like you're walking to the bathroom. Okay, now turn around and do it again. When you get here, I want you all to walk backward until the end of the room."

Andy spoke in a soft, warm voice. He had ash-blonde hair, cut short on the sides with a long mesh in the front—not quite a fringe. He was not very tall but walked ever so daintily, almost swinging, almost dancing. Abby loved him instantly. He was just so sweet.

They walked barefoot back and forth for a good hour.

"Now we're going to spice it up a bit," he quipped, smiling all the while. "I will place an empty plastic cup on each of your heads. You will walk across the room with the cup on your head. If you drop the cup, I will fill it with water and place it back on your head."

Needless to say, all four girls dropped the cups after only a few steps. True to his word, Andy filled each plastic cup with water, placed it on their respective heads, and made them walk—and walk—and walk.

He kept "spicing it up a bit" every few minutes: walking with outstretched hands, walking with eyes closed, right hand on the nose, left hand on the nose—all the while with water in the plastic cups. After more than an hour, the girls were drenched, and Andy ordered a water break. Coffee was not allowed, but green tea was. So water or green tea was offered at the break.

The three girls and Abby walked barefoot for four hours, with Andy continually pushing their limits. Just when they thought all the walking was over, they were given flat shoes to wear, and it started all over again.

At the end of the first day, Group A left with swollen feet, unable to walk, while Group B complained of strained necks and shoulders. Nevertheless, Abby was excited and enthusiastic. She couldn't wait to FaceTime her mom and sister. She had to tell them all about walking with the challengers and actually not spilling a drop. She was absolutely thrilled with herself. She was so ecstatic that she promised herself she would give it a full week before contacting Robert about leaving.

On day two, the groups switched. Group A headed off to composure while Group B practiced their walking skills.

In composure, the girls had to sit still while makeup was applied. Then, they had to sit on a stool facing the camera with bright lights focused directly on them. The lights made them hot, sweaty, and itchy.

"Don't move. Hold it! Hold it still now. Lick your lips. Eyes to the camera. That's it, don't move."

They heard this for hours on end.

"Okay, now swirl, turn around, head facing me, eyes into the camera! Somebody touch up the makeup; it's running. Okay, next! Look like you're running. No! Not like that. Running. Run! Run! Now turn around. Smile, don't smile."

It was stressful.

Applying the makeup was fun for Abby. She'd never bothered to wear makeup to school—or anywhere, for that matter. Here, she actually had someone do it for her and show her how to enhance her facial structure. The makeup artist showed Abby how to apply eyeliner and eye shadow, how to raise her cheekbones or lower them with liner and contouring. She loved that part, but the twisting and twirling and holding her eyes into the camera were too much.

Each day, they were shown how to improve their composure, their walking, their posture—all the while honing the subtleties of when and why.

Days turned into weeks, and weeks into months. Abby forgot about calling Robert; in fact, she forgot about Robert completely.

Each day, without fail, she called or texted home. With each FaceTime and message, Abby told her mother and sister that she loved and missed them. Frank was sometimes in the background, blowing kisses, but he didn't look in the best of health. Abby was a little worried about her dad, but her mother reassured her that he was fine—just tired from working the ranch.

Abby missed home, home cooking, and the banter with her sister and her cousins. The girls here were great fun—a second family—but nothing could replace the first and real one.

Robert almost never came to the FAC, and she had forgotten about him. She dedicated her time to learning as much as she could about the fashion and modeling world. She wanted not just to be a part of this intriguing place; she wanted, even more, to succeed—to be approved, to be recognized as having the required talents to be accepted.

Abby was driven by a strong desire not to fail, not to be deemed as just average. She wanted to graduate at the top of the class. Valedictorian.

She memorized the rules, scrupulously adhered to them, and ensured that Anna followed them too.

Abby had persuaded Radka to switch rooms with Anna so that Radka and Helen became roommates, and Abby and Anna roomed together. It didn't take much convincing, as all the girls got along really well, and there was no issue switching roommates.

Abby was a little more talkative with Anna, especially when they were both excited about the day's routine and couldn't sleep— or when they were experiencing severe discomfort caused by menstruation. They would often comfort each other, tell each other stories, or prepare a hot drink for the one who was feeling a little under the weather.

Such was the camaraderie between the two. They pushed each other, leaned on each other, and helped each other. There was no question of seeing the other be released because of a technicality, a misunderstanding, or a lapse in judgment.

Abby recited the rules in her head when she awoke in the middle of the night and couldn't sleep:

Rule No. 1: No alcohol consumption, ever!

Rule No. 2: No smoking at all—tobacco or otherwise.

Rule No. 3: No boyfriends.

Rule No. 4: No visitors to the apartment.

Rule No. 5: No sleeping out unless consent is expressly given by DiAnna McDermott

Rule No. 6: No clubbing, partying, or music festivals

Rule No. 7: No nutritional indulgence—adhere to the strict nutritional values provided.

Rule No. 8: No weight gain.

Rule No. 9: No fighting or violence in the FAC, anywhere or anytime.

Rule No. 10: No stealing or taking each other's belongings.

There were also strong recommendations, such as not lending belongings to each other, as this could eventually cause tension. Additionally, the girls were strongly encouraged to help each other whenever necessary, as they were not adversaries. They were also expected to protect each other at all times.

Abby didn't think she was protecting Anna for any particular reason—she just liked Anna. Anywhere in the world, under any circumstance, she would have reacted the same way, whether it was her friend or her sister.

Chapter Seven
Abby

There was no summer vacation, as this was not a school or a college. The girls were often reminded of this. Most of the girls didn't really have a vacation to go on—except for Abby, who missed her sister terribly. Sometimes, after FaceTime, Abby would cry herself to sleep, thinking of how much she missed her family. But the next morning, she would look at Anna—so young, resilient, and determined, whose family wasn't even in the United States. Anna never complained, even though Abby had once heard her crying herself to sleep. Abby never mentioned it or asked if she was okay.

The course was physically and mentally challenging, to say the least, but the girls survived, remaining focused on their respective goals. None of the eight girls was prematurely released; all excelled in the tasks assigned to them. As a group and individually, they flourished and vindicated the FAC's confidence in their abilities.

Before the final months of the program approached, Dee summoned Abby to her office. She knocked on the door and waited.

"Please come in, Abby," invited Dee. "You've met Robert here. He came over to your family ranch to recruit you."

"Yes, I have," Abby said, turning to Robert. "Hello, Robert. Nice to see you."

"Hello, Abby. How are you?" he replied.

They exchanged pleasantries until DiAnna got straight to the point.

"Abby, I'm not sure if you're aware of why you are here."

"No, nobody mentioned anything to me."

"Well, Abby, Robert and I—and I can assure you, Robert, even though you haven't seen him around the FAC, he's been following your progress very, very closely."

"Well, I'm flat—"

"Please let me finish," DiAnna McDermott continued. "You see, Abby, you have all excelled in all departments of the program. We are thoroughly pleased with the tremendous amount of work ethic and discipline you've all invested in our program. And we are pleased with you all. But we have never—and I repeat, never—had a candidate here at the FAC who has achieved the level that you have achieved. All the advisors, technicians, and choreographers have nothing but the highest praise for you. The highest!" Turning to Robert, Dee asked, "Where in the world did you find her?"

Smiling back at Abby, while Robert mumbled some self-praise under his breath, Dee continued, "It gives me great pleasure to present you with this plaque. We have never given this out to any candidate. Ever! Robert and I would like to award you with the most highly rated achievements by any candidate in the FAC. This is for you, Abby. Well done, girl. You came here a girl, and you leave a woman—a lady. Make that a catwalk Queen!"

"From the first time I saw you, I knew. I just knew," said Robert, smiling, his whole face glowing, showing off his brilliant white teeth. "Abby," he continued, "we don't usually go to great lengths to make a graduation ceremony for the girls, but this year, we'll make an exception. After graduation, it will be my great pleasure to fly you back home on my private jet. Would you like that?"

"I don't know what to say…" Abby said—and burst into tears.

"Oh, come here, my dear," said Dee, rushing to take Abby in her arms. "There, there. Let it all out."

"Perhaps this can wait a little," said Robert. "But I have more good news. You have your first professional assignment in one month. Of course, a short visit home, see your parents—then off to Paris. Oh, did you mention Paris before? Chanel? Hmm, silly me for forgetting!"

Abby pulled back, opened her sea-blue eyes, and tried to speak—but just sobbed louder. It was all too much for her. The concentration, the rules, the privation, the hard work, and the absence of her family all came to a head in that moment. She sat down, buried her face in her hands, and bawled. Both Robert and

Dee came around to her, kneeling beside her and speaking in soothing tones, encouraging her to release the tension and just let it all out.

After a while, still hiccupping back her sobs, Abby dried her sea-blue eyes—now red from howling—and stood up.

"Thank you," she said meekly. "Thank you. I just tried to do my best. I never expected an award. I just didn't want to be released prematurely."

Dee smiled softly. "Abby, there was never any question of you ever being released prematurely. Never! I can assure you of that. You've done well. You put in a lot of effort throughout the whole program. Not once did you slack. But most important of all, you are the one with the most talent. So natural you didn't even need to be here to enter this program. Born to be a catwalk Queen. I'm happy to have met you. I'm happy to know you." Turning to Robert, Dee added, "I turn her over to you now. Make her a star!"

"She's already a star. The world just doesn't know it yet," Robert chimed thoughtfully.

"I have a small request," said Abby.

"Sure, go ahead," said Robert.

"I've invited Anna to meet my family and stay at the ranch for the vacation—or the break—we're about to have. First of all, is that okay with you? Second, can she join us on your private jet, please?"

"Hmm... let me think on it," joked Robert. "Of course! No question. She can join you, and she can ride on the private jet with us."

"Thank you. Thank you both." She hugged them and kissed them both on the cheek. "Paris! Wow!"

Abby walked out of Dee's office wet and red-eyed, but smiling, holding onto her award. It was a gold-colored pewter statuette of a walking model. She was so proud of the award that she couldn't wait to FaceTime her mom and Katherine. She also desperately wanted to show it to Anna but was hesitant, in case it created a negative sentiment between her and the girls. So, she decided to be discreet about it.

When she got to the FAC lobby, only Anna was waiting for her. The others had left, tired and just wanting to escape the memory of the day. Anna looked jaded, with sad eyes, drooping shoulders, and a dejected look about her person. Abby was glad she had safely put the award in her bag before heading to the lobby. She was hoping they had all left—but Anna, faithful friend, little "sister," was there waiting.

They rode the subway uptown, sitting next to each other and chatting about the day's events. Nothing in particular—just commenting on their own little errors or misgivings. Abby brought up the subject of vacationing at the ranch, and she was excited to have Anna with her. The three of them would have fun horseback riding, going out to San Antonio, shopping, or just hanging out.

Abby had introduced Anna to Katherine and her mom via FaceTime, and they, too, were looking forward to having Anna stay with them. This perked Anna up a little. They still had two weeks to go before the break. All eight girls had acquired the skill sets necessary to hone their talents and were ready to face the world, the cameras, and—most importantly—the catwalks, wherever they were.

Two weeks passed without the girls even noticing. Graduation came; it was more like a farewell party, where the girls could indulge—well, just a little. Not much more than fruit juice and flavored water, still or sparkling, was on offer. Alcohol-free champagne was then offered for the toast by Dee and Robert, celebrating the success of the program as well as the success of the FAC for turning out such talent.

Hip! Hip!

Chapter Eight
Isabella

The next morning, straight after breakfast, Isabella walked out to her car. Her new car—a black European model Audi S8 with a white interior—had been replaced by a standard white Chrysler 300C. Her new driver had also been replaced by a middle-aged, leather-faced Mexican man named Ramiro. He was short, plump, round-bellied, and almost bald. He wore a too-tight brown suit, brown shoes, a brown shirt, and a brown tie. Somebody's idea of a joke—dressing him in head-to-toe brown to please the client. He had that irritating, fake-but-warm grin plastered on his face, aimed to please. Always bowing, grinning incessantly: "Yes, madame, if you please, to my pleasure," even as he opened the door for Isabella. Speaking for the sake of speaking, never making any meaningful sense.

Isabella stepped into the car, not acknowledging the changes. As she fastened her seatbelt, Ramiro closed the door and drove off.

Punishment, she thought. *Punishment for last night.*

This was his way of making his point—being the Alpha male, the Alpha dad, the head of the establishment. He had to make his mark, establish his rule. He just had to make her obey, show her and her mother who was boss, who made the rules, who enforced them, and—most importantly—who paid for everything. The breadwinner. The moneymaker. The patriarchal chief. The Czar. All who stood before him were beneath him. No conversation, no discussion, no debate. Just bow down, kneel, and follow orders.

Javier was not just Javier—he was His Excellency, King Javier. He alone made the rules. He would show her and teach her to obey her father. Girls were nothing. Boys—sons—yeah, they were the future. To be disobeyed by a girl, a nine-year-old girl, brought him shame and humiliation. He would dot the I's and cross the T's. No more treading lightly. He'd come down hard and fast. Take away the luxuries: no new car, no American driver. Ramiro was old and reliable. He knew he could count on Ramiro to bring her home straight after school. No more dilly-dallying with friends. Straight home. Then schoolwork. Then chores. Like all girls should learn and do.

I'll show her who runs this house. Who the father is. Who the adult is! Javier had thought to himself as he stood by his bedroom window, watching her leave for school with Ramiro.

Good old Ramiro. He would follow orders. He would bring her straight back—or else.

Isabella had glanced up and seen her father standing at the window before getting into the car. She waved and smiled as she stepped inside. New car, new driver. She hadn't asked for any of it. She didn't care one way or the other.

"What's your name again?" she asked the driver as they pulled onto the main road.

"Yes, if you please, my name is Ramiro, señorita. For your pleasure! I drive you."

"What happened to the other driver?" Isabella asked, purely out of curiosity.

"Yes, if you please, I think work for only one day. Temporary job. One day. Grand Señor Javier tell chief driver to send back to Hamerica. Not pass test!" Ramiro replied, trying his best to be polite.

"What test?" Isabella asked, sitting forward, a little more curious now.

"Err, yes, if you—"

"Cut out the 'yes if you please' and just get to the answer. Okay?" she said, growing impatient.

"Please... err, I don't know the test. I'm driving you now. Test for me. Grand Señor Javier tell me so. Test!"

Isabella sat back, clearly annoyed and bordering on frustration. She preferred the Mute. Injured at war, he couldn't speak. Still, he was intriguing. She'd never met anyone like that before, with such uncommon injuries. But one day on the job—one day obeying her orders—was not enough to declare war with the Tyrant, as she often referred to her father, though only in her private thoughts.

He was still her father—an archaic, patriarchal, monolithic, self-indulgent, obsessive tyrant of a man. Did she love him? The real love was in the acceptance of the fact that she shared strong traits with him. Outwardly, she looked like her mother, but deep down, she resembled her father. That was the root of their antagonism, the true cause of their friction—the reason they constantly repelled each other when in the same room.

At just twelve years old, Isabella didn't think much further than her resentment of being bullied or ordered around. Her mother Abby, on the other hand, was the softest, gentlest person in the world. Isabella felt a duty to defend her mother's sweetness from wolves like her father.

Not a word more was spoken between Isabella and Ramiro on the drive to school. When they arrived, she instructed him to turn into the driveway and drop her off at the main entrance.

Silently, he obeyed. He shot out of the car, ran around to Isabella's side, and opened the door.

"Ye—" Ramiro began, grinning again.

"Enough. Not a word. Just drive off, okay? Drive off." She brushed him off rudely and arrogantly.

Isabella walked into the school entrance, glad that Carmen wasn't behind her to further annoy her with chitter-chatter about Whiskeybar—or whatever her stupid horse's name was.

But alas, waiting for Isabella in the hallway by the lockers was Carmen.

"You'll never believe what happened to me yesterday after school!" Carmen exclaimed as soon as Isabella was within earshot.

"Hello, Carmen. How are you? What happened to you after school yesterday?" Isabella asked in her most sarcastic voice.

"Okay, well, now that you ask—mind you, I wasn't going to say anything—but since you asked so nicely, I'll tell you. Well, after school, when—"

"Yes, after school... I got that," Isabella interjected.

"Oh, Bella, don't be so catty. You did ask, so let me start at the beginning. Anyway, we were on our way home with the driver when I felt in the mood for an ice cream. I wish that you could have been there. We could have gone together."

"Yeah, me too. I wish I could have been there. Wow... eating a delicious vanilla, chocolate, strawberry, pecan, cookies and cream ice cream."

"Oh, stop mocking me! Do you want to hear the rest of the story or not?" Carmen said, grabbing Isabella by the shoulders to stop her from entering the classroom.

"Not really, no. But you'll tell me anyway. No escaping. So summarize, okay?"

"Okay, well, I didn't want to go in, but the drive was so long, so many cars, so I told the driver to park, and I went in. Guess what happened?"

"No more ice cream!" Isabella shouted with a feigned look of shock, eyes wide.

"Bella! Come on!"

"Okay, okay . . . my bad. Go on!"

"Well, sitting there in one of the booths was none other than Ricky Martin, the singer. Ricky Martin, right here in town. I just stood there. I couldn't move. I froze."

"Like the ice cream!" retorted Isabella as she walked into the classroom. "Probably just a look-alike. Everybody wants to look like a star these days. Gets them noticed. Did you ever hear the theory that Elvis is still alive? Sightings of Elvis all over the United States."

"Who's Elvis?" remarked Carmen, disappointed that Isabella wasn't too impressed with her "encounter" with Ricky Martin.

Before either could say more, Miss Sarah walked in and class began. It was the usual curriculum, with English Literature as the first subject of the morning, followed by Math, American Geography, General Science, and finally, Language Skills.

As usual, Isabella was the most knowledgeable in every subject. She had the highest grades in class. In some subjects, she would even politely and respectfully correct the teacher when it appeared the teacher had limited knowledge of the topic.

Miss Sarah really liked Isabella. Here was a student with everything—one who didn't ever have to work for money, who didn't need a career. Yet here she was, the brightest, most focused student. A gift to any teacher, professor, or instructor. Totally focused and sharp, with a sense of humor that most people didn't understand.

What was she doing being best friends with simple-minded Carmen? The two were like oil and water—chalk and cheese, as the more common expression goes—but Sarah preferred "electricity and water." Not that they would explode, but there was a short circuit in their personalities. The funny part was that Isabella was both the water and the electricity, and Carmen was the item being electrocuted.

The final bell came quickly as Isabella really pushed herself in her Russian lessons. She was so motivated to speak Russian, though these were still early days. She planned to ask her family to vacation in Moscow—at least for two weeks—so she could improve her basics.

Ramiro was waiting for her with the rear door open, but he wasn't grinning. He was bowing his head, not saying anything, just like they do in Japan.

He would fit in real nicely there, she thought.

They drove down the driveway and onto the main road.

"I'd like you to go to this address, Ramiro," she said, showing him the address on her cell phone as she leaned forward.

He half-turned to look at her phone and then said, very quietly, almost in a whisper, "I must drive you straight home. Grand Señor Javier strict message to me. So sorry, madame miss."

"Grand Javier, or whatever you call him, is not here, right? *I* am here. *I* am giving the messages. And I'm giving you a message right now that you should follow. Okay? Go to this address! Turn the car around and drive to this address. Now!"

Ramiro wouldn't budge. He just kept driving, heading straight home. Obviously, he was more afraid of Grand Señor Javier than of Madame Missy.

When they got to a traffic stop, Isabella opened the rear door and got out of the car with her gym bag. Across the road was a bus stop. She ran to it just as the bus was pulling in. She stepped up, bought her ticket, and sat down. She never looked to see what Ramiro was doing. The bus drove off.

She had to change buses twice more before arriving in the neighborhood. She was still wearing her school uniform, but she didn't mind. The kids knew enough not to comment on what she was wearing.

"Princess . . . princess, you look like a princess!" they chanted. "Isa, Isa!" they kept calling as she made her way to the sports center.

Once inside, she went straight to the changing rooms and geared up for Aikido—Japanese martial arts, the art of mastering energy and movement. The outfit was all white with an orange and green belt. This was an art: the art of immobilizing your opponent in a sporting manner.

Was it a sport, or rather a sophisticated method of self-defense? Yet the objective was to maim, hurt, and destroy one's opponent with swift, elegant moves. The "Ki" in Aikido meant "energy." Yet the real "key" was to immobilize the opponent in hand-to-hand combat using skilled techniques and movements that physically and mentally unbalanced the aggressor.

After Aikido, Isabella prepared for Eskrima—the art of fighting with batons. This was a very dangerous sport. While in the dojo it was practiced with extreme care, out on the street it could be deadly. She loved it.

The form of Eskrima she was training in originated from the Philippines. Of course, there were many forms of Eskrima—or Kali, as it was sometimes called. Many disciplines, many disciples. But since her instructor was a Philippine national, they practiced Philippine Eskrima.

Isabella was still in the early stages, but she was a fast learner and had quickly mastered the basics. Aikido demanded a high level of concentration, and all techniques were referred to in Japanese. One had to remember the Japanese term for each technique—they were not translated. The Sensei would call out techniques in Japanese, and students would have to perform them. *Ayami Katadori*, for example, required students to perform the *Ayami* technique.

In Eskrima, the techniques had no names—they were numbered. Attacks ranged from one to seventeen, each targeting different parts of the body: head, arms, knees, and so on. When sparring, students wore thick gloves, knee and elbow guards, and helmets to avoid injury. For her level, Isabella didn't have to wear headgear yet, as they were only instructed to target hands and knees. Later, when they had mastered the art of restraint, they would target all seventeen areas of the body.

At 5:30 p.m., as the sun headed slowly toward the western horizon, Isabella left the sports center and got into a waiting car. She had pre-ordered the ride via the internet and prepaid by credit card to ensure pickup at the exact time and location.

Once safely seated, she gave the driver the address and sat back. A little restless, she began reviewing her Aikido session in her mind. In one month, she would be tested for her next grade level and hoped to move from orange and green to a full green belt. She needed to practice and remember the Japanese terms for each technique.

She closed her eyes and replayed the moves of the day, over and over again, in her mind.

She didn't realize she had dozed off and woke with a jolt, a little disoriented, when the driver announced that they had arrived. They were outside the front gate of the Hacienda, the mansion where she and her family lived. The driver asked if he should ring the gatebell and drive in.

"No, it's fine here," she said to him in fluent Spanish. "Here, please take this," she added, offering him a cash tip.

"Gracias, señorita, gracias." He smiled as he opened the door for her to exit the car.

"Maybe again tomorrow. I'll let you know. If you let me have your number, I'll call you directly," she said, still speaking in Spanish.

With that, she walked through the side gate and up the driveway toward the house. When she reached the front door, it was locked, so she walked around the side of the house, across the lawn, to the kitchen door entrance. Standing in the doorway, waiting for her, was Corella.

Frowning deeply and speaking in Spanish, the older woman asked, "What happened today? You caused quite a stir, quite a commotion. Your father almost had a heart attack, screaming and shouting. I honestly thought he was going to bust a vein. His veins all popped out on his face, and he was changing colors—from red to pink to crimson, then to pale, ghost white. Only you can bring out the chameleon in him. Come in, you must be starving. I'll cook up a snack for you, then you can go bust a vein!"

"Oh, don't worry about him. He doesn't even frighten the chickens running around in the coop," chimed Isabella, walking into the kitchen, washing her hands, and sitting down at the kitchen dining table.

The kitchen was huge; in fact, it was in two parts: the cooking area, with all the electrical cooking installations, and the informal seating area, where Isabella often had her breakfast and most of her meals, except when called for dinner.

The cooking area had two six-plate gas stoves, four ovens, six microwave ovens, six fridges, six deep freezers, numerous appliances, kettles, coffee machines, tea machines, and handheld vacuum cleaners. Shining copper pots and pans, along with wooden cooking spoons, lined the walls and shelves. Every inch of the space was spotless.

The dining area had a large rectangular table in the center of the room with six chairs around it. No more were needed, as this space was for informal dining, and only Isabella and her mom ever dined there. Javier never did. The walls featured original paintings from Mexican and Spanish artists— not well-known, but carefully selected by Corella. There were cookbooks on the shelves, along with glasses and art objects like crystal ornaments scattered throughout. The walls were white and gray marble, and the floor was deep blue marble with white streaks. Corella sometimes teased

Isabella by calling her "Marble Eyes" after the color of the kitchen floor.

One door led off the kitchen into the hallway, directly in front of the staircase to the upstairs rooms. Another set of double doors led directly into the formal family dining room. On the first floor, directly above the kitchen, was the ballroom. A large food elevator connected the kitchen to the preparation room adjacent to the ballroom. There, staff would receive the food, plate it, and serve it during formal events.

Isabella sat at the table eating a salty crepe filled with melted mozzarella cheese, chicken ham, and sliced tomatoes. Her glass was filled with sparkling water. As Isabella and Corella chatted about the day, the door from the hallway opened, and there stood her father. Noticing him—but without looking up—Isabella continued eating her crepe.

"Corella, please leave us," he ordered. Then he turned to Isabella and bellowed:

"Where did you go after school today . . . and every day? You disobeyed me! You tried to trick the driver I put in charge of your security! You were supposed to come straight home from school, not go wandering all over town, spending my money with I don't know who! That stupid horse friend of yours! I am your father. I make the rules in this house! You are just a child—you obey! You cannot, and will not, decide for yourself! I decide for you and everybody in this house, including your mother! I decid—"

Isabella stopped eating, pushed her chair back, and stood up.

She didn't like it when he involved her mother in their quarrels. She didn't like it one single bit. In fact, it struck a nerve. Grated it raw.

She stood up and faced him squarely, staring deep into his eyes—further still, into his brain—burning through whatever debris lounged in the channels. Her stare moved from his brain down to his chest, searching for him. Past his lungs, to the side where his heart beat faster and faster, blood spurting in all directions, no control, no order. Still, she stared—past his clumsy heart—and there he was.

There was his soul, cowering like a boneless, spineless, single-cell amphibian.

Still, she stared. Now that she had found him, she closed in. Relentlessly, she pressured him back, further and further into his ribs. There was no hiding now.

With a swift and sudden surge of her inner energy and willpower, she yanked his soul out from its crouched position and slammed it against the kitchen wall.

There, splayed on the marble—naked, unprotected, sorrowful, and completely and utterly defeated—was Javier's soul.

Without a word, Isabella walked toward the door, brushed past Javier, and went upstairs to see her mother.

Javier just stood there, rooted to the spot. No movement. No sound. No words. His eyes stared straight ahead, not blinking, not focused on anything in particular. His face had turned ghost white, the blood drained from it.

As Isabella walked past him, his knees buckled. He grabbed the wall to stop himself from collapsing. Slowly, he sank down and finally sat on the kitchen floor.

His breathing was steady now, but his heart was still racing. Faster and faster.

He had to slow it down, but he didn't know how.

His focus began to fade, when Corella silently handed him a glass of water.

"Señor Javier! Are you alright? Please drink this."

Corella hadn't left the kitchen as Javier had ordered. She had witnessed the meltdown. Señor Javier was no longer a señor—just a weasel of a loud-mouthed, fear-mongering, power-grabbing wannabe. Nothing but a mama's-boy playboy. He was a pitiful sight as he sat there, crumpled on the kitchen floor, struggling to comprehend what had just happened to him.

Thank God for Corella. No! Where did she come from? Had she witnessed it all? Could she explain what just happened? Would she tell everybody? Anybody? Was she complicit? She had to be!

These were the thoughts running through Javier's mind as he took the glass of water and drained it thirstily. He struggled to his feet and walked out of the kitchen to his personal study.

Isabella ran up the stairs to her mother's room.

"Hi, Mom, I'm home!" she called out as she reached the bedroom. She pushed open the door and shrieked, "Mom! Mom! Corella, Corella! Come quick!"

Isabella was hysterical as Corella came running up the stairs and joined her in the room.

"Oh my God!" Corella breathed. "Okay, help me here. I need you to help me, okay? Calm down and help me. She's just passed out!"

"Then why is she bleeding?" asked Isabella, noticing the blood on the side of her mother's head.

"She probably hit her head when she fell," offered Corella. "Here, help me lift her up and put her on the bed."

"No, let's take her to the bathroom," suggested Isabella.

"Why?"

"She's drunk. Can't you smell the alcohol?"

"Yes, I can, but she can sleep it off. We put her on the bed, she'll sleep it off, and she'll be fine in the morning."

"No, she may get alcohol poisoning. I read about it. We even discussed it at school in our science class."

"You drink alcohol at school now?" joked Corella.

"No, silly—just the effects of excess alcohol in the bloodstream."

"Okay, so what do you want to do in the bathroom?"

"We have to stick our fingers down her throat and get her to throw up. This will bring out the alcohol and whatever she ate. When it all comes out, she will stabilize."

"Gross! I'm not doing that!" Corella said, walking around and lifting Isabella's mom from under her arm.

Isabella took the other side, and they half-dragged Abby to the marble bathroom.

The floor and tiles—top to bottom—were the most beautiful pink marble. Not girlish pink, but decorative deep pink.

"Bathtub or toilet bowl?" asked Corella.

"Toilet bowl."

"Okay, here we go. Wait!" said Corella. "This is going to gross me out, and we'll have a throw-up contest here."

"Okay, I also read somewhere that black coffee helps. So, while I stick my fingers down Mom's throat, please make her some black coffee. If we can get her to drink that, she'll bring all the alcohol up. It's more effective than the finger poking."

Corella left the room to make the coffee while Isabella tried in vain to get Abby to throw up.

After a few minutes, Corella returned with a steaming mug of coffee.

"It's too hot," said Isabella, "and we need a spoon to help her get it down her throat."

"Here, use the teaspoon," said Corella.

Isabella scooped up some coffee, blew on it to cool it, then opened her mom's mouth to force her to swallow. She cradled her mom's head in her lap. Corella helped by blocking Abby's nose so that she was forced to swallow. It worked. When they managed to get half the mug down, a rumbling noise came from Abby's stomach.

Isabella barely had time to turn her mom's head into the toilet bowl when it all came pouring out like a volcano erupting. Inevitably, Isabella was sprayed with some alcohol, but she didn't mind. She loved her mother unconditionally.

Five minutes of nonstop rumbling, then calm. More coffee. More rumbling. Bigger volcano.

This went on for almost an hour.

Then quiet.

The volcano was dormant, and Abby was awake. Coughing, spluttering, and spitting, she tried to stand, but her knees crumbled beneath her. Fortunately, the two helpers were there to support her.

They stuck Abby in the shower—clothes on—and left her there, slumped on the shower floor, unable to support herself. After about fifteen minutes, they turned off the shower and wrapped two towels around her. She was shivering from withdrawal rather than cold, but she was lucid. She stared at her two "first responders," her two "emergency aides," fire in her blue eyes—but said nothing.

When Abby came out of the bathroom, Corella had gone, and Isabella sat on the bed waiting for her. There were tears in Isabella's eyes as her mom came out dressed in her pajamas. She stood up and ran to her, crying.

"Mom, oh Mom, I was so scared when I saw you lying there. Are you okay?" Isabella was sobbing now—partly from sadness, fear of the worst, and relief. The stress of it all brought tears, and they wouldn't stop. She grabbed her mom around the waist and buried her head in her chest.

"Thank you. Thank you both. I don't know what came over me," Abby said in response to her daughter's sobbing. "I'm sorry you had to see that—to witness me at my weakest. I promise you'll never have to go through that again. This is my promise to you, my darling. I love you so much. You are my life!"

"I love you too, Mom. I love you so much. Just get well, okay? Please get well."

"I promise, my baby. I promise! I'll be okay. Now, get along to bed. I'll be in to kiss you goodnight."

Isabella brushed her teeth and hair and jumped into bed wearing her mom's matching pajamas. They had bought them together at the shop where parents and children dressed identically.

She didn't hear her mom silently slip into her room, tuck her in, kiss her ever so lightly on the forehead, and whisper gently, "Goodnight, my baby. Sweet dreams," then leave and close the door on her way out.

Chapter Nine
Javier the Prince

When Javier Carlos Esteban Ozabel-Reyes was born, both his father and grandfather celebrated in true noble fashion. The initial celebration was held at the family domain, roughly two hours from the city.

The domain, aptly named *La Castillo*, was a vast estate consisting of a main structure with several detached dependents situated in close proximity. The massive edifice, adorned with intricately carved stone sculptures, represented the main household. It comprised five double-story apartments: two on the second floor, two on the third floor, and the main apartment covering the entire fourth floor. Each apartment contained four bedrooms with en-suite bathrooms, spacious dressing rooms, and a private spa. Children and close direct relatives were usually housed in these.

The main living quarters were situated on the second floor. Two elevators serviced the entire house, with a discreet service elevator connecting every level. The layout of the fourth floor featured two large bedrooms on either side, each with a bathroom, two toilets, and three dressing rooms. Between the bedrooms were two expansive lounges, each connected to a library and office space. This entire floor was the private living space of Juan-Carlos Senior and his wife—the grandparents.

On the ground and first floors, there were three main lounges, two guest receiving lounges, two dining halls, and one banquet hall that could seat over fifty people. Other amenities included a saltwater aquarium that housed sharks among other marine species, an indoor pool, and a squash court.

Outdoors, the grounds boasted four clay-surface tennis courts, a horse stable with an equestrian training ring, dog kennels, a forest, a stream running through the property, and a man-made dam stocked with freshwater fish, where the family sometimes held fishing competitions. The entire estate spanned two hundred hectares, with a mix of rugged terrain and mountainous landscape.

The cottages—several in number—were spread out on either side of the main castle, all facing away from it. They shared the same architectural design as the main building, with intricate stone carvings depicting characters from Spanish culture and heritage. Impeccably maintained gardens linked each cottage to the main structure. Each cottage featured four spacious bedrooms, a large receiving lounge area, and two dining rooms—one intimate and the other accommodating sixteen chairs. They were all similarly furnished with fourteenth-century Spanish antiques and included a private swimming pool, spa, sauna, and gym room.

As afternoon wore on into evening and dusk settled, guests were ushered into a large marquee. Fifty tables were arranged, each seating eight guests. A stage was set at the front of the marquee, with a podium and microphone. To the right stood a long rectangular table with seven seats—reminiscent of a wedding table for the bride, groom, and close family. No one was seated there initially.

On stage, in front of the podium, stood a Catholic priest dressed in long white robes, reminiscent of a Pontiff. Speaking with a firm yet gentle voice, he called the congregation to attention.

"Please!" the priest said. "Can I have your undivided attention, please!"

Silence fell over the gathering as guests turned their seats to face the front.

"Let us arise and welcome our hosts."

Everyone stood, eyes forward, waiting for the grand entrance of the host family. The air was still; one could hear a pin drop. Finally, there was movement at the front as the grandparents entered, followed by a nurse carrying baby Javier, then Juan-Carlos, Sofia, and Maria Ysabel. They all approached the main table, standing behind their respective places, and turned toward the priest.

"Please be seated," the priest announced into the microphone. Chairs scraped lightly as everyone sat.

"Will the parents and godparents please bring the baby boy?"

Juan-Carlos, Maria Ysabel, a man named Raoul, and his wife, Carmen, stood and walked to the podium.

"Let us all stand, please," said the priest again, prompting more shuffling of chairs.

With baby Javier nestled in his mother's arms, the group ascended the stage. The priest called out, "Let us sing."

Everyone joined in the first hymn:

Glory, glory, praise Thee Father,

We all worship but no other.

Jesus, son of Mother Mary,

Bless us all, our souls are weary.

Welcome us into Your bosom,

Guide our acts and make them fulsome.

Praise Thee Lord, O praise Thee Father

Glory, glory, praise Thee Father!

The priest continued:

"We are gathered here today to welcome Javier Carlos Esteban Ozabel-Reyes into the realms of Heaven. Our Lord Jesus Christ, who sacrificed Himself for our sins—for the blemish of the sins of our babies—so that we can be born pure. With this water, we will wash away the blemish, the sins, the impurities of Javier Carlos Esteban Ozabel-Reyes."

Turning to the godparents, he requested the baby be brought to the Holy Water basin. Carmen and Raoul jointly held Javier as the priest continued the baptism.

"In the name of the Father, the Son, and the Holy Spirit. Amen," he said, dipping his finger into the water and making the sign of the cross on Javier's face. Then, he gently wet the top of Javier's head with the Holy Water.

"Let us sing," he said once more.

Two more hymns were sung before the priest invited everyone to be seated again. At the ceremony's conclusion, he asked the congregation to come forward to pay their respects to the baby.

The godparents descended the podium with baby Javier, standing at the bottom of the stage beside a large donation box.

As guests filed past, each made comments on the baby's beauty and innocence, slipping banknotes of various denominations into the donation box. The proceeds would be split between the parish and the family. One could only imagine the final amount collected by the end of the night. Thus, Prince Javier was introduced to the world.

As the years passed, each of Javier's birthdays was celebrated with an elaborate party. Most attendees were political acquaintances of his father, grandfather, or both. One could hardly expect the young boy to have his own friends at such grandiose events. Instead, the parties served as a platform for showing appreciation for political loyalty and confirming one's place within the inner circle of influence. Perhaps "lucky" was too generous a word to describe those invited, as guests were always expected to donate via the ever-present donation box. Over time, the proceeds were no longer shared with the parish—they were set aside for Javier's college fund.

Each year, Javier's birthday welcomed the Spanish elite to another extravagant affair in honor of the young prince's New Year.

His sister, on the other hand, celebrated her birthday with her school friends—it was more of a "girl thing." Little effort went into the occasion beyond the traditional protocol of making a guest list, distributing invitations at school, and preparing the house to receive the attendees. The men of the house barely acknowledged the event. It was Maria Ysabel who took charge, fussing over her daughter and her daughter's friends, ensuring the celebration was special in its own right.

At sixteen, Javier was quite an avid polo player. The horse stables at the domain accommodated four horses that belonged to him. No one was allowed to mount them except Javier. These were strict instructions handed down from his grandfather at each acquisition. Each horse was acquired for a specific purpose and sport.

Javier's first horse was given to him on his tenth birthday. It was a gift from his grandparents for his show-jumping activity. He had started show jumping at the age of five. Five years later, he was competing in a junior competition—hence, the gift of his own horse, one that understood him.

His second horse was for Spanish horse dressage. From the age of seven, Javier performed dressage with his horse for their guests. His parents were immensely proud of him and the way he mastered the activity. It was quite a spectacle. On rare occasions, his sister, Sofia, would mount her own dressage horse as a supporting act. However, Javier was always the star—the main attraction.

The third horse was gifted to him as a pony, which he rode only when he had friends over. They would often ride around the vast property, racing each other. Javier considered this horse his best friend. He didn't feel the need to show extra care while riding or pamper it when taking it out of the stables.

The polo horse was the fourth, and the pride of the stable. Javier was enrolled in a polo club from the age of ten and was pushed hard to become a champion. By sixteen, he was already playing competitive polo with adults. He was quite the player—tall and elegant as he sat in the saddle, whacking the ball and outriding his opponents.

For his sixteenth birthday, Javier was presented with an open-top Ferrari Spider. Since he was still a minor, the car was gifted to him at the domain and was to remain there until he was legally allowed to drive it. However, because the domain was so vast and the side roads mostly belonged to the family, Javier drove his friends around the countryside. It was his social "Coming of Age," a moment that marked his entry into certain family obligations as a young man. During this event, he was also permitted to invite his official girlfriend and her family to the estate.

Four years later, Javier lost his grandfather, Juan-Carlos Senior. He was completely devastated and withdrew from all his activities. He stopped polo practice and declined all invitations for match-day games and show-jumping competitions. He even offered his dressage horse for sale.

He brooded constantly and refused to attend any family functions at the property. As second in line to the family fortune, Javier was encouraged by his parents to take on greater family responsibilities. His parents, Juan-Carlos II and Maria Ysabel, were at a loss in trying to steer him out of his depressive mood and guide him back on track. Javier and his grandfather had been best friends. They were incredibly close.

The melancholy persisted for a couple of years. During this time, he saw very little of his girlfriend of four years, and eventually, they broke up. His friends filled more of his time, and they partied hard. At home, he was sullen and miserable—but out in public, he became a notorious partygoer. With his undeniable charm and aristocratic posture, Javier was a magnet for all the sophisticated young women in Madrid. There was never a shortage of female companionship wherever Javier and his friends went. They were always surrounded by the most beautiful, elegant, well-educated young women of high society. Promiscuity followed—and with it, indifference.

The death of his grandfather, while plunging him into unprecedented grief at such a young age, served to steer Javier into a socially delinquent spiral that was pulling him into an abyss—without him even realizing the danger.

One night, after one of these social outings, Javier failed to return home. His absence was only noticed when his father needed him urgently for an administrative matter that required his signature. The maid informed Juan-Carlos that Javier's room was empty and that his bed had not been slept in. The gardener was summoned to check if the Ferrari was still in the garage, as would usually have been the case. It wasn't—Javier had not returned home.

His cellphone went straight to voicemail. Fraught with fear, Maria Ysabel called the main hospital, asking if her son had been admitted for any reason. While she was on hold, a police car pulled into the courtyard. Juan-Carlos stepped out to meet the two officers.

The police reported that Javier had been in an accident. The Ferrari was a complete write-off. Javier was lucky to be alive. Excessive speed and alcohol were the primary causes of the crash. Javier, the driver, lost control while maneuvering around a bend and collided with an oncoming truck. The truck driver was unharmed. Javier was taken to the hospital with serious injuries—but, tragically, his passenger, a girl, had died at the scene.

Juan-Carlos collapsed on the spot, and Maria Ysabel let out a loud, piercing scream, dropped the phone, and rushed outside to her husband.

Due to the family's social and political standing, they were driven to the hospital by a police escort. Javier was in the ICU, with breathing tubes and an oxygen mask covering his face. The sight was too much for Juan-Carlos, who collapsed again. This time, nurses at the hospital took him away for resuscitation.

Maria Ysabel and Sofia remained steadfast at Javier's bedside. Their red eyes, tear-streaked faces, and tense, somber expressions revealed the deep anguish and endless sobbing they had endured. Maria Ysabel sat close to Javier, prayer beads in hand, reciting the Hail Mary over and over, begging God to spare her baby and bring him back to her—unscathed.

Two weeks later, Javier was discharged from the hospital. He had been made aware that his passenger had died. He couldn't recall her name or where he had picked her up. His parents intervened on his behalf with the girl's parents and offered a substantial financial settlement, which was accepted. No case or civil litigation would be instigated against Javier.

Whether the consequences of his arrogant and selfish behavior—his complete lack of respect for the well-being of others and utter disregard for the law—had awakened some form of responsibility in him was open for debate. Javier hadn't shown the slightest remorse upon his release from the hospital. His main concern was whether his beloved Ferrari could be repaired, and how soon.

Exasperated by the entitlement shown by her son, Maria Ysabel sat down with him and addressed his actions and attitude, especially toward those around him, including his family. She strongly suggested that Javier travel to Mexico, her birth land, to acquaint himself with the suffering and humility of her people.

Juan-Carlos was completely against the idea and expressed his disagreement in no uncertain terms. It took several weeks before he came around—largely due to unprecedented pressure from both women in the household. It was eventually agreed that Javier would travel to Mexico for six months, then to Texas for one month, and afterward to any European capital of his choosing.

Two years later, Javier still had not returned to Spain, despite his father's constant ramblings. When he finally did return, it was to inform his father that he was branching out on his own business venture. He explained to his parents that while sojourning in London, he had met wealthy individuals who approached him to organize a special event involving politicians, aristocrats, and entertainers.

It was to be a private event held in an upscale, secluded venue, with each guest purchasing a seat at a table for one hundred thousand euros. Two hundred people were invited, and the guest speakers included ex-presidents and prime ministers from developing countries and abroad.

Javier proudly announced to his parents that he had succeeded and felt this was his calling. He suggested to his father that his sister,

Sofia, be appointed Vice President of the family organization. Juan-Carlos was opposed to this, but under pressure from within the household, he relented and appointed Sofia to the role. This decision somewhat released Javier from any immediate obligation to join the family corporation. Nevertheless, he retained the title of Executive Vice President.

Javier began traveling from city to city, promoting his companies—several of which were incorporated in various tax havens. During a visit to Moscow a few years later, Javier met the son of a prominent Russian politician. The two quickly became friends and entered into a joint venture. It helped that the friend had a younger sister to whom Javier was intensely attracted. They began dating.

The joint venture gained significant momentum, and the three of them became inseparable. It was the first serious relationship Javier had experienced, and he was happy.

For his twenty-fourth birthday, Javier organized a lavish party through his Russian subsidiary at the Metropol Hotel in the Russian Black Sea port of Gelendzhik. It was an exclusive affair, with guests flown in by chartered planes from across Europe's capitals. Two hundred guests were expected.

As was customary with such elite events, there was a strict dress code, a gift list, a "no singles" rule, and several other conditions that all attendees were required to follow. Naturally, all the guests were from high-net-worth families, and their invitations were largely a result of their financial stature.

However, despite the strict "no singles" policy—where everyone had to arrive with a partner—Javier, the birthday boy, flirted openly with all the women. His girlfriend (or fiancée, as she liked to call herself) was livid. She spent the evening desperately hanging onto his arm, trying to fend off would-be suitors and flings.

Javier, true to form, managed to slip away and seduce a young guest—the very one invited by his Russian associate. This incident caused quite the scandal and left a mark long after the party ended. The tryst occurred in the hotel restroom and was witnessed by the associate's brother.

Javier's girlfriend, utterly embarrassed, left the party. She refused to be humiliated—especially in front of so many strangers. The young girl in question, however, didn't understand what all the fuss was about. She was there to have fun, shrugged off the incident, returned to her boyfriend, and continued flirting with Javier whenever their eyes met.

Despite the scandal, the party was a success and lasted until midday the next day. Javier, having consumed countless shots and indulged in a few illicit substances, staggered around with a different woman on his arm. When he awoke, there were two previously unknown women lying naked in his bed. He couldn't recall how or when he had ended up in that situation.

He had burned his bridges in Moscow—especially with his associate, whose father was immensely wealthy. Upon returning, all that remained was for him to collect his personal belongings from the office and apartment and head back to Paris.

In Paris, Javier revived one of his event planning subsidiaries and embarked on a new venture. Within a short time, his inbox was flooded with inquiries for various events. One such request was for a videography package for a sixteenth birthday party, complete with extravagant add-ons.

The event was to be unique, and Javier had to think outside the box to ensure exceptional ratings. He met with the sixteen-year-old girl, got to know her preferences and those of her friends, and then began planning the celebration.

The girl's parents were Russian oligarchs living in Paris. There was no budget cap. With an unlimited expense account to manage the planning, Javier invited several established artists to perform, along with multiple public relations professionals, DJs, and popular influencers.

Three artists were booked to perform, each paid one million dollars for a one-hour set. Influencers were paid slightly less, and PR figures—such as top models—received over a quarter of a million dollars each.

If the parents intended to make their mark among the elite and the Parisian jet-set crowd, this event certainly delivered. It was unique and innovative. Javier flourished once again and shook Parisian high society with his avant-garde approach to event planning, setting the bar incredibly high.

Success bred more success. Soon, Javier became the most sought-after event planner in the French capital and beyond. His reputation spread rapidly among nobles and aristocrats, each desiring an exceptional, one-of-a-kind event for their special occasions.

Inundated with a plethora of requests, Javier was eventually contacted in person by an envoy to organize a sixtieth birthday celebration for a Russian oligarch. It was another no-budget-limit affair, with only one constraint—no minors were to attend.

This condition set the stage for an adult-oriented theme that required a mindset focused on indulgence and entertainment. From planning a sweet sixteen to a sixty-year-old's birthday, Javier remained unfazed. He recalled the details and challenges of organizing his own extravagant twenty-eighth birthday bash.

This time, with unlimited funds, an unprecedented entertainment program, and a smorgasbord of exquisite cuisine, Javier was in his element.

For the occasion, Javier secured one of the largest and most luxurious yachts available. He enlisted singers, entertainers, a full orchestra, top models, magicians, and even pole dancers. Four hundred adult guests were expected to attend.

It took Javier a full twelve months to plan and prepare the event. The stage was set for the most exclusive—and most expensive— sixtieth birthday party ever thrown.

Chapter Ten
Abby

At eighteen, Abby had become the headliner—the star attraction of the academy. She was constantly in demand all across the country. The rise to the top of the modeling world had been gruesome and tiresome for Abby. Exhausted, feeling flat and unable to perform, Abby insisted on taking a break.

Robert, seeing only lost revenue, reluctantly agreed to let Abby return home for a short rest before her next assignment: Paris.

The flight to San Antonio took a little over six hours. During the first hour, the girls chatted excitedly, but after two hours, they fell asleep. Robert woke them up just before landing.

In the arrivals hall, Abby ran into Katherine and Anne's arms. All three were crying, hugging, and kissing. Frank was there too, and he flung his arms around Abby, holding her tight and kissing her on both cheeks.

"Well, lookatcha!" exclaimed Frank. "Skinny as a broomstick, but as beautiful and elegant as ever. Welcome home, my sweetheart."

"Mom, Dad, Katherine—this is Anna, my roommate and best friend in New York. I invited her to spend time with the family since her own family isn't in the United States."

"Hello, Anna. Welcome to Texas," said Anne, opening her arms to hug her daughter's friend. "You're both so skinny. Didn't they feed y'all back in New York?"

"Don't forget, these young girls are now world-famous fashion models. And y'all know that the demand for fashion models is based on the very fact that they fit the clothes they present," chimed in Robert, who had, until now, stood back not wanting to impose.

"Nonsense. These girls need to put some meat on their bodies. This calls for a family barbecue. Will you be joining us, young man?" Frank asked Robert.

"Thank you, kind sir. Duty calls. I must head back to prepare for Paris. Not too much red meat now, girls." Robert hugged the girls, turned, and headed back through the departure gates.

The vacation flew by too quickly for Abby. Two weeks felt like two days. She felt like she was caught in a tornado. Her head spun with turbulence that didn't seem to stop. There was so much rest she needed to catch up on, and so much lost time with her family to make up for, that she found herself constantly bouncing between events, invitations, hangouts, and pastimes.

Anna, her guest, was equally swept up in the whirlwind and thoroughly enjoyed her stay with her newfound family. All in all, it was a positive and refreshing break. Abby needed to recharge her batteries, so to speak, because now came the real deal. This was camera-roll time. The real world. Make-or-break. See-what-you're-worth time. There would be no hiding place.

Much to her disappointment, the two-week vacation came to an end. Abby and Anna spent the last two days of the trip, along with Katherine, at the ranch, seeing no one else. Long horseback rides. Picnics by the river. Chatting about everything and nothing. This was chill-out time—the calm before the chaos. Their mental prep for what lay ahead: city after city, cameras flashing, dressing and undressing at lightning speed—all in a day's work. This was the world that awaited them.

Deep down, Abby was apprehensive, still questioning whether this was what she truly wanted. Would she be a success? Was it all worth it—leaving the things she loved behind for a life of uncertainty? Part of her was ready to quit, return to her old life, graduate high school, go to college, and become a veterinarian.

"Did you pack everything?" asked Anna, snapping Abby back to reality.

"Huh? Oh—yes. Yes, I did," Abby replied, a little embarrassed by her absentmindedness.

"Are you excited about Paris?" asked Katherine.

"Hmm. I'd much rather stay here on the ranch with you, Mom, and Dad. But I feel a little responsible for Anna, making sure she doesn't get sidetracked by shady offers. We look after each other, really."

"She's my big sister, and you're my twin sister," Anna said happily, content from having spent time in a warm, loving home for the past two weeks.

"Well, twin sister and older sister, I'm sure I'm gonna miss you both to the point of depression," said Katherine—more seriously than Abby was comfortable with.

"FaceTime, Kate! FaceTime! And a little souvenir from wherever we go. How about that? Might ease your depression a little?" Abby offered.

"Well, if you put it that way, Abbs—if you bribe my ass that way—then yeah, bring it on! No time for grime!" Katherine said, half-joking.

"You two angels ready?" asked Anne, walking into Abby's bedroom where the girls had gathered to help finish packing.

"Ready as I'll ever be, Mom. Which is... not ready," Abby replied. "I don't wanna go. I barely got here, and now I'm back on the road—literally. I'm not sure about all this, Mom. Just having doubts. I missed you guys so much. I'm not sure I can go through that again." Tears welled in her eyes as she looked between Anne and Katherine.

"FaceTime, Abbs. FaceTime! If I recall, somebody promised diamonds and jewelry," Katherine said, trying her best to lighten the mood and ease the growing emotional tension.

"Well, I'm ready," Anna chimed in, reminding them she was there and helping to break the heaviness in the room.

The car ride to the airport was quiet and heavy with emotion. This time, there was no chaperone to assist them. The girls were on their own.

What few knew was that Anna hadn't even been on the official flight schedule. It was Abby who had insisted she come along to Paris. Anna had been the sweetener—the one who convinced Abby to take on this particular assignment. Not that she really needed a sweetener. For Robert, Anna was more of a "scratch my back" card he had tucked up his sleeve. He had his reasons.

It was the first week of March, and Paris was still very much in the midst of winter. It snowed the morning Abby and Anna arrived, but it didn't last long. By early afternoon, the snow on the ground disappeared, replaced by a light drizzle that was irritating as it stung their faces when walking outside. It was almost like the rain was frozen and melted just as it pounded your face. *Ice rain,* if she'd ever seen it, thought Abby.

But this was Paris! Nothing could take away the excitement, the feeling of being in another world. Everything about this place was mythical; it was the birthplace of fashion, with legendary fashion houses, world-famous historical buildings, museums, streets, and parks. It was all just fantastic.

The girls had taken a taxi from the airport to the hotel. They quickly checked in and went out walking to get the feel, to breathe the Parisian air. They walked around for an hour before deciding that they needed transport to go from site to site. Two gullible teenagers, gasping at everything they saw, laughed at themselves as they tried to pronounce the street and shop names. Paris did not disappoint. They took a taxi to the Eiffel Tower, the first stop. It was mid-afternoon when they got there and found that there was still a long queue.

After spending three hours at the Eiffel Tower, the girls headed back to the hotel. Dee had called and left a message for Abby to call her back, which she did.

"Hello, is this Dee?" Abby asked when someone answered at the other end.

"This is she," came the reply. "Who is this? Abby? Abby, is that you?"

"Hi Dee, yes, this is me, Abby. You left a message for me to call you back. Is everything okay?"

"Yes, yes, everything is okay, nothing pressing. How is Paris? Are you enjoying yourself? Met a young romantic Parisian yet?" teased Dee.

"Yes. I mean, no. I mean, yes, we're enjoying Paris. We just arrived today, and no, we're not looking for boyfriends, Parisians, or others," giggled Abby. "Is anything wrong?"

"No, no, actually. I wanted to speak to Anna."

"Okay, well, she's right next to me. Maybe you can tell her directly."

Abby passed the phone to Anna.

"Hello, Dee," said Anna meekly.

"Anna, listen to me. Write this down. We have an important mission for you in Seoul. Have you ever been there? Hmm, no, you haven't. Why would you go there? Okay, anyway, you are to leave on the next direct flight from Paris to Seoul. We have an agent there who will meet you, take care of you, and explain the mission. Your fees have already been negotiated, and we'll talk about it when you return to New York. You are to stay there for three days. Two all-day photo shoots for some new electronic gadget. Then you fly back here. Is this okay and clear for you?"

"Yes, it is. I'll look for flights right now. Thank you, Dee. Thank you very much. I'm so looking forward to my very first modeling assignment."

"Pass me Abby, please," said Dee.

Anna passed the phone back to her friend.

"Hello, this is Abby."

"Abby, you are not to worry about Anna. She's absolutely being taken care of. I know how close the two of you are, but no worries at all. I want you to focus on Paris. This is a big one. Okay?"

"Yes, I understand."

"Focus, okay. Focus! Bring it home, girl. You can do it!"

With that, Dee hung up.

"Ahhh! Eeek!" screamed Anna. "I just can't believe it."

"Believe it, girl. You've earned it!"

They danced and shrieked for a good while, and they chatted excitedly about how things were taking off for them. They had hit the big time; this was their time! They talked until late that night, eating very little as they were so excited and anxious about the next day. Anna had found a flight leaving Paris early evening the next day, while Abby was expected at nine the next morning.

The next morning, they had a light breakfast of All Bran cereal, non-buttered brown toast, fresh fruit, dried fruit, and a glass of freshly squeezed apple, carrot, and orange juice cocktail. Straight after breakfast, a car pulled up outside the hotel's front door to drive Abby to the photo shoot, while Anna stayed to pack up before embarking on a sightseeing adventure on her own.

Abby was driven to the studio, owned by an internationally reputable photographer, which was situated behind the Arc de Triomphe, at the top of the Champs-Élysées. It was very close to the famous George V five-star hotel. Driving past the hotel, Abby wondered what it would be like staying there and mingling with international dignitaries and famous people. She smiled to herself for allowing herself to be drawn into the world of opulence, which was totally out of character. Still, a little pampering never hurt.

After maneuvering for what seemed like ages to Abby through the relentless Parisian morning traffic, they finally arrived at the famous Feuille d'Or photographic studio owned by none other than internationally renowned photographer Artur Placetillini.

Abby entered the fifth-floor studio and was instantly greeted by an assistant.

"Hi! Are you Abby? My name is Giovanna, and I work with Art. Please, call me Gio." She spoke perfect English but with a thick French accent.

"Ermm, hi, Gio. Yes, I'm Abby. Nice to meet you."

"Please follow me. Art is really excited to work with you. He has heard so much about you—all positive, I assure you."

"Well... I don't quite know what to say, except that I'm flattered."

Abby followed Gio through a fairly wide corridor filled with photographs on both walls—obviously the work of "Art," or whatever he called himself. They entered a large, spacious room fitted with spotlights all over the ceiling. A large sofa sat at the back of the room, next to a bar area with a coffee machine and cooler fridges, no doubt stocked with all kinds of drinks. Two doors led off the back wall, which Abby assumed were the gender-separated bathrooms.

Seated on a stool at the bar counter was Artur Placetillini. He jumped off his stool as Abby and Gio entered and, with a huge grin, walked over to welcome her.

"Haabby! It's so nice to see you. Please come, welcome to my humble studio. Do you want to drink something—coffee, soda, water maybe? Yes?" He spoke with a pronounced Italian accent and a hint of French.

Abby found it amusing that he pronounced her name with an "H" at the beginning.

"My name is Artur Placetillini, but you can call me Art. Art Place. Get it? This is Art Place. I create art in this place. Issa nice joke, right?"

Overwhelmed, Abby chose a glass of water to be polite—not that she was thirsty after having just finished breakfast.

"Nice to meet you, Mr. Artur. Thank you for having me."

"Nonsense, it is I who thanks you. And please, I insist—call me Art. Mister Placetillini is my father. Hokay, now I will start right away. Time is money, and money is in my blood. If I give it up, I will bleed to death. Ha! Issa nice joke, right?"

Gio took Abby aside and explained what was required of her and how the shoot would proceed. Abby clarified to Gio that, as per the terms of the agreement in the contract, she was not willing under any circumstance to do any topless or nude shoots. Gio reassured her that none were planned in the program.

Abby followed Gio into the female dressing room to prepare. There were hangers of different clothing, ranging from beachwear to evening and cocktail dresses, with matching footwear for every ensemble. The first shoot was swimwear, so Abby suited up and returned to the studio area.

She was a little startled by the transformation. There were more assistants moving furniture around, but what surprised her most was the sandy beach that had been prepared for the shoot. Lights were on everywhere: direct spots on the "beach," overhead spots, backlight spots—all lit up and waiting for her. Two other girls, already dressed in swimwear, stood nearby.

Okay, let's do this, she thought.

The morning session focused on the swimwear shoot. Most of the shots featured Abby alone, with a few including the two other girls as auxiliaries. Art was a genius—taking shots from all angles, highlighting Abby's beauty, matching her golden blonde hair with the golden sand, and all the while showcasing the swim attire. The lights were perfectly arranged to imitate natural sunshine, further enhancing Abby's features and talents in a relaxed, fun-filled atmosphere. The beach sand was real and felt soft and smooth on Abby's feet. It was fun.

At lunch, sandwiches and light snacks were ordered and delivered by one of the many food delivery companies now invading the city. This was the new norm—the new chic: order out and have the food delivered. Prawn sandwiches, salmon, maki sushi, California rolls, and tempura were all laid out buffet-style, along with still and sparkling water, light sodas, and freshly squeezed fruit juices to round out the refreshment spread. Abby, not a big eater, indulged herself—especially enjoying the sushi assortment.

After the lunch break, the photoshoot shifted focus to evening wear, cocktail apparel, footwear, and jewelry. It was long and demanding—much more intense than the morning's beachwear session. Still, Abby endured. It was her first real paid assignment. She was full of adrenaline and raw excitement.

It was late when Art finally wrapped up the session. Everyone clapped, and Art was beaming. He showered Abby with praise for her talent. By this point, Abby was exhausted and wanted nothing more than to return to the hotel, kick off her shoes, and soak in a hot bath.

Art, thrilled by the day's success, insisted that everyone stay for a final celebratory drink at the bar counter in the studio. They all raised their glasses as Art proposed a toast to Art Place, Abby, and the staff.

"I thought the studio was called *Feuille D'Or*," Abby whispered to Art.

"Last owner. New owner—me. I changed the name to *Art Place*," he replied. "*Arturo Placetillini Studio*—too long. *Art Place*—trendy. No?"

"Yes, much better. Very trendy," Abby offered, hoping to be released soon so she could take that much-needed bath.

"Haabby," said Art, pulling her aside and lowering his voice. "I have anotha gig for you for tomorrow. Are you hinterested? When you go back to New York? You stay one day? Two day?"

"Err, well... yes, I'm booked for tomorrow evening. I have another assignment in New York, yes. Why? What's this new assignment? Did you speak to Robert about this?"

"No, no. No Robert. You direct. You want? Pays well. But you must decide now. I must give answer for tomorrow. You see these girls here," he said, referring to the other models used as background stand-ins. "They think, 'tall, skinny, no eat, then I'm model.' No talent. You! You, Haabby, you have *beeg* talent. I want to work with you all the time. So—tomorrow is good for you? No Robert. Me and you, direct."

"Well, this is very short notice, and I'm really flattered, Art—really, I am. But... right now, I can't think straight because I'm a little exhausted from today. I'll call you after I've had a bath and relaxed, and I'll give you my answer. Before midnight—is that okay?"

"Yes, yes, *hof course*. But please, don't mention to anybody—not Gio. She very good assistant, but I tell her my way. Hokay? We good?"

"Sure, no mention to anybody. But if I agree, we *must* talk business first. Usual remuneration, how long—one day, two days? Expenses? And most importantly, the actual assignment. Sounds exciting, but let me get back to you later this evening."

Abby kissed Art lightly on the cheek, walked over to the rest of the crew, and thanked everyone for their support. She kissed Gio lightly on the cheek and gave her a warm hug. Then, she left.

Chapter Eleven
Abby

There was a driver waiting for her downstairs in a black BMW 6 Series with tinted windows. She eased herself into the rear seat, took out her phone, and called Katherine. They talked excitedly about the day's events. She repeated everything in detail to her mom, and then again for a third time to her dad, as the phone was passed from one family member to another.

Then there were questions about Paris: Were there handsome Parisians on every street corner? Were they as romantic as everybody said they were? They chatted about the food she ate, and then Abby told her mom about the session Art had proposed. Her mom told her to be very careful about what she agreed to and promised to email her a draft contract. Abby was relieved that her family supported her and would provide logistical help in the form of a contract, cell phone monitoring via the internet, and "Location" tracking.

Abby walked through the hotel lobby and straight to the elevator. She put it down to fatigue when she heard her name being called out. She continued her brisk march to the elevator, oblivious to all around her, half-dreaming about the day's events and half longing for the hot bath that awaited her.

There it was again—louder and closer. Abby turned to see Robert running toward her, calling her name.

"Abby, Abby, how are you? It's good to see you! I've been waiting all afternoon for you. I arrived late morning on the red-eye from New York. How was your day, girl? Tell me all about it."

"Robert! What are you doing here?" exclaimed Abby, shocked, the color draining from her face. If there was an emergency, it wasn't her family—she had just spoken to them in the car.

Oh God, no, not Anna, she thought.

"Well, you don't look too excited to see me, girl. I flew halfway across the world to be here for you. And that's all I get? 'Robert, what are you doing here?'" he said, mimicking her expression and tone.

"New York to Paris isn't exactly halfway across the world. What are you doing here?"

"Duh, girl, I came to see you."

"Why? Is anything the matter?"

"Is there? You'll tell me if something's wrong, won't you?"

"Robert! Why are you here? Stop turning around the subject with your insincere concerns! Is something the matter? I'm really tired from a long day of studio shoots, so please, stop draining what's left of my patience and energy."

"Okay, okay, smile a little, will ya! Nothing's wrong. Tell you what—let's move to the bar area, and I'll explain it over cocktails. Heh? How about that?"

"I'm tired. I need to shower, relax, and digest the day's events. My conversation will not be coherent. Perhaps breakfast will be more appropriate."

"Oh, nonsense. You're always coherent. If I may suggest an alternative—why don't you do what you have to do: shower, relax, have a glass of wine or whatever, and let's meet, err, shall we say in two hours for dinner in the hotel restaurant? Will that be okay for you?"

"I guess I can make the effort. After all, you flew halfway across the whole wide world to see little old me!" said Abby, batting her eyelids and smiling innocently.

"Great! Time check—it's a little after six p.m., six twenty-five to be exact. Eighteen twenty-five, military time. Hmm, let's say we meet around 8:30 p.m. Okay for you?"

"More like nine p.m.—or twenty-one hundred hours, military time, if you like. You don't need to call; I'll be down. See you."

The elevator door opened, and Abby walked in. She pressed the eighth-floor button and leaned back against the side as the door closed. She was alone in the elevator.

Once in her room, Abby called her mom and asked how the draft contract was going. She then got undressed and ran a hot bath. She poured herself a soft drink from the minibar and stepped into the tub with her drink. She drained the glass, leaned her head back on the headrest, closed her eyes, and dozed off.

Abby was awakened by the loud ring of the wall phone fitted in the bathroom. Disoriented, she couldn't quite figure out what the ringing noise was or where it was originating from. Slowly, she came around and recognized the ringtone. She stretched above her head to reach for the phone, then thought better of it. She didn't want to electrocute herself by accident, lying in the bathtub. So she stepped out and answered. Besides, the water had gone lukewarm.

"Hello," she answered in a soft voice.

"Hey girl, where are you? I've been sitting here alone for the past thirty minutes. Do you want me to come upstairs?"

"Oh, Robert! It's you! Hmm, okay, give me a few minutes, and I'll be down. So sorry, I dozed off in the bath. I'll be down." She hung up and started brushing her teeth.

Twenty minutes later, she was sitting opposite Robert at the dinner table in the hotel restaurant.

"You look amazing! Even wearing newspapers and cardboard, you'd be amazing. Would you like an aperitif? Wine? Red, white?"

"Water will be fine. Sparkling, please."

The waiter came, took their orders, and left them to their conversation.

Abby looked at Robert, sighed, and said, "Okay, Robert, I'm listening."

With a serious expression on his face, Robert explained to Abby what exactly he was doing in Paris.

"Thank you, Abby. Thank you for listening. I came out here to have a chat with you about the academy. We're in serious financial difficulties. At present, we're unable to recruit new candidates. Your class was the last we could afford. The situation was so bad that we were due to shut down and file for Chapter Eleven under the Protection Against Creditors Act until we were able to return to a profitable base.

"We borrowed from friends and family to finance the year under the pretext that we had discovered the rarest of gems. The unflawed diamond. *You!* We are confident that you will be the biggest star in the world. All the other girls you graduated with—I know that you have a tender spot for Anna—but none of them have the talent, the charisma, the beauty, and the charm that you have to make it as a world-class model. They just don't have it.

"But we needed them to make up the numbers for the academy and the school year, albeit at a cost to us. We invested heavily in you, mostly, but we hoped that maybe one or, optimistically, two of the other girls could cover costs with medium assignments."

"I came out to reach you for your support, your understanding and empathy regarding our situation—and for your help. These are difficult times, and please don't misunderstand my reasoning. We are not asking for handouts. We... I am appealing to your kindness, your consideration, and your business acumen in extending a personal financial commitment to sustain the continuance of the academy.

"I'm not even checked into this hotel—way beyond budget. I'm checked in—well, not yet, anyway—to a bed-and-breakfast near the Gare de Lyon metro station. You know, low budget. I came to speak to you face-to-face, to lay out our predicament, and to hope that you will commit. I've put our cards on the table. No fancy sales pitch. What do you say? Will you help?"

Abby sat across from Robert, her face stern. She didn't move, didn't speak—just stared at him. They sat this way for a while. The waiter brought their orders, placed their meals in front of them, and asked, "Can I get you anything else? More wine?"

"This is just fine. That will be all, thank you," replied Robert.

Abby's appetite had vanished after listening to the academy's predicament. She would have gladly skipped dinner altogether but had agreed to join Robert and had managed to work up an appetite. Now it was gone. She toyed with her filet de rouget and fresh vegetables, sipping her sparkling water with ice.

Finally, she spoke.

"What business acumen are you referring to?"

"Well, I know that you study the contracts scrupulously before accepting and signing any commitment. In this instance, I know you'll expect compensation for any financial outlay you may pledge."

"I have conditions. These conditions must be met rigorously."

"Yes, of course. I ask for nothing less than a legally binding agreement—a contract that stipulates all the terms and conditions by which we enter into our commercial arrangement."

"I assume that you have already prepared a draft of such a contract?"

"Abby—"

"Robert. Please don't patronize me. Do you or do you not have in your possession a draft contract?"

"I'm sorry. Yes, I do."

"Okay then. Let me have it. I'll look it over and get back to you."

"Can we go through the main points now and continue after dinner in the bar area—coffee, tea?"

"I have to sleep early. I have an assignment tomorrow. I have yet to confirm my acceptance to Art."

"What? A follow-up assignment with Art? Wow! You must have blown him away—and all his assistants too!"

"Apparently so. But I haven't agreed to anything yet. I guess I will do it."

"Wow! This is great, Abby. Art is the best photographer in the world right now. He wants to work with you on a follow-up assignment. That's just fantastic!"

"Yes, well… he said not to mention it to you."

"Why not?"

"I don't know. Maybe he thought you'd mess it up with your meddling and demands. He probably just wants to keep it simple. Anyway, after dinner, I'll email him my acceptance, with a copy of the contract that my mom emailed me."

"Not wanting to mess it up, as you so crudely put it, can I suggest a few pointers?"

"Sure!"

"Well, first of all: expenses. All expenses must be covered—from the moment you sign the contract, you're assigned, and all travel and living costs from wherever you are must be included.

"Second, security. Your security must be guaranteed—from the moment you agree to the moment you leave. All arrangements must be pre-approved by you, and all related charges should be assumed by the hiring party.

"Third, your fee. Always agree on a net fee, post-tax. As an American citizen, U.S. taxes must be factored in when setting a fee, and the fee must be paid in full up front.

"Fourth—and this is where I usually 'mess it up'—ask for certified, accredited makeup artists, hair stylists, wardrobe coordinators, etc. Also, include a clause allowing you to keep the clothes you model. It's difficult to get it approved, but we always include it. Often, it gets removed. Other minor items—sparkling water, ice bucket, still water, wine or no wine—these are the typical 'Prima Donna' demands that appear in such contracts."

"Thank you for the pointers. I'll certainly include them. Oh, and by the way, two things come to mind. First, let's get you booked into this hotel. And second—you can accompany me to the follow-up assignment. If you want to, of course."

Robert was all smiles as he cleaned his plate—and some of Abby's unfinished meal. He ordered a glass of champagne for himself and more sparkling water for Abby. They chatted about world events, the weather, Paris, Europe, and nothing in particular. The evening's discussion had already been heavy enough.

After dinner, they both went to the reception area to book a room for Robert. After about thirty minutes of haggling, they secured a single room on one of the lower floors. They bid each other goodnight and agreed to meet for breakfast at 9:30 a.m.

Once in her room, Abby emailed Art, accepting the follow-up assignment. She included all the pointers Robert had suggested as part of her terms and conditions. For her fee, she requested an hourly rate of $50,000 USD, starting from the moment she was picked up from the hotel. This fee, she underlined, was non-negotiable. Additionally, she stipulated that the hourly rate would double after midnight for the first two hours, and then quadruple for every hour after that.

Art replied almost immediately with big smiley faces and laughing emojis. At the bottom, he added one word: **"Okay!"**

Abby replied, **"Good!"** with one smiley, and added a postscript:

"P.S. Robert is here and will be joining me."

Art replied with an upside-down smiley—clearly not thrilled—and typed,

"Okay! Please be ready by 2 p.m."

Abby jumped into bed after her bathroom routine and read the draft contract Robert had given her.

The next day, they were picked up from the hotel and driven to an airport that catered to private jets. After check-in formalities, they boarded an Airbus ACJ319 outfitted with a conference room, VIP suite, first-class dining area, and other luxurious amenities. Abby was taken aback by such splendor and extravagance. She had flown thousands of miles before, but never in her wildest dreams imagined an aircraft outfitted with such opulence.

She felt almost guilty having such extravagance at her disposal, especially when a standard flight would have sufficed. Her guilt—and slight reluctance—stemmed from two basic concerns forming in her mind.

First, the environmental cost of using a massive private jet for a short-haul flight, when regular air transport would have been perfectly   adequate. Second, Abby wondered what kind of compensation would be expected of her in return for this excessive luxury.

Maybe she was overthinking the significance of flying private— and her own self-importance.

She decided to sit back and enjoy the ride. After all, a ride was all it was.

Chapter Twelve
Isabella

RYAN - The New Driver

The next morning, Isabella prepared herself for school. Before going downstairs for breakfast, she checked in on her mom. Her dad, Javier, was nowhere to be seen. Her mom was lying in bed, checking her phone for text messages when Isabella entered.

"Oh, hi, hon!" Abby exclaimed, beckoning for Isabella to approach. "That was a very brave thing you did last night. You were so courageous and level-headed. Thank you, my sweet baby. I just want you to know how sorry I am that you had to witness that. I'm so sorry and embarrassed. Can you forgive me?"

"Oh, Mom! Nothing to forgive. If anything had happened to you, I don't know what I would've done. I was so scared when I saw you motionless on the floor. I'm just glad you're okay."

"Come sit next to me for a second. You are my world. I live and breathe for you. If anything should happen to you, I'd die!"

"I love you, Mom. Promise me you'll beat this, please. Promise me! Please?"

"With your love, strength, and support, I can beat anything, my baby. My sweet baby."

"Thank you, Mom! I will be your strength and boundless support through everything. I just need you to be courageous and have the willpower to beat this. Promise me, Mom! Promise that we'll work on this together."

"Seeing you battle—unwavering, fearless—gives me all the strength and willpower I need. I promise we'll work this out together, my darling baby girl."

"Thank you, Mom. I have to go to school now."

Isabella left her mom's bedroom and headed down to the kitchen. She had no appetite, so she decided to skip breakfast. As she passed through the kitchen on her way out, Corella called out to her.

"Breakfast gives a warrior strength to fight and defeat enemies. With no fuel, an engine—a machine—can't run. It stutters and splutters and dies down."

"To go!" Isabella called back, hesitating before exiting the kitchen.

"To go, it is!" smiled Corella.

Corella instantly handed Isabella a small carry bag containing a small bottle of orange juice, a toasted egg and chicken sandwich, an

136

apple, and a banana. Two cereal energy bars were also tucked in the bag.

Isabella looked up at Corella, who added, "Afternoon sports require a great deal of concentration and physical energy."

"Thank you, Corella."

As she walked to the courtyard, Isabella noticed Ramiro fussing over the car assigned to her. It was the same one as the previous day, but not the one driven by the Mute. He was wiping it down with a leather cloth, ensuring there was no dust or scratches. For Ramiro's simple brain, the "test" began with a clean, spotless car. Next would be a faultless drive to school, safely dropping off the "client," then driving back to await further instructions.

For Ramiro, passing the test meant executing the boss's orders to the last detail. Any deviation would be considered a failure, likely resulting in immediate dismissal.

Ramiro had substantial financial obligations and needed a steady income to support his family. Losing this job was unthinkable and would lead to disastrous consequences. Thus, he was bound to maintain employment by being obedient and subservient. The dichotomy of his contract meant that while Isabella was his client, Javier was his employer—and Javier's orders were absolute. However, Isabella's wishes also had to be respected. Under normal circumstances, where employer and client were the same or not in conflict, these terms wouldn't matter. But in this case, they did.

Isabella hurried to the car and opened the rear door herself, getting in before Ramiro could reach it. By the time he got there, she was already seated, pulling the seatbelt across her chest. Ramiro rushed back to the driver's side, climbed in, and started the car—driving off slowly and carefully.

As the city approached, Isabella instructed Ramiro to continue down the interstate, through downtown, and into the rundown city backstreets.

"My instructions from Señor Javier are to take you straight to school. No dilly-dallying. No stopping for anything," he warned.

Isabella leaned forward and placed her hand across Ramiro's eyes, blinding him. In a panic, Ramiro slammed on the brakes, and the car screeched to a halt in the middle of the street. Horns blared in protest. Calmly, Isabella opened her door and stepped out right there in the street. More honking. She stopped, placed both hands on her hips, and stared at the drivers. The honking stopped. She picked up her bag and crossed the street to the sidewalk.

Ramiro, sweating and panicking, quickly parked the car with two wheels up on the curb, about five meters ahead of her. He jumped out and begged Isabella to get back in, fearing he'd lose his job if she didn't.

Isabella simply put on her headphones, turned up the volume, and kept walking briskly toward the city center. Remembering the events of the previous day, Ramiro realized he wasn't in control and that resisting would only make things worse. His only option was to follow Isabella's lead.

"Please, Señorita Isabella, I take you where you want. I take you! Please, please return to car. I follow your orders!"

Isabella stopped walking, turned to Ramiro, and simply pointed. She pointed to the car, then turned around and walked back to it. She opened the rear door and stepped in.

Ramiro, flustered and teary-eyed, scrambled into the driver's seat. He sat silently for a few seconds, wiping the sweat from his brow before starting the car. He turned around, waiting for instructions.

Isabella told him to drive through the city center and toward the outskirts, heading for the ghetto backstreets. They drove through street after street until she instructed him to stop and park.

Ramiro didn't argue. He complied silently and closed his eyes, praying. He prayed that neither Isabella nor he would be harmed.

Boldly and confidently, Isabella walked to the street corner where five young men were sprawled on the sidewalk. Ramiro closed his eyes—then opened one—ready to drive off if there was any trouble.

Hands on her hips, Isabella stopped just two feet from them and appeared to address the group.

"What happened to you?" she asked, addressing one of the men who was flat on his back, staring wide-eyed at nothing. He lay there motionless, barely breathing, not answering, not acknowledging her.

One of the other men struggled to sit up, pressing his back against the wall for support. He was clearly intoxicated.

"Who are you, little bitch? Buy the drinks, then fuck off. Maybe we keep you here and sell you!"

Completely ignoring him, Isabella addressed the motionless man again.

"I said, what happened to you, Mute? Think you'll find your tongue at the bottom of that bottle. What's that—rum? Whiskey?"

"Just buy both," said the man slouched against the wall, who had tried several times to stand but kept falling back down.

Mute just lay there motionless—numb from excessive drinking, smoking, and whatever other illicit drugs he had consumed.

Isabella bent down, grabbed his arm, put it around her shoulder, and tried to lift him. He was too heavy and nearly pulled her down with him. As she bent forward to let go, one of the other men tried to grab her. She kicked him in the ribs with a side-kick, and he went sprawling in the dirt.

He grinned and said, "I like it when you play rough." Then he closed his eyes and passed out.

Isabella put two fingers in her mouth and whistled for Ramiro to get out of the car and give her a hand.

Ramiro came running, muttering prayers to "Mother of God" for mercy and forgiveness. When he reached her, he shut his eyes and pleaded for her to leave immediately—they were in imminent danger.

"Grab his arm. I'll grab the other. We need to lift him."

"No, señorita, this a bad decision. We die here . . . too dangerous, this area . . . please, we must go now. School calling."

Isabella grabbed Ramiro by the shirt collar and pulled him toward her.

"I said grab his arm. He's too heavy for me to lift alone."

Together, they lifted the Mute and half-dragged him to the car, putting him in the front seat. Isabella climbed into the back, and they drove off. Mute was passed out—possibly overdosing.

"Where to now, señorita?"

"Home!" she answered.

"Oh no, no, no! Oh no. Please no. Señor Javier kill me for sure. Today, I die."

"If you don't drive me home, you will surely die today. I'll kill you myself. Home!"

They drove in silence. When they arrived at La Aldea—The Village, as the estate was called because of all the dependencies and staff residences—Isabella instructed Ramiro to drive around to the Cuidador residence, which was reserved for the most senior and trusted personnel.

Ramiro parked right up close to the front door. He and Isabella got out and went to the passenger side. Together, they dragged Mute from the car, his feet dragging along the ground. They pulled him into the house, straight to the bedroom, and laid him on the bed, fully clothed.

"Go fetch Corella! Quick!"

Without hesitation, Ramiro ran from the bungalow and headed to the main house. He entered through the kitchen, where Corella was preparing lunch. She looked up at him quizzically, without saying a word.

"Señorita Isabella needs you urgently. Please come," he said in Spanish. Then he paused, smiled, and added, "Smells good. What are you making?"

"Where is Isabella?"

"Residence Cuidador!"

"Okay, let's go."

When Corella entered the bungalow and opened the bedroom door, she immediately understood the gravity of the situation.

"Turn him on his side," she instructed Ramiro. Then she turned to Isabella. "Get a wooden spoon and hold his tongue down so he doesn't swallow it. I'm going to give him a herbal drink that will violently convulse him. Let's go!"

Ramiro turned the Mute onto his side while Isabella held his tongue down tightly. A few minutes later, Corella returned with a strange-looking bottle filled with even stranger-looking herbs.

"A tablespoon won't be enough," she muttered.

"Sit him up!" she ordered.

They lifted the Mute until he was sitting upright, though he slouched forward. His breathing was shallow, and his pulse weak.

"Okay. Hold him firmly when he starts to shake."

Corella opened Mute's mouth, poured half the bottle of her concoction down his throat, clamped his mouth shut, and pinched his nose. The only path for the liquid was down.

Five seconds passed.

Ten. Fifteen. Twenty. Thirty...

Then Mute's eyes shot open. He gasped for air, sucking in deeply. A violent shudder wracked his body—a convulsive attack. Then came a sudden, forceful surge of energy, as though he were fighting off invisible enemies, lashing out at whatever was holding him down.

Isabella and Ramiro were no match for his Hulk-like strength. He roared, pounding his chest as the liquid scorched its way down his throat and into his bowels. He jumped up on the bed and roared again, still beating his chest, bouncing in place like he was running on a treadmill.

Then—silence.

No more pounding. No more roaring. No more movement.

He collapsed backward on the bed, eyes wide open, staring blankly at the ceiling. Slowly, his eyelids lowered. His breathing was heavy—but steady.

Isabella stood in total shock, struggling to believe what she had just witnessed. But deep inside, she trusted Corella.

Corella looked over at Isabella and said, "He wasn't going to make it through the night. I know where you found him. You did well bringing him here. He needs rest. Keep an eye on him, and I'll do the same. Call me when he wakes. He'll need a follow-up potion."

Ramiro, pacing back and forth, moaned endlessly about how Señor Javier was going to skin him alive before tossing him, naked, to the alligators. He complained that he had never imagined being dragged into such an incident—and how desperately he needed his job to support his heavily indebted family.

Corella took him in her arms, gave him a hug and a kiss on the cheek, and assured him that none of that was going to happen.

Isabella pulled up a chair and sat next to the bed, watching over the Mute.

Corella looked at her and asked, "Why? Why this one?"

With a stern look on her face, clearly concerned, Isabella looked up at Corella and answered, "You know why."

"I'm sorry that you have two to deal with at the same time."

"I can manage. Thank you, my dear Corella. You are my second mother." Isabella stood up and kissed Corella lightly on the cheek.

Corella turned to Ramiro and said, "Now, let's get some lunch for you."

The Mute drifted in and out of consciousness for a few days. Each time he opened his eyes, Isabella was there, sitting next to him, watching over him.

When he was finally able to get out of bed, he walked out in his shorts and sat on the cottage's veranda. Isabella was not home yet. Corella walked across the green and sat beside him on a lounge chair. She was carrying a tray with food she had prepared: a bottle of still water, some fruit, and a homemade apple tart. She placed the tray on the glass garden table between the two of them. The Mute sat there, unmoving, just staring straight ahead.

Corella pulled out a half-liter bottle of herbal mixture from her apron pocket. She handed it to him and said, "Drink!"

He took the bottle and set it on the table.

Slowly, she turned his head to face her. "You're wondering what the hell you're doing here, right? You died—overdosed on alcohol, cocaine, heroin, and whatever other shit you took. You died, *cabron*! I brought you back to life! Now drink this preparation—all of it. And I mean *all* of it, every last drop! It will make you sick. Your body will be on fire, your head will explode, and when it's done, you'll be as good as new. I promise you that. Why? You better ask that little girl who went out of her way to find you dead on a street corner and brought you here. *Here*! To *me*, so I could fix you. Why? All I can tell you is that Isabella saw something in you. You'll have to ask her what. Maybe she'll tell you, because she certainly hasn't told me."

Corella stood up. She placed her hand on his shoulder and said, "Drink. Now!"

The Mute took the bottle, filled with roots, leaves, and berries, and drank it all down. He handed the empty bottle back to Corella, who said, "Now eat, then go back to bed."

She turned and left.

It took the Mute two full weeks to regain enough strength to get out of bed and walk around the lawn surrounding the cabin. His steps were still slightly wobbly, but he could feel his strength slowly returning. Corella no longer brought food to his door, so he had to walk to her kitchen when hungry.

He had lost a great deal of muscle; he resembled nothing more than skin and bones. He was, to say the least, a shadow of his former marine self. All the strength, muscle, shine, and body mass were gone. In their place was a ragged, skin-and-bone ghost. Still, he was glad to be alive—and he knew he had Isabella to thank for that. He would repay the debt, he vowed, whatever it took—even if it meant paying with his life.

One evening, three weeks later, while the Mute was heading to the kitchen for supper, he spotted Isabella on the green that separated his cabin from the main house. She was dressed in black tights and a pink gym crop top, practicing Tai Chi. Her moves were smooth, precise, nimble—and beautiful. He just stood there, mesmerized by her lithe movements.

While he stood there transfixed, Isabella never once acknowledged his presence. She practiced for an hour, and Ryan stood there the entire time, watching, admiring, completely consumed by the combination of physical beauty and disciplined movement. Isabella was lithe, flexible, and strong—each movement displaying her power.

When Isabella finished, she picked up her towel, wiped down her face, and entered the main house without so much as a nod or a glance in his direction.

For his part, Ryan walked up to the kitchen, and before he could even knock, the door opened. There stood Corella with his dinner. She smiled at him.

"I see you got caught up in traffic. Food's almost cold."

She handed him the covered plate and closed the door without inviting him in. Ryan turned and left.

It had now been roughly six weeks since Ryan was brought back to life by Corella, and he had regained nearly seventy percent of his strength and range of movement. Isabella's parents had traveled to

Spain, where Javier checked in on the family businesses he managed—and visited his sister, Sofia. Isabella often thought about her parents, wondering where they were and if they were okay. Especially her mom. She knew her dad enjoyed the travel, the hotels, and all the first-class pampering on the planes.

Ryan trained rigorously every morning, going for long runs on the main road outside the property. In the evenings before dinner, he followed a carefully designed muscle gain program. During one of these evening workouts, Isabella walked up to him, interrupting his routine, and stood right in front of him.

"Today, we will train together," she said, dressed in fitness attire. She was all seriousness—no smile, no visible emotion.

Ryan nodded, and they got to work. After an intense hour and a half of nonstop exercise—mixing cardio with strength training—he sat down on the green, smiling. He clasped his hands together, looked up at the sky, then back at Isabella, and nodded with a grin.

He picked up his towel and walked back to the cabin. He headed straight for the shower. He wanted to clean up all the sweat before heading over to the kitchen to pick up his dinner.

He pulled on a pair of comfortable sweatpants and a soft T-shirt, then headed toward the lounge. As he opened the closet door to enter, he froze. Isabella was standing right in front of him, in the middle of the room, her eyes locked on his. For a moment, he felt like a deer caught in headlights—stunned, motionless, unable to do anything but stand there, caught off guard by her sudden presence.

"Look at me!" she said. "Look at me."

Ryan cast his eyes down, unable to look at this twelve-year-old girl—his boss.

"I'm looking at you. You lift your eyes and look at me! Look at me!" she said firmly.

Ryan slowly lifted his gaze and looked at Isabella standing in the middle of the lounge.

"Look at me," she said again. "I am, and will be, the last female you will look at in this way. As of this moment, you will never set eyes on another woman—naked, undressed, or in any other state. You will never touch or feel another woman, whether dressed or undressed.

"As of this moment, with our eyes locked, we are unified as one. I, Isabella Katherine Reyes, on this day, at this moment, give my mind, my soul, my love, my commitment, my loyalty, and my protection to the man before me. The man that I have chosen to stand by my side as my future husband, partner, soldier, lover, and father to my future children.

"This man is standing in front of me right now. There will be no cover, no shield, no secrets between us. Just as he entered this world—pure and untainted—shall he bequeath himself to me. I stand in front of him just as I entered this world, pure and untainted, with no cover, no shield, and no secrets. Today, our spirits combine and unite as one. They can never—and will never—be untangled or separated."

She stared directly into his eyes for a full minute more. Then, as unexpectedly as she had appeared, she turned and swiftly left the room.

Still shaken by the events, Ryan went straight to see Corella for an explanation. He felt strange about the entire encounter and needed to either block it out or fully understand where it came from. He no longer had an appetite.

He knocked on the kitchen door. Corella opened it, smiling—yet her eyes were watering. She looked at Ryan and said, "You have been chosen. You're confused, and you need to understand what just happened, right? That's why you look like you've just had your first encounter with an alien."

Corella was still smiling, but the tears flowed even more.

"Yes. What was that all about?" asked Ryan, visibly shaken, holding his head with both hands and muttering to himself.

"Isabella is a special young girl. She belongs to the bloodline of an ancient Aztec people. She has chosen you to be her lifelong partner at this young, early age because she sees all the good in you. You will be protected by the Ancients. Don't fight it. Go in peace. Go with God! I'm so emotional right now. You two are the perfect couple. You will marry when the time is right, but I'm already crying with emotion. That's all. Now go!"

Corella stepped back into the kitchen and closed the door.

Ryan, still stunned and confused, walked slowly back to his quarters. He showered and went straight to bed.

The next morning, Ramiro woke him and informed him that his vacation period was over and that the boss required him to start work. He got dressed quickly and was ready when Isabella walked out. Ramiro had already prepared the Audi A8—the car Ryan had driven only twice before.

Isabella sat in front, in the passenger seat. As they turned onto the main road, she looked at him and said, "Every morning, on our ride to school, you will train your voice. For the first exercise, I want you to roll your tongue to the back of your throat and make a gurgling noise. Like this—uuurrrgggglllle!"

Ryan dutifully complied.

Six weeks later, he was able to pronounce the letter "R" from deep in his throat. He could roar like a ferocious lion, much to Isabella's amusement. His speech was returning at a rapid pace, and communication was progressing comfortably. In the evenings, they practiced Tai Chi, yoga, and fitness together. But Isabella never ventured into his cabin again. The initial ritual was done—and could never be undone. Corella understood this, but she never let on to Isabella that she did.

One morning, on her way to school, teasing Ryan about his slow, hesitant speech, she instructed him to deviate from their usual route to a less desirable part of the city. The Mute said nothing—but broke out in a cold sweat. His face turned stern and focused; his eyes grew smaller and wide open, as if he had been tasered.

Isabella directed him to their destination—an abandoned match factory. Many years ago, the factory had produced stick matches. But with the rise of cheaper and more practical lighters, the match factory had shut down and never reopened.

They entered the factory building with the car and drove to what used to be the office unit. She instructed Ryan to turn off the engine and follow her. They walked up the metal staircase to the main office door. Isabella stopped, turned to him, and told him to enter while she waited outside.

Inside the office were two couches in despicable condition, a television mounted on the wall, and a large office desk to one side. Sitting around the room were his old mates.

They looked up, jaws dropped, eyes wide in shock—staring at their friend, alive and in remarkably good shape.

Ryan, too, was stunned. Frozen. Just as speechless as his friends.

Then came the roar—everyone shouting, screaming, laughing, insulting, and hugging one another.

"Ryan! Ryan! We thought you were dead, bro!" were the only coherent words amid the roaring.

Then the door opened, and Isabella stepped in.

Total silence followed. They all stood straight—almost at attention—bowed their heads, and mumbled, "Ma'am."

Ryan looked back at Isabella, then at his friends, and then at Isabella again. Before he could utter a single word, Isabella patted him on the shoulder and said, "Hello, boys. Nice to see you all behaving."

Ryan was at a complete loss. "What?"

"He speaks! He speaks!" his mates shouted all at once.

"Yes, he does, guys. Yes, he does! Get yourselves ready. We'll meet at ten at the coffee place outside."

Chapter Thirteen
Isabella

B reakfast at the coffee place was a happy reunion. Laughter rang out almost incessantly as they exchanged stories and relived their past glories. The darker stories were avoided. Breakfast lasted almost until noon.

Before leaving, Isabella stood up and addressed the group.

"You all have been granted a second chance in life. You all know, deep in your own minds, the deep, dark place you were in. You all know what took you there. What kept you there. But look at you today. You have survived death. No! Death would have been a blessing—you survived the enchantment of the devil himself. You are among us now. Welcome back to the living. Take this chance. Make a difference. Build on that difference. Make yourselves proud, for you can only thank yourselves for your rehabilitation.

Let us pray. Dear Lord, you have tested us to the utmost, knowing we are but weak souls. Lord, we broke, we caved into the temptation of the Cursed One, and yet you have plucked us from our demise, stood us straight, and pointed us in a steadfast direction. Lord, let us never again be led astray. Amen."

"Amen!"

Back in the car on their way to martial arts practice, Ryan looked at Isabella questioningly.

"After picking you up and taking you home, Ramiro came back with a few friends and picked the boys up and took them to the factory. Corella prepared a batch of potion for them all. Between school and martial arts, I brought the brew to them and made sure they all drank it. The rest is history."

Ryan stopped the car and turned in his seat to stare unblinkingly at Isabella.

"Thank you," he stammered. "Thank you."

Isabella leaned over and kissed him on the cheek. "I know. They are your family. They are my security now."

Ryan pushed the gear into "drive," and they continued to the martial arts academy, where Isabella was considered a local hero by the kids who attended classes there.

The Boys—as Isabella affectionately referred to them—were moved from the factory and re-settled in prefabricated bungalows, more like individual trailers, on land adjacent to the residence. There, they were provided with a support staff, which consisted of a cook and cleaning crew. Their daily routine involved jogging, exercising, target practice, and unarmed combat training.

Between driving Isabella to school and picking her up for extracurricular activities, Ryan joined his buddies—the Boys—in their training. He earned the nickname "Captain," or Cap for short, even though he was the youngest and the lowest-ranked member of the group. When the Boys were confident enough to resume active duty, two were assigned each day to escort Isabella—albeit from a discreet distance—to school. They remained in the vicinity all day, providing security.

When Javier and Abby eventually returned from their trip to Spain, they were both bewildered by the transformation of daily operations and execution of tasks at the Hacienda. Staff moved with purpose; tasks were executed almost in military fashion. There was no lounging about. The Hacienda had a somber, serious atmosphere.

When they stepped out from their armored Mercedes-Maybach, Javier and Abby were met by middle-aged female staff who ushered them into the house. Gone were the young girls in mini dresses catering to Javier. Young men attended to their baggage, and the vehicle was immediately whisked away, washed, and inspected. No orders needed to be given.

Before entering the house, Javier turned 360 degrees to take in everything he was seeing. This was not the home he had left behind. As if reading his mind, his chief of staff appeared from the office across the courtyard.

"Welcome back, señor. How was your trip? How was your stay?" said Manuel Ortega.

"Am I in the right place here, Manuel?" asked Javier.

"Sí, señor, you are in the correct place. This is the Hacienda—your home."

"It certainly doesn't feel like home. What is going on here? Looks like a military camp."

"Señorita Isabella has given new orders. New security. New army. We must obey—all of us. Otherwise, *cortarte la garganta*," he said, imitating slitting his throat with his forefinger.

"Well, I'm back now. I give the orders. This is my house, my rules, okay?"

"Señor, for your own safety, speak softly."

"What?!"

Javier turned and stormed into the house.

Later that evening, Isabella returned home—later than usual. Her mother, Abby, was waiting at the front entrance to welcome her daughter. Before the car had come to a complete stop, Isabella had already exited the passenger door, screaming, "Mother, Mother! You're back! Oh, I missed you so!"

"Oh, my baby. Oh, my baby," was all Abby could mutter.

They locked in a long and tight embrace. Abby kissed her daughter all over. They wouldn't let go of each other, and tears of joy flooded Abby's face.

"Oh, Mom. I missed you so much. I love you," Isabella repeated.

"What about me?" Javier's voice came from inside as he walked to the entrance.

Reluctantly, Isabella let go of her mom and hugged her dad. "Hi, Dad. Did you have a good trip?"

"Didn't you miss me?"

"Of course I did. Why do you ask?" replied Isabella, frowning.

"Well, apparently, you couldn't wait for me to leave to completely change the daily operations and functioning of the house. All my orders were thrown out the door. What's going on?"

"See why I don't miss you? Straight down to business."

"Well, at least you're open about not missing me. Now, who are these people? Where are the regular personnel I hired?"

"Oh, you mean the very young girls with short skirts that bend every two seconds to show that they're not wearing any underwear? Well, I hired them. They work for me now. Only not here, and no longer half-naked."

"What do you mean?"

"Mom, tell me all about Spain."

Mother and daughter walked into the house, completely ignoring Javier. When he tried to utter something, Isabella waved him away.

"We'll talk later," she shouted over her shoulder. "In the meantime, try not to wander around the property."

Days passed into weeks, and weeks into months. Javier was never at ease at home. He felt threatened by the invisible army he never saw—but that everyone had told him about. Warned him about. He traveled more frequently, often staying away for weeks at a time.

He had recognized Ryan but never questioned what he was doing back at the Hacienda. He noticed that Ryan was treated favorably by Corella and that he and Isabella spent a great deal of time together—training, exercising, or whatever. Javier came to terms with the situation at home and used the tension as an excuse to stay away from Abby and Isabella.

Late one evening, Javier was returning from a trip that had kept him away for almost a month when the driver slowed a quarter of a mile prematurely. At that time of night, the driver had strict instructions not to slow down until the very last minute and then speed through the gate, which would be open. But this time, the driver slowed early.

Javier, texting on his phone, didn't notice the change in speed. Out of nowhere, dressed in full camouflage and ski masks, two men appeared in the middle of the road and shone bright flashlights at the driver. The vehicle came to a stop. Javier realized they had stopped and began shouting at the driver to run them over.

From both sides of the road, more men appeared. They signaled for the driver to get out and open all the doors. He complied, much to Javier's disgust. One of the men opened the back door and asked Javier to step out of the vehicle.

"Sir, you are in breach of protocol. Given the time and your lack of escort, you are strongly advised to contact the base and inform the security detail of your exact movements. You have neglected to follow this simple protocol set in place for your own well-being. There will be consequences should you or your driver neglect these simple rules again. You may continue. One of my men will assume the task of commanding the vehicle to the base. Good night, sir."

The men disappeared into the night with the driver. One man remained and drove Javier the rest of the way home.

He had finally made the acquaintance of the invisible army.

As soon as he was safely within the confines of his home, he rushed to the bathroom. For three days, Javier did not leave his room. Meals were placed in front of his bedroom door, and no one was allowed to enter. He met with no one and conducted no business with the outside world.

Javier was traumatized to the point of succumbing to his mental anguish. He had lost control—control of his personal security, control of the discipline he had tried to install to ensure the safety of his family, and finally, control of his business operations. The most challenging element to grasp was the fact that he had lost it all to his twelve-year-old daughter—not to any outside pretender.

For three days, Javier pondered how to retake all the control he had lost. He had a plan, but it would take time to implement.

Chapter Fourteen
Abby

Once securely seated in the VIP lounge area, they were flown to Monaco. They arrived at midday after a one-hour flight that felt like ten minutes. The plane was equipped with all the trappings of extreme luxury, coupled with personalized in-flight service befitting such affluence.

At the exclusive private jet airport, Abby and Robert were met by a sleek black Mercedes Maybach, driven by an impeccably dressed chauffeur waiting at the aircraft's doors. They were swiftly driven straight to the iconic Hôtel de Paris in Monte Carlo. The hotel, with its beautifully intricate design, was originally built in the eighteenth century and had recently been renovated and modernized. It offered a majestic edifice—grandiose, imposing, and filled with splendor beyond imagination. Even the most revered royalty and gentry coveted the opportunity to reside on the premises. Its historical significance was rooted in secret meetings between Europe's powerful monarchs during negotiations of alliances and allegiances in the wars that shaped modern Europe.

Abby was astounded to be accorded accommodation by her bookers at such an iconic and revered hotel. It gave her pause—was she deserving of such lavishness, or would she need to earn this extra VIP treatment?

Upon arrival, Abby was greeted not by bellboys but by the hotel management. There was no check-in. Staff escorted her directly to her suite and introduced her to a personal concierge who would be at her service throughout her stay. Robert, on the other hand, was driven to a different, albeit still luxurious, five-star hotel. They would not be staying at the same location, nor would Robert accompany Abby to the cocktail party planned for that evening.

Once settled in their respective rooms, Abby and Robert met at the terrace restaurant of the Hôtel de Paris about an hour later. They ordered a light lunch of grilled chicken salad, avocado on toast, sparkling water, and fresh fruit.

After lunch, an elegantly dressed young woman, about Abby's age, approached and politely asked if she could join them to discuss the evening's protocol. Her name was Yelena. She detailed the day's schedule and outlined where and when Abby was expected to be. Robert, she clarified, would not be participating in any of the proceedings.

Essentially, Abby and Robert had a chauffeur at their disposal for the rest of the day should they wish to explore the city and surrounding areas. By late afternoon, Abby was to begin preparations for the evening's events. At precisely 6:00 p.m., the driver would await her at the hotel entrance to drive her back to the private airport, where a helicopter would whisk her away to a private yacht named *Youtan Poluo*.

Once the debrief with Yelena concluded, Abby and Robert instructed the driver to take them across the border to the tiny Italian village of Ponte San Luigi. Shopping hadn't been on the agenda, but Abby couldn't resist buying Italian shoes for Anna, her mom, and her sister.

At 5:00 p.m., Robert dropped Abby off at her hotel, said goodbye, and had the driver return him to his own accommodations. He would be flying back to New York the next morning and wouldn't see Abby again. He reminded her that her hourly rate would begin at 6:00 p.m. when the driver picked her up. She didn't need the reminder.

At 6:30 p.m., Abby descended in the elevator, crossed the lobby, and exited the hotel, where the driver was waiting. She wore a black evening gown designed and handmade by Donatella Versace, paired with gold open-toe heels and a matching gold Versace purse clutched at her side. Her golden blonde hair was loosely brushed down her back. Her makeup was impeccable—gold and silver eyeshadow lightly dusted above her lashes, not caked; a deep, dark lip gloss; and a pink-red blush that gave her a radiant flush. She was glowing.

Her stride across the lobby was breathtaking—flawless and confident. Behind dark sunglasses that shielded her brilliant blue eyes, she moved with quiet grace. As she stepped out of the elevator, silence descended, broken only by the click of her heels on the marble floor. Nobody moved. Jaws dropped as all present turned to take in the rare, naturally beautiful vision before them.

The driver had been waiting in his car for a full forty minutes, having arrived ten minutes early just in case. When Abby exited the hotel, he jumped out and rushed to open the rear door. There was no eye contact, no conversation. The twenty-minute drive to the airport gave Abby ample time to text her family back home. She FaceTimed her parents and sister, who were all curious about where she was headed, seeing her so dressed up. Her mom, of course, already knew—she had a copy of the contract.

The helicopter ride was a bit bumpy and loud. Abby had to wear noise-canceling headphones to protect her ears from the intense noise. She felt a little nauseous during the flight and fought hard to keep herself composed and prevent her stomach from regurgitating everything she'd eaten that day.

The flight lasted a long forty-five minutes before landing shakily on the helipad of *Youtan Poluo*. The yacht was anchored roughly twenty nautical miles out at sea, and the gusty conditions had made the flight rough.

Upon landing, Yelena met Abby and promptly escorted her to her overnight quarters to freshen up. They would not return until mid-morning the following day, and Abby had wisely packed an overnight bag.

The *Youtan Poluo* is named after one of the rarest and most beautiful flowers found in Latin America. Botanists claim it only blooms once every three thousand years. The exciting news was that this year, the *Youtan Poluo* was scheduled to bloom brightly. When it does, delicate white stems extend from the leaves, transforming elegant green vines into snowy white floral cascades. A truly magnificent and impressive phenomenon.

Needless to say, the yacht was aptly named.

Woozy and wobbly in the knees from the helicopter flight, Abby barged into her room as soon as the door was opened and rushed straight to the bathroom. Dropping to her knees, she gagged into the toilet bowl. She heaved uncontrollably, tears streaming down her cheeks, stomach acid rising into her esophagus, and the lingering odor of her recent snack provoking further nausea. The room spun around her. Abby felt weak and helpless. She shut her eyes tightly, panic creeping in—until she felt a hand lightly on her shoulder.

It was Yelena.

She placed a cold, damp hand towel with ice cubes tucked inside on the back of Abby's neck and held it there for several minutes. Then, she began gently rubbing Abby's neck, moving around to her forehead, then back down her spine, all the while supporting Abby, who leaned back against her.

Abby slowly opened her eyes. Her face was ashen white, all color drained. She looked at Yelena and whispered, "Thank you."

"I've had the same experience before. I should've warned you not to eat anything solid before the flight," Yelena replied.

"I wasn't expecting such a choppy flight. I felt every dip, every gust of wind—it was worse than a roller coaster," Abby said.

"Take your time, freshen up, and come up to the deck when you're ready."

Yelena helped Abby to the bed, then quietly left the room.

Abby curled up on the extra-large bed, clutching the cold towel to her forehead and neck. The nausea had begun to subside, but a headache had taken its place. Her head throbbed. She took an aspirin and lay back down.

An hour later, Abby lay on her back, staring at the ceiling of the suite, completely disoriented. It took her a good ten minutes to place her surroundings and reorient herself. She looked around and saw she was in a large, luxurious suite—complete with a dining area, lounge space, sauna, jacuzzi, bathtub, shower, and even a second bedroom. The opulence only added to her feeling of gloom.

Shaking off the unease, she showered, brushed her teeth vigorously, and rinsed her mouth with mint-flavored mouthwash—once, twice, then a third time. Finally, she got dressed. She wore a sleeveless, just-above-the-knee black dress, trimmed with lace around the bust. She paired it with sheer stockings and closed-toe black heels. Her makeup was simple: rose-pink lip gloss and matching eyeshadow. She looked stunning.

Up on the deck—her earlier wooziness and embarrassment now a fading memory—Abby joined the other guests for an evening cocktail. With a glass of sparkling water in hand, she moved gracefully among the crowd, charming the other models with light conversation. She mingled group to group, as was expected of her. Representational duties.

Abby was contracted to be present—her role was to enhance the ambiance, to elevate the guest list, to lend glamour and status to the event. So she mingled, chatted, and laughed—while steering clear of any personal revelations.

A live band began playing soft, jazzy music in the main hall just off the primary deck. The yacht was full. Abby estimated about a hundred people on board, herself included. The night promised to be long and cumbersome, weaving through clusters of people, engaging in light, superficial conversation as she table-hopped.

After about an hour, she had her first glass of champagne, still avoiding solid food—especially anything fish-related.

One of the girls—a model, Abby assumed—seemed to attach herself to Abby and followed her around as she mingled and chatted.

"Which agency do you work for?" the girl asked. She couldn't have been older than nineteen.

"New York Academy," Abby replied.

"Wow! You are beautiful! How many of you are from New York?" she asked again.

"Just me," Abby replied, a little taken aback by the girl's intensity. She turned to face her with a surprised and curious look, lowering her chin and staring at her with a stern gaze.

"What's your name?" continued the girl, envious of Abby's modest, composed demeanor.

"Abby," she replied, now slightly irritated by the young woman's persistence and intrusion.

"Well, my name is Yulia. It's short for YuliAnna, which means 'youthful.' What is Abby short for?"

Abby turned to face Yulia head-on, making full eye contact.

"Abby is short for Abigail. Abigail means 'Power of the Wind,' which is exactly what I'm feeling right now. We both have work to do—interact with the main guests, chat, and represent the host of this party. You should get to work."

"How much are they paying you?" Yulia asked, wide-eyed, completely unbothered by her own bluntness.

"YuliAnna, that's none of your business. You should read your contract before signing it. Now, I have to go," Abby said firmly, clearly annoyed.

"Please... I'm afraid. I don't have a contract. I was just told to get on a helicopter. I'm told what to wear, where to place the jewelry, and where to return everything afterward. I'm scared," Yulia confessed.

Abby stared at her in disbelief, then softened. She put an arm around the girl's shoulders and said gently, "If you ever find yourself in a situation that makes you uncomfortable, come find me. Okay?"

"Okay. Thank you," Yulia said quietly, walking away feeling slightly lighter, a little more assured.

As Abby resumed circulating, she began to notice more young girls who looked around Yulia's age—barely adults, wide-eyed, nervous. She suspected they might be in similar predicaments. She couldn't save them all—maybe they didn't need saving—but they stood out to her as she glided through the crowded deck.

She moved into the main hall for a quick chat with a few of the male guests, then stepped back onto the deck to continue mingling with the public relations models.

It was during one of these mingling walkabouts into the lounge area that Abby recognized a familiar face. At first, she thought she was experiencing a hallucination, provoked by the sight of so many very young girls hired as PR agents to engage and entertain the male guests. Abby blinked twice, totally in denial, then slowly walked toward whatever had caught her attention. She stood with her arms on her hips, her gaze cold and unyielding. All she could muster was:

"Anna?"

She tried to follow up with a question, but words failed her as she stood motionless, towering over the three people seated on a loveseat—two older men with Anna in between.

"Hello," said one of the older men.

Abby didn't respond. Her cold, hard stare remained locked on Anna, who was nestled between the two men.

"Nice of you to come join us; come sit," said the second man, patting his lap.

Without saying a word, Abby leaned forward, grabbed Anna by the hand, and yanked her to her feet.

"Hey, what are you doing?" yelled the first man, standing in protest.

"Ow, Abby! That hurt!" Anna cried, stumbling forward as she was pulled up.

Abby took a step back, keeping her distance from the man who had stood up. She yanked Anna behind her and said in a harsh, forceful tone:

"She is fourteen years old! This is my sister! Go find someone else, you perverts!"

Turning to Anna, Abby hissed, "You've got some explaining to do!"

Still clutching Anna's hand, Abby stormed out of the lounge, dragging her behind. The sun was setting as they reached the deck, and a sea breeze had picked up, rendering the air slightly chilly. The crowd was still gathered there, gasping and marveling at the beautiful sunset. Abby pulled Anna through the throng to the far end of the deck, an area mostly ignored by the other guests. She turned Anna to face her.

"What are you doing here? You were supposed to be in Tokyo. I set it up for you. What happened? Why are you here?"

Anna burst into tears. Fear flooded her eyes as she clung to Abby, sobbing uncontrollably.

Still flustered, Abby pulled Anna away at arm's length, shook her shoulders, and hissed venomously, "I set you up for a well-paying gig in Tokyo. Why didn't you go? How did you end up here?"

Tears streamed down Anna's cheeks, ruining her mascara and smudging her pink blush. Her face was a mess.

"The Tokyo gig was canceled at the last minute. I was already at the airport when I got the call," she sobbed, rubbing at her eyes to wipe away the black streaks. "I was lost and scared, Abby. I didn't know what to do."

"Why didn't you call me? You should've told me what happened."

"Before I could think, I got a call asking if I wanted a gig that paid double the Tokyo job. I said yes. They told me to catch a flight to Monaco—it was leaving in forty-five minutes. I barely made it. I told myself I'd call you once I landed, but I couldn't. Everything moved so fast. Next thing I knew, I was on this ship."

"Yacht," Abby corrected.

"What?"

"It's not a ship. It's a yacht."

"Oh. Okay."

"Who called you? How are you being paid? How much?"

"I don't know who it was. I was told I'd be paid ten thousand dollars in cash—an envelope would be sent to my room the next morning."

"Where is your room?"

"Somewhere on the lower deck. I share it with two other girls. It's a bit small for three people, but I guess it'll be okay."

"Okay, come with me," Abby snapped, still furious as she pulled Anna behind her. "We're going to get your stuff. You're moving in with me. I have plenty of room. We'll get to the bottom of this later."

After moving Anna's belongings into Abby's suite, the two girls returned to the upper deck. Abby wrapped a shawl over her bare shoulders and did the same for Anna. Anna had washed her face, scrubbing away the mess of mascara and blush streaked from her earlier tears. This time, Abby applied the makeup for her. Despite being just fourteen, Anna looked stunning.

Abby insisted that she change out of the short black dress she had been wearing and into elegant white pants, a matching white blouse, and a soft pink shawl. On her feet, she wore white heels that made her nearly as tall as Abby. Together, the two of them looked astoundingly radiant.

"Listen to me carefully," Abby said firmly. "You stick right next to me and don't talk to anyone without my approval. Got it?"

"Yes. I'm really sorry, Abby. My mother has been hospitalized. She needs emergency surgery. Her kidneys are both damaged from all the vodka and alcohol she's consumed over the years. I need to send her money for the operation. They found her a kidney, but it'll go to the one who pays first. That's not all—she has CADASIL! Do you know what that is? It might complicate the kidney surgery."

"Yes, I know what it is. I'm sorry to hear that," Abby replied, her voice softening. "CADASIL is a rare, inherited vascular disease that can lead to dementia. It stands for *Cerebral Autosomal Dominant Arteriopathy with Subcortical Infarcts and Leukoencephalopathy*. It's caused by a faulty gene. You need to take care of yourself, Anna. You'll need regular checkups."

She took a deep breath.

"I'll schedule a full, comprehensive medical evaluation for you when we get to New York. I'll also open a bank account in your name and make sure you have enough money for personal expenses. The cash I've received in the two envelopes will be deposited safely. I'll send enough for your mom's medical needs. You won't have to worry about that anymore."

"I won't let you sell yourself just to buy your mother a kidney or pay for her treatment," Abby said, resolute. Then she smiled faintly and added, "Now, let's go rock this party. Make everyone drool and be envious of us. Remember..."

"Yes... stick by your side, not talk, just smile," Anna interrupted.

"I didn't say smile. I said..."

"Yes, big sister. I got it."

Abby held Anna's hand, and they took the elevator to the upper deck. They made a grand entrance—though unintentionally. Conversations stopped as everyone turned to watch them join the group.

The dinner bell rang roughly three hours into the evening, and the cocktail portion of the night's event was suspended. Everyone was ushered into a large, spacious, well-lit dining hall with a huge crystal chandelier hanging over the largest dining table Abby had ever seen.

Seats were assigned and indicated by crystal name tags, each guest's name laser-printed in elegant handwriting. Abby was assigned a seat next to a young, smartly dressed, and very handsome man named Javier Reyes, seated to her left. To her right, the name tag suggested a Russian man with whom Abby had no interest in conversing. She pulled Anna into the seat to her right and placed the name tag face-down.

"This is somebody's seat," whispered Anna.

"Yes, it is. Yours now. Sit here and stay seated next to me, no matter what."

"Okay, Sis," said Anna, smiling and enjoying the protection and attention.

Javier Reyes leaned over and whispered to Abby, "That is the Birthday Boy's seat. He specifically requested to be seated next to you. Let's not create drama."

"I agree. Let's not create drama. Why don't you vacate your seat? That way, his request will be granted—not that I have any particular desire to be seated next to either of you, Birthday Boy or not."

Abby turned her attention to Anna, and the two gossiped and giggled about everything and nothing.

The Birthday Boy made his grand entrance into the dining room once everyone was seated. He looked around slowly and noticed his requested seat was occupied. He frowned, forehead wrinkling, and shot an unpleasant, dissatisfied look in Javier's direction before seating himself in the only remaining unoccupied place. He studied the name tag in front of him, which said "Anna." He looked up toward Abby, smiled, and nodded ever so slightly. Masking his displeasure, he turned to the model seated next to him and started a conversation. To Javier's relief, the Birthday Boy would not make a scene.

Water—both sparkling and flat—was served first in one-liter designer glass bottles. Then came the vintage white wine for those who preferred it. Abby hastily turned both wine glasses in front of her upside-down to signal that she didn't want any. She did the same for Anna before the server could fill her glass. Then came the champagne.

"No wine, madame?" the server asked.

"No, water will be fine, thank you," she replied. "For both of us—she's a minor," Abby added, referring to Anna.

"Absolutely, madame."

The meal began with the amuse-bouche. While the first of what Abby sarcastically estimated to be about one hundred servings was being presented, Javier—mic in hand—introduced the Birthday Boy in the most flattering way. It turned out the Birthday Boy's name was Ivan Kuznetsov, who had turned sixty the previous day.

"Can I have your attention, please? Ladies and gentlemen, attention! Thank you, thank you very much. Now, we are all here— as you may or may not know—to celebrate tonight's special guest, seated across the table from me, my good friend Ivan Kuznetsov, on the occasion of his milestone sixtieth birthday. I ask you all to please stand, raise your champagne glasses, and wish Ivan a very special happy birthday!

"Ivan, we are gathered here today to celebrate this momentous, joyous occasion with you. We raise our glasses to you and praise the man you are. I am grateful to call you a personal friend. Congratulations, Ivan—and happy birthday!"

"Happy birthday, Ivan!" sang the guests.

"Big round of applause, please! Hip, hip! Hoorah!" Javier shouted.

Everyone clapped incessantly and finally sat down for another amuse-bouche—or was it an hors d'oeuvre? Abby lost count, nibbling politely on whatever was placed in front of her.

She turned to Javier and whispered, "We're fashion models. Are you trying to fatten us up so y'all can eat us after?" She was clearly teasing, referencing the Hansel and Gretel fable.

Javier whispered back, "You have a dirty mind!" and winked at her.

Abby abruptly turned her seat toward Anna and didn't speak another word to Javier for the rest of the meal.

Twelve-course meals were more exhausting than satisfying, and Abby was bursting to relieve herself after consuming so much water.

"Finally," she whispered to Anna. "I need to powder my nose and freshen up my makeup."

Anna stood and followed Abby to the ladies' room.

Dinner rumbled on—or was it Abby's stomach, rebelling from the endless succession of tiny, rich plates in such a short span of time? It was an opulent affair, flawlessly presented, set in sublime décor. *Overkill* was the word her mind landed on to describe the whole scene—and many of the people in it.

Still, she felt content overall and especially relieved to have rescued Anna from the jaws of the wolves.

Finally, dessert was to be served: a birthday cake specially prepared by a renowned three-star Michelin chef in Paris and flown in by private jet. The cake was wheeled out by three female servers dressed in skimpy black skirts, white aprons, white blouses, black stockings, and black heels. It stood six stories tall—one for each decade—with ten candles on top, in case anyone hadn't done the math. The candles were lit as the cake was wheeled to Ivan.

Before Ivan could blow them out, Javier took the mic again and asked all the models to stand. Abby remained seated, and when Anna tried to rise, Abby pulled her back down.

All the young girls stood, except for Abby and Anna.

"Ivan, it is tradition," Javier began. "When you blow out the candles, you must make a wish. Well, before you make your wish…"

Ivan gestured to the standing girls.

Right on cue, they all chimed sweetly, "Your wish is our command!"

Beaming, Javier started the countdown. "Three… two… one… Happy birthday, Ivan!"

Ivan blew out the top-level candles, and the three servers extinguished the rest.

That made two strikes for Javier, in Abby's book.

Abby and Anna shared one portion of the dessert.

Hot drinks—coffee, tea, cognac, and more champagne—were served in the mini-lounge adjoining the dance hall. The music's decibels surged, and conversations grew louder as alcohol lowered inhibitions. The dance floor filled, the rhythm intensified, and several of the girls began to gyrate to the beat.

Anna was eager to dance. She swayed her hips and sang along, folding her arms across her chest, completely immersed in the music.

Chapter Fifteen
Abby

Abby, sensing the teenage party-urge overwhelming Anna, gave in and pulled her to the middle of the dance floor. Laughing and rejoicing that her wish had been recognized, Anna let herself be seized by the tempo and danced like any teenager at a party. Abby allowed herself to be inspired by the mood, the atmosphere, and Anna's enthusiastic dance routine.

The two danced, smiled, and laughed until Birthday Boy tapped Abby on the shoulder and politely asked to cut in. Ivan, who seemed to have an insatiable craving for Russian vodka and was clearly working to satisfy it, stood wobbly on the dance floor and asked a second time if he could intercede.

Surprised by the intrusion, Abby recoiled and placed both hands on Anna's shoulders. Facing Ivan, she opened her mouth to express her annoyance when Javier appeared almost out of nowhere.

"Ah, Ivan the Great! My Birthday Boy! I was looking for you. Here you are!"

Javier's "Ivan the Great" was a reference to the fifteenth-century Russian ruler, Ivan III of Russia, the Grand Prince of Moscow.

His remarks brought a huge grin to Ivan's face. Obviously, being compared to such a great ruler was a compliment that fed his ego, suggesting power and influence.

"I was just asking this most beautiful girl in the world to dance with me," Ivan said, turning to face Javier.

"Which one?" joked Javier.

"True, too true. They are both exceptionally beautiful beyond belief. But this young beauty here is a minor, I am to understand. A mere baby. Too young for..."

"Yes! She is too young to be present at such a gathering, too young to be in the presence of uninhibited alcohol consumption, and exceedingly too young to be around intoxicated, perverted older men," Abby cut in, her voice calm but cold.

"Come, Ivan. I have somebody I would like you to meet. It's just what you need. Come with me," Javier urged, gently pulling Ivan away from the girls by the arm.

"But I already have what I need standing right in front of me," Ivan slurred, clearly inebriated and unable to control his actions or emotions. He stumbled forward, trying to approach Abby and kiss her.

Abby stepped back, putting out her hands protectively. That was the last straw. She grabbed Anna by the arm, and the two girls left immediately, retreating to Abby's room to retire for the night.

The next morning, there was a gentle knock on the door. The suite, being so spacious, with the bedroom door closed, muffled the sound. A louder, more persistent knock followed, along with a voice calling out, "Room service."

Anna stirred and went to wake Abby. Abby slipped on a bedroom cloak, walked to the door, and called out, "Who is it?" before offering to open it.

"Room service, madame!" came the reply.

"But I didn't order room service, and I'm still sleeping. You are disturbing us," Abby responded.

Then a male voice interjected, "Abby, it's me—Javier. I've taken the liberty of ordering breakfast for us. I hope you don't mind. Allow me to apologize profoundly for last night—for Ivan's behavior."

"Us?"

"Yes, you, Anna, and myself. I hope it's not too presumptuous on my part, but I owe you an explanation—and Anna a check."

Abby checked her appearance to make sure she was decent, then called out to Anna to get dressed. She stepped aside and opened the door. Five room service trolleys were rolled into the suite's dining

182

area. Javier followed the last trolley, dressed in white loafers, a navy blazer, white flannel pants, and a light blue shirt untucked.

Before Abby could respond, Javier leaned in and kissed her on the cheek.

"Good morning, ladies!" he chirped. "I hope you're both hungry!"

In minutes, the dining area was transformed into a beautifully set room, closely supervised by Javier. Drawers and cupboards were opened, and the food from the five trolleys arranged into a grand buffet. A complete smorgasbord—lavish and excessive—was laid out, buffet-style. The five staff members who had brought in the trolleys stood by the walls, hands behind their backs, ready to serve.

Anna entered the dining room, freshly showered, her wet hair cascading down her shoulders.

"Wow! Is this just for us, or is everyone else coming to join?" she asked, completely overwhelmed by the amount of food, the layout, and the attendants waiting to serve.

"Breakfast—or brunch, if you like—for my two most beautiful favorite ladies!" beamed Javier, clearly proud of himself and hoping to impress Anna. Now, he waited for Abby's reaction.

Abby walked into the dining room, dressed casually, her wet hair falling loosely around her shoulders, wearing light makeup and designer sneakers. Even in casual wear, she was stunning.

She looked around the room, then turned to Javier and said, "You do know we're catwalk models and need to constantly monitor our body mass and weight gain. Your insensitivity to our persistent daily struggles is duly noted, and I'm contrived to decree you a strike-three offense—the consequence of which would doom you to a perpetual injunction from ever contacting either of us."

Javier's eyes widened, but before he could speak, Abby added, "But, since you've gone to such lengths to redeem yourself from last night's events, I'm willing to overlook your foolish underestimation of the situation and partake in this dreadful lapse of consciousness and gorge away. Besides, this all smells good—and I'm hungry. So, let's eat. Come on, Anna."

Jeez! thought Javier. *What a pompous, pampered, pretentious pain-in-the-ass!*

"Well, that's music to my heart," he said aloud.

"You mean *music to my ears*," quipped Abby.

"No—my heart!" insisted Javier. "Because there are two things close to my heart: you and good food."

"Hmm. Charmer. Watch yourself."

The two girls indulged in the smorgasbord guiltlessly, chatting between mouthfuls, reaching across each other for whatever they wanted. There was no time for polite "please pass." It was as if they'd been given a reprieve from responsible eating.

Javier, meanwhile—forever the raconteur—charmed his way back into Abby's esteem, telling stories about his childhood and upbringing in Spain with his parents and younger sister. He recounted tell-tale stories from his teenage years, always making light of his youthful experiences and how he eventually ended up running his own successful venture. He spoke about the important political figures he had met through his father and family connections.

He nattered relentlessly while the girls, eager-eyed, listened and were clearly impressed.

It was difficult to tell whether Abby approved of all his self-centered tales or simply brushed them off as desperate. Still, the conversation remained light and very pleasant. Coffee and *miniadise* were served, and the discussion drifted back to business.

Abby looked at Javier, smiled, and asked if he had remembered to bring Anna's check.

A huge grin spread across his face.

"My dear Abby, would I overlook such an important element of our *rencontre de petit déjeuner*?"

"I don't know. Would you?"

"Come now, Abby. I am a man of honor and dignity. My word is my bullet. Should I release a word, it will head straight for the recipient just like a bullet—without reverse."

He turned toward one of the young girls serving breakfast and nodded. She came forward and handed him an envelope. Javier turned toward Anna and handed it to her.

"It's all there. Would you care to verify?"

Abby stretched out her arm and intercepted the exchange. She grabbed the envelope from Javier's hands and said,

"Of course! Charmer! Or should I add *snake* before that?"

"Hmmm... the old Abby is back, I see."

"Never left!" retorted Abby.

The three retired to the lounge area to discuss the matter confidentially while the dining area was cleared out. Once seated on a comfortable two-seater sofa, Abby beckoned Anna to sit beside her. She emptied the envelope and meticulously counted every dollar bill.

"This is only half!" said Abby, turning sharply to face Javier. "May I remind you that you hired an underage girl and plied her with alcohol?"

"I didn't ply her with anything."

"You certainly didn't supervise and constrain her consumption. In fact, you left her unsupervised until I came along. I should charge you chaperone fees."

"Thought you might go down this alley."

Javier took a small bell out of his jacket pocket and gave it three little rings. The same young girl approached again. She handed

Javier a second envelope and walked out. Javier immediately handed the envelope to Abby, sat back in his sofa chair, and smiled while she counted the contents.

Abby looked up, smiled, and said,

"This is acceptable."

She rose from the two-seater and walked into the bedroom area to deposit both envelopes in the room safe. She re-entered the lounge area and sat in a single sofa chair facing Javier.

"This has been an experience. It lacked a certain degree of professionalism, smelt of sexual abuse of minors, and barely legal-age teenage girls from the pleasure of rich, wrinkled, bald-headed oligarchs, using their wealth and fortune to corrupt needy young girls. The fact that you organized such an event, with the full intention of satisfying your sweaty, over-weight clients, without the tiniest bit of concern for the girls you recruited, disgusts me to the point of wanting to thrust my hand down your throat and reaching past your heart, down to your testicles and pulling them up, forcing them down your throat, slamming your mouth shut thereby crushing said testicles and causing you to drown in your own semen. I never want to see you again. Please leave!"

Javier stood up, brushed himself off, and walked to the door. When he got there, he turned around and looked at Anna, then at Abby. He locked eyes with her and said,

"Ladies, I will see you in New York."

With that, he stepped out, closing the door behind him.

In the lounge, Anna stared at Abby in total shock—jaw dropped. She just stared, not uttering a word.

"Well, that should put his jabbering motor-mouth in place," said Abby, sitting back down and staring back at Anna.

"I can't believe you said all those things to him. I mean, wow! First of all, nobody has ever defended me for anything; people always wanted to offer the world and take advantage of me. Thank you, Abby."

Anna rose from her seat and went over to hug and kiss Abby, sobbing quietly.

"Well, we have a plane to catch as soon as this boat docks," said Abby. "Come on, let's pack and get ready to disembark quickly."

"Will we go directly to the airport?"

"No, I have stuff to pick up from the hotel. So we'll go there first. I should imagine that there's a driver waiting for us at the port."

The big yacht docked without further ado, and, true to Abby's assumption, a black Maybach Mercedes with their names on it was waiting at the dock.

"Courtesy of management, madame!" said the driver as they entered the car.

"What management?" Abby asked.

"I am not at liberty to divulge."

"Thought as much."

The drive back to the hotel was silent, both girls evidently lost in their respective thoughts. Abby broke the silence.

"Do you have all your stuff? Clothes, shoes, makeup, etcetera?"

"Yes. I came directly to the port from the airport. No hotel."

"Okay, we'll go straight up to my room. I don't have to re-check in, since I didn't check out. Then we'll go down to the lobby to figure this all out. You can enjoy the full spa while I make some calls and try to book you a flight back to the United States."

"Oh, I'd love that. Full mud bath, sludge bath, steam bath, sauna, jacuzzi—wow! I'm really gonna enjoy it."

"You're forgetting gym room, pool room, massage room—work off all the junk food we indulged in."

Anna leaned over from where she was seated and kissed Abby on the cheek, eyes watering. She whispered, "Thank you, Abby. Thank you. I love you so much. You are my big sister."

Anna had no family she could rely on. She had no one; she was alone in this cold, lonely, wolf-infested forest.

Abby would take her under her wing and guide her through the pits and traps until she was able to manage herself—which would never be the case. It was such a lonely, dangerous jungle, with snakes crawling all over, just waiting to strike.

Chapter Sixteen
the Grandmother

Maria Ysabel Catalina Reyes-Diaz was born to Mexican parents. Both her parents were descendants of the powerful Mayan tribe. The Mayans were the dominant tribe in Central Mexico. Maria Ysabel was proud of her Mayan heritage and culture.

Her parents, particularly her mother, were strong believers in the traditional religion of the Mayans, as passed on by the local priests. They were frequent attendees of the rituals and ceremonies practiced habitually. During these sacraments, the priest would often assemble the congregation and call upon the gods and spirits to heal the worshippers of their woes and physical struggles.

One such séance had the priest quivering as he pleaded for the healing spirits to descend upon his gathering and shower them with mercy and forgiveness. He begged for an appearance to prove to his followers that the spirits were, in fact, present and merciful.

It was then that the priest fell into a trance. He collapsed to the ground, eyes and mouth wide open, in what appeared to be an epileptic seizure.

Maria Ysabel's mother, sitting in the front row, rushed to his aid, lifting his head and praying for his salvation from whatever he was experiencing. The seizure subsided, and the congregation fell to its knees—praying and crying—feeling privileged to have witnessed a miracle.

After church, the priest approached Maria Ysabel's mother to thank her for coming to his aid. He told her that he had seen a light hovering over her head. It was so blinding that he couldn't see or speak and felt extreme pressure on his chest, making it difficult to breathe. It was then that he blacked out, remembering nothing afterward.

She asked repeatedly what he had seen. He remembered a bright light followed by a vision of a very beautiful woman with light behind her. The light was so bright it temporarily blinded him, and he couldn't recall much else.

The priest told Maria Ysabel's mother that all his life, his father had spoken of such appearances, though he had never really believed in them—until now. Today, he had experienced it.

The legend said such an appearance occurred once every five hundred years. A light and a vision would appear above the Chosen One.

"Chosen for what, exactly?" she asked, curious.

"I don't really know. My father always said the vision would appear when the people needed guidance and saving. The direct descendant—whom we were not aware of—would suddenly appear before all. This chosen person, legend says, is a woman. She will be the most powerful woman on Earth. She will correct all the injustices the people face and provide redemption and forgiveness for the sinners."

"So, Reverend High Priest, you're saying I've been chosen to lead the people from their misery?"

"You or your descendants! That's all I know. Please don't ask me more. You! You are the one to provide answers from now on. Please don't come to the seminars anymore."

Maria Ysabel's mother was deeply hurt by the parting comments from the Reverend High Priest, but she obeyed and abstained from attending congregation on Sundays.

When she fell pregnant for the first time, Maria Ysabel's mother knew right away that it was a girl. She felt it. Her husband told everybody he was expecting a son, but his wife knew that she was carrying a girl.

Often, she would cry silently to herself at night, cradling her huge belly and thinking about how beautiful her daughter would be. Such was her contentment.

True to her conviction, she gave birth to a beautiful, healthy baby girl. However, there were complications during labor, and she had to undergo a life-saving operation. The result was that she could no longer bear children.

Her husband completely fell apart—not only had she given birth to a daughter, but she would never be able to bear him a son. How embarrassing. How humiliating for him. How could he ever face the village men? What would they think of him? They would certainly mock him for celebrating the birth of his "son" eight months earlier. This was surely the end of the road for him. No longer could he walk through the square with his head held high. It was a disaster.

When it was time to name the baby, a vision appeared in her mother's dream and spelled out the name clearly: Maria Ysabel Catalina. There could be no deviation from that name.

As the years passed, Maria Ysabel grew into a beautiful, intelligent young woman. Her mother never told her about the incident at the congregation, nor did she mention the origins of her name, which was steeped in Mayan tradition. Her father was absent for months at a time, which allowed mother and daughter to form an inseparable bond.

On her sixteenth birthday, Maria Ysabel wanted to celebrate at school with her close friends. Her father, rarely present for any occasion, insisted on inviting the whole village. His daughter was about to become a woman, and such an important rite of passage called for a communal celebration.

On the day of the celebration, the whole village was decorated with brightly colored garlands strung across the streets and buildings. Colored lanterns were placed in windows overlooking the village square. Traditional music was played by local musicians, who were more than happy and excited to have a fête.

A cortège, led by the Reverend High Priest and all the village children, came up the main street leading into the square. A music quartet rounded out the procession.

Maria Ysabel was dressed all in white from head to toe, accompanied by her parents, who flanked her. Her father had ordered the slaughtering of two goats, and local wine was offered, along with the usual homemade food and offerings. It was a huge festival, and everyone was pleased and excited to participate.

It was as if the commune was offering a sacrificial lamb in return for blessings and good tidings—except Maria Ysabel was not being sacrificed in any form or shape. She was the one blessing the village for nurturing her during her pre-adolescence.

The cortège proceeded slowly, snaking its way into the village square, then formed a circle around Maria Ysabel and her parents. The trio made their way to the church, climbed the few steps, and turned to face the crowd. Everybody cheered. What a beautiful sight.

The Reverend High Priest raised his hand, and the music and chanting ceased.

"We thank the High Priestess, we thank the Powerful Queen, and we thank the Revered Goddess. Our beautiful child has reached the age of womanhood. Our child, your child, O Revered One, has blossomed into the most beautiful of us all. It is with your guidance, your protection and security, your blessings and kindness, and your mercy that we have arrived at this day. Oh Divine Spirits, we present you with your daughter. Oh Divine Spirits, continue to protect us, to bless us with your kindness and mercy."

The crowd bowed their heads and each said a silent prayer.

Then, Maria Ysabel's father stepped forward, his voice steady and proud. "My daughter has reached her age of maturity. From this day forward, she will step out into her own light and make her own decisions. Form her own destiny. You all have been gracious in your protection of her. Thank you! Let the festivities begin and never end!"

Immediately, the music started, and people danced. The party lasted for three days, and most of the men suffered relentless hangovers from all the local wine and brew.

Maria Ysabel sat down with her parents and informed them that she wanted to be a teacher. Not just any teacher, but a cultural elite teacher. She wanted to teach proper Spanish, history—Mexican and world history. She wanted to prepare the youth of the village for the world that awaited them.

In order to achieve these goals, she had to leave—travel abroad, attend college or university, then return and build a proper school. Her father merely nodded without uttering a word. Her mother smiled and talked excitedly about which country she wanted to go to.

Maria Ysabel had long decided on traveling to Spain to learn about the culture, history, and proper Spanish language. Her destination was already set. To finance the trip, her mother sewed, baked, cooked, toiled, brewed, and sold her wares in the neighboring villages. Maria Ysabel helped. Her father was absent.

After six months of hard work, Maria Ysabel and her mother had earned enough to pay for the trip. She traveled to the port by bus, then boarded a liner to Spain.

It was on the voyage across the ocean that Maria Ysabel met a wealthy elderly Spanish couple from Madrid. One morning, while sitting in the canteen having breakfast, the couple approached and sat opposite her. They engaged in conversation about who she was, where she was going, and why. Being the shy, timid person she was, Maria Ysabel responded mostly with one-word answers like "yes," "no," or "thank you" when they praised her.

At the end of the two-and-a-half-hour, mostly one-sided conversation, the couple were pleased to offer Maria Ysabel accommodation and financial aid in exchange for housework and the occasional babysitting of their nephews and nieces, as they were childless. This was all too good to be true. Maria Ysabel trusted her instincts and graciously accepted their offer.

During the remainder of the voyage, the trio ate all their meals together. From an outsider's perspective, they resembled a close-knit family.

When they arrived at the port of Valencia in Spain, they were met by family, all overexcited to see them. Maria Ysabel was introduced to everyone as the *fille-au-pair*. She was welcomed with open hearts and warmly embraced by all.

Once in Madrid, Maria Ysabel settled into her new dwelling and began familiarizing herself with the immediate surroundings. Later, the elderly couple took her on a tour of the city, showing her the center and all the important colleges that she might be interested in.

After a week of touring the city's colleges and universities, Maria Ysabel created a top-five list of the finest colleges based on curriculum, distance, and cost. She intended to visit at least two colleges from her list each day.

For the first week, she was away all day, learning her way around the city and calculating the pros and cons of each day trip. Finally, she settled on a college that was quite a distance from her residence but offered the closest match to her academic requirements. The college she chose was one of the pricier options, but it was accredited and highly reputable among young city dwellers. She discovered this by chatting with actual students attending the college.

As for the tuition fees, the elderly couple offered to help in any way they could, but Maria Ysabel politely turned them down. She set a daily timetable in which she would complete her chores early in the morning before heading out to the city, where she would take on a student job. This was the blueprint for how she intended to study and pay her way through college.

At college, her study timetable was rather full, leaving her very little time for non-curricular activities. So, it was morning chores, school, work, home, and evening chores. Maria Ysabel was ecstatic with her new life in the big city.

One afternoon, when Maria Ysabel was at the end of her shift, waiting for a table at a popular student café, she waited on her last table. Seated around it were five young students from a different college than the one she attended. There were three boys and two girls, all perhaps one or two years older than her. They ordered refreshments without looking up, all deep in conversation about some sporting event.

When Maria Ysabel served their order, one of the young lads looked up and stared at her uncomfortably. The young girl sitting beside him reached out, touched his face, turned his head toward her, and kissed him. After the brief kiss, he turned back and asked:

"What's your name?"

"Maria Ysabel," she replied.

"I've never seen you here before. Isn't that right, guys? We've never seen her here before, right?"

They all nodded their heads and continued their conversation—except for the young man who had asked her name.

"What is your name?" asked Maria Ysabel, staring straight into his eyes with a slight smile. She was defiant, she was self-confident, and she was fearless.

The conversation stopped; all eyes were on Maria Ysabel. They all had the "how dare you speak to us" expression on their faces.

"Hmm, let me see, what is my name? Oh! Yes," he said jokingly. "My name is Juan-Carlos the Second, but you, my dear, can call me Loverboy!"

The girl beside him punched him in the shoulder and turned her back to him. The others all laughed and teased Juan-Carlos for being a flirt.

It became a regular after-school meeting place for Juan-Carlos and his friends. The girls accompanied them less and less until they stopped coming altogether.

One day, after her shift was over, Maria Ysabel was met by Juan-Carlos, who was waiting on the street for her. He had with him a bouquet of pretty summer flowers. He approached her, handed her the flowers, and kissed her on the cheek. He then slipped his arm through hers, and the two walked to the train station where Maria Ysabel usually boarded.

The gesture was so relaxed, so unrehearsed, that one could quite comfortably assume the two had been dating for a while—which, of course, was not the case.

When they arrived at the train station, Juan-Carlos kissed her lightly on the cheek again and told her he would be waiting for her the next day. True to his word, he met her every day after work, and they walked and talked about everything and nothing.

Finally, during one such after-work meeting, Juan-Carlos invited Maria Ysabel to a family event on the weekend. Apprehensive of the significance of such an encounter, Maria Ysabel declined the offer and counter-offered that he join her at her place of residence to meet the elderly couple. They compromised, agreeing to visit each other—Maria Ysabel would attend the function, and then Juan-Carlos would escort her home.

On the day of the event, Maria Ysabel arrived at his home by taxi, as there were no trains or buses to the neighborhood.

"Come," he beckoned to her, "meet my mom."

To his mother, Juan-Carlos said, "Mom, I want you to meet my future wife."

To Maria Ysabel, he said, "Darling, this is my mom, Dame Leonora Ozabel Di Maria Sanchez. Of course, my mom has more than one first name, but Leonora is sufficient." He laughed as he said this.

Leonora stepped forward, her eyes softening as she looked at Maria Ysabel.

"My son is obsessed with you. He talks about nothing else all day. I must say, you are truly beautiful. Come with me. If you are to be my future daughter-in-law, then come meet the family and my friends."

With that, Maria Ysabel was taken, arm in arm, by Leonora to meet as many friends as she could. All had the same first impressions: Maria Ysabel was exceptionally beautiful, and she would make beautiful grandchildren.

Two years later, Maria Ysabel and Juan-Carlos were married. Her parents were unable to attend the wedding due to health and financial reasons; it was the elderly couple that "gave her away," and the old man walked her down the aisle.

Maria Ysabel continued her studies, graduated one year later, and almost instantly fell pregnant. Hence, the prospect of finding a job, working independently, and building a career was temporarily frozen.

Throughout the pregnancy, Juan-Carlos boasted to all who were willing to listen that he was expecting a son—the heir to the Ozabel empire. The conviction was so intense that he categorically refused to discuss girl names, just in case. For Juan-Carlos, there was only one "just in case." He was as certain as the sun shining the next day that he was expecting a son. He was expecting a son.

When Sofia Catalina Maria was born, Juan-Carlos went into a drunken stupor and an alcohol-induced semi-coma. He was in total denial, and not even his best friend, his childhood "blood brother," could communicate with him. He spent weeks, sometimes months, away from home, absent from his respective social circle.

Maria Ysabel, in the meantime, buried herself in motherhood and loved her daughter enough for two.

After almost twenty-four months of rare home appearances, disappearances, tantrums, and numerous domestic aggressions instigated by alcohol abuse, Juan-Carlos accepted that fathering a girl was not demeaning and did not question his manhood.

He sobered up, but was still plagued by sexually transmitted diseases, which drove him to seek expert medical attention—all the while abstaining from any form of intimacy with Maria Ysabel. Such was the intimate state of affairs of the young couple.

Juan-Carlos discreetly integrated into the family corporation, as well as his father's political party. His allegiance to all that his father represented was tantamount to him assuming his role as heir apparent of the family fortune. He had no other siblings to rival his claim.

Maria Ysabel, with all her charm and patience, nurtured Juan-Carlos back to his former self. He sobered up, spent less time away from home, and participated more in family-oriented activities. Maria Ysabel pardoned his philandering and allowed him back into the connubial bedroom. Whether his actions and behavior embarrassed him at all, Juan-Carlos did not let on. He smiled more often, spent time with his daughter, and even took her for walks.

When Sofia Catalina was three years old, Maria Ysabel invited her husband and daughter out for a family dinner. She ordered a glass of champagne for Juan-Carlos and sparkling apple juice for Sofia and herself.

Raising her glass, she smiled at her husband. "Cheers, my darling. Soon, we will be four!"

Juan-Carlos froze, his glass halfway to his lips. "What? What did you just say? Did I hear you right?" he asked.

Maria Ysabel beamed. "Yes, my dear, you heard me right." She then leaned toward Sofia, whispering softly in her daughter's ear, "Soon, you will have a little brother to play with."

Juan-Carlos pushed back his chair slightly, his excitement barely contained. "Come here. Come over here and sit on my lap."

"We are in a restaurant, in a public place."

"Yes! Yes, I know," Juan-Carlos replied. "I want the world to know and to see how happy I am."

Happily, Maria Ysabel walked around the table and sat on her husband's knee. She threw her arms around his neck, hugged him tightly, and kissed him passionately.

"Are you sure?" he asked again.

"I am, dear husband. I am. I waited to be one hundred percent sure before telling you both. This time, it's a boy!"

His eyes darkened a little, his face tensed, and he spoke in a low, serious voice. "I so wanted a boy the first time that I was completely consumed by the fact that you were pregnant with a boy—and that I would make my father proud by giving him an heir to the Ozabel empire. It was such a selfish and absurd attitude that led me to the brink of self-destruction. I will not repeat that again. So please, let's not discuss whether it is a boy or a girl until birth. Promise me that, please."

"I promise I will not discuss with anybody except you, dear husband, whether it's a boy or a girl. But I can tell you, right here, right now—I'm carrying a boy!"

Juan-Carlos closed his eyes, drew his wife closer, hugged her tightly, and kissed her again and again until his daughter made exaggerated gagging noises to show her embarrassment at this public display of affection.

"Thank you," he said. "Thank you so much for believing in me. Thank you for our family, and thank you for our son. I believe you—but no one must know."

Nine months later, Maria Ysabel gave birth to a son. They named him Javier Carlos Leo Reyes Ozabel. The heir was born—a prince was born. The Ozabel family name would live on.

Chapter Seventeen
Abby

In the weeks that followed, Abby returned to New York after a brief visit with her family. Constantly FaceTiming her mother and sister made her feel like she had never left home. The love, the companionship, the support—and most of all, the banter— really alleviated whatever burden may have come from being away from her family for extended periods. Anna didn't have this—just the constant demand for money, and more money.

Undoubtedly, the pressure was unbearable for such a young, naïve, and lonely girl, expected to save her family from hardship. Anna had not traveled with Abby to Texas but stayed in New York to practice, improve on her flaws, and hang out with the other girls roughly her age.

In her absence, Abby had instructed Robert to prioritize Anna for any new assignments. So, when Abby returned to New York, Robert was pleased to announce that Anna was away on assignment in Tokyo. This pleased Abby and allowed her to focus on the business side of the academy.

One morning, upon arriving at the academy—Abby, who loved the bustle of early New York commuting—arrived at the office earlier than usual. She skipped her habitual stop in the coffee room and headed straight for her office.

She opened the door and, to her astonishment, found the entire room covered, from wall to wall, with the most exquisite bouquets of flowers. She shut the door, took a deep breath, and reopened it, almost as if she were hallucinating and expected the image to vanish. But the flowers were still there.

She entered her office slowly, taking in every bouquet, every flower arrangement, and every petal as she made her way to where her desk normally was. The room was full—not an inch to spare. Yet, strangely, there were no delivery message cards. Not that she needed to know who sent the flowers—she already had a pretty good idea. It was just the normal thing to do when sending flowers, chocolates, or presents: you usually add a note, a "congratulations," or some other message.

The deluge of flowers, all so sublimely arranged without the slightest flaw, were placed so delightfully around her office that the air was vibrant with a whirl of intricate, pleasant aromas. The fragrance tingled not just the nasal palate but also provoked a timeless sense of heavenly extravagance. The blend of scents, like an unseen rainbow, meandered around the room, soothing even the most aggravated mood. Yet, Abby still couldn't find a single delivery card—not even the name of a florist who had prepared the arrangements.

The door opened, and Robert walked in, smiling. Abby turned around to face him, and his grin froze in place, his eyes betraying his apprehension based on her reaction.

"I can't seem to find one card—not one—from any of the florists, as I assume these didn't all come from just one."

"That's because they had to leave their calling cards at the reception."

"Were you here when all this happened?"

"Hmm, yes!" Robert replied, smiling again. "I politely asked each delivery agent to leave their respective calling cards at the reception."

"Can I have them, please?"

"Sure, just go get them. In the meantime, enjoy! I wish somebody would send me flowers—or anything, for that matter."

"Go!" Abby said, cutting him off.

"Okay, okay," Robert replied, holding up his hands in mock surrender before heading out to retrieve the cards.

When he returned, he handed Abby a stack of business cards from seven different florists scattered across the city. Without a word, Abby took them and marched into the conference room. She sat down at the table, spread the cards out in front of her, and began calling each florist one by one.

"Hello, this is Abby. I received a delivery from your shop today. Could you please tell me who placed the order?"

Seven times, she asked the same question. And seven times, she received the same cryptic response: "12:30 at Tiffany's."

Frustrated, she hung up the last call and summoned Robert to the conference room.

"You called, m'lady?" said Robert, clearly enjoying the drama of the day.

"You're enjoying this, aren't you? Figures—always the drama queen!"

"Not every day do we get all of New York City's floral arrangements delivered!"

"Okay, here's what we're gonna do. First, I want you to distribute a bouquet or arrangement to every office—two at the reception. I want two in the conference room. Put some in the training room as well, please.

"Next, I want to know who has made a reservation at Tiffany's for 12:30. Get the manager on the phone if you have to. I hate surprises. I got my fair share for the whole year today. Book me a ride—a discreet town car—for 1 p.m. Where is Anna?"

"Anna is on assignment in Australia."

"Who's with her?"

"Merika!"

"The Swedish girl? I like Merika. She's a little older and will take good care of Anna. Good choice. Merika and Anna are like sisters. Follow up on the remuneration for both girls and let me see it."

"Yes, m'lady. Your wish..."

"Oh, stop it, Robert!"

"Sorry, just milking the day."

"Well, enough already. Now, I need to call my mom."

Robert exited the conference room and set about executing Abby's request to distribute the flowers. Abby shut the door and called her mom. She FaceTimed her mother and younger sister Katherine. They spoke for over an hour. At first, it was girl talk—chatting about life in the city, whether she had met someone, when she was coming home, and the usual banter. In return, Abby asked about life on the ranch, her horse, and her cousins.

The discussion soon drifted to business matters. Abby's mom inquired about the open contracts of all the girls on assignment, current and potential new recruits, budget adherence, and all the relevant pending financials.

Her head spinning after the interrogation, Abby left the conference room and walked around the office, admiring the floral décor Robert had overseen. As she strolled through the scented corridors, her mind still deeply focused on the discussion with her mom, Abby felt confident that she was in the right place, doing the right thing, and that this project was destined for success.

One o'clock came fast, and Abby got the call that the driver was waiting for her. She was thirty minutes late. She made a quick bathroom stop, brushing her loose shoulder-length blonde hair into place and touching up her makeup. Her makeup was light and minimal—pink blush, ever so thinly applied to enhance her high cheekbones, and light pink lip gloss. That was all.

She changed her earrings, choosing her heart-shaped yellow gold, diamond-encrusted pair—a gift from her parents for her twenty-fourth birthday. She kept them in the office safe.

Apart from that, Abby wanted to give the impression that she had not made any extra effort to be especially presentable for the occasion. So she wore blue jeans, a little torn around both knees, a blue Armani T-shirt that matched the color of her eyes, and a white Armani jacket. Ordinarily dressed, she was not. She checked her makeup again as she rode the elevator down. She smiled to herself—this was going to be fun.

Abby strode into Tiffany's, hesitated a little as she glanced around, then headed for the elevated table situated by the large, tinted window. The young restaurant hostess scampered behind Abby, inquiring whether she had a reservation or was meeting someone. Abby completely ignored the hapless hostess and continued on her path.

As she approached, the single occupant stood up and gestured for her to take a seat opposite him. The restaurant manager rushed over, pulled out the chair for Abby to sit, then gently pushed it back in once she was seated.

Still standing, the man stretched out his hand and offered a greeting.

"Hello, Abby."

"Hello, Javier. I guess it's a little too late for breakfast at Tiffany's."

Abby then turned to the hostess as she was departing and said, "I'll have bottled sparkling water with a slice of lemon and ice cubes."

The hostess, slightly flustered, replied, "Oh no, ma'am, I don't take the orders. I'll have someone—"

Abby cut her off. "Okay, fine. But please let your colleague know that I will have the light seafood salad, grilled halloumi, grilled chicken breasts in thin strips, baked sweet potato, and vaporized carrots and marrow."

Closing the menu card and handing it back to the hostess, Abby added with a slight smile, "Thank you!"

The hostess bowed ever so slightly, took a step backward, then turned to leave and place the order when Javier interjected with a grin.

"I'll have the same. Please make that times two."

"Ma'am... will that be all?"

"Thank you, that'll be all," Abby said, turning her attention to Javier.

She looked at Javier—no smile on her face—her deep, crystal-clear blue eyes dancing as she scrutinized his expression while she spoke.

"Quite the announcement you made today," she quipped. "I'm not easily impressed by flowers. I'm more of a horse girl. The ranch is in my blood."

"Yeah, well, it would be quite impossible to fill your office with horses," he quipped back.

"Touché. Thank you for the flowers. Robert just loved them."

"What about you?"

"Hmm, let's just say you got my attention. Now what?"

The drinks were served as ordered, and then the seafood salad was brought in a single bowl and placed on the adjoining serving table. Plates were set in front of each person, and the salad was evenly divided onto each plate.

The waiter stood, both hands behind his back, and explained the composition of the salad and the chef's special salad sauce. Neither spoke as they were being served.

When the waiter finally departed—after making his lengthy speech on the source and composition of everything placed on the table—Abby looked at Javier, both hands under her chin, eyes fixated as she stared at him quizzically, waiting for a reaction.

Chapter Eighteen
Isabella

THIRTEENTH BIRTHDAY

For her thirteenth birthday, Javier convinced Abby to organize a surprise party for Isabella. Nothing that Javier ever proposed to Isabella was accepted or even considered. Thus, Abby was his way of accessing what his daughter liked. Even though his influence was largely undermined by Isabella's control over the security and daily operations of the Hacienda, Javier still maintained a fair amount of leeway in conducting business. He was grateful for this and exploited all organizational commands he could get away with.

Javier planted the birthday "seed" in Abby's mind. Their daughter was turning thirteen—a teenager, beginning her passage into adolescence. What better way to mark this milestone than to celebrate with family and friends from afar? When Abby agreed, Javier tasked her with organizing the event, not wanting to appear involved in the planning in Isabella's eyes. Hence, the stage was set for Javier's master plan.

Abby invited her parents and her sister Katherine to the celebration, organizing all the transport logistics for them. She also invited a few of Isabella's friends from school, reminding them that it was a surprise party and that they should not mention anything to Isabella or discuss the event within her earshot. Abby also sought out Ryan, explaining the event and the potential guest list. She requested total silence and discretion from him, instructing him to increase the security arrangements. With Ryan on board, Abby was sure there would be no lapses and that the celebration would go smoothly.

Javier, on the other hand, invited a few of his business associates under the pretext that it was mutually beneficial for all concerned to congregate and discuss future business amalgams, measures, and proceedings. Two significant guests of note were Benito Alvarez Dos Almeidas, a very powerful Colombian mass farm producer of cocaine, and Ramon Miguel José Gilles, a Mexican arms dealer and territorial controller. Compared to these two personalities, Javier was just a small-time wannabe. He wanted to be recognized as a big player. Javier wanted more than anything to be respected and feared internationally. He wanted his name—and his family name—to instill fear into those who interacted with him. But he had nothing to offer, nothing to arouse even the slightest interest from either party. He had a master plan, but would it work?

Isabella strolled down the path leading from the Hacienda to the lake on the property. She often walked this path, which cut through the shrubs and rocky terrain, over jagged boulders, and down to the lake shore. The shore was covered in reeds and sharp, rocky edges that were uninviting for bathing or leisure activities. Isabella, not allowing nature to dictate the terms of her enjoyment, cut a huge patch through the reeds, cleared whatever rocks lay in between, and created a tidy beachfront for herself. It was to this private spot that she would often descend to practice and train her katana skills.

With her headphones blaring music in her ears, she walked nonchalantly down the path toward her beachfront. About fifty meters ahead, she noticed a figure walking in the same direction. No one had ever dared to walk here, as it was considered her private space. Yet there, right in front of her, was a man walking slowly, unsure of his steps, toward the lakefront. Then, as suddenly as he had appeared, he vanished from view. Surprised, she quickened her pace.

Just over the ridge, the man was lying on his side, moaning and holding his foot. Isabella rushed up and saw a rattlesnake slither away into the underbrush. It crawled over a rock and disappeared. She followed it, caught up, and sliced its head off in one swift swing. She rushed back to the man, who was now convulsing, foaming at the mouth, and groaning. Isabella used the tip of her katana to slice open the man's ankle, where she had noticed the snake bite marks.

She bent over and sucked the blood out, spitting and sucking repeatedly until she was satisfied that she had drained a significant portion of the venom. The man passed out from the shock and pain.

Isabella then tied a tourniquet just below his knee with the belt she was wearing. She then pulled out her shoelaces and tied a second, tighter tourniquet above the knee.

The man was too heavy for Isabella to carry alone, so she called Ryan. Together, they half-carried, half-dragged the man back to the Hacienda. They placed him on the couch in Ryan's quarters and called Corella.

Corella arrived with an anti-venom injection kit and a bottle of her homemade potion—more of a "one-size-fits-all" type of concoction that seemed to heal everything. She injected the man while Isabella lifted his head and made him drink the potion. They then laid him down, wiping his face with a cool, wet towel.

Corella rummaged through the first aid kit, looking for a needle and nylon thread to stitch the wound. She found none. Then Isabella found a small tube of superglue. While Corella pieced the cut together, Isabella applied the glue in a thin streak. They both held the wound closed until the glue began to dry. Isabella then applied a second coating for good measure. Corella wrapped the wound in a clean bandage. Ryan placed a pillow under the man's foot to elevate it. All they could do now was wait. He was certainly out of danger.

Isabella and Ryan kept watch over the man while Corella returned to the main house to prepare lunch.

It was late afternoon when the man eventually opened his eyes. He stared at the ceiling, totally disoriented and in a great deal of pain. He couldn't pinpoint where exactly the pain was coming from, or even which part of his body was injured. He just knew he was in terrible pain, and it was attacking him from somewhere.

He heard muffled voices in the distance. At first, they were distorted, like they were emanating from inside a drum—distant, hollow sounds coupled with blurry images he couldn't quite make out. The voices continued, increasing in volume as he regained consciousness.

"Hey Benito, welcome back to the living!" Javier's voice broke through.

"Benito, Benito, you're gonna be okay. Thanks to the quick thinking of my sharp-minded daughter, you're alive. Still with us! Benito, can you hear me, man?"

Javier gently shook Benito's shoulder as he spoke. "My daughter saved your life. You were bitten by a western diamondback rattlesnake. It's a very dangerous and deadly snake. You probably had only a few seconds to live, but thankfully, my daughter was on hand to suck the poison out. Otherwise, my friend, we'd be preparing your body for shipment back to your family."

"Diamondback rattlesnakes are very venomous, but it takes two to three days to die if unchecked. The body starts to shut down after thirty to forty minutes if untreated," said Isabella, correcting her father.

She turned to Benito and added, "You already suffered the typical symptoms—shock and collapse, nausea, extreme pain and swelling, and difficulty breathing. I got to you almost immediately, so there will be no long-term organ damage. But you do need to rest. Corella and I will check up on you, make sure you heal nicely."

She nodded to Benito, turned, and walked out of the room, heading straight to the kitchen to consult with Corella, who was waiting for her.

As Isabella entered, Corella looked up and smiled. "You've just made yourself a very powerful friend—someone who'll be indebted to you for life. Do you know what it means to save someone's life? Well, multiply that by a million, and that's what it means to that man and his family. They'll kiss the ground you walk on. Trust me, they'll never forget what you've done."

Isabella raised an eyebrow. "What do you know about that? Have you ever saved someone's life?"

"I am of Colombian origin. I know the culture. My grandmother was Colombian, so I know. I know I can tell you, I know! Not only did you save his life, but you killed the attacker with one swift strike. You cut off its head. No loose ends. Snake, attacker, or whoever— dead! No loose ends. Then you tend to him like a professional field agent, fighting somewhere in the desert! Improvising and administering first aid to a wounded colleague!"

"Oh, stop, Corella! You watch too many Hollywood dramas. I just did what anybody would do, given the circumstances. I'm no hero—just a Samaritan, nothing more!"

Corella was smiling and wanted to continue the banter when Javier walked in and said to Isabella, "That was a very brave thing you did today. I'm so very proud of you. You brought honor to our family. You gave us prominence. Thank you, my darling. Come here, let me hug you."

Isabella just stood there—expressionless, motionless—staring at her father. Javier walked over to her, took her into his arms, and hugged his daughter real tight.

"Tomorrow," he said, "we will celebrate your thirteenth birthday with a real bang and celebrate for three days—music and dancing and eating and drinking."

He let go of Isabella and walked out of the kitchen, into the main house, and up to his quarters.

Chapter Nineteen
Isabella

THE PREPARATIONS

True to his word, Javier hired a twenty-piece brass band featuring all kinds of instruments, just like in a traditional classical orchestra. He also hired a local Mexican quartet for traditional Mexican and Latino music. Spanish Flamenco dancers with castanets, Spanish Bolero dancers, and Cuban salsa dancers were flown in. The very best Spanish wine was shipped directly from the family cave. The caviar came from Russia, the smoked salmon from Norway, and sushi chefs were flown in from Japan. The list was seemingly endless.

The birthday cake was to be prepared by the most renowned French baker from Paris. The extravagance of it all was mind-boggling. After all, in Javier's eyes, Isabella was becoming a teen—a rite of passage from being a school-aged pre-teen to a bona fide teenager. That meant she was becoming a young woman. Her thirteenth birthday needed to be proclaimed to the whole world.

In general, school kids celebrated their birthdays by simply inviting friends and classmates for an afternoon dance party. They rarely, if ever, called for such extreme extravagance. Nor did they last for three whole days.

The motivation behind Javier's efforts was clearly not just the milestone of his only child entering her teens. Rather, it was the celebration of the successful implementation of a strategic future alliance. Benito Alvarez Dos Almeidas—the most important alliance that anyone with even the slightest aspirations of entering the distribution phase would need. Not only was Benito's recognition, trust, and approval of vital importance, but it also served as a testament to entry-level status within the syndicate.

Benito Alvarez Dos Almeidas was a very discreet and private man who rarely ventured outside his compound—let alone his native Colombia. To be graced with his presence at a birthday celebration bordered on miraculous. And yet, here he was—attacked and injured. Had the incident not been resolved the way it was, the consequences for Javier and his family would have been dire. Accusations of a deliberate attack on Benito—or even an attempted assassination—would have followed.

Fortunately, the situation was resolved to Benito's satisfaction. He had nothing but pride and praise for Isabella.

Part one of Javier's master plan was shaping up. Hence, the extravagant celebration. Isabella's thirteenth birthday was merely an excuse. Now, for the second piece of the jigsaw to fall into place.

Chapter Twenty
Isabella

THE PARTY

The next morning was total chaos at the Hacienda. There were people everywhere—trucks, vans, and buses coming and going nonstop. It was a Saturday, so there was no school. All the noise that had started at 5 a.m. had woken Isabella. She opened her shutters slightly and observed the hustle and bustle from her room. It was a nightmare for the security logistics team, and Ryan and the crew were inundated with tight security measures being enforced. A ten-mile queue of trucks lined the main road leading up to the Hacienda, all waiting to deliver and offload.

A large tent was erected in the back garden, capable of seating almost a hundred guests. This would be the dining area. On the side of the tent, a wooden dance floor with an elevated podium was assembled to serve as the stage for the orchestra. Huge base pots filled with the most beautiful flowers were placed throughout the tent interior, as well as around the outside dance floor and stage area. Hanging flowerpots were installed inside the tent. Around and on the main table, vases overflowed with stunning white flowers. The arrangements were designed by florists from Miami. Javier, who had directed the celebratory arrangements himself, was reminded of his own childhood birthday celebrations organized by his grandfather.

From the outside, it was simply a continuation of family tradition—something he wanted his daughter to experience and appreciate. Nonetheless, Isabella hated every aspect of these preparations. She resented having her birthday manipulated by her father to further his sinister operations.

The trucks that had delivered the equipment, musical instruments, flowers, and all the other decorations finally departed. As the noise and chaos simmered down, a sense of familiar calm began to return.

Isabella spent the morning with Benito. She went to his quarters to check on his condition and well-being. They walked down to the lakeside—a gesture of reassurance that what had happened a few days ago was a freak accident. They talked about her educational interests and career goals, if she had begun to form any. All the while, Benito was mesmerized by this elegant, exquisitely beautiful, intelligent, and brave young girl. How he wished one of his sons possessed even a portion of the integrity and spirit of this girl who had saved his life.

In his heart and mind, Benito had adopted the daughter he would never have. During their two-hour walk, Isabella did most of the talking while Benito smiled, admired, and quietly hoped he could have this graceful young woman in his life forever. The only way to make that possible, he thought, was to initiate a union between her and his younger son. He would speak to Javier about it.

That evening began with classical music playing softly as guests arrived. Just where all these guests had come from intrigued Isabella. As she stepped out of the main house—dressed in white pants and a white jacket with subtle pink lining along the edges and inside—she noticed that most of the guests had already arrived and were taking their seats in the tent. To complement her outfit, she wore a deep pink button-down shirt with matching shoes. Her mother placed a pink flower in her hair before she stepped outside. To match her daughter's ensemble, Abby wore pink pants, a pink button-down shirt, a white jacket, and white shoes. Standing side by side, the two beauty queens were stunning.

Soft, discreet classical music filled the air as the guests mingled, feeling privileged to be invited to such a special occasion. The outfits, the jewelry, the cars, and the chauffeurs on display betrayed a clear undercurrent—each guest was trying to outshine the other.

At the main table sat Javier, Abby, Benito, Ramon, José-Manuel, Carmen's father, his wife Maria Catarina, the deputy governor of the region, and the federal interior minister. Isabella sat with Carmen and their school friends at a table close to the dance floor. Between courses, guests wandered over to the dance floor to dance—mostly classical waltz.

As the evening progressed and the main meal was served, the orchestra took a break, and the Mexican quartet took over. They played traditional songs while walking between the tables. When the music turned to salsa, the dance floor filled up, and the guests thoroughly enjoyed themselves.

Then came the Flamenco dancers from Spain. It was a special performance, and all guests were requested to take their seats. The orchestra returned, and the music transitioned to Spanish Bolero and Flamenco. The female dancers were dressed in flamboyant red and black-lined long dresses, castanets in each hand. The performance began with the strumming of the guitar, and then the dancers entered, encircling a single figure as she strode confidently across the dance floor. They opened up into a singular line formation.

In the middle of it all stood Isabella, dressed in a long red and black dress with a black shroud over her head. She wore black heels and held castanets in each hand. She was sublime and poised—pure talent.

Javier jumped up in utter and complete surprise. He clapped his hands vigorously and began raising his voice in praise of his daughter.

Abby pulled him down and whispered, "Sit down and stop embarrassing her. Let her dance!"

"Did you know about this?" he asked, reluctantly sitting.

"Of course, she's my daughter. I know everything about her! Now watch!"

Javier opened his mouth to respond, then thought better of it. He turned his attention to Isabella—now the center of the performance. As the guitar played and the dancers moved in harmony, Isabella strutted flawlessly across the wooden dance floor, her castanets clicking rhythmically. Her movements were seamless and expressive. She was focused, composed, and clearly in her element. The dancer had become the dance.

Benito, sitting next to Javier and still on crutches, leaned in and whispered that he would like to propose a marriage arrangement between Isabella and his youngest son, Jimmy.

Eyes sparkling—perhaps more from the wine and alcohol consumption than from admiration for his daughter's performance on the dance floor—Javier turned to Benito and said aloud, "You are too late with your proposal, my friend. I have already accepted a wedding proposal from my friend Ramon. Ramon has proposed a marriage between my daughter and his son, Miguel, and I have accepted. I am so sorry, my friend, but if I had a second daughter, I would gladly entertain your request."

Abby stood up and said, "How dare you make such preposterous arrangements for my daughter? You are—"

Javier jerked Abby's arm hard, forcing her back into her seat. "Sit down and stop embarrassing me!" he growled.

Abby pulled her arm away from Javier, stood up again, and declared, "Isabella will marry who she wants and when she wants—without interference from anybody!" Then she left.

"Women!" said all three men at the same time, and they laughed.

Part two of Javier's master plan was in place. His alliance with Benito was secured, thanks to Isabella's brave and selfless act of saving his life. Now, the arranged marriage between Isabella and Ramon's son, Miguel, would solidify his pact with Ramon. Javier was all set to become a key player in the market and would be respected throughout the region. His status and influence were guaranteed.

He patted himself on the back. "Well done, Javier, well done!"

Three days of festivities followed. Neither Isabella nor Abby took any further part in the celebrations.

It took three weeks to dismantle and remove all the infrastructure that had been brought in. The security operation, which had once been a nightmare, was ultimately deemed a success. Isabella ordered the crew to take a well-deserved rest and recuperation break. Half the team complied.

Back at school, Carmen and her friends could talk about nothing but the party—and Isabella's dancing. The question they all had was, "Where and when did she learn to dance like that?"

Isabella's answer was simply, "Private lessons at home." Still, they were all envious.

Chapter Twenty-One
Isabella – Abby

EIGHTEEN MONTHS LATER

After the night Javier sold out his daughter for business pacts with ogres, Abby began her descent into hell. She ate less and less and drank more. By the time lunchtime approached, she was heavily under the influence of alcohol. When evening came, Abby would ingest several lines of cocaine. This had the effect of immediately sobering her up, rendering her presentable for Isabella's return home from school.

Each day, each week, Abby consumed more alcohol and, subsequently, more cocaine. Javier encouraged her to indulge, often taking her on trips away from home for days on end, spoiling her with excessive luxury shopping, all the while plying her with alcohol and drugs. Abby's condition visibly worsened.

Now, eighteen months later, Abby was in free fall. She was dependent on both drugs and alcohol but denied her condition. She lived in constant denial, convincing herself that she could recognize her limits and would act without hesitation if things became uncontrollable. She lied to herself, believing she drank merely as a reprisal against Javier, and used the drugs to maintain a relatively measured state of mind when Isabella got home. Under no circumstances should Isabella ever see her inebriated and incoherent, as she often was. Hence, the early development of her drug use.

She kept telling herself that she was not an addict. She simply sought escape—from Javier and the trade he was deeply involved in. Isabella was the only thing keeping her in that house, in that situation. So, she endured. And she consumed.

Isabella hadn't noticed her mother's inebriation, as the sobering effects of cocaine masked the signs. On one occasion, extracurricular activities were canceled, and Isabella returned home straight from school. Eager to see her mother, she went upstairs to her room, hoping to greet her and perhaps plan an afternoon outing together.

What she found, however, was a scene that would haunt her forever.

Her mother lay unconscious on the bed, completely naked and unresponsive. On top of her was one of Javier's trusted employees, raping her. Behind him stood another man, his pants down, impatiently waiting for his turn.

Isabella stood frozen in the doorway, completely in shock. Her mind raced, but her body refused to move. She tried to scream, but no sound came out. Her knees buckled, and she gripped the doorframe to steady herself.

When she finally regained her composure, a surge of rage and adrenaline coursed through her. She let out a piercing scream and lunged into the room. Without hesitation, she kicked the second man hard in the groin. He crumpled to the floor, writhing in pain.

The man on top of Abby turned, wondering what the commotion was about, when he received an open-palm slap over both ears. His pants were down to his knees, so he couldn't move freely. As he turned fully around, Isabella punched him directly in the throat, cutting off his respiration. He went down, holding his neck and gasping for air. Isabella then stomped both feet on his groin and kicked him in the side of the head. The force of the kick slammed his head against the corner of the bed, rendering him unconscious.

The first man could only shout, "Por favor, para, por favor, para. El señor Javier nos la ofreció. Ése era nuestro bono, autorizó el señor Javier, nos animó. Por favor, solo estamos realizando pedidos."

In English: "Please stop, please stop. Mr. Javier offered her to us. This was our bonus. Mr. Javier authorized it and encouraged us. Please, we are just carrying out orders."

Those were his last words as Isabella, in a rage of uncontrollable fury, punched him repeatedly in the head. She screamed and struck the man until Corella, who had come upstairs to investigate the screams, pulled her away.

Isabella sobbed into Corella's shoulder. Corella hugged and kissed her gently on the forehead, speaking in soft, low tones to calm her down. Then the two of them dragged Abby into the bathroom, ran the water, and placed her naked body in the tub. Afterward, they called Ramiro to clear the room of the two men. One was still breathing; the other was unresponsive.

After the cold water bath, Abby regained consciousness— groggy, disoriented, and sobbing. She looked around for Javier, unable to understand where she was. She couldn't process her surroundings and kept calling for him.

Isabella sobbed uncontrollably, unsure of how to respond. She jumped into the bathtub, fully clothed, sat behind her mother, and cradled her head in her arms.

"I'm here, Mom. I'm here. I'll never let anything like this happen to you again. I promise. I'm here, Mom," she repeated over and over.

Abby dozed off in Isabella's arms. Corella walked into the bathroom, and together they dressed Abby. Once both Isabella and Abby were dry and dressed for bed, they carried her to Isabella's room, where she would spend the night.

At the time of these events, Javier was on a business trip to Spain to oversee the family's operations there. He had been gone for a full three months. When he returned to the Hacienda, Abby was not there.

He ate dinner alone the first night. After not seeing or hearing from Abby the entire day, Javier summoned Corella into the dining room that evening.

Instead of Corella, Isabella walked in.

Javier looked up, surprised, and forced a smile. "Well, to what do I owe this lovely surprise?"

Isabella didn't say a word. She pulled up a chair close to Javier and sat facing him directly. A nervous smile spread across his face, but his eyes showed real fear. He put down his fork and stared at his plate, avoiding her gaze.

"Three months ago," Isabella began, "I caught two of your most trusted henchmen raping Mom. She was clearly comatose, unable to defend herself from such an attack, from such abuse—in her own room. But do you know what's so disgusting, so horrendous, so intolerable about all this? It was what one of the men said to me before I beat the life out of him.

"He had this surprised look on his face as he said that *you* authorized and encouraged them. That *this*—raping Mom—was their bonus. Their **bonus**! You are nothing but a horrible, despicable worm. Not a man—a God-condemned worm! No spine, no legs, no head, no brain—a worm! Crawling in the undergrowth, scrounging for leftovers from other, lesser insects.

"How does that make you feel? I'll tell you—*it makes me feel repulsed* knowing that we share the same bloodline. But God knows the big picture, and He will enlighten me. I hope it's soon. You despicable invertebrate phyla—you *Sipuncula.* Do you know what a Sipuncula is? It's a peanut worm! A stupid worm! Of all the worms, **you** are the most stupid!"

"Enough!" Javier shouted, slamming his hand on the table. "I said enough! I am your father. I provide for this house. I provide for you, for your mother! Where is she?"

"Mom is away. In rehab. I put her there!"

Laughing out loud, Javier said, "Your mother won't last in rehab. First chance she gets, she'll call me—and I'll go pick her up. Then no more rehab. Just more of what she had. But—"

"But what, you creep!"

"You can fix this. I'll keep her in rehab. And when she gets out, I'll send her away to a monastery I know that will help her stay clean—away from all this."

"Why would you do that?"

"In exchange for you agreeing to marry Ramon's son. His name is Miguel."

Isabella stood up, her face red with rage. She moved stealthily behind Javier, just as he was about to put food in his mouth, and twisted the fork toward his throat.

"I'll kill you right here and now and feed your body to the pigs on Carmen's farm."

Javier didn't flinch. Instead, he smirked.

"You won't do that. You see, I moved your mother from the rehab center *you* sent her to. Now she's in *my* rehab center. Anything happens to me, she doesn't come out of there. Not dead. Not alive. So sit your disobedient ass down and listen to my proposal."

Isabella hesitated, her hands trembling with fury. But eventually, she sat down—still seething.

Javier laid out his plan: she would marry Miguel—who, he casually mentioned, was gay—live with him for two years, and then get a divorce, which he would arrange. In return, Abby would receive the full rehabilitation treatment she desperately needed.

Reluctantly, Isabella agreed. She would do it for her mother's sake—but she made one thing clear: if Javier didn't hold up his end of the bargain, she would strangle him with her bare hands.

Without another word, she stood up and left the room.

Javier patted himself on the back with both hands. "Well done, Javier, well done. You are a Master Planner," he said to himself.

Upstairs, Isabella locked herself in her room and collapsed onto her bed. For the first time in as long as she could remember, she cried herself to sleep.

Chapter Twenty-Two
Isabella - Miguel

THE WEDDING

O n her fourteenth birthday, Isabella was married to Miguel. To mark what he saw as his ultimate triumph, Javier orchestrated the most lavish ceremony imaginable. Family members from both sides were invited, including his older sister, Sofia Catalina, who traveled all the way from Spain. Isabella's grandparents, Frank and Anna, were present, as was her Aunt Katherine. They stood as somber, disgruntled figures, their silent protest palpable amidst the opulence of the event. Abby, still too physically and mentally fragile to leave the rehab center, was notably absent.

It was Aunt Katherine who had practically forced Isabella's grandparents to attend, insisting they show solidarity with their young granddaughter. Katherine, who knew the full extent of the sacrifice Isabella had made for her mother's well-being, admired her niece's strength. She stood firmly by Isabella's side, helping her prepare for the day, assisting Corella in dressing her, and offering quiet words of encouragement.

It wasn't a union sanctioned by either the state or the church but rather a civil engagement between consenting parties, crafted to safeguard any future legal reclamations or allegations regarding Isabella's age. The marriage was to be officiated by Javier's sister, Sofia, who had long aspired to become an ordained pastor. The Catholic Church, however, did not allow female priests, so Sofia had abandoned her Catholic faith and embraced a more flexible denomination. She loved her brother and fully supported the union. She felt deeply honored to have her faith recognized by Javier and to be given the opportunity to practice it. Sofia had spent weeks preparing for the ceremony.

Javier would walk Isabella down the makeshift aisle. The guests would rise, the orchestra would play soft wedding music, and then Sofia would take control. She would call everyone to order, deliver her speech, give her blessing, and pronounce the couple married. She had dreamed of this moment and looked forward to it with great anticipation.

Katherine, Isabella's beloved aunt and stand-in mother for the day, stood behind Isabella as she stared at herself in the mirror for a final appraisal.

Beauty at its utmost perfection, Katherine thought as she admired her niece.

"Come on, let's go, my darling," she said gently.

Corella began to sob uncontrollably, her voice shaking with grief.

"Dios mío, Dios mío, ¿por qué le ha hecho eso el señor Javier? Es una bebé, es demasiado joven, Dios mío, Dios mío. No, no... Por favor, Dios, no... Detén esta locura."

In English: "My God! My God! Why did you do that to her, Mr. Javier? She's a baby, she's too young. My God! My God! No, no... Please, God, no... Stop this madness."

Isabella turned to Corella. She wrapped her arms tightly around the weeping woman, then reached for a tissue from the dresser and gently dried her tears.

"You take care of my mother when she returns, okay?" Isabella said softly. "Take care of her while I'm away. Promise me that. Just take care of my mother. I can take care of myself. Promise me, Corella. Promise me you will protect my mother from this monster."

"Te lo prometo, Dios es mi testigo, te lo prometo, mi bebé. Eres mi bebé. Desde que naciste te tuve en mis brazos. Te prometo que Dios me castigará si fallo."

In English: "I promise you, God is my witness. I promise you, my baby, you are my baby. Since you were born I held you in my arms. I promise you that if I fail, God will punish me. But I won't fail."

Isabella turned to Katherine and said, "I'm ready, Aunt Katy. Will you walk with me?"

"Of course, my darling," Katherine replied.

The two hugged long and hard. Then, with Corella in tow, they walked to the side entrance that led onto the path toward the arbor.

Everything was white: the flowers around the arbor, the petals on the walkway, the ribbons, even the balloons. In stark contrast, Isabella wore a long, blood-red dress with black lace trimmings. Her flat shoes matched the dress, and a black veil covered her face. She wore her mother's long white-gold diamond earrings. Her makeup was striking—red blush and black lipstick. Isabella belied her tender age of fourteen.

Her choice of attire had met resistance from both Katherine and Corella, who had urged her to wear a traditional white gown. But Isabella had been firm.

"This isn't a traditional wedding," she had said. "It's a betrayal by my father, and I intend to show that to everyone."

Despite the pain and defiance behind her appearance, Isabella was breathtaking. She was beauty incarnate—her slender frame radiating a quiet strength that left an indelible impression on everyone who saw her.

To the right of the doorway stood a white horse-drawn carriage, harnessed to two stunning white horses. Javier had arranged for the carriage to take Isabella on a short ride around the main house before dropping her at the start of the walkway to the arbor.

As Isabella, Katherine, and Corella stepped outside, the driver quickly opened the carriage door, bowing slightly as he waited for Isabella to enter. True to herself, she ignored both the driver and the carriage. Instead, she walked the shortest path to the beginning of the walkway.

Javier, standing at the top of the pathway, was visibly shocked and disconcerted by Isabella's choice of attire. His mouth opened, as if to comment, but he hesitated. Then, unable to contain himself, he spoke.

"Red and black?" he asked, holding out his arm for Isabella to take.

This was his proud moment—the joy, the immense pride of walking his daughter down the aisle to give her away to her groom.

Only Javier wasn't giving his daughter away in marriage. He was selling her.

"What happened to the white wedding gown I ordered from Paris?" Javier continued. "It was a custom-made designer gown by the most talented designer in the world!"

"Well, you should have worn it," quipped Isabella.

Javier's face flushed with anger. "Why? Why this insolence? Red and black—for your own wedding?"

"This is not *my* wedding. This is *your* wedding. Your arrangements with your associates. Red and black? Well, the red is for the blood that will spill if you renege on our agreement. Black is for my heart! When it comes to you and your family, my heart is black. There, now you know."

Isabella turned around and beckoned for her Aunt Katherine to join her.

"Come on, Aunt Katherine. Please walk with me, and let's get this farce over with as soon as possible."

She completely ignored Javier, who stood there with his arm in a sling.

Katherine stepped up, hooked her arm into Isabella's, and the two women walked down the makeshift aisle to the arbor, where Miguel was standing. Next to Miguel stood a young man Isabella had never seen before—likely the best man.

Embarrassed by the unfolding events, Javier marched up to the front of the seating area and stood by his designated seat.

As the women walked slowly to the wedding music and reached the arbor, Katherine took her seat next to her parents, and Isabella stood facing Miguel. He held out his hands to take hers, but Isabella offered nothing. Her arms remained by her sides.

"Please be seated," said Sofia, Javier's sister, who had been nominated as the wedding minister by her brother.

With outstretched hands, she continued, "Welcome! Welcome, dear family and friends. We are gathered here today to unite, to join, to celebrate the coming together of these two young, beautiful souls standing here in front of us all. We seek God's blessing, God's approval, and God's divine intervention to seal this union in His glorified Heaven above and to declare this union absolute.

"Oh God, O Father, watching over us all, send down Your angels to protect this marriage for eternity. Let not those with evil intentions inhibit this union. Let not those with envy in their hearts interfere in this union. Cast away the devil, our declared enemy, from his influence in this union. O Father, let's not—"

"Aunt Sofia," Isabella interrupted, "just get on with it, please. I want this over as soon as possible, so cut your speech and finish this."

Sofia paused, then smiled nervously at the guests.

"My respected family and friends, the bride and groom are so impatient to be in each other's arms eternally that I must ask you all to please stand."

The guests all stood.

Sofia turned to Miguel. "Miguel Jimenez Calderon, do you take Isabella Katherine Reyes to be your heaven-chosen partner in marriage? To love and protect, to provide for, to care for in sickness and in health, to befriend, to respect, to obey, until death do you part?"

"Sí. I do," said Miguel in a soft, inaudible voice.

"Please speak up, Miguel. Say it out loud for all to hear."

"I do!" shouted Miguel.

Sofia turned to Isabella. "And do you, Isabella Katherine Reyes—"

"I do!" shouted Isabella.

Sofia frowned. "Please let me read it all out. Let me finish."

"Just get to the end part," Isabella said flatly.

Sofia's eyes narrowed, and she muttered under her breath, "You little shit." Then, regaining her composure, she declared loudly, "By the power God has invested in me as Minister of the Jesuit Faith, I pronounce you husband and wife. Miguel, you may kiss the bride!"

"Don't you *dare*," Isabella growled at Miguel.

She turned and threw the bouquet she was holding to Corella, then walked briskly to her grandparents and her Aunt Katherine. She hugged them tightly and buried her head in her aunt's chest.

The four of them left the ceremony abruptly, not making any further appearances.

Isabella had kept her end of the bargain.

Now, it was up to Javier to hold up his.

Chapter Twenty-Three
Isabella

MARRIED

Six months into her marriage, Isabella began to encounter inappropriate behavior from Ramón Calderon, Miguel's father. While the ground rules had been set between Isabella and Miguel, it was Ramón—the perpetrator—whose advances antagonized her. His innuendos and humorless quips incensed Isabella to the point of completely withdrawing from all forms of contact with every member of the household, including the staff.

Isabella practically isolated herself, often taking her meals alone. On the occasions when Miguel sought her company to share a meal, Isabella rebuffed him.

One evening, while Isabella was in her kitchen preparing her own meal, Miguel walked in unannounced and sat down. Bemused, Isabella stopped what she was doing and stared at him questioningly.

"I'm gay," he muttered. "My father suspects it, which is why he wanted us married so soon. Now he's pestering me to start a family.

'I want a grandson,' he keeps repeating. 'If you can't do the job, then I will. You're wasting a woman. Looks to me like you're a woman yourself.' What a pathetic rodent."

"You want a quesadilla?" Isabella asked.

"Oh yes, please. I'm avoiding the main house, my father, and all his slaves."

"Okay. Sit down while I prepare. But—" she turned and faced him squarely, expression stern—"don't ever walk into my space unannounced. You ask me first. You check with me first. Ever. Understood?"

"Yes. I'm really sorry about barging in like this. I feel so depressed. I really needed someone to talk to. I know you'll understand. You have a kindness in your eyes."

"Don't mistake my calm and solitude for weakness and kindness. I'll cut your throat without a second's hesitation."

Weeks turned into months, and Ramón's obsession with his son's wife intensified. It reached the point where he instructed the maids to leave notes in Isabella's quarters while they cleaned and arranged her belongings.

One early evening, Isabella stepped out of the shower, her hair wet and glistening. She had just washed it and applied a super-soft conditioner for blonde hair, leaving it in for ten minutes before rinsing it out. She always took great care with her hair—

meticulously washing, conditioning, and drying it with a cold-air blow dryer.

She still had a towel wrapped around her head when she walked out of the bathroom—*her* private bathroom. Her husband had his own quarters across the hallway, almost as large, fitted with similar amenities. He often crossed the hallway for a chat and always to say goodnight. They were friends, but nothing more.

Isabella stood barefoot in the middle of her room, wearing black, tight-fitting sweatpants, an oversized gray T-shirt, and a towel around her head. It had become a habit to dress in the shower before entering her bedroom, ever since Miguel had once surprised her by walking in without announcing himself.

She had been so furious with Miguel that she absolutely castigated him for his total lack of respect for her personal space. She vowed, with all the rancor she could muster, that she would remove his manhood with one slice and feed it to the pigs on the ranch. Such insolence and disdain for her privacy were utterly unacceptable, and he would not go unpunished if he ever repeated such a lapse in judgment. Isabella, with ice-cold eyes, only had to relay her anger once. The message was received.

The door to her room opened.

There was no knock.

No calling out.

No asking for permission to enter.

It just opened—and in walked Ramón.

Isabella froze. She stood in the middle of the room, staring first at the door, then at Ramón. She said nothing—just stared. Shock, disbelief, and then rage stormed through her mind.

"Aha, you're here. Fresh out of the bath, I see. And you smell so good," he said wryly, smiling and flashing his gold-capped teeth.

Isabella said nothing—just returned a cold, hard stare. Her blue eyes revealed irrepressible contempt.

"You're alone, I see. This is good. I was hoping to get you alone—not have my soft, dainty son in here, interrupting our encounter. Let him play with his boyfriends; give *us* our space, hehe." His laugh grated like iron on concrete.

Isabella shuddered. His words, his insinuations disgusted her. A cold shiver ran down her spine. Her nerves fired up every bit of adrenaline her body could produce. Her cheeks flushed with heat, but she still said nothing. Slowly, deliberately, she turned to face him squarely, arms folded across her chest, eyes locked on his— unblinking.

Ramón stepped further into the room, striding nonchalantly toward Isabella and talking all the while.

"You smell good. I can smell you from here. I love that perfume. My wife uses a different one every day, like she's still choosing— or maybe she's just a peasant who never had perfume before.

Splashin', splashin' all over the place—I can't even get used to her smell. Not that I want to.

"But you—your soft, delicate, sweet smell—I'm already used to it. Makes my heart beat from the other side of my chest. Which side? I don't even know anymore. Come, my dear. Don't look so surprised—or is this your way of showing you're happy to see me?"

He got within touching distance and reached out to push Isabella down onto the bed.

"Ahh, this feels good already—just thinking it, even before touching you."

Ramón placed his hand on Isabella's chest to push her down. In that instant, Isabella stepped forward and locked his hand where he had placed it. Then, twisting slightly and stepping backward, she placed her elbow behind his outstretched arm—just above the joint—and jabbed hard.

Ramón was caught off guard.

He spun in the direction of the thrust, but the sharp jab and relentless pressure she applied to his elbow joint caused it to snap. A loud *crack* filled the room.

Still gripping his arm, Isabella stepped behind him and wrapped her arm around the front of his neck, using her other hand to push his head backward. She spun her body again, further stressing the shoulder, and pressed her upper body into the back of his elbow.

Then came the final snap.

Crack!

The sound of his arm breaking.

Still holding onto his hand, she stepped back, pulling on his outstretched arm. With her free hand, she slammed Ramón's upper shoulder with her elbow—right where the arm met the shoulder.

Crack! She broke his collarbone.

Finally, she struck him with the back of her hand across his throat. He went down, howling and screaming in pain, then choking. The pain was so unbearable that Ramón passed out.

"What's the matter? Don't want to play anymore?" said Isabella. "Too physical for you? You little soft, dainty pussy. You ever come back in here, I'll break your little chicken neck!"

Then she opened the door to her room and ran out screaming, "Help, help! Ramón is hurt! Help! Somebody call an ambulance. He fell down and broke his arm and shoulder, I think. Miguel! Miguel... somebody!"

Ángel, Ramón's chief confidant and bodyguard, came running from downstairs.

"What happened? Where is he?"

"In my room."

"How did it happen?"

"He slipped on the wet floor. He came into my room; the floor was wet from when I came out of the bathroom. He tried to break the fall with his arm and just fell—real hard. Is it bad? Can you tell?

Oh, I feel so bad. We were... well, anyway, he fell! Did you call an ambulance?"

"Yes, I did. It's on its way."

"Oh my God, I feel so bad. Please don't tell Miguel and Sally where he was!"

"Don't worry. It's my job to arrange the fallout, pick up the pieces, and clean up his mess. Don't worry—nobody needs to know anything."

"Oh, thank you!" exclaimed Isabella, feigning relief.

In her mind, she replayed: *I'll clean up this mess! So, I'm a mess,* she thought. *They ain't seen nothing yet!*

The ambulance arrived within twenty minutes. Isabella, still pretending to be distraught over the evening's events, continued her charade.

"I'm accompanying Ramón in the ambulance," she said to no one in particular.

To the ambulance assistants: "Is there a place for me? I need to be with him."

"Yes, yes, sure. No problem, miss. You can sit there, right next to him," said one of the attendants, who would be riding in the back with them.

Before climbing in, Isabella turned to Ángel and said, "Get two guys and follow us in a separate car. I want you to establish a protection perimeter around the hospital and on the floor outside his room."

Ángel just stared at her blankly, not moving, watching her climb into the back of the ambulance. He waved the ambulance away and set about doing exactly as Isabella had instructed—not because she had told him to, but because this was standard protocol under such circumstances.

He didn't need the precocious little bitch giving him instructions—least of all telling him how to do his job.

At the hospital, the charade continued. Isabella shouted instructions at the security team that had followed behind the ambulance, while Ángel ignored her and ordered his men into place.

Hospital staff rushed out, grabbed the gurney, and wheeled Ramón into the emergency room. Ángel followed, but Isabella insisted his job was outside with his men, and that *she* would monitor Ramón's condition and relay it to him. She also told him to locate Miguel and Ramón's wife, Consuela.

Again, the blank stare.

Only this time, Isabella stared back—and in his eyes, she detected an element of bitterness.

In his mind.

In his soul.

Ha! Let the games begin, she thought.

She turned and followed the nurses into the emergency room. The doctor was already waiting. He took one look at Ramón's condition—without a thorough examination—and immediately ordered the operating theater to be prepped. As he walked out, he called a colleague, insisting it was an emergency and instructing him to meet him in the OR.

Isabella was directed to the waiting lounge, rather than the standard waiting room. The lounge had long, comfortable sofas, cushions, free coffee machines, and light snacks—crisps, nuts, biscuits, and fruit. A large flat-screen TV on the wall played 24-hour international news.

She made herself comfortable and asked a male nurse if she could borrow his cell phone to inform the family. He practically tripped over himself in his eagerness to help. She looked up at him, silently asking for privacy.

"I'll come back in a few minutes, miss. Please, take your time."

"Thank you for your kindness."

Isabella made two calls.

"M? Don't hang up. B here! Yeah, it's me! ACTIVATE. Repeat—ACTIVATE." Then she hung up.

The second call lasted a bit longer.

"Hello? Mom? Is that you? It's Bella. Can you hear me? Yes, *Bella*, Isabella—your daughter. Yes! I'm fine, Mom. How are you? Is everything okay? No, this is not my new number—don't write it down. Yes, it's a friend's number. Hello? Yes, okay, Mom. I'll call back later."

She hung up. She was about to make a third call when the male nurse returned and asked if she was finished.

"Thank you. Thank you very much. How much do I owe you? I don't want to jeopardize your forfeit. Will a hundred cover it? Dollars, not pesos!"

"No, no charge, miss. My monthly forfeit is just fine. Thank you for the offer, but it won't be necessary. The doctor asked me to inform you that the operation will take up to eight hours to repair all the fractures. He also said to ask if you witnessed the fall, because the injuries aren't consistent with slipping. More like an attack. Do you know if he got into a fight with anyone and *then* fell?"

"No," was all Isabella said.

The nurse looked taken aback by the curt response.

"Well... the doctor will speak with you directly after the operation. Please make yourself comfortable. Can I get you anything?"

Isabella shook her head, pushed herself back on the long couch, put her feet up, and turned her eyes to the news on the television. The nurse quietly left the room.

Miguel and Consuela—known more commonly as Sally—were finally located and brought to the hospital under Ángel's orders.

They found Isabella asleep in the waiting lounge and gently woke her.

""How is he? Is he awake? What happened? Did you see what happened?" asked Sally frantically.

"What did they tell you?" queried Isabella.

"Well, only that he was in the hospital and that it was an emergency, life-and-death situation, so I came straight here. Oh my God! Oh my God, what will I do? I can't cope. This is too much for me. I can't stay here. I need to go home. Can I see him?"

"They are still operating. Two hours to go. You go home, Sally. Miguel and I will wait here, and we'll call you when he comes around. Okay? You tell Ángel to take you home now."

"Well, I don't really want to stay either," said Miguel.

"You stay!" said Isabella, half growling at Miguel and staring him down.

She turned to the television and didn't say another word.

Sally left the room, and Miguel found a comfortable sofa and sat back glumly. He stared at the television on the wall for a while, then fell asleep. Isabella stayed awake the entire time.

She had her reasons for not wanting to go home. She wanted to be the first to speak to Ramón when he eventually came around. She had nothing waiting for her at home—no plans, activities, or projects. So, she waited.

The eight hours came and went, and still no news. Finally, in the early hours of the morning, at 5 a.m., the doctor walked in— exhausted and weary, barely able to keep his eyes open.

"Ms. Calderón, the operation was a success. We were able to insert tiny metal rods into his arm. The bones in his wrist, elbow, and upper arm were splintered. We inserted pins in the wrist and metal rods in the elbow and upper arm to keep the bones from shattering. We also inserted metal rods in his shoulder, as his shoulder blades were cracked pretty badly. They needed stabilizing.

"Now, as the nurse informed you earlier and subsequently inquired whether you were actually present when the accident happened, the injuries are not consistent with a simple fall down the steps. These injuries are consistent with blunt force trauma—as if he was in a fight and had his hand and arm deliberately broken. Did you actually witness the fall, Ms. Calderón?"

"No, I just assumed he fell."

Miguel stared at Isabella, not daring to contradict her version of the events leading to the "accident" and subsequent injuries. He knew—he was certain—what had happened to his father.

He had, on a few occasions, caught his father snooping outside Isabella's quarters. When he confronted him about his actions and behavior, he was met with a verbal and physical rebuke. A firm grip on his throat and a harsh whisper in his ear, telling him he was nothing but an unequivocal and total embarrassment to the family.

Furthermore, his father had made it clear: Miguel couldn't give the family an heir, so Ramón would do it himself—by sleeping with his son's wife and impregnating her.

Miguel knew. He knew his father had probably entered Isabella's room, tried to force himself on her, and she had reacted.

Miguel had, himself, tried to consummate their marriage on the first night, knowing full well that his father and the entire entourage expected him to. But when he approached his bride with a macho gesture, trying to oblige her, he was met with a swift and efficient martial arts maneuver that left him gasping for air and crying out in pain. Fortunately, it was just a warning—one that he had taken seriously ever since.

Miguel knew what had happened to his father. He stood behind Isabella and said nothing.

Finally, Ramón was allowed visitors, and Isabella went in alone. She ordered Miguel to wait in the lounge until her return, and he was glad to oblige.

Ramón lay under an oxygen mask, his entire right arm encased in a massive plaster cast, suspended in a sling attached to a lever above the bed. He was slightly turned onto his left side. He was awake when Isabella walked in.

She made her way around to face him. When he saw her, his eyes widened, and he began breathing rapidly. Isabella looked at the drips fixed to his left arm and casually fiddled with them, snapping the IV tube with her thumb and forefinger as if encouraging the flow of liquid.

She turned to look at him. Ramón was hyperventilating under the oxygen mask.

Isabella slowly bent over and whispered in his ear.

"This is what happens to dirty, uncultured macho pigs who think they can take whatever they want, whenever they want. Not gonna happen. Never gonna happen.

"You will be held accountable for your grotesque comportment. Now, you'll soon be having visitors. My advice to you is: do not disclose our little encounter to anybody—least of all Ángel. Besides—and I'm sure you already know—Ángel is fucking Sally. Word has it that he fathered the twins, not you. How about that? Macho gone straight out the window, right there!"

Isabella chuckled at the sight of Ramón squirming in his hospital bed, unable to move or adjust himself. It wasn't true, what she told him—but let the games go on.

"Your life," she said loudly as she straightened up, "your life as you know it, as it was before the *accident"—*she chuckled again, emphasizing the word—"is over, my dear father-in-law.

"Here's what's gonna happen. What's gonna change for you.

"Miguel—you leave him alone. No more 'fairy' or 'dainty' comments. You leave him be.

"Ángel—he's history. Gone. Invisible. Evaporated. Whatever—just *gone.*

"Sally—well, I think she likes the money, the jewelry, and the attention. So she's yours.

"Finally... me. Yes, your beloved daughter-in-law. *I* am the boss. *I* run the business. *I* am *your* boss! You take your orders from me! I tell you when to shit, piss, eat, sleep, breathe, fart! I will monitor every move you make and every muscle twitch in your body. One false move. *One!* Just one—and you're history. You hear me? Nod your head if you hear me. Like this!"

Isabella grabbed the back of Ramón's head and nodded it back and forth for him.

""Remember—*accident!* You fell, or I'll break every bone in your body and throw you into the jellyfish tank to satisfy the male jellyfish that can't find mating partners."

Isabella turned and walked out of the room, having relayed her message directly to Ramón. Whoever came after would no doubt hear the details of the accident—she was sure of it.

One of the drivers took Isabella and Miguel back to the Hacienda. Nobody spoke during the ride. No conversation was necessary.

When they arrived, Isabella went straight to Ramón's private business quarters. It was more than just an office. The quarters included a reception area, although there was never a receptionist.

To the right was a waiting lounge with soft, comfortable individual sofas. A door behind the reception desk led to a fairly large hallway, lined with various paintings—originals, no doubt.

The door at the end of the hallway opened into a spacious lounge, with oversized sofas and two beautifully crafted couches. It all matched perfectly in soft pastel colors. On the main wall stood a massive fireplace, though it was rarely lit. To the right of the lounge was a bathroom with men's toilet facilities. To the left, a door led to Ramón's private office. Beyond that, a separate sleeping area held a king-size bed, complete with its own bathroom.

Isabella entered the office, walked behind his desk, and tried to open the drawers. Locked. She searched frantically for the keys, then remembered—they hung around his neck. She'd have to return to the hospital tomorrow to retrieve them.

She sank into his large leather armchair and leaned back, taking in the room.

Just then, the door opened—and there stood Ángel.

"What are you doing here?" he asked.

"I could ask you the same thing," Isabella replied.

"You're not allowed in these quarters. This area is strictly off-limits. I'm here to enforce that restriction."

"Family business! Last time I checked, I *was* family. You're not," Isabella shot back.

"You're right—*family* business. But this is a business that belongs to *the* family. Not the family you think you're part of. And last I checked, *you* weren't part of the business. *I* was. You think you've fooled everyone. Maybe you have, maybe not—but you can't fool me. I know Mr. Ramón didn't fall like you claim. I know you had him beaten up—or used some kind of weapon to break his arms. You—"

"*Arm.*"

"What?"

"*Arm,* as in singular. Not *arms,* like you're incorrectly insinuating. *One arm.*"

"Whatever, jeez. That doesn't change anything—one arm, two arms, whatever. You broke his arm! It was no accident. You can't fool me. You see, I went to see Ramón after you left, and he *confirmed* what happened. He said he went to your room looking for Miguel, and you jumped him. Said he didn't even have time to react or defend himself. Just—wham! You hit him with a metal rod you keep hidden in your room somewhere. I searched while you were playing daughter-in-law at the hospital, but looks like you already got rid of it, you whore.

"He also told me you threatened him. I figured I'd find you here, going through his private business papers. Mr. Ramón made two major mistakes with you. First, he underestimated you—thought you were just a little girl who'd be his whore. Big misjudgment. But the major mistake—the *big* one…"

Isabella didn't move. She stayed reclined in the oversized armchair, calmly staring at Ángel.

"Don't you want to know what big mistake Mr. Ramón made?" he asked.

"I guess you're going to tell me whether I ask or not," Isabella replied coolly.

"Well…"

"Say what you have to say. If you're gonna tell me, then tell me. Otherwise, get the fuck out of *my* office."

Ángel scoffed. "*Your* office? Oh, that's rich. That's *funny!* I'll tell you what the major mistake was—bringing your fuckin' whore ass here. *Big* mistake! Now get the fuck outta *my* fuckin' office!"

He reached inside his jacket, clearly going for a weapon—likely under Ramón's instructions.

Isabella looked past him and nodded.

Confused, Ángel turned to see what she was reacting to.

Too late.

One silent bullet to the head. One to the heart. Execution-style.

He never saw it coming.

He also didn't notice he'd stepped onto a plastic sheet laid over the carpet.

"Get somebody to clean this mess," Isabella said as she walked out. No more games. Game time was over.

Operation ACTIVATE was in motion.

"Oh—and ACTIVATE Phase Two," she added before leaving the office.

Isabella returned to her room and took a shower but didn't wash her hair—it still smelled fresh from two days ago. Afterward, she dressed in light, sporty clothes, knocked on Miguel's door, and entered without waiting.

"Miguel, my love," she teased, "where are you, dear husband?"

"Right here, behind you, my beloved dearest wife," he teased back.

"Miguel, listen carefully. I want you to go to the hospital *right now* and visit your father. See if he still has the key around his neck—a single key, on a gold chain. Bring it to me without telling *anyone*. Not the doctor, not the nurse, not Sally. *Nobody.* You hear me? *Nobody.* Bring that key straight back here. No toilet breaks. No quick visits to your boyfriend. *Straight back.* Understand?"

"Why? What's going on? What key? What's it for?"

"Sheesh, Miguel. Why can't you just do what I ask without a million questions and pointless explanations that mean nothing to you? Should I send someone else instead? I ask *you* because you're the *only* one in this wide world I trust. But if you think someone else is more trustworthy for such an important mission, fine. Goodnight. Sweet dreams."

Under her breath, she muttered, "Asshole."

Miguel hesitated, then stepped forward, stopping her as she turned to leave.

"Okay, okay. I'll go. I know you trust me—just like I know you broke Dad's arm with your Japanese-Chinese martial arts moves. I've seen it firsthand. So yeah, I know. I just thought that since we're in this together, maybe you'd share some secret stuff with me."

"First of all, we're not *in this together!*" she snapped. "*I'm* in this—but not together with you. You do as I say, we stay friends. You cross me, disobey me, ignore me, confront me, or just simply get on my nerves in *any* shape, form, or way, and you'll pay the price. Got it? Now, be a good little boy and run along to the hospital and fetch me that fucking key. *Now!*"

Miguel was out the door in a flash. He summoned a driver and was gone.

Isabella went to the kitchen, fixed herself a snack, and returned to the office. She sat behind the desk like before and began eating. She pressed a buzzer on the desk, and a subservient voice came through, full of eagerness.

"Send me Gonzales," she ordered.

No sooner had she sat back than there was a knock at the door. A squeaky, high-pitched feminine voice announced that Gonzales had arrived and asked if she should send him in.

Ah! The receptionist, she thought.

"Send him in."

The door opened, and a diminutive man with a goatee and a bald head was ushered in. The door closed behind him. Gonzales stood there, clearly fazed, looking around in all directions before turning his gaze back to Isabella. He was about to ask what she was doing there and why she had summoned him when Isabella raised a finger to her lips, shushing him.

She let him stand there, completely puzzled and unable to comprehend the situation. Isabella leaned back in the big armchair, silently studying the man—not saying a word, not giving away anything through gesture or facial expression. After what felt like an eternity—though it was barely ten minutes—Gonzales finally stopped shifting and stood still, facing her but avoiding direct eye contact. With both hands behind his back, he looked like a little schoolboy summoned to the principal's office for misbehavior.

Then she spoke.

"Are you Gonzales?"

"Yes, I am," he said proudly.

"Let's start again. *Are* you Gonzales?"

With a puzzled look, he hesitated. Her eyes locked onto him—piercing, stripping away any arrogance he had entered with—leaving him bare. Meek. Humbled.

"Yes, I am Gonzales, Señora. You requested—"

"Please only answer the questions I ask you. Not any questions you may have in your head."

"Yes, Señora. I apologize."

"Why are you here?"

"You requested my presence, Señora."

"No. *Why* are you here—at the ranch? What is your job here? Who do you report to?"

"I am a man of many talents, Señora. I report to Ángel and to Mr. Ramón, Señora."

"Not anymore. From now on, you report directly and only to *me*. Understood?"

"I will be of kind service—"

"Just answer the question I ask you. I won't tell you again! You report directly and only to me. Understood? That's a question. Understood?"

"Yes, Señora. Understood. Only to you."

"Good. We're getting there. I want you to take a very old farm truck—*an old one*. Take some chickens in a pen, a few hens—say, five or six—and take a woman with you who can pass as your wife. I don't care one way or the other.

"Drive down to Belize. If you're stopped for any reason, pretend to be a chicken farmer. When you get to Belize, I want you to *observe*. No intervention. Just observe. Do not interact. Do not make your presence known *for any reason*. Do *not* be obvious. Take a cell phone—an old first-generation model with a camera. I want you to take pictures of everything and everyone coming across the border from Guatemala into Belize—and *vice versa*. Do you know what *vice versa* means, Gonzales? It means 'and the other way around.' People going to Guatemala."

She continued.

"Now, there will be an old farmer with three mules selling animal skins near the central market. He is my mule. Follow his movements. See who he interacts with. Even if he *just looks* at someone, I want pictures.

"Two young girls—very young, about my age—will lead the mules from the old man and take them to a cantina. They'll tie the mules outside and leave. The old man will enter the cantina and exit through the back door.

"Do *not* enter the cantina. Stay outside and take pictures of the policeman who leads the mules away. The policeman will take them to the back of the police station, where someone will relieve the mules of their load, load it into the trunk of a car, and drive off. I want pictures of the car—and the plates. Is that clear?"

"So, I go this place—"

"You must have a hearing problem," she snapped. "Or maybe my English is really bad. *Or maybe*—just maybe—you have the mentality of a *retarded moron.* Or *all of the above!*" she shouted, pulling out a set of Kung Fu sticks as she rose from her chair and walked around the desk toward him. She flipped the two batons, tied together by a short chain, back and forth as she approached.

"Yes, Señora. Yes, it is clear."

"You just used up your *last* chance, Gonzales. No more thinking. No more questions. No more—*okay?* No *more.* Follow orders. Answer my questions. That's it. That's *all* I want from you."

"Yes, Señora. My mission is clear, Señora. I am at your disposition."

"I know you are. Now *go.* Two days to drive down, one day of observation, and two days back. I want you *back here* with a full report in five days. *Go!*"

Gonzales was about to speak when Isabella raised a single finger—*don't say a word.*

It was late at night when Miguel returned from the hospital with the key. Upon his arrival, he was directed to the office. Isabella had left instructions for him to report there immediately.

He had never been to the office before—it was strictly off-limits to him, and he had never ventured into that area. This was his first time, and he was apprehensive.

The whole space felt daunting, from the receptionist area through the hallway to the lounge, where he was instructed to wait until summoned. He didn't know whether he was allowed to sit or stand, but he knew one thing: he wanted to run as fast and as far away from this place as possible—especially from Isabella.

She freaked him out right down to his boots, made him sweat when it was freezing, and froze him when it was sweltering. She had this effect on him just by staring with those marble-blue eyes.

He was here, but he wished he were anywhere else.

Even his father, with his brutal physical abuse, never drew more than scorn from Miguel. But Isabella? She was something else— terrifying, intimidating, daunting, manipulative, imposing, powerful, strong, sharp—and the list went on.

The fact was, Miguel really liked Isabella as a friend, but he couldn't help these reactions when he was in her presence.

Finally, the red light outside her office door turned green, and he was led in by a woman he had never met or seen before. He didn't even know where she had come from.

"Did you bring me the key?" Isabella asked the moment he entered the office.

"Wow! Is this where he conducts his business from? Sheesh. I've never—"

"Miguel! Did you bring me the key?"

"Oh, yes, yes, I did. It was among his personal belongings, so I didn't have to search his body for it or ask anyone. I did good, right? I did good, huh, Isa?"

"Yes, dear husband, you did good. Now give me the key and get out!"

Miguel dutifully complied and retired to his quarters, exhausted from the trip.

Isabella opened the top drawer with the key. There were lots of papers and insurance policies in the name of his wife, Consuela. There were birth certificates for the twins, who would be two years old in a few months.

At the bottom of all the papers were bank statements and regular bank movements—nothing noteworthy.

She unlocked the second drawer: pens, yellow stickers, and a stapler.

The key didn't open the bottom two drawers. They were locked but with a different key. Isabella reopened the top drawer, took all the papers out, and emptied everything onto the desk.

Then she painstakingly combed through every paper, reading every word, looking for the slightest clue as to where the key for the bottom two drawers might be. She was almost certain that was where Ramón kept his important documents.

Taped to the inside of a brown envelope, hidden at the bottom of the pile of papers, was a key. She removed it and opened the bottom two drawers.

The last drawer held the most interesting information. There was an invitation to the Annual General Conference between Heads of States. Last time she checked, Ramón was not a head of any state— but the invite clearly had his name, and his name only. No partner or spouse was mentioned.

Why did he hide this? Why did he lock it away so that nobody could see it?

There was a number on the back of the invitation. It had too many digits to be a phone number. First, there were two digits—1 and 6—followed by a space. Then came five: 08521. And then four: 1825.

Puzzled, Isabella tried to figure out if this was some sort of code, but she failed to break it.

She put the card back in the last drawer and walked over to an elevator. Before she could press any button, the doors slid open. Still holding the card, she stepped into the elevator.

There were no buttons to push. The doors slid closed, and the elevator descended. It stopped on what Isabella thought was an underground bunker.

When the elevator opened, Isabella staggered back, unable to comprehend what she was seeing. She walked out slowly, holding the sides of her head in shock and disbelief.

There were stacks and stacks of pallets wrapped in plastic, filled with U.S. dollar bills.

She examined each stack closely and noticed that there were stacks of one-hundred-dollar bills on one side, and on the other, pallets of fifty-dollar bills. No smaller denominations.

One thousand square feet, ten feet high, filled with U.S. currency. There was easily one hundred million dollars stacked up on those pallets.

"Bingo! Sweet Jesus! What have we here? Ramón's pension fund! Well, I'll be…"

Isabella walked from pallet to pallet, examining the denominations wrapped in each stack of bills.

When she finally processed what she was witnessing, she made her way back to the lounge, shutting everything down behind her as she retreated.

There was one more thing to decipher: the invitation.

Isabella couldn't sleep that night, so she went out for a walk in the courtyard. Several bodyguards were positioned around the house and likely down by the property entrance.

She pondered the significance of the numbers on the invitation—undoubtedly some sort of communication.

She took out her burner cell phone and texted:

"Codebreaker, 62 08523 1825."

"Advance ACTIVATE!"

"Will GIT."

GIT for *Get In Touch.*

She then stomped on the phone, took out the battery and SIM card, pocketed them, and threw the phone away.

She went back to bed, feeling slightly less anxious.

Chapter Twenty-Four
Ramon Demise

Ramon was discharged from the hospital after three weeks. He insisted that he only wanted Angel to drive him home. Consuela was there to pick him up with a driver.

"Hello, my love! How are you feeling? I came here straight from yoga. I missed Pilates, and I came straight when the hospital called to say that you could go home. Oh, you poor thing, are you in pain? Did you take your medication? Here, let me help you."

"Where's Angel?" was all Ramon said.

"Angel is not around."

"What do you mean, not around?"

"Angel vanished. Disappeared. Gone. Maybe liquidated—I don't know. I'm here, my sweet. I'll have the driver take us home."

"Liquidated? Liquidated?! By who? By who?! It's her, it's her. I gotta send her back home. Angel warned me about her, but I didn't listen. I should've listened."

"What are you talking about? No—who are you talking about? You're delirious, my sweet. You must still be in pain."

Consuela helped Ramon out of the wheelchair and into the waiting car. They drove off and headed home.

Thirty miles out of town, on a quiet stretch of road, the driver accelerated. He edged up to a hundred miles an hour, cruising comfortably in the super luxury Mercedes 600 S.

BOOM!

It was a deafening sound as the car exploded, lifting six feet into the air—nothing but a huge ball of flame. When it came down, it was a massive rolling fireball. It rolled for fifty yards off the road, into the brush on the side. The gasoline tank had exploded and burned everything within a thirty-foot radius. The car and its occupants were carbonized.

The explosion was heard all the way back in town, and the ball of flame was seen for miles around. By the time the ambulance and fire brigade arrived, there was nothing but a white-hot metal frame still smoldering. There was no trace or presence of anything or anyone in the car. It was totally carbonized.

The call came immediately to the residence. All the staff were in total shock—speechless. Security around the house was doubled.

Miguel howled and howled, needing a double dose of tranquilizers to calm him down. In spite of everything—the bullying, the disrespect, the humiliation—he loved his father. This was devastating news.

How was he going to cope without his father? Who was going to take care of the household, the business, and the personnel? It was too overwhelming for him. He was not strong enough to manage everything.

He would certainly need Isabella now. She was strong enough. She would take care of the business. She *had* to take care of the business.

Phase Three, thought Isabella.

She took out another burner cell phone and texted:

"Phase Two confirmed!"

"Codebreaker?"

The answer came back:

"May 8th, 2023, 6:25 p.m., 18:25."

"62??"

"Seat number? Not sure!"

"Activate Phase Three. Pick me up ASAP."

She stamped on the phone vigorously, smashing it to pieces. Then she took the battery and SIM card, pocketed them, and walked back into the house.

She called for the nanny

"Where are the twins?" she asked.

"Sleeping, madame. I fed them, bathed them, and put them to sleep. What will happen to them?" she asked, tears welling up in her eyes. Then she started crying.

"I will take care of them. But I need your help, of course. Will you help me to take care of the twins?"

"Yes, madame. With all my pleasure. I love them. I can't leave them. Señor Miguel—he cannot take care of them. But you are too young to be their mother."

"You don't worry about me. I just need your help to prepare their meals, bathe them, and sometimes put them to sleep. Okay?"

"Yes, madame. Very good."

"I will be going away for a few days. You stay close. Put a bed in their room and sleep there. Nobody should come near them—understood? Nobody. Not even Miguel. Just you. Okay?"

"Yes, madame. I will go arrange for a bed. Good night, madame."

Isabella turned and walked upstairs to her room. She had been there for less than a minute when Miguel walked in. No knocking, no announcing himself—just barged in.

He stood in the doorway, teary-eyed, nose running, hands on his hips.

"Why? Why Consuela? What did she ever do to you?" he sobbed. "Why, Isa? Why? Look what you've done. You created a mess—a real mess! Am I next?"

"Listen to me, Miguel. Listen very, very carefully. Consuela wasn't supposed to be there. She was at the spa. Yoga, spa, Pilates. Then home. Not to the hospital.

"As for Ramon, he put out a contract on me. First Angel tried, then one of the drivers. Now, I fear that one of the other members—outside members—will come at me. And no, you are *not* next. This is a private war.

"Do you know why your father brought me here? Arranged our wedding? Set me up like a princess? Do you even know?"

"Why?"

"Oh, please stop. Your father knew full well that you were gay. He told me the day I broke his arm. He wanted me for himself. Have me as his trophy wife without officially declaring. An object that he just had to have.

"He fantasized about me. I was to be his sex slave, all the while acting out the dutiful wife to you. He was nothing but a self-righteous, egocentric, arrogant pig! You hear me? He was a pig. A lowdown, disgusting, short, fat pig! He deserved what he got—believe me!"

"And Consuela? Did *she* deserve what she got? And the twins? Orphans! Do they deserve to be fucking orphans?!"

"Take a look at these." Isabella threw an envelope at Miguel.

He opened it and pulled out several pictures of Consuela.

The first picture showed Consuela entering a hotel room alone. The second picture showed her in the room, kissing a mystery man. The next one showed them both naked on the bed. Three other pictures showed them in compromising positions.

She threw another envelope at him—similar pictures taken on different days and at different times, all explained away as yoga, Pilates, or the spa.

"Ramon knew! Ordered a hit on her. It was delayed until he was released from the hospital. He knew, goddammit! You hear me? He was going to liquidate her. What about the twins, huh? You think he cared? Do *you* care? Ever play with them, hold them, talk to them? Nah! Poor Miguel, always the victim.

So don't fucking lecture me, okay? The twins—they are now *my* responsibility! I will take care of them. Where I go, they go! I'm their mother now! Got that? I'm *their mother!*

As for you, you will do whatever I say. I say jump, you say, 'With pleasure!' No questions. Just execute. Got it?"

"Why would I follow your orders and do whatever you say?"

"Well, it's real easy. You get to choose. Right here, right now! You get to choose: stay or leave."

"If I stay, I have to listen to you. But this is *my* house now—*my* home. I inherit my father's business. I get to deal with the other members now. So the way I see it, *you* get to choose—stay or leave.

Stay, you follow my orders. Or you can go back home to your family."

"Miguel, Miguel, Miguel! I've listened to your dribble for longer than I ever envisaged! Your diatribe is provoking an acid build-up in my throat, creating a nauseous reaction.

Shut the fuck up and listen.

Your problem is, you always listen with your mouth open and ears greased closed. It should be the other way around, my dear husband. Mouth shut! Ears open!

You get to choose: stay, you follow my orders and instructions *to the letter,* no questions. Leave—you're on your own. No protection. No financing. You relinquish all ties. Change your fucking name for all I care—but you're out!"

"What do you mean, 'out'?"

"Shit, Miguel! What does *out* mean?! It fucking means *out!* Out of your room, out of the house, out of the ranch, out of the family. *Out!* Okay? *Out!*"

"Who made you boss?"

"I did! *I'm* the boss. I give orders and make decisions—like I'm making with you right now. I decided *not* to liquidate you but to let you choose your own fate.

What's it gonna be, husband?"

"Stop calling me husband!"

"The only thing keeping you here is the fact that you're still officially my husband. In reality, you never were—never going to be. Gay or not.

Now get the fuck outta my room. Fuck out, go! If you're still here in the morning, in this house, then you follow my orders… or you'll get to know what *no protection* means!"

Miguel turned to leave. He held onto the door handle just a second longer, contemplating. Then he turned to Isabella.

"Isa, I know my dad was a pig. He never tried to hide it. His behavior disgusted me. *He* disgusted me. He liked little boys too, you know. I saw him.

He did get what he deserved.

But I'm really sorry about Consuela. She was always nice to me.

Isa… I'm staying. You're the boss. I'll do whatever you say. I'm sorry for being rude, but I was hurting. Still hurting. For Consuela—not for my father.

Good night, Isa. Good night, boss."

He closed the door behind him as he left.

The next morning, Isabella walked down the long driveway to the private road that led to the main highway. Waiting for her outside the gate was a rusty red old farm truck.

In the back were rusted farm tools, some of which were broken. The front windshield was cracked right across, the back tires were smooth, and the seats were torn.

She got in through the passenger door and slid over to the middle so she was seated close to the driver. She kissed him on the cheek and said, "Hi!"

"Hi," came the reply. "It's an address. A location! Some sort of location."

Isabella looked at him with a puzzled expression.

"62," he said. "It's an address or a location."

They drove in silence for a while, both pondering the implication of the two numbers.

"How've you been? I'm really happy to see you—and get to be with you for a few days. That was an astounding discovery I made: over a hundred million U.S. dollars in a bunker under Ramon's office.

All secured in huge bundles and stacked on wooden pallets. The room was filled with these pallets. I estimated there to be over a hundred million… but it could be closer to two hundred million.

What's your take on that?"

"Hmm. Ramon was too cavalier, too blasé to have the *savoir-faire* to accumulate such a take.

My guess is, he was just a middleman. A temporary storage site. Like a transit point."

"You mean like the banker?"

"Nah. Not smart enough to be the banker. Transit warehouse. I'm sure of it."

"That means someone will come calling—looking to collect, and then deliver to the final destination. Probably trusted lieutenants. Then the heavies. Then the owners with the army.

I'll be waiting."

"We'll be waiting.

How's the fallout on the incident?"

"Painful—as the wife was where she shouldn't have been. She went to pick him up at the hospital, acting like the good, loyal wife, when she should've been with her lover.

Collateral damage, unfortunately. I now have two kids to raise," she said, turning to look at him for a reaction.

He chuckled, looked straight ahead, and said nothing.

"Hey…" she said and punched him on the shoulder. "Ain't you gonna say something? Maybe, '*We've* got two kids to raise'?"

He just chuckled again, turned slightly to her—keeping his eyes on the road—and kissed her cheek.

"Can't go against the boss's wishes."

She laughed and said, "Better not!"

Chapter Twenty-Five
Javier's Demise

Isabella went straight up to her room. She was hot and sticky from the ride to the hospital and back. She undressed, showered, and then powered up her old computer. She browsed around, looking at old pictures of herself and her friends at school, horse riding with Carmen, and at her famous eleventh birthday party.

She searched for high schools across the border in the United States. She found ten high schools, checked them all out, and researched their curricula, faculty, facilities, sports programs, neighborhoods, and comments from alumni and parents. She shortlisted three when there was a knock on her door.

She didn't call out but rose from her seat and went to open the door, curious to see who was foolish enough to disturb her when she was in her private quarters. Both her mom and Corella were absent, so it could only be her father. She opened the door and was not disappointed to see him standing there.

"Isabella!" he beamed. "My men told me that you were here. How are you? When did you come?"

"I'm pretty sure they told you when I arrived, with whom, and what I've been up to since I came. So please cut the small talk. You were away. Did you just get back?"

"Now look who's engaging in small talk," he said, smiling nervously.

"It's not small talk; you went away, and you left Mom with nobody to care for her. She collapsed, and I took her to the hospital in La Mesquite. I didn't know she was using, but *you* did."

"You accuse me of deliberately intoxicating my wife—the mother of my daughter, *your* mother—to what end? What benefit? I am saddened by all this."

"Javier…"

"*Javier? Javier?* I am your father! My blood runs in your veins! I'm your father, goddammit! Don't I at least get that respect? I raised you, fed you, clothed you, educated you, and all that means nothing to you! You call me *Javier!* Not Dad, Pa, Daddy, or Papa, like other good, respectful children call their fathers. No—you… you take it upon yourself to disrespect me in my own house, under my own roof, and call me by my name! I should call you a whore!"

"You lost the right to be my father when you sold me to your fucking partner, Ramon, for an equal share of the supply route. 'Family ties,' you called it. 'Uniting the two families under one trademark!' you said. 'The sky's the limit to what we can achieve together as partners and not as adversaries or competitors.'

You sold me. Forced me to marry his son, Miguel, whom you both knew was gay—so effectively, you sold me to that fucking weirdo, Ramon! I should call you a motherfucking son of a bitch. Make that *son of a fucking whore!*"

"I'll... I'll..."

"You'll what? You stuttering fucking coward. We had a deal. I did as you asked—married the fucking Miguel—on the condition that you take care of Mom. No more drinking, and absolutely no drugs of any kind. You promised that you would personally see to that. That was our deal. *Me for Mom!* I do what you ask in exchange for Mom's freedom. Rehab. Clean bill of health! That was our deal.

But you lied. You lied to me. You had no intention of keeping your end of the bargain. What did you do instead? You gave her away to your fucking morons! They fed her drugs and raped her!"They kept her intoxicated, drugged up, and raped her at will while you fucked their fourteen-year-old daughters. You sick fuck! You take one step closer, and I'll wring your chicken shit wiry little fucking neck. Get the fuck out before I take a step closer."

"Ungrateful little whore, just like your mother. You watch your back. That's right, watch your back... bitch! You think I'm afraid of you... you bring it on. We'll see who gets who."

Isabella stared at him, her eyes boring into his. Then a thin smile curled her lips as she said coldly and dryly, "Things to do when you're already dead. Go do 'em."

She slammed the door in his face.

She waited until the footsteps faded in the hallway, opened the door, and then crept downstairs to her father's private lounge.

Javier had gone to his room to freshen up before heading out. Isabella had long since made a skeleton key to her father's private lounge. A door to the left led into his office. Using the same key, she entered the office, went behind the desk, and proceeded to open all the drawers. She was looking for something specific this time.

She didn't have to look far. In the bottom, unlocked drawer was a similar invitation to the one she had found in Ramon's office. Bingo. It had the same numbers—most of which had been decoded by Ryan, except for the first two digits: 1 and 6.

She folded the invitation and put it in her pocket. She looked around and noticed a personal bathroom off to the right of the office. She went in, not quite sure what she was looking for or what she would find.

Then it struck her. Javier had developed an addiction—one that he had gotten himself deeper and deeper into. This was their game, their forbidden fruit. Except that nothing was forbidden to these degenerates.

She looked frantically through the bathroom cabinets and found a pack of blue tablets. Fifty-gram doses.

"Son of a bitch," she muttered to herself. "Fucking Viagra addict."

She took the fifty-gram doses and replaced them with one-hundred-gram doses. Before leaving, she carefully pricked a tiny hole in the back of each pill. Then, she dipped the whole pack into liquid poppers that she had crushed and mixed with water. The blue pills absorbed the colorless mixture. When they were saturated, she took them out and blow-dried them. She carefully placed them where the fifty-gram packet had been and left the bathroom.

She spent all of fifteen minutes in the office. She left, making sure that everything was as she had found it—nothing displaced that could arouse suspicion. Isabella locked the doors and went to the kitchen to fix herself and Ryan something to eat.

In the kitchen, Javier had summoned his most trusted security personnel. They were checking everything, tasting everything, when Isabella entered. Without a word, they all left.

Outside, sniffer dogs were checking for explosives around all the cars. Javier had his drivers line up six cars, not letting anybody know which one he would be using. Electronic equipment was deployed to check for explosives or any tracking devices. Nothing was found. Javier came out the front door and jumped into the fourth car without hesitation. Two security guards—one on each side of him—sat in the back with him, and the car sped away.

Heavily armed guards were placed from the front door along the driveway to the main gate. Nobody was to exit or enter the house. Isabella found this very amusing, as none of the guards could prevent her from doing whatever she wanted.

Isabella returned to her father's study and calmly entered the lounge. She looked for a trapdoor to the safe room but found nothing. She went through every piece of paper in the office but found nothing of interest. She took out the invitation, laid it out on the desk, and studied it.

She took out her burner and texted Ryan:

"In the office. JM (join me)."

A reply came almost instantly:

"OMW."

Ryan and Isabella sat together, reading and re-reading the invitation, permutating all possibilities of what the numbers might mean.

"It's definitely a location. But where?" Isabella thought out loud.

Ryan sat silently for a while, staring at the ceiling, leaning back in the big armchair, hands clasped behind his head. He closed his eyes, no expression on his face.

"It could be an area code or a precinct, or..."

"That could be it," Isabella said. "Let's look at geographical indicators or precise locations. Lines of longitude and latitude, for example."

"I thought about that, but Mexico is on the 100-degree longitude. The one hundred and tenth is way off to the left. On the latitude front, we're between the twentieth and twenty-fifth lines. No sixty-two."

"I'm looking at the map right now, and there's Highway 62 here. Somewhere near the San Luis Potosí vicinity, so to speak. Let's see here... hmmm. Take a look at this."

"What is it?"

"Highway 62 is deep in the high mountainous region. A place called Real de Catorce. Right on Highway 62. You thinking what I'm thinking?"

"Hmm, yeah, that sounds real plausible. Worth checking out."

"I'll stake my steak on that."

"You mean you'll *bet your ass* on that being the location?"

"Undeniably. We should stake it out."

"You hungry or something? That's the third time you mentioned steak."

"Stakeout... not as in cookout, but as in buy doughnuts, sit in a big, conspicuous car, eating said doughnuts while watching a suspect's movements."

"Donuts! Jeez, you really *are* hungry. I'll order in."

"No, I'll get Corella... oh, I forgot, she's not here. Okay, but who will deliver? We're a long drive from any decent food."

"I'll get Ramiro to go."

"Okay, marvelous. Now let's get planning. You need to send an advance reconnaissance team—like yesterday already—to lay the groundwork. We need eyes on the ground, in and around the whole village. If they've chosen this place, they know it, trust it, believe in it, and control it—top to bottom. This is the real task: countering what they are contemplating.

We need Harry Potter and his invisible cloak to get us in and snoop around without being seen or heard. A fly on the wall, so to speak."

"We have time," said Ryan, standing up and walking toward the door. "What do you want to eat?" he asked Isabella.

"Something light, like a chicken breast salad. Italian salad sauce. With sparkling water. Thank you."

Ryan left the room to find Ramiro and have him pick up the order.

A few minutes later, Isabella stepped out of Javier's office, satisfied that they had broken the code—if it really was a code. Now, planning ahead would occupy both of them in the days to come. She passed Ryan, who was on the phone with the restaurant, and headed for the kitchen. They would eat there.

Javier's convoy turned left onto Highway 85, heading in the opposite direction of Nuevo Laredo. There was one car in front and two following. After driving at high speeds for approximately twenty minutes, the car transporting Javier and one of the trailing cars turned onto an unpaved, grassy double-track path, while the other two cars sped on.

Javier and his escort continued for another ten minutes before reaching a grassy clearing. Right there, in the middle of the field, was a transport helicopter that could seat at least nine people. Javier and his escort vehicle pulled to a stop at the edge of the field, unwilling to proceed any further until it was safe. Javier remained in his car and waited.

The other two cars headed for a small village, a further ten minutes of driving, to pick up two female guests for Javier. They lived in the same area but barely knew each other—perhaps by sight, visual recognition, nothing more. Each girl boarded a separate car. As for their ages, one was sixteen, and the other barely seventeen.

None of Javier's mistresses were older than nineteen. He relied mostly on the relatives of his multi-task workforce, always insisting on being presented with family members for "security reasons," while often offering bonuses to staff members with young female relatives. This was the bait on the hook to snare his victims.

He wasn't even discreet in luring young girls into his warped web of abuse. Families were so destitute, and the situation so desperate, that if these young girls did not volunteer their company and humor, their parents would offer them up in the name of survival.

Javier's hunting ground was rife with eager young teenage girls vying to be noticed and chosen for his company. Often, it was a luxurious getaway for a short period, laden with pampering, gifts, and bonuses. Thus, the two girls in question were over-eager and willing beyond comprehension to be first selected—then offered a unique opportunity, if one could even consider these abusive escapades as such. While undeniably life-altering, the outcome could be either devastating or, in rare cases, beneficial.

Javier waited a full twenty minutes in his car when he heard vehicles approaching. He silently exited the car and stood behind a thick brush, concealed from view. The vehicles turned out to be his security staff, delivering his two companions for the weekend—or however long he chose to stay.

He had intended to stay longer to relieve his mind and anxiety from the events at the house with his daughter. He would deal with that situation immediately upon his return. For the moment, it was a question of "out of sight, out of mind."

The two cars drove right up to the helicopter. Javier got back into his car and instructed the driver to follow.

Seated quite comfortably in the helicopter were Javier, four security staff members, the two companions, and the pilot. It was a powerful Boeing C-135 helicopter designed for troop transport. He instructed the pilot to head for Playa Carabonera in the Gulf of Mexico. They would be staying at the Doña Clarita Hotel and Restaurant, a quiet, family-oriented, luxurious hotel with excellent local food.

The hotel had a private beach area where Javier issued instructions that he did not want to be disturbed by the public. This had all been prearranged with the hotel manager and his wife. No one knew who the owner was.

The helicopter ride took two and a half hours. It landed on the main shore, and three cars were waiting to drive Javier and his guests to the hotel.

After a sumptuous dinner and dessert, filled with countless glasses of the most exquisite champagne, Javier discreetly swallowed a blue pill. He then coaxed the girls to follow him to the Regal Suite. It featured a sauna, jacuzzi, and an indoor pool on a patio overlooking the Gulf of Mexico. A private butler was available to serve cocktails and snacks upon request.

Finally, Javier and the girls were alone, having relieved the butler of his evening duties. Javier offered each of the girls a white gold necklace with a heart-shaped pendant—a diamond in the center—matching white gold, and two-carat diamond earrings. Sublime.

Shaking with joy and the pleasure of receiving such an exquisite gift, the girls shed tears of gratitude. Was it the gratitude, or simply the intoxication from the champagne they had incessantly consumed? Still, Javier was the man. Javier was the hero. And these two young girls, armed with the cliché *"Diamonds are a girl's best friend,"* were devoid of any inhibitions—assuming they had any to begin with.

They were all over Javier—hands, lips, and tongues.

Javier excused himself to the bathroom, where he took the second pill. This was going to be a long night for all concerned.

No, he was going to take a third. He wanted to keep going, over and over, non-stop, until he dropped.

Fifteen minutes into his erotic dreamscape, Javier began to see everything around him turn blue. At first, he thought they had turned on blue lamps to set the tone and mood. Then he noticed the girls were blue, and soon everything around him turned blue.

This had never happened to him before. His breathing became heavy, and his pulse raced.

Oblivious to Javier's discomfort, the girls—now naked—undressed him, kissing and nibbling him all over as they gently ushered him toward the huge triple bed.

Something was wrong.

This was not the first time he had indulged in the blue pills. Surely, it was not the alcohol. He could most definitely handle his alcohol.

What was happening to him?

Javier's mind raced, causing his heart to follow suit. His body temperature sharply escalated, compounding the complications he was experiencing. By this time, he was frothing at the mouth. Finally, Javier collapsed onto the bed, unable to move—semi-paralyzed.

The girls mistook this for some sort of orgasmic ecstasy that Javier was enjoying and kept going. But Javier couldn't feel anything. He was numb. His heart exploded—a massive coronary attack. He lay there on the bed, on his back, sharp, desperate breaths almost nonexistent, eyes staring at the ceiling but not seeing.

When one of the girls looked at Javier, expecting further encouragement, she noticed that his eyes were not focused, and she pulled back, grabbing the other girl with her.

"He's not breathing," she said. "Oh my God… he's not breathing. He's not breathing—oh my God!"

The second girl screamed at the top of her lungs as she ran to the door, forgetting that she was naked. The door burst open, and the four security guards rushed in. They grabbed the second girl near the door by the throat and flung her back onto the bed. The first girl, covering her ears and screaming, received a sharp slap across her face. The shock of it all silenced her. The guard put his forefinger to his lips to quiet them both. They were still naked, sitting next to each other at the foot of the bed.

"You! What happened?" one of the guards asked, pointing to the girl he had grabbed by the door.

"I—I don't know. We thought he was enjoying… having a good time… but his eyes…"

"His eyes just stopped seeing. They just stared at the ceiling," said the first girl.

"Okay… get dressed and go wait downstairs. Don't talk to nobody. Hear me? Nobody! Not even a hello! Got it?" he said, pointing his forefinger at them.

The girls picked up their clothes and went to the bathroom to get dressed. Once dressed, they left the room silently.

"Shit, shit, shit. Now what do we do?" said Ignacio, one of the guards.

"Is he dead? I mean, we didn't even check his heart and stuff like that," offered Dave, the European guard.

"His eyes are fucking staring wide open at the ceiling, not fucking blinking. Is that not dead enough for you?"

"Okay. First, we close his eyes, get him dressed, and then call an ambulance. We need to make this official, get the cops in here, take him to the hospital, and have them do an autopsy. Then we'll know what happened. I know he was a blue pill junkie. Took it all the time, like fucking aspirin. Are we all clear on that?"

This was Sergio—chief of security and Javier's most trusted guard, guide, influencer, and advisor.

The four of them moved with purpose and swiftness. Ten minutes tops, and they were downstairs, waiting for the police and the ambulance.

Ignacio went over to the girls to comfort them and issue instructions not to acknowledge any of the evening's events. They were to state that they were the guests of the guards.

The ambulance came, picked up the now-defunct Javier, and took him to the nearest hospital. The police interrogated everyone at the hotel, including the manager and his wife, who testified that they had not seen anything unusual and had retired to bed shortly after dinner.

The girls were regarded with suspicion, interrogated harshly, but released as the guards insisted that these were their dates and that they had spent the evening in each other's company. Javier had retired to his room alone, feeling fatigued and weary after the trip.

Thus, the interrogation subsided with the reserve to recall all persons of interest at a further stage of the investigation, pending a comprehensive autopsy report.

"We need to call this in," said Dave.

"To who?" queried Sergio.

"To the family, to the partners," continued Dave. "People have to know—his wife, his daughter, the members. Everybody linked to him."

"We keep this quiet for the moment. Nobody needs to know. I need time to work this out. Proceed carefully."

"What about his daughter? She should know," insisted Dave.

"That cheap whore! Never! She's the last person that needs to know. I'll handle her when the time comes. We start early tomorrow. We need to get some sleep."

"What about the girls? What do we do with them?" Oscar asked, genuinely concerned.

"Help yourself," said Sergio, and went to bed.

Oscar went over to the girls and suggested they share a room as far away from the Regal Suite as possible, and that should they feel insecure, they could come wake him up.

With that proposal, everybody retired to bed.

It was too costly to organize separate transport to return the girls home, so it was decided that they wait with the rest of the crew until Javier's body was released to be taken home. Sergio suggested that they enjoy their time at the beach and forget about the night's troubles, which they dutifully did.

Organizing the release of the body and securing police clearance to return home was left to Sergio. On the third day, Javier's body was released, and they were allowed to return home to Nuevo Laredo.

The girls freaked out, sobbing and hugging themselves, just knowing that they were traveling with a dead body in the back. What a nightmare! It had all started off so beautifully—a Cinderella affair—only to turn into an Alfred Hitchcock movie.

It was a long, long two-hour ride back.

Chapter Twenty-Six
Abby

OVERDOSE

Nothing surprised Isabella. She had awaited the news on the outcome of her father's adventures, but when nothing filtered through, she and Ryan resiliently prepared for the advanced ghost crew to Real de Catorce. Deep down, she knew that Operation FW (Free Willy)—the code name for Abby in this case—was a success. She and Ryan were about to activate the most dangerous and daring phase, which could result in her expiration and that of her crew, with Ryan being the principal.

Implementing the logistics of PHASE IV, Operation DT (Death Trap), was daunting. But it was also the most exciting phase. Mom was secured. Next was **SEIZURE!**

They drove for fifty miles and then turned onto a dirt road. The road twisted and turned through dense brush until it came to a clearing. There, waiting on a stretch of low-cut grass, was a small plane. They parked the battered truck under some trees and boarded the aircraft. Once they were safely seated, the pilot took off. They were heading home to the Hacienda, and Isabella couldn't contain her excitement at the thought of seeing her mom.

The plane landed on a similar stretch of low-cut grass in a wooded clearing. There was a white Chrysler with a few scratches and dents, weathered upholstery, and an engine that had seen lots of road time. It was a warm, familiar sight. Isabella recognized her old banger. She had that contented feeling of being home.

The drive home would take approximately two hours. Isabella sat back, closed her eyes, and fell asleep. She awoke when they pulled into the driveway. It was early evening, but already dark. Passing through the security check was no problem. There was no apparent additional security presence for any perceived alert or threat. Perhaps events from the south were isolated and had no bearing on activity further north. Still, even if there was any perceived unidentified threat, Isabella was home—and she was recognized.

They drove up to the front entrance, where two heavily armed security guards paced, keeping alert and not paying attention to Isabella and her companion. Nobody came to meet her. She was not expected, yet a car pulling into the driveway warranted extra attention and created a buzz within the household.

Isabella entered the house alone. It was dimly lit, gloomy, and uncannily quiet. She took the private elevator to her mother's floor and went straight to her bedroom without making a sound.

She opened the door to her mother's bedroom and walked in. She didn't call out like she usually did—she just walked in. Abby was in bed, asleep. Isabella crawled in next to her, wrapped her arms around her, and lay there. The emotion was too strong for Isabella, and she started to cry. Her mother looked frail and thin, the smell of alcohol on her breath. She was just a shadow of the person Isabella once knew, and that made her cry even more. She cried herself to sleep right there, lying next to her mother.

The next morning, Abby woke up befuddled, disoriented, and amnesiac. Someone was lying next to her, but she couldn't remember who or how they had ended up in her bed. All she saw was the top of the person's head—blonde. Juan-Pedro, her supplier, was not blonde.

She slid out of bed, not wanting to know who was there, and went to the bathroom. She was shivering but not cold. Hungry, maybe—but not cold. She could smell her own breath as she rinsed her face with cold water, trying to bring herself to her senses and focus.

She brushed her teeth, rinsed her mouth, brushed again, then used mouthwash. Cupping her hands over her mouth, she smelled her breath and looked in the mirror. Satisfied that her morning breath wasn't nauseating, she tiptoed back into the room.

Sitting up in bed, checking her phone for text messages, was Isabella. When Abby saw who it was, she shrieked.

"Oh my God! Oh my God! Bella? Bella? Is that really you? What are you doing here? Bella! Oh, my Bella, come here."

But before Isabella could move, Abby ran toward her, still sitting up in bed.

"Oh, my baby. Oh, my baby! You're back. You're back, my baby. You're back. Oh, how I missed you so. When did you come? Why did you come? Here, let me look at you! Wow! You've grown so much. A full-grown woman now!"

"Mom! Oh, Mom! I came last night. I came to see you here in your room, but you were asleep already. So I just laid here next to you. I missed you so, so, so much."

The two hugged and kissed each other and clung to each other. Isabella sobbed, shocked and saddened to see her mother in the state she was the previous night.

"Mom, let me wash up. The bathroom is up, and we can go downstairs and get Corella to fix us breakfast. Is that okay with you?"

"Perfect. Hurry, 'cause I'm shivering with hunger."

Corella was already in the kitchen when Abby and Isabella got there. She smiled and greeted them both. Before they could request a breakfast meal, Corella imposed her menu.

"I have scrambled eggs, fresh from the chicken coop, sliced avocado, turkey ham, grits, freshly squeezed orange, carrot, and apple juice, freshly cut fruit—kiwi, strawberries, mango, raspberries, and banana. Coffee, herbal tea for you, Bella. Brown toast, corn tortillas, croissants, and freshly baked scones. How about that? I hope you're both hungry."

"Ooh, I'm starving," said Abby.

"Hmmm, yummy," said Isabella.

The three chatted as they ate, with Corella joining at the insistence of both Abby and Isabella. They ate heartily and chatted in a friendly atmosphere. Finally, Isabella got around to asking where her father was. When Abby offered no response, both Isabella and Abby turned to Corella for an answer.

"I'm not sure. I heard he had to travel south for business. I don't know what business it was. But some of the drivers…"

"You mean Ramiro," butted in Isabella.

"Errr…" Turning bright red in the face, Corella offered a lame confirmation that the driver in question, supplying the information, was in fact her partner, Ramiro.

Corella felt bad that she had let Isabella down when it came to looking after Abby closely. She regretted this and kept apologizing.

Content that her father was out of town—or more precisely, out of the house—Isabella moved to activate her next plan of action. She let her mother ascend to her room to shower and prepare herself, while she remained in the kitchen and began texting:

"Tide is out!"

"Heard!" came the reply.

"Hair on end alert!"

"Always! ☺"

"Activate Code FW!"

"HOE alert confirmed. Code FW activated. Ready to rumble."

"RS! MIP!"

The "RS" stood for *Radio Silence,* and the "MIP" stood for *Meet in Person.*

Isabella took the battery out of her cell phone and stamped on it vigorously until it shattered into bits of plastic all over the kitchen floor. She carefully picked up every piece and threw it in the trash. She then went upstairs to check on her mom.

She entered her mom's bedroom and froze, her knees buckling. There, lying on the floor, was her mom, with the breakfast she had just eaten spilled all over herself and the floor. Isabella shouted for Corella, took out another burner phone, and sent a text:

"Urgent, come upstairs . . . CODE RED FW!"

Corella came running up the stairs, and right behind her—taking two, sometimes three steps at a time—was Ryan. He rushed past Corella and burst into the room. Abby was passed out on the floor, close to the bathroom door. Ryan quickly knelt beside her, and Isabella did the same.

The three of them lifted Abby and dragged her into the bathroom, where they placed her in a sitting position in the bathtub.

Once she was secured, Ryan left to clean up the mess on the bedroom floor. Isabella and Corella proceeded to undress Abby from her sports tracksuit. Corella ran the bath while Isabella placed the soiled clothes in the washing machine.

At first, they used warm water to clean her, then rinsed the bathtub. After that, they ran cold water to wake her up. She was having a seizure—her eyes rolling, holding herself tightly, and shivering. Isabella went into the bedroom while Corella dried and dressed Abby.

"Withdrawals," said Ryan. "Real heavy stuff. Gotta get her to a hospital before she gets alcohol poisoning."

"Get me some methadone, please. It'll calm her down until we get her to the hospital. Same state we found her in last night. Two guys came in trying to feed her habit, but I threatened them. We need to move now. We are now active and operational FW. Start the clock."

Corella called out to both Ryan and Isabella to come into the bathroom to help move Abby. Corella wanted to put her to bed and call a physician, but Isabella said no.

"Get the car to the kitchen door, please. We'll meet you there."

"Sure. The two of you can manage?"

"Yes, we're on the clock. Let's move," said Isabella to Ryan. Turning to Corella, she added, "Help me get her downstairs. When we're done, please come back here, clean up thoroughly, and put everything in place."

"Yes, I will. I'm really sorry that I didn't pay more attention to what was going on here. I was distracted by my loneliness and by the attention from Ramiro. When you left, I got so depressed that I just let everything go, including myself. Ramiro was my salvation. Please try to understand."

"Corella, you were always there when I needed you. I need you now, so please, let's get Mom to the kitchen."

Each holding Abby under their respective arms, they managed to half-drag her down the stairs and into the kitchen. Ryan was already waiting with the white Chrysler. They gently placed the still-passed-out Abby in the backseat. Corella insisted on going along. Isabella sat in the front seat, and Ryan drove.

At the border, they were stopped, asked to produce valid identification, and questioned about their destination. Judging by Abby's state, they were let through with little trouble and sped to the hospital. Isabella had called ahead, so they were met at the entrance with a stretcher, two nurses, and a doctor. Abby was taken straight to the ICU. Isabella, Corella, and Ryan were ushered to the waiting lounge.

"Oh, stop your crying, Corella," Isabella said abruptly, giving a stern look. She was clearly annoyed at Corella for her self-pitying act. "This should never have happened for a variety of reasons, the main one being I counted on you to have my back. 'My back' being watching over my mom."

"You don't understand. You don't understand . . . They took you away from me . . . I wanted to die. I didn't want to live anymore . . . Then Ramiro showed me kindness, showed me how to live and breathe. I was lost. He made me find myself! Selfish, I know, but I thought that I deserved a second chance . . ."

"Second chance—with eyes on your head and on the ground, not in the sky."

"Please—"

"Enough. Stop crying. We are here now!" Isabella walked out. Ryan followed, leaving Corella alone in the waiting lounge. "Fetch me when the doctor has news!"

Ryan and Isabella went out the service entrance to the back of the hospital, into a quiet alleyway.

"When's the tide in?" queried Ryan.

"Not sure. Day or two. We stay here, in town, until then. Corella will take a bus back across the border, then Ramiro can pick her up. I'm still mad at her. If Mom doesn't make it, I'm not sure I can forgive her."

"Your mom will make it. I've seen countless cases—worse—that made it. Plan ahead."

"He probably knows already that I'm in town. Sure he's planning ahead as well. Changes are too big for him to ignore. We need to accelerate FW. Jump to Phase Three. You think we can still execute efficiently?"

"With precise planning, it can be done. No slack!"

"Okay, in that case, I have a call to make."

Isabella put out her hand to Ryan, who slapped a burner phone into it. They both looked around, up and down, and walked away from any building doors. Once clear, Isabella made the call.

"Hello... Aunt Kate, is that you? Hello... okay, yes, I can hear you better now. Not a very good line, but I can hear you. Yes, Aunt Kate, it's me, Isabella. Your favorite niece. Hahaha! Yes, it's been a long time since we last spoke.

"Listen, I don't have much time. This isn't good news. Yes, it's about Mom—yes! Aunt Kate, Mom's in the hospital. Possible overdose. Hard stuff, yes. Not sure exactly what, but I came home and found her passed out. We're at Mother Theresa Memorial Hospital. It's a private institution on the Mexican border, USA side, in a town called La Mesquite.

"Aunt Kate, can you please come and be with Mom? Then take her back with you? No, no, no Mexico—not for a while. I'd like to make it more permanent, if you don't mind. Where? California? Oh, okay. What about Grandma? Just for a while. I need time to figure this out. Rehab. Yes, I'm organizing a stint in rehab—soon. Hmm, I don't know... three weeks' time? You'll come? Great. Thank you, Aunt Kate. I won't be here when you come, but I'll personally pick her up and take her to rehab. Oh, thank you, Aunt Kate. Yes, me too. I'm looking forward to seeing both you and Grandma. Bye."

Turning to Ryan, Isabella said, "My mom's sister Katherine will pick her up from here and take her to California with her. Then I can pick her up from there. We can leave Corella here until Aunt Kate comes. I'll talk to the doctor and get his contact details for an update on Mom's condition."

"You ready?"

"For what, Phase Three? Yes! Let's move!"

Ryan left to prepare the car while Isabella returned to the waiting lounge to brief Corella. After giving her precise instructions, Isabella sought the doctor. She explained that she had to leave urgently and unexpectedly, and that her Aunt Kate would be picking her mom up from the hospital. Isabella instructed the doctor to present Corella with all the details concerning Abby's condition.

Fifteen minutes after leaving the hospital, Ryan and Isabella crossed the border back into Mexico. Both had American passports, so the cross-border procedures were routine. They were soon on the highway headed for the ranch.

They arrived in the late afternoon. Isabella went straight to her room, while Ryan drove the Chrysler around the back and parked it inconspicuously. He then proceeded to his old quarters, where he changed into his fitness outfit. Out on the lawn behind his quarters, he began his stretching routine, followed by slow, flowing Tai Chi movements. It calmed him, recalibrated his brain and senses, and improved his blood flow.

Ten minutes into his routine, and he was lost to the world—except not quite. He was awaiting instructions. His mind was on full alert. Phase Three, Code FW. Fully operational. *Focus, focus, focus!* No distractions. Ryan was ready.

Mug in hand, Isabella headed for her father's office after she awoke—her office now. She walked past the lounge area and into the adjacent office, where she sat behind the huge mahogany desk. She placed the satellite phone in the top drawer and took out a burner phone.

"Hello, Aunt Kate. It's me, your favorite niece."

"Hey Bella, where are you? Heard about Javier. You okay?"

"Had it coming!"

"Damn right, he had. Abby is doing good. We're in Corpus Christi. Abby's out of the coma. You know it was medically induced, right?"

"Yes, I was aware of that. Does Mom know about Dad?"

"No. Won't tell her till she's strong enough. Right now, her health is more important than any mourning she's expected to go through."

"I agree. Aunt Kate?"

"Yes?"

"I really miss you. Thank you, Aunt Kate. Thank you for Mom."

"My best friend... she was always, and still is, my best friend," Kate said, sobbing as her voice trailed off.

Isabella heard the sniffing, and a lump formed in her throat. "Don't know how I could've managed without you, Aunt Kate. Is Grandma with you?"

"Yes, she is. We're a family again."

"How is she taking it?"

"Bad! But she's a tough cookie. She's showing a strong face for Abby—encouraging her, supporting her. We just want her back."

"Yes, I want her back too. But not here. Somewhere safe and somewhere happy. With you and Grandma."

"I know, sweetie. But you need to come here too. You're too young to stay there alone. Who would take care of you?"

"I'm a tough cookie too, Aunt Kate—just like Grandma. Please give Mom and Grandma my love. Kiss them both for me."

"I will, sweetie. Are you sure you're okay? Should I come get you?"

"Oh no, Aunt Kate. I'm good, really."

"But you're so young to try to manage all this on your own."

"I'll be fine. I love you."

"Love you right back, sweetie."

"Oh, and one last thing."

"Shoot."

"Do you still need Corella over there?"

"Hmm, not really. She isn't actually doing anything."

"Please send her back—whichever way is easiest: plane, train, or bus. Thank you for everything."

"You're welcome, sweetie. I'll send her back today. You take care now, and don't hesitate if the burden gets too much, okay?"

"Yes, I promise."

They both hung up.

Isabella called Sergio to the office before stomping on the burner and removing the SIM card.

Chapter Twenty-Seven
Javier

DEAD

"I was looking all over for you," Sergio began nervously.

"Good morning to you, too," Isabella said stoically. "Where did you look? My bedroom?" she quizzed.

"Yes, sorry—good morning—and no, I didn't look for you in your bedroom."

"What do you want?"

"I don't quite know how to relay this to you. How to even pronounce the words."

"Well, if you can't pronounce the words, maybe you should just write them down on a piece of paper, like a mute! You want a pen and paper?" Isabella said mockingly, while remaining expressionless. Her eyes never left Sergio's. She locked onto them and held them there.

"Err... no, that won't be necessary. What I have to say is that there has been an accident involving your father, Mister Javier."

"What kind of accident?" said Isabella, feigning alarm.

"Miss Isa, your father, Señor Javier, died last night. We received an initial, non-official autopsy this morning with the release of his body. He died from medicinal complications, Miss Isa."

"Medicinal complications? What an interesting way to phrase that! You mean he had a blue pill overdose? How many were there?"

"Excuse me? How many pills?"

"Oh, don't play the fool with me, Sergio. You are loyal, even in death. Admirable—truly admirable! I commend you for this. But how many girls were there this time? You think I don't know about my father's philandering?"

"Two."

"Age?"

"Of age."

"How old were they?" said Isabella, irritation creeping into her voice.

"Sixteen and seventeen."

"You mean fourteen and fifteen. Oh, never mind. What does it matter now? He got his just desserts. Where is the body now?"

"We took it to the local church in the village of Cuchilla. We asked the local priest—whom your father knew very well—to organize the obsequies. I hope you don't mind me taking the initiative on this. If you would like to prepare and organize the memorial service and burial, I'll let Father Tomaso know, and he can halt the proceedings. Please just let me know. I'm sorry for your loss."

"Thank you, Sergio. I'd like to be alone, please. Thank you. Father Tomaso can proceed. I'd like to have my father cremated. Let him be aware of this."

As Sergio was stepping out of the kitchen, Isabella called after him.

"Sergio, please ask my driver, Ryan, to come in here. I would like to pay my respects to my father."

"Yes, certainly, I'll call him right now."

With that, Sergio left the kitchen, closing the door behind him. Shortly after, Ryan walked in and sat down.

"What was that all about?" he said.

"Javier is dead. Fucking blue pill pedophile junkie. Had it coming anyway. Get the car and let's drive out to Cuchilla. That's where they left his body—in the local church. We'll go pay our respects and give final funeral instructions to the local priest. I have a plan on how to get into Real de Catorce. Meet me outside in five minutes; I'm going to change into my blacks. We will talk in the car."

Isabella walked over to her father's office and sat down in the huge armchair.

Sergio knocked on the door to the lounge and waited. Such was his respect for protocol that he waited patiently at the partially opened door until being called in. Five minutes passed. Then ten. It was fifteen minutes before Isabella appeared in the lounge doorway and invited him in. She didn't want to receive him in the office; that was going to be her private domain. Under no circumstances would the hired help ever be allowed into her personal space. She intended to demonstrate her authority and impose her will from the outset.

Isabella seated herself in the Louis XIV armchair and gestured for Sergio to sit on the visitor's two-seater couch facing her. If that was not how her father received his guests or business associates, this was how it would be from this moment on.

Her governance over all her father's affairs, associations, interests, and personnel would be communicated directly—beginning with the submission of the chief of staff, head of security, and undoubtedly the most trusted man in her father's entourage. She pretended to be looking at some "important papers" while Sergio sat patiently, watching her.

Finally, she looked up at him and said, "Sergio, what is your role here?"

"I'm sorry, Miss Isabella, I don't understand the question."

"Simple. What is your role here? What exactly do you do for my father? Start with your day-to-day activities."

"I'm head of security. I ensure that all safety precautions are taken care of wherever we go."

"Yet my father still died. Murdered even, maybe."

"I saw the autopsy. The doctors handed it to me directly. I was the first one to read it. It said myocardial infarction, coronary artery spasm, or silent heart attack. The main artery was completely blocked, resulting in first a coronary artery spasm, then a STEMI. He also had an abdominal aortic aneurysm caused by a rupture of the aortic valve. Three semi-digested blue pills mixed with a foreign stimulus agent resulted in extremely elevated blood pressure. Cause and effect: excessive consumption of blue pills. Nothing any security agent could have prevented."

"A heart attack! Do you know that heart attack victims can recover if treated promptly and effectively? Of course, one would have to administer said intervention immediately if the patient felt discomfort. Why were you not on hand to administer effective first aid immediately? Why did you wait? Where were you when my father was having a heart attack and dying?"

Sergio's response was a blank look and a reddening face. He shifted in his seat, rubbed his hands together, and scratched the side of his face. He looked down at his shoes and then up at Isabella. He opened his mouth to speak.

When no words came out, Isabella raised her hand, gesturing for him to stay silent.

"Sergio, I also read the autopsy report. I understand that it's not the first time you and your crew assisted my father in his 'adventures,' and there was no reason for you to suspect that events such as the night in question would deviate from what you've witnessed before. Am I right?"

As Sergio was about to respond, Isabella raised her hand again and continued.

"I have a few questions for you, and based on your replies, I will decide on the reorganization of the establishment.

"Two of your comrades, Dave and Oscar, who were part of the security detail when my father died, have been abusing my mom. Feeding her incessantly with high-level narcotics, keeping her in a constant state of submissiveness—almost slavery—in return for sexually abusing her. Were you aware of this? Think carefully before you answer."

"Miss Isabella, I went everywhere with your father. I was always by his side. He loved Señora Abby very much. But since your departure, Señora Abby stopped speaking to your father. She once attacked him with a knife while they were eating dinner. That was the last time they were together in the same room."

"Were you or were you not aware of what was going on with my mom? And who else was aware?"

"Miss Isabella, I was not aware of the abusive treatment of Señora Abby. I swear to you on my children's hearts and heads."

"Good. Good for you. Do you know the two girls that were with my father that night, and the three girls he was with the previous time?"

"Yes, Miss Isabella. Yes, I know where to find them. I don't know them personally, but I organized the transportation."

"Hmm. Okay. How long have you been with my father, and what will you do now?"

"I've been here fifteen years. First as a driver, then as your father's personal driver, then personal assistant. I am still in shock. Maybe I don't show it well, but I'm in disbelief. I am lost. I'm lost without my boss. It is all just too quick—too quick, Miss Isabella—and I can't handle it. I haven't thought much about what I will do or where I will go."

"You do know that once this gets out, we are all targets. We will all be swallowed and spat out."

"Yes, this is the reality."

"Sergio, you said you were my father's bodyguard and head of security. What do you know about security? Do you have any skills?"

"Not really, Miss Isabella, but I can control the team. I've learned a few things, and I carry a gun."

"Yes, but can you shoot straight? Anybody can shoot, but can you shoot straight and hit the target?"

"Yes. I've been practicing over the years. I've learned a lot since I first came here."

"Do you want to continue working here?"

"How? What will I do—go back to being a driver?"

"I want you to work for me. I am head of this family now. Everybody works for me. I want to know if you are interested in staying and working for me. Of course, you will not be head of security, but you will be responsible for the team—all the drivers and outside staff. You will report directly to me and me only. You will do as I say, with no questions or secrets. Just complete and utter loyalty. Are you in?"

"Yes, Miss Isabella. I am in without hesitation. This is my family. I pledge my life to this family—to you! My allegiance is to you and you alone."

"Good. This is what I want to hear from you. Do you know Ryan?"

"Yes, I do. He is your personal driver and confidant."

"He is my future husband. My life. We are one unit, and obeying him is obeying me. Are we clear on that? Think about it, Sergio, before answering."

"Nothing to think about, Miss Isabella. Your wishes, your orders, and your commands are what I live for. Nothing to think about. It is my honor to serve you in any capacity!"

"Good. Now, listen carefully. This is what I want you to do for me.

"First, I want you to execute Oscar and Dave for what they did to my mother. Immediately. Bring me their heads. I will feed them to the pigs.

"Second, I want you to bring me the girls that were with my father—all five of them. Bring them to me here tomorrow. Understood? Tomorrow.

"Third, I want you to arrange with the Sicarios to take Ramiro across the border to the United States. Get him a house in a discreet neighborhood for him and Corella. Get him a job working as a landscaper. I will provide you with the necessary funds.

"Finally, I want you to organize a new breed of explosive sniffer dogs.

"Is that understood? Are any of these orders going to be a problem for you?"

"No, Miss Isabella. I will take care of everything as you desire. Your orders will be executed immediately. Thank you!"

"For what?"

"Thank you for your trust in me. Thank you for accepting me back into the family. And thank you for not holding me personally responsible for your father's death. I will never let you down. I will be prepared for all eventualities."

"Don't worry, I'm not a blue pill junkie. You are excused. You are on the clock, and it is ticking!"

"Yes, Miss Isabella. My watch begins now, and I'm on it. May I please be excused?"

"You are excused, Sergio. Please send me Ramiro."

Sergio bowed out, lowering his body at the waist as he exited the lounge. Upon exiting the office annex, he summoned Ramiro and two other drivers.

He told Ramiro that Isabella awaited him in the office, and ordered the other two drivers to transport the girls in question to the Hacienda. Once there, they were to await further instructions.

Under no circumstances were they to exit the vehicles or communicate with each other or any other individual. Their respective cell phones were to be confiscated, SIM cards removed, batteries removed, and phones destroyed upon location.

Ramiro entered the office, knocked on the door, and waited. He stood in the hallway, not even daring to venture into the lounge. The hallway was dim, with no natural light. There were no seats or any objects one could use to sit while waiting. So Ramiro stood upright, not leaning on the walls, and waited until he was summoned.

After an hour, Isabella buzzed on the intercom for Ramiro to enter the lounge.

"Miss Isabella, so sorry. Condolences, Miss Isabella. My big, deep condolences for your father."

"Thank you, Ramiro. I'll be quick. Corella will return to the Hacienda tomorrow or the day after. But you, my dear Ramiro, will be taken across the border into the United States. Sergio will arrange everything. You will be taken to a house—it will be yours. You will be assigned a job, and you will work. Corella will join you eventually. Do you understand what I just said?"

"America? I will not drive anymore? Are you not happy with me? You are not satisfied with Ramiro, Miss Isabella? Why? What have I done to make you angry with me?"

"Ramiro! Shut up and listen! Okay? Do not question me. Okay?"

"Yes, Miss Isabella. I listen. You say, I listen. You tell, I obey!"

"Whatever. You will go live and work in the United States. You will work for me, dumbhead—but in the United States. You will leave in two days. Pack a few things—very light. A few clothes, a passport, a driver's license, and stuff like that. Sergio will organize everything for you. He will pay the Sicarios. When you cross the border, you will be taken to a house. You will live there. You will have a job. You will work. And you will not talk to anybody. Clear? You don't talk to anybody. Nobody. Clear?"

"Yes, señora. I listen. I obey. I am happy I still work for you!"

"Okay, Ramiro, you can go now."

"Thank you, señora. Thank you very much. I'm happy. Thank you."

When Ramiro left the office, a call came through on the satellite phone. It was Ryan. They had landed safely and were about to begin their hike through the dense jungle to the target point. She listened attentively to the details of their progress, then hung up.

She removed a burner phone from the drawer in the office—the same one she had returned after Ramiro had left—and made a call. Then she made a second call, this time to Miguel.

"Miguel? Where are you? Stay put. Don't leave the ranch for any reason. You heard me. Yes! SYS." (See You Soon).

She hung up and destroyed the burner.

She stayed in the office all day, going through every drawer and examining all the papers, searching for a safe or any other hidden compartment that might reveal confidential transactions her father was involved in. She wasn't interested in finding a cache of banknotes or precious stones. Isabella was more focused on assuming control and leadership over the activities her father had instigated—the potential outcome of which could lead to acclaimed status.

She sought a triumphant conclusion for any affair that would guarantee glorification and, in turn, solidify her power and status.

She was intrigued by how her father was implicated in the Sixty-Two affair. What did it entail? Soon, she would find out. She had never heard of it before, except for the identical invitation she had discovered in Ramon's office. Ramon and her father were associates, and she had been the pawn used to accomplish this feat. They had not necessarily liked each other, but their alliance had flourished, and both parties had benefited immensely.

She had located, albeit by accident, a cash bunker in Ramon's office. Why was there no such chamber in her father's office? She doubted that Sergio would be aware of such a chamber. She would return tomorrow and continue her search.

She left the office, secured it by setting the alarm, and went to the main house. She made herself a sandwich, ate, and went up to her personal quarters.

The satellite phone rang, and she chatted briefly with Ryan. By this time, it was late. She showered and retired to bed. Tomorrow would be a busy day.

Chapter Twenty-Eight
Abby Rehab

Corella had not yet returned from Nuevo Laredo. Perhaps she had accompanied Abby to her next destination, which had been carefully selected by Isabella. Abby would be transferred to a private clinic in Corpus Christi. There, she would spend all the time she needed to physically and medically heal—or at least begin to heal—and then she would be transferred to an undisclosed rehab center. It was all meticulously arranged by Isabella, with instructions relayed via Corella to Katherine. Nothing was left to chance.

Operation FW (Free Willy) had been successful so far. The remaining activation phases were executed according to plan. The ball was rolling, and there was no turning back. The biggest test of all lay in the assessment of Isabella's analytical intuition and the subsequent organization and implementation of her strategy, which were about to be put to the test. Any slight deviation from the prescribed action plan could prove costly—if not disastrous—for all involved, especially Isabella and those who depended on her.

To describe her current mental and emotional state as "exciting" would be a massive understatement. Isabella was thrilled beyond character just contemplating the possible outcome of her venture. She was entering uncharted territory—whether by reckless impulse or meticulous planning, it defied belief. Needless to say, she remained undeterred in her pursuit.

After Ryan left, Isabella ran upstairs to her room to change into appropriate mourning attire. She returned downstairs wearing a long black dress that reached her ankles, a black hat, and a black veil to cover her face. When she stepped out the front door, a line of personnel was waiting to offer their sincere condolences.

"Miss Isa, oh, so sorry to hear about Señor Javier…"

"I can't believe Mister Javier is gone…"

"Oh God, it's too quick. Such a kind and generous soul."

"In the name of the Father and the Holy Spirit…"

"Our Father, who art in heaven…"

Each person had something to say as she walked past them, shaking every hand that offered a kind word. Most of the women were crying—whether sincerely or for show, Isabella didn't pay much attention, nor did she care. Still, she played her part, walking slowly, stopping at each hand, nodding graciously, thanking each one in turn, and assuring them that their employment at the Hacienda was guaranteed.

Finally, she made it through the throng of mourners and got into her Audi. She sat up front next to Ryan, and they sped off.

Chapter Twenty-Nine
Javier

THE FUNERAL

Javier's funeral was a somber affair. Everybody knew where Abby was, so it fell on Isabella to bear the brunt of the responsibility for the funeral arrangements and lead the mourning. She did so with panache and the dignity befitting royalty. The entire personnel of the Hacienda were present in the small church. Villagers were encouraged to partake in the memorial service from outside, as there was limited space inside the church.

Ryan parked directly in front of the church entrance, and Isabella stepped out of the car. Father Tomaso rushed to greet her, offering his deepest condolences and stating that he shared in her grief. He met them at the church entrance as they disembarked.

"Your father was one of my sheep."

Do they still call them sheep? thought Isabella to herself.

Her father was certainly not a sheep—a fox, maybe. Or worse still, a wolf. She almost burst into uncontrollable laughter at the thought of her father as a sheep.

"Thank you, Father," she offered instead. "I would like to discuss the funeral arrangements with you, please. Do you have time?"

By this time, Ryan had joined them.

"Father, this is my husband, Ryan O'Connel-Garrison."

"I don't see a ring on any of your fingers," retorted Father Tomaso. "A wedding band is a symbol of attachment and fidelity to the vows of union that you make, especially in the faith." He stared at Isabella quizzically.

"Father, I am to blame. I have not earned enough money yet to afford the ring of my wife's choice. Please don't see this as blasphemous or a blatant disregard for tradition," Ryan interjected immediately.

"Father," said Isabella patiently, "I would like to have my father cremated and to distribute his ashes in the very religious village of Real de Catorce, high up in the mountains. This was my father's wish."

"Certainly, my child. If these were your father's wishes, and if these are your wishes as well, then the Church shall comply accordingly."

The three of them walked slowly inside, with Father Tomaso leading. He walked straight up to the pulpit, while Isabella and Ryan sat in the front row.

"Followers of Christ our Lord, sheep of Christ our Lord, fear not as we walk through the dark valley of death, for our Lord Jesus Christ walks with us—our Savior.

"Brother Javier, fear not your new path to the fruits of Heaven, for our Lord Jesus Christ, who sacrificed His soul for our sins, walks beside you. As you lay here, eyes closed, all dressed up, ready for your final journey to meet our Lord—know... know that your sins are forgiven.

"Our brother Javier was a sincere man, an honest man, a pious man, and he was loved by all—most of all by his family, and his beloved daughter Isabella, mourning the terrible loss of her father here before us. Let no evil word be spoken about our guide, Brother Javier. For he will lead the light, clear the path, and prepare the way for our own eventual journey. He will pave the way for us, my brethren.

"Let us pray... Heavenly Father, we send You our brother to pave the way for us to follow in his footsteps. Heavenly Father, accept his soul among those You have unburdened from past sins. Accept his soul among those You have forgiven. Heavenly Father, let not our brother Javier's soul dwell in the dungeons of darkness. Heavenly Father, guide us—each and every one of us left here on Earth—guide us onto the path of goodwill and righteousness.

Heavenly Father, lighten the burden of our little sheep, Isabella. Take away the pain and suffering from this fragile sheep and keep her safe from the dangers of the dark matter.

"Isabella, please come up here to lead us in prayer."

After the funeral service, Isabella and Ryan sought out Father Tomaso to discuss Javier's interactions with the Church and the villagers. When Isabella asked about the events on the night of Javier's death, Father Tomaso looked down at his feet and remained silent for a moment. A deep frown formed on his large forehead—he was bald—and his wrinkles extended halfway up his head. Isabella hadn't thought wrinkles could go that far. She silently vowed never to have wrinkles and never to go bald—she'd rather die first.

They all stopped walking, standing in silence as they waited for Father Tomaso's response. Finally, he spoke.

"Your father purchased a piece of land from the Church, way at the back, near the big tree at the far end of the churchyard. He said he wanted to build a family mausoleum where you would all be buried. There was never a question of him being cremated. Of this, I am sure."

"You are an upholder of the staunchest, most revered teachings of Christ our Lord. Let he who doubts your word fall on his sword this instant. Hath he no such weapon, let the demons relieve him of his tongue."

"Now, now, my dear, this is the house of Christ our Lord. We teach forgiveness and mercy—kindness and humility. There is only us here. My thoughts are directed to you, my dear."

"Father, I question not the words you speak. Perhaps my father failed to settle on a final death wish, believing that his transit on this Earth was still to endure. Alas! The old cliché comes to mind: 'Tomorrow is promised to no one.' Perhaps my father believed he was someone special. The Chosen One. Hence, he believed that tomorrow was promised to him.

"But forgive me, I digress. Is the mausoleum already built and ready to accept corpses?"

"No, my dear. Work still has not yet begun."

"Then we cremate him. Tomorrow, please. I would greatly and humbly appreciate you accompanying me in disseminating his ashes in Real de Catorce. Would that be okay, Father?"

"Why so hasty, my child?"

"I have my mother in the hospital to tend to, Father. I will be leaving the day after tomorrow to care for her in Nuevo Laredo."

"In that case, we shall have the obsequies tomorrow, followed by the cremation ceremony."

"Thank you, Father. I will make a considerable contribution to the Church, both for your upkeep as well as for the upkeep of your sheep—especially the younger generation, to protect them from fast words and flashy promises of a better world away from here."

"Well spoken, my dear. Thank you for your kindness, your thoughtfulness, and your generosity."

Turning to Ryan, Father Tomaso said, "Marry this girl. Be quick before another suitor steals her from right beneath your nose."

Father Tomaso smiled and walked toward the altar. He knelt before it, made the sign of the cross, and disappeared into his private quarters.

Isabella and Ryan left the church. Ryan drove, and Isabella sat up front. They were both silent for a moment as they slowly made their way out of the village and back to the Hacienda.

Chapter Thirty
Isabella

SUMMIT I

When Isabella and Ryan drove up, the Hacienda was in total darkness. There was no sound and no movement. Ryan was already packed and ready to leave. He confirmed his rendezvous point with the rest of the crew—they would take off from the airstrip, thirty minutes from the Hacienda.

Ryan went to the kitchen looking for Isabella, even though he knew she wasn't hungry. They had served food for the entire village after the funeral services, and the villagers were still feasting when they left.

Isabella wasn't in the kitchen, so Ryan went upstairs to her room. He knocked gently, waited a few seconds, and the door opened.

"Spend the night here tonight. I need you close, and I know you need my reassurance before the mission."

"You think that's a good idea?"

"All my ideas are good ideas," she replied, smiling.

"Are you hungry?"

"Ooooph... after all that food—tortillas, burritos, chicken breasts, and all that soda—I feel like I'm going to blow up into a million tortilla pieces."

She closed the door behind him and went to the bathroom to do her nighttime routine: remove her makeup, shower, brush her teeth, and get ready for bed. She came out wearing pink, flowery pajamas. Then she walked over to her clothes hanger, picked out an oversized T-shirt, and slipped it on over her pajama top.

She jumped into bed and sat up with pillows behind her back, drawing up plans and jotting down notes while waiting for Ryan to freshen up in the next room, as she had done.

Dressed in loose-fitting sweatpants and a top, he knocked on her door and entered. He sat beside her on the bed, and they went over the plans for what felt like the umpteenth time.

Isabella and Ryan chatted back and forth, reviewing the strategy for attending the meeting in Real de Catorce on May 8th—barely two months away. The advance crew of five would depart with Ryan after the funeral and parachute into the treacherous mountain area, then hike to within five miles of the village and camp there for two months.

They would scout the area on foot, looking for vantage points, escape routes, hideouts, and possible bunker locations, noting any and all human presence in their vicinity. Two months was barely enough time to set up such an operating outfield reconnaissance camp. Ryan would need a few burner phones to call in some favors.

Finally, assured that they had covered all the security details they could control, they fell asleep—Isabella on the bed, Ryan on the couch.

The next morning, around 4 a.m., Ryan quietly closed the door behind him and walked out through the kitchen. He headed to his quarters, grabbed his duffel bag—packed with all the essentials he was so accustomed to—and made his way to the main entrance.

It was a brisk fifteen-minute walk to the main gate. He exited the property, turned left onto the side road, and walked another twenty minutes. At the junction to Highway 85, he entered the wooded area, removed the leaves, branches, and camouflage from the white Chrysler, and drove to the rendezvous meeting point.

Chapter Thirty-One
Sofia Catalina

THE SISTER

Sofia Catalina Maria Ozabal-Ramos landed in Mexico City early in the morning, around 6 a.m. She had been born Sofia Catalina Maria Reyes Ozabal—Reyes being her mother's maiden name and Ozabal her father's last name. Now, she had added her husband's last name and removed her mother's, so she went by Sofia Catalina Maria Ozabal-Ramos.

When she stepped off the plane, Sofia was tired and restless after an eleven-hour non-stop flight from Madrid, Spain. Her stomach growled with hunger—the in-flight meal had been bland and lacked any recognizable or authentic flavor. She hadn't eaten on the plane. In her mind, she questioned whether the food had been haphazardly prepared in an airplane hangar rather than a kitchen—or any place resembling a proper cooking environment.

She was tired, irritable, and, most of all, impatient—impatient with the country, the people, the authorities, and especially impatient to reach her final destination, which was a further two-hour flight to some remote village up north. It was the family compound she had never visited—or rather, didn't recall ever visiting.

When Sofia presented her travel documents to airport authorities, she was ushered into an adjoining room. Her immediate thought was that she was being detained for some unknown reason. Her temperament was quickly tested as she demanded answers.

"Is there a problem?" she asked. "Do I need a visa? Look, I'd like to speak to the manager, please."

"This is not a restaurant. There is no manager."

"Well, I'd like to speak to the person in charge. The boss, the director, the president, or whoever the hell gives the orders around here. I want to know why I'm being detained in this smelly, unclean little shithole. And where is my luggage?"

"You are not being detained. Please! Please, come this way."

Sofia stood defiantly and followed the female border agent through a passageway into a VIP lounge.

"Please take a seat. Your passport and luggage will arrive shortly. In the meantime, make yourself comfortable," the border agent said, then promptly closed the door behind her, leaving Sofia alone in the lounge.

A few minutes later, the door opened, and a smartly dressed man appeared.

"Good morning, ma'am. I'm sorry for the confusion and misunderstanding. Please come this way."

Sofia stood, her patience worn thin, and followed the man out without saying a word. Right outside the door was a huge Mercedes limousine waiting for her. The chauffeur opened the door and seated her in the back. Before she could ask, he gestured that her luggage was already in the trunk and handed her an envelope containing her passport. They drove through the airport perimeter and onto the freeway toward the outskirts of the city.

"Where are we going?" she asked. "I need to catch my connecting flight. Some village in the middle of nowhere."

"Ma'am, with all due respect, I'm taking you to your connecting flight. It's a private jet waiting at a private airfield outside of town. Because of traffic, it will take us roughly an hour to get there. Please make yourself comfortable. There are refreshments in the cabinet in front of you. If you need anything else, please don't hesitate to instruct me."

Instruct me? Sofia thought. *Well, that's reassuring to know.*

She leaned back and relaxed a little. Somewhere deep inside, she was thrilled to realize she had just received VIP treatment at the airport. Somebody was well connected—her brother, no doubt.

Sofia dozed off for what seemed like a few minutes before the chauffeur gently woke her, explaining that they had arrived. The car had stopped beside a large private jet, where a hostess stood at the foot of the steps, ready to welcome her aboard. At the top of the steps, the plane's captain awaited, greeting her as she stepped inside.

The plane featured a spacious lounge area with six tables—three on either side. Each arrangement seated four people. A total of twenty-four passengers could be comfortably seated in the lounge, yet Sofia was the only one on board. At the back was a private sleeping area for the main guest, complete with a double bed and bathroom amenities. If she needed rest, it was available.

After showering and changing into fresh clothes, Sofia settled into the lounge, feeling reassured, comfortable, and relaxed. The hostess indulged her with food, champagne, reading material, and anything else she desired.

When Sofia looked out the window, she saw nothing but dry, arid land—no airport, no landing strip.

"Do I have to parachute out of this plane?" she asked sarcastically.

"Ma'am?"

"Well, I don't see any airport, aerodrome, or landing strip anywhere, so I'm guessing I have to parachute out to get to my destination," she retorted, without even the remotest hint of a grin.

"We'll be landing in just a few moments directly at the private residence. It's not an airport, aerodrome, or landing strip, as you mentioned. It is the private residence of QIR."

"Who?"

"QIR, ma'am."

"Who the hell is QIR?"

"Kindly fasten your seatbelt. We are beginning our descent and will be on the ground in five minutes. You can ask the appropriate ground attendants your questions. Here, let me help you with your seatbelt."

Before Sofia could protest, the hostess had fastened her belt, pushed her seat upright, and prepared the area for landing.

The landing was smooth—no discomfort, just a slight bump—and they were on the ground, racing down the runway before turning off.

Sofia was intrigued, looking left and right, trying to fathom where she was, how she had landed, and what this place could possibly be. On the ground, about ten staff members waited as the plane door opened. She was ushered into another limousine and driven a quarter of a mile to the main compound.

When the gates opened, her jaw dropped, and her eyes widened in shock, astonishment, and amazement. Right there in front of her stood a magnificent Spanish architectural mansion. It was striking in its grandeur and exquisite in its intricate sculpting. The carvings on the stone walls were an exact replica of the Royal Palace of Madrid—only on a smaller scale.

Chapter Thirty-Two
the Female Brigade

Isabella woke up the next day, preoccupied with her slate for the day, which entailed meeting with the young females who had been her father's addiction—his personal downfall that contributed to the demise of his union with his wife, Abby. It was the primary motivation for the willful dismissal of Isabella from the household. This obsession with underage females—for dominance and particular erotic pleasure—had finally caught up with him, and he paid the ultimate price... with a little outside impetus.

She ate a hasty breakfast of cereal, a glass of milk, and a bowl of fresh-cut fruit. Then she headed straight to the office, where she would set the ball in motion—directing and managing her day from there. She summoned Sergio to the office and rebuked him for the delay in presenting the girls. She also inquired whether any of her previous day's orders had been executed. She was uncharacteristically impatient. Ryan had checked in regularly, which allayed her concerns, but time was of the essence. Her schedule was unyielding, and she needed to tick the boxes before proceeding.

"The girls are here, Miss Isabella. They have been here all night."

"Okay, I want you to bring them in one at a time. Now, let's go."

"Yes, Miss Isabella."

Isabella waited in the lounge. She didn't want to engage in any official activities with anyone in the office. The lounge was the meeting area; the office was off-limits.

The first girl to enter was a very young, timid girl.

"What is your name?" asked Isabella.

"My name is Clarissa," came the reply.

"Okay, tell me, Clarissa, how old are you?"

"Fourteen. Fifteen later this year."

"Why are you here?"

"Please, señora? I don't understand. You bring me here."

"I only summoned the girls who were my father's prostitutes. Were you one of my father's girls?"

Clarissa looked down and didn't answer. Tears welled up in her big brown eyes. She fidgeted nervously with a button on her blouse, never looking up. She was completely mortified to be in Isabella's presence and to be questioned so directly. She felt shame, self-disgust, guilt—and suicidal. She wanted to run and never stop.

"Clarissa, look at me. I said look at me," Isabella said sternly. "Now tell me, were you one of my father's whores?"

Without looking up, Clarissa nodded her head. She wanted to be invisible at that precise moment.

"Do you have a family? A mother, father? Brothers or sisters?"

Finally, Clarissa spoke. "I live with my parents. My father is not working, and we are very poor. So my parents speak with the driver and get me to go with Señor Javier. Señor Javier pays, and I give my parents the money."

Then she burst out crying uncontrollably.

"I so sorry for Señor Javier. So sorry he dead. So sorry to you."

"Go. Wait outside and send me the next girl."

Without a word, Clarissa left, still sobbing, and sent in the next girl.

The questioning went on in similar fashion with the other four girls. Gabriela was fifteen, Maria Luisa was sixteen, Esther was sixteen, and Carmen, the oldest, was seventeen.

Isabella was not surprised by the troupe of young girls her father had indulged in for his personal fervor. But she was saddened by the willingness of parents to coerce their young daughters into promiscuous activities to support their families. She was not surprised—her own father had negotiated a pact with Ramon to offer his daughter in exchange for business benefits.

She met all the girls and questioned them on their respective rationales for willingly participating in what were, at least in Isabella's eyes, despicable acts with an older man for financial gain. Still, she wasn't judging them.

After the last girl, Carmen, left, Isabella stepped out of the office and instructed Sergio to assemble the girls.

"You all know why you are here, why you were brought to me. When I look at you—how young you are—I can only say that my father was a pig. He used you and abused you. But you were all willing participants. Does that make it right? No.

"I want you all to turn the page. Close that chapter. It's time to regain your dignity and self-pride. As of today, you will all work for me. Not as sex slaves, but as soldiers.

"As soon as I'm done with you, you'll be taken to a camp where you'll be taught everything you need to know about being a soldier—my soldiers. Your families will be paid regularly and taken care of in the best possible way. But you can never go back there. None of you can ever return to your families as of this moment.

"Sergio will take you to a place, and from there, you'll be transported to the camp where my generals await you, ready to mold you into the most lethal striking force in the world. Money will never be a problem for any of you once you successfully complete the training. Do you have any questions?"

One of the girls slowly raised her hand.

"Yes, Clarissa, what is it?"

"I want to go home. I am too young. I want my parents."

"Clarissa, your parents sold you to my father—for what, one hundred dollars? Some of you were sold for two hundred dollars. Maybe you were given a little present that your parents later sold to pay for your father's tequila. Am I right?

"Your father is a fat, lazy, ignorant, alcoholic peasant. He sits around drinking tequila all day, and you—yes, *you*—have to pay for that with your body. And you want to go back to your parents?

"What parents? They are animals. Pigs! Just like my father. No! You are not going home to that family, to that household that will continue to use you to pay for everything.

"Anybody else? No? Good. Sergio, get Rosario to get them washed up, give them all a change of clothes, feed them, and get them ready to move out. Nobody stays. They all go. Okay?"

"Yes, Miss Isabella."

"Good luck, girls. See you in one year."

She turned and went back into the office, locking the outer door behind her. There, she set about searching earnestly for a safe, a bunker, a closet—someplace where her father might have amassed valuables and cash.

The satellite phone rang, and she promptly answered. Ryan explained that they had set up an observation post from a vantage point where they could monitor all the comings and goings in the village.

When she hung up, the desk phone rang. It was Sergio. He confirmed that he had executed all her instructions—nothing was pending. He would confirm when the girls had left.

She hung up the desk phone, ripped the cable from the wall, dumped the phone unit in the trash, and returned to her fixation: locating the safe.

She walked into the hallway, stopped, and turned a full circle, looking for possible openings, loose floorboards—anything that might indicate a hidden compartment. Satisfied that she had examined all possibilities in the hallway, she returned to the lounge.

She inspected every inch of each wall, top to bottom, ripped out the carpets, and moved the furniture. Still, nothing.

She was intrigued. How could her father not have a safe? It was customary for business elites to have easy access to crucial stored information, valuables, and important documents. It was unfathomable for such a basic precaution to be ignored.

Perhaps he was considered a member of the business elite. Or perhaps he was just a glorified peasant with financial clout. She preferred to think of her father as the former rather than the latter.

He had to have a safe, a closet, a bunker—*something*.

Eliminating each possible hiding place in the lounge, she retreated into the office and set about examining the obvious spots first: wall paintings, carpet, desk, chair, cabinets—everything.

She sat back in the big armchair, threw her head back, and closed her eyes.

Where? Oh, where?

When she opened her eyes, what appeared to be spider trappings caught her attention in the corner of the ceiling. She noticed a tiny smudge. Retrieving a broom handle from the reception area, she cleared the cobwebs and uncovered a minuscule infrared camera hidden behind them.

She passed the broom handle in front of the camera lens, and the office door suddenly shut and auto-locked. Then, the entire floor—desk and all—slowly descended into a massive bunker, warehouse, or storage room. It was huge, twice the size of the office, extending beneath the house.

At the far end of the room, a stairway led directly to the study in the house. Her father could access this area from either his office, like she just had, or his private study in the main house.

Along the main wall, the back wall, and down the center of the room were stacks of U.S. dollar bills piled to the ceiling. A narrow path in the middle led to the other end, where one could access the house. The office floor acted as a concealed elevator.

Once the floor reached the bottom, Isabella stepped into the bunker room and looked around. On the left wall were paintings still in their frames, wrapped in brown paper. There was also a door in the middle of the left wall.

Isabella stepped up to the door. It was unlocked. Presumably, the security protocol was managed on the upper level, and once the activation process was granted, security was assumed to be granted.

She opened the door and walked in. The light came on instantly, and there, before her eyes, was a walk-in safety deposit box.

Glass cabinets lined three sides of the room. Each cabinet displayed a unique set of exquisite, diamond-studded jewelry. All the major jewelry fabricants were represented.

One side displayed only watches—men's watches, as well as women's—diamonds and gold, all arranged and documented as if it were an upscale, exclusive jewelry store.

On another wall, the cabinets exhibited jewelry sets such as necklaces, earrings, and bracelets. Then there were engagement rings, diamond, ruby, and emerald rings, more bracelets, and necklaces again. It looked like an Alibaba cavern.

Out of the corner of her eye, Isabella noticed a medium-sized metal safe with a combination lock on the front. As a first attempt, Isabella used the same figures from the invitation. It worked, and she opened the safe door.

She took out the three trays that were stashed inside. Laid out on the trays were strange trinkets—no watches—just solid gold, arranged with precious stone antique pieces. These were not of this era—priceless collector's items, hidden away in the safe of a safe.

Out of the corner of her eye, Isabella noticed a medium-sized metal safe with a combination lock on the front. As a first attempt, she used the same figures from the invitation. It worked, and she opened the safe door.

She took out the three trays that were stashed inside. Laid out on the trays were strange trinkets—no watches, just solid gold, arranged with precious stone antique pieces. These were not of this era—priceless collector's items, hidden away in the safe of a safe.

Isabella was mesmerized by a strange ring. It looked more like a wedding band, given its width. There were two rows of small diamonds running all around the band. In the middle of these two rows was one row of larger diamonds that encircled the ring. On each edge of the ring was a row of emeralds of the highest quality.

Isabella picked up the ring and tried it on. It was slightly too big, but it fit her slim, lithe finger. She admired her hand. *This was to be her wedding ring.* She would give it to Ryan to put on her finger on their wedding day.

Now, I want to find something similar for Ryan, she thought. *A matching ring, if at all possible.*

But there was nothing. This ring was unique.

She tried on the other trinkets—necklaces and bracelets—but nothing caught her fancy quite like the ring. Carefully, she placed it back on the tray and returned it to where she'd found it. Then she retraced her steps out of the walk-in safe.

She returned to the desk and said, "Close sesame!"

Smiling to herself, she looked for a button to return her upstairs to the office. *Her* office. *Her* safe. Well, she would manage. She ticked off her to-do list.

Ryan called on the satellite phone, and she explained the situation—about the girls, the exterminated bodyguards, and Sergio's reaction to being employed.

Ryan was intrigued by the scenario involving the girls. He hadn't seen this coming and thought it was an ingenious idea.

Well, he was dealing with a genius, after all.

They discussed it for a while, and then Isabella suggested they maintain radio silence for the sake of prudence and security.

Chapter Thirty-Three
Sofia

THE SISTER

The driveway was immaculately paved with similar stone. Neatly trimmed hedges and trees lined the driveway. The building was in a "U" shape, just like the Royal Palace. Sofia closed her eyes, blinked a few times, and opened them again, only to find that she was not dreaming.

As the limousine pulled up to the front entrance, Sofia was met by Isabella. She stretched out her hand in greeting, but Isabella grabbed her and hugged her tightly. They embraced and lingered until Sofia pulled back and stared at Isabella.

"I'm so glad you could come. How was your flight, Aunt Sofia? Oh my God, you must be tired. Have you eaten? You must be starving! Come, we will eat, and then you can rest. I'm so happy to see you after all this time."

"Well, good to see you, Bella. You have grown so much. You've grown into a very beautiful young woman. Still married to what's-his-name, Mikael?"

"Miguel! And no, I'm not married to him. Never was, by the way. Just a sham wedding ceremony with a fake priest."

"I conducted that ceremony, if you remember correctly. And may I remind you that I am not a fake priest, as you claim. I am an ordained minister in Spain."

"If you say so. And may I remind you that we are not in Spain. If you'll follow me, I'll show you to your quarters."

Sofia was shown to the guest rooms, which were essentially an entire apartment. Isabella assigned five housemaids to be available to Sofia twenty-four-seven for all her needs. This was a bit excessive and unnecessary, but nonetheless, these maids had been given a task, and under no circumstances would their duties be diminished.

Still, Sofia didn't intend to demand any extreme tasks from these women, regardless of their orders. She was perfectly capable of managing her own needs. She decided that she would take a short nap, then explore the surroundings as far as she could—unattended.

She woke with a shock, totally disoriented, unable to determine where she was or how she got there. Panic consumed her as she jumped out of bed, desperately searching her mind for answers, for clues—for anything to explain the situation.

She sat back on the huge bed with its soft eiderdown and ultra-soft pillows. She lay her head back, fervently trying to control her mental state. Then it dawned on her: she was in Mexico, in some lost remote village, with a palace in the middle of nowhere. The birthplace of her mother.

The recollection was just as violent a jolt as the panic.

She sat up. It was dark in the room. She turned on the light to check the time. It wouldn't be the same time as in Spain. Then she heard a voice that jolted her even more and sent her heart racing.

"Can I get you anything, madame? Maybe prepare you a bath?"

"Jeez! Where did you come from? What are you doing here?" asked Sofia.

"I am your honored chief maid. I was waiting for you to awaken so that I may be of service. Can I get you anything, madame?"

"You already asked me... never mind. Err, no! I'm fine. I'm okay, but what time is it?"

"It is 3 a.m., madame."

"Three in the morning? How long have I been asleep?"

"Quite some time, madame. QIR has already retired for the evening."

"Now that you mention it, who is QIR, and what does it really mean?"

"Perhaps you can ask Miss Isabella in the morning, madame. Can I prepare you something to eat?"

"Is that all you people ever do here—eat?"

"You are our guest. We must serve you and ensure that you want and need nothing."

"Fine! I am not hungry. Unlike you lot, I don't eat every minute of the day. I would like to go for a run. You know, exercise... alone!"

"At this time of day, security will not allow this. But we have a gym room downstairs. Perhaps you can run on the machine."

"Very well. I might just do that—run on the machine, as you say."

"Very well, madame. I will have the girls prepare you the appropriate clothes."

Sofia dressed in the clothes provided, which were very comfortable, though nothing overt or revealing. She went down to the gym and spent over an hour working through her usual routine. But her energy levels were testy, and she tired easily.

She showered and returned to her quarters.

Unable to sleep, she stepped out into the courtyard and walked around, admiring what she saw.

How? How could this be here? she wondered.

After wandering for what felt like ages, she finally returned to her room. She took out her laptop and FaceTimed her children. They were thrilled to hear from their mother, and they talked for over an hour.

Around 6 a.m., Sofia started to feel drowsy. She lay back on the covers and fell asleep again.

She awoke the next day at five in the afternoon. She felt a little embarrassed, but nobody seemed to notice or care. When she had freshened up, the chief maid was there to escort her to the study.

There, she found Isabella seated on a huge single sofa, drinking a cocktail of fruit juices. She was talking on the phone, beckoned Sofia over, and gestured for her to take a seat on one of the other large single sofas. When Isabella hung up, the maid poured a similar cocktail for Sofia.

"Try it," said Isabella. "They are just so refreshing."

Sofia obliged, and the two women clinked glasses and drank.

"Thank you so much for being here," said Isabella to Sofia. "It's been so difficult for me to accept. I still can't believe that he's no longer with us."

"I'm totally devastated! Dumbfounded! How could this have happened? Have they released the toxicology report yet? I need to see that.

There are also many administrative matters that I need to address, such as the inheritance and distribution of all the family assets. My brother was the heir apparent to many of my late father's assets and possessions. All of this needs to be sorted appropriately and distributed to all the family heirs. I'm sure you understand.

First, I need to know what exactly happened. Also, ever since I landed in this backward wasteland, I've heard about QIR! Who or what exactly is that?"

"First, tell me, have you traveled well? Why didn't you travel with my cousins? Why didn't you bring them along? Oh, I would have loved to meet them and hang out for a while."

"I couldn't take them out of school, even for such an unexpected tragedy."

"Have the maids treated you well? Do you need anything?"

Turning toward the door, Isabella called out, "Maria Dores! Come in here!"

The chief maid entered, head bowed. She curtsied and stood there, not looking up or speaking. She was trembling slightly, but only Sofia seemed to notice.

"Are you taking care of my aunt?" Isabella asked.

Maria Dores curtsied again, bowed her head, and said nothing. Fear was in her eyes—but again, it seemed only Sofia noticed.

Isabella turned to face her aunt and asked if everything was to her satisfaction. Sofia replied that she wanted nothing more than what was already available.

Isabella sat down in the largest of the sofas. Turning to her aunt, she said, a little more excitedly, "How is Madrid, Aunt Sofia? How is Spain? How is Europe? Oh, I so want to visit soon!"

"I will get directly to the point. What happened to my brother?"

"Maria Dores, you can leave. Close the door behind you," ordered Isabella.

Once the maid had gone, Isabella turned back to Sofia and said, "You know, Aunt, nobody really knows. He was on a business trip and had a heart attack. That's all we know. Mom is still totally in shock; she can't believe it. Total denial. She still keeps thinking he'll just walk in the door and we'll all go back to normal. Just a bad dream. But that's not the reality. You know it, I know it."

"You don't seem shocked or devastated. You—the apple of his eye."

"Father had many apples in both his eyes."

Chapter Thirty-Four
Javier - Cremation

It was early evening when Isabella summoned one of the auxiliary drivers. Ramiro had left, not to return anytime soon, and Corella would be arriving the next day. What a shock that would be for her. Isabella smiled at the thought. At least she was looking out for Corella, even if Corella didn't look out for her—or more precisely, for Abby.

The driver took Isabella to the village to collect her father's ashes from Father Tomaso. When she arrived, the priest was in the middle of mass, which Isabella attended—for the first time in she didn't know how long.

Afterward, the two walked into the village square, where Father Tomaso, curious and courteous, questioned her about her age, her mother's whereabouts, her plans, and her intentions with the villagers and the house staff. Isabella smiled politely, answered the questions she deemed appropriate, and gently declined to answer the rest.

After what seemed like an eternity of walking, they returned to the priest's quarters to retrieve the ashes. Isabella reminded Father Tomaso that they had barely two weeks before the trip to the village in the mountains of Real de Catorce.

"I've been there in my youth," she said. "Stayed a few nights when there was a carnival and a meeting of important people."

"Tell me about the carnival, please, Father," said Isabella.

"Well, my dear, it was a long time ago, but I can tell you that the whole village looks forward to celebrating the coronation of the Aztec king. That's what the carnival is all about. The meeting was just a coincidence. I don't know much of what happened, except that the security was very jittery—with all the people out on the streets, loud music, and dancing. It was crazy. One poor boy was shot by the security staff. They said they mistook him for a gunman. He was about twelve years old and holding a homemade wooden pistol. The whole village turned on them, and the meeting was abruptly cut short. For many years, they held their high-level, secret meetings someplace else. I say, good for the villagers."

"When is the celebration, Father?"

"In two weeks!"

"Do you think we'll be shot like the twelve-year-old boy if we find ourselves in confrontation with security?"

"Well, first of all, I'm not sure if they've returned the meetings to the village. And second, we don't carry wooden pistols. So, I can safely say we'll be okay."

"Thank you for coming with me, Father. I'm so afraid to be up there, in a place I've never been, all alone. Lord Almighty knows what they'll do to me."

"Lord Almighty will keep you safe."

Isabella picked up the urn holding her father's ashes, stood, and prepared to leave.

"Father, I would very much like you to marry Ryan and me here in your church. Please! Is that okay with you?"

"Yes, my child, it would be an honor. I will have the whole village prepare the festivities. I will marry you. It is highly recommended by the Holy See and the Church."

"Thank you, Father."

Isabella got back into the car and returned to the house. She went straight to the kitchen to prepare herself a snack before going to bed. The next day, she would tick more boxes off her to-do list. Exhausted, she fell asleep almost immediately.

Chapter Thirty-Five
Sofia Catalina

THE SISTER

Sofia looked at Isabella with cold, unblinking eyes and said, "Where is my brother's body now? I'd like to see him. Pay my last respects."

"Cremated. Ashes spread over the mountaintop behind the property."

"What?!" Sofia jumped up, red-faced, eyes watering. "What did you say? You cremated my brother without even consulting me? My brother was to be buried in the family mausoleum in Spain—next to my parents! How dare you! I hold you all responsible!"

She stormed out of the room, but when she reached the door, Isabella said in a low, cold voice, "Sit down. You don't get to come here, in our house—*my* house—and give me orders. Javier was your brother, but he was *my* father. I am his next of kin. You didn't know your brother as well as you pretended to. You had questions for my mom. Well, sit down, and I'll answer them. You wanted to discuss the inheritance? Let's get to it," said Isabella, red-faced, eyes fixated on her aunt, ready for battle.

"Listen here, Aunt, I'll address what's pressing in your mind first. Your brother died of a Viagra overdose mixed in a cocktail of poppers, cocaine, and alcohol. Your brother—my father—was not on a business trip, as my mother would like to believe. He was on a sex trip. He flew to a resort where he booked out the whole complex for himself and his troop. They were a party of twelve. You flew in on the same jet.

"Of the twelve, six were young girls—two of whom were underage: one seventeen-year-old and one sixteen-year-old. The other four were between eighteen and twenty. There were two bodyguards and three friends and business acquaintances. The six girls were divided among the four men. Since they were passing the girls around, they needed extra vigor. Hence, the cocktail of sexual sustenance. The mixture proved too strong for my father, and he had a seizure—but succumbed by the time the ambulance with the resuscitation kit arrived. An autopsy was carried out here, at the local hospital, along with a toxicology test. That's how I know."

"You didn't need to cremate him."

"Aunt, my father was an uncontrollable, selfish, immature, macho degenerate who married my mother and then abandoned her to be his trophy wife after I was born. He wanted a son. I felt unwanted and abandoned all my life. My father searched for that son desperately in all the women he slept with. He wanted an heir—a boy. Girls were useless. To be given away, just like *you* were."

"What did you just say? You think I was given away? Me? Do I look like someone who was given away?"

"Aunt, you chose Spain. But your mother—my grandmother—was Mexican. Reyes. That was her maiden name. *Reyes!* You were ashamed of your Mexican heritage. You were Spanish. Told your friends and schoolmates that you were Spanish."

"What do you know about my upbringing? My father was Spanish. I took my father's culture and nationality, which is perfectly normal. Besides, we were living in Spain. What do you suggest I should have done—denied my Spanish heritage instead? No! I was proud and am still proud of my choice to be Spanish."

"Your brother embraced both. He was both—Mexican and Spanish. Just like I am Mexican and American. The culture that you are so proud of—the culture you so desperately clung to—*abandoned* you."

"What do you mean?"

"Under Spanish law, during your grandfather's time, and during the time you were growing up in Spain, the law clearly stated that only male children could inherit the family fortune. Female children would inherit only from their spouse's family. Thus, all the boys inherited. Nothing was set aside for *you*. But your grandfather loved you, cared so much for you, that he found a good family—and gave you away."

"Shut up! Shut up! I don't need to hear any more of this tripe coming out of your mouth, you hear me? Tripe, I say! You're just a baby. What do *you* know, huh? What do you know about me? About my family? What do you know about my father? My mother? Huh? Who do you think you are?"

"Aunt Sofia—"

"Oh, just *stop* calling me that! Stop! Stop! Stop! I'm not your aunt. I don't even know you!"

"Get off your high horse and listen. You *are* my aunt, but I'll call you Sofia. You see, Sofia, when my father was born, Grandfather celebrated for months. There was a huge barbecue, and all the top political and social personalities attended. Prominent members of the business community—the elite of the elite—were invited. When Grandfather was invited to the United Nations General Assembly, he briefly congratulated Grandma on giving him a son, to which the whole Assembly applauded for a full five minutes.

"Yes—boys were important to the whole world, not just in Spain. You were three years older, but there were never any overjoyed celebrations for you. Javier, yes—he gave Grandfather his manhood. For this, he was ever grateful to Grandma. She was proud of herself too. From the time of his birth, Grandfather began the steady transfer of all his assets to Javier—my father. When Grandma intervened to speak on your behalf, Grandfather told her to hush and not to interfere.

"On your sixteenth birthday, Grandfather hosted a massive party in your honor. Political and social celebrities were invited. It was the Spanish version of the *Bal des Débutantes.* It was then that Grandfather *gave you away.* You see, he invited all those celebrities, political allies, and personalities to choose a family for you—one that would allow you to inherit a similar fortune to what was due to your brother.

"Alfonse Ramos was a powerful political figure and a highly successful businessman at the time. His son, Alejandro Ramos—your husband—was in attendance at your sixteenth birthday party. That's where the two of you met for the first time. Negotiations were underway almost immediately for the alliance and marriage between the two of you."

"By the time you reached twenty, Ramos was in political decline, and his business ventures were struggling. Grandfather bought a minor interest in one of the ventures. He provided financial support to prevent it from going bust.

Alas, he was dragged into the other businesses that were folding and ended up owning all the Ramos businesses. You see, Ramos was a womanizer and a gambling addict. His incessant gambling instigated the downfall of all his business ventures. Grandfather had backed the wrong family for his daughter.

To remedy this, he unconditionally supported Ramos, paid off his gambling debts, quietly squashed his political misgivings, and supported the family financially. Grandfather paid for Alejandro's law school. He set up Alejandro's law firm when he graduated. Grandfather even pushed clients toward Alejandro's firm so that he could sustain his family.

When Alfonso Ramos racked up over one million euros in gambling debt, Grandfather decided that enough was enough. Alfonso had a car accident and died on the spot. There was no investigation—it was deemed an accident."

"Now you're accusing my father of murder?"

"Grandfather supported Alejandro, his mother, and his sister financially until his death. He made Javier promise to continue supporting Alejandro and his family until they no longer needed it. My father agreed.

Aunt, here is the financial package set up for you: You have the family home—the one you grew up in—ceded to you. I have the paperwork for you to sign. Initially, your father inherited it along with all of your grandfather's assets and possessions.

A trust fund has been set up in your name. This fund will pay you one hundred thousand euros per month.

A separate trust has been established for your two children. This fund will pay each child ten thousand euros per month from the age of sixteen until age twenty-five. When each child reaches the age of twenty-five, the fund will increase to forty thousand euros per month.

The Ramos family home—which, by the way, was owned outright by my grandfather and passed on to my father—has been ceded to your children jointly. I have the paperwork for you to sign as their legal guardian.

Alejandro's office building has been ceded to both of you jointly. Grandfather's watch—a collector's item valued at five hundred thousand euros—has been ceded to your son, as it was inherited by my father and should go to the next male member of the family.

That's it. I don't think I've left anything out."

"If you think I'll settle for the peanuts you're throwing at us, then think again. I'll fight you to the bitter end. You and your mother are nothing but gold-digging trash. I don't know which lawyer you've been talking to, but nothing you say here is valid. You are not even Spanish! You can't inherit anything from my country. You hear me? Nothing! I'll see you in a Spanish court—not a donkey court like you have here in this donkey republic. I'm leaving right now, back to civilization!"

"Be my guest. But my father inherited everything from Grandfather a long time ago. You didn't contest—couldn't contest. You were given—no, sold—to the Ramos family. For what? Gambling debts?

Alfonso Ramos was a gambling, womanizing drunk. Grandfather paid him to give you a good home. That's the reality, Aunt Sofia. Ramos begged his son to marry you. Told him Grandfather would make him prime minister one day. Yes! That was the promise to Alejandro: become a lawyer, learn the law, and be a politician. Then, all of Grandfather's political allies would back him. Ask him! Go ahead—call him and ask him! Ask what Grandfather and Alfonso promised him if he married you."

"You are pure evil! The devil!"

"My grandma stands beside me—showing me the way, opening the right doors. *You* turned your back on all of this. This was meant for you! Your true inheritance. But you turned your back on your own mother.

'I'm not Mexican, I'm Spanish.'

Well, little Miss Spanish—you lose. Go back to your life that *I* own. I own you and your family. You, your two children, and your husband.

Oh—do I own your husband? He has two main clients. Ask him about that. Both of those clients are *me!* Yes, me! I am his client, so I can support you *through him.*

Get off your high horse, little Miss Muddy Princess. Swim out of the mud you find yourself in—with dignity."

"I curse the day you were born. For all I know, you killed my brother and burned his body because you didn't want anybody to find out how you killed him."

"Your brother was nothing but a little wimp. All he focused on was having a son. Forcing himself on poor peasant women with no means to survive, in return for money, food, and shelter.

Then he got to *like* raping these underage girls—flying them around in his private jet, plying them with alcohol, giving them presents to take to their destitute parents—parents who were only too willing to see their daughters with a rich, powerful man.

Karma! Yes, karma, my dear Aunt Sofia. Karma got to him. He only got what he deserved. I have no empathy for either him or you. I couldn't care less whether he rots in hell or not."

"I'm done. I wish you to die."

"Oh, I will... just not tonight," retorted Isabella, laughing sarcastically.

Sofia jumped to her feet and strode hurriedly to the library door. She pulled it open and turned around for one last comment before parting—but Isabella beat her to it.

"Aunt, those trust funds I mentioned? Just got canceled. Your husband's law firm just lost its two most important clients. Your children will have to attend public school like everybody else.

Tomorrow morning, you'll take the ten-hour bus ride to Mexico City. There, you'll take your flight back to Madrid. There is no coming back from this.

Goodbye. Don't let the door slap you in the ass on the way out."

"I will make sure that you never set foot in Spain. Ever!" hurled Sofia as she slammed the door on her way out.

"Hmm... I don't need to go to Spain. *Spain will come to me!*" said Isabella with a chuckle.

The next morning, two limousines were lined up in the courtyard outside the palace entrance. Two coaches were standing by in the service parking lot around the back, unseen from the front courtyard.

Up in her room, Sofia was awake, showered, and readying herself for the trip back home. All five maids were in the room, preparing her luggage, cleaning and arranging the space, and offering support for whatever was needed. They moved around swiftly and silently—packing, vacuuming, changing the sheets, and re-arranging the room for the next guest.

Sofia quietly accepted their assistance and managed her own personal affairs. When her luggage was finalized, it was taken down to the courtyard, where the chauffeur placed it in the trunk of the vehicle and waited politely.

Sofia was the first to descend and hurriedly made her way to the waiting limousine. Before she could enter the vehicle, the front door opened, and Abby and Isabella stepped outside. Abby walked over to Sofia, gently placed a hand on her shoulder, and said softly:

"I'm so sorry that you're not attending the memorial service. You are the only blood family he has. Growing up, the two of you were best friends."

"I don't feel comfortable here," Sofia replied. "I don't feel any family affiliation with any of you. I will mourn my brother in my own way, on my own. I will hold a private memorial service for him back in Spain when I return."

Isabella walked over to the limousine assigned to her, got in the backseat, and looked straight ahead. She was stunning—all dressed in black with a black hat and veil. If there had been any cameras, advertising agents, or modeling scouts nearby, this moment would have been their dream shot. A picture that could be viewed and sold over a billion times on any platform.

Her vehicle drove off first.

Sofia, sitting in the backseat of the second car, followed at a safe distance behind. She was taken to the same village where the church ceremony was being held. Right there, in the esplanade in front of the church, was a bus stop.

Sofia was dropped off there with her luggage. Nobody paid her any attention; nobody gave her a second glance. She was deemed *persona non grata*.

When everyone was seated inside the church and the memorial service began, the bus noisily arrived, picked up its sole passenger, and headed toward Mexico City.

Sofia never returned to the region again.

Chapter Thirty-Six
Corella

When Isabella awoke the next morning, Corella had already arrived at the house. Oblivious to this, Isabella went down to the kitchen to fix herself a snack before tackling the day's activities.

There, sitting at the kitchen table, she found Corella—with her face in her hands and her eyes redder than the Martian depiction of an alien by pro-extraterrestrial-life scientists. They were bloodshot around the pupils, almost as if a kindergarten child had colored them for a competition. Her pupils even seemed to shift in color, adapting to their surroundings—blank and unfocused on any particular object.

Corella looked up as Isabella, still in her pajamas, walked into the kitchen. Upon seeing her, Corella stood up straight, saying nothing, and stared at her uncertainly. She wasn't sure whether to run and hug Isabella or to be angry with her, so she simply stood still and silent, tears streaming down her cheeks.

"Corella!" shouted Isabella, jumping for joy and running to hug her once-second mother. "I'm so glad to see you! How was the trip? Are you okay? Welcome home. How's my mom? How's my Aunt Katherine? Did you get to see my grandma? Oh, all these questions are so silly of me! You must be tired. Come! Sit! Let's have cocoa."

"Isabella," whispered Corella. "Good to see you. Good to be back home. Miss Abby is doing great and improving every day. Miss Katherine and your grandma are both fine. Miss Katherine is such a wonderful person."

There was no enthusiasm in Corella's words. She spoke quietly, truthfully, and without malice. She dried her eyes on her apron, pulled away from Isabella, and sat back down again, head in her hands.

"Corella, what's the matter? Why are you so emotional?"

"I heard about Ramiro," she said, looking up at Isabella. "I heard you sent him away. Why, Bella? Why? To punish me for Miss Abby?"

"Oh, Corella, no! Of course not. It's not a punishment. It's a new development—a change of scenery, a new life. Why would you think I'd want to punish you? You've always been like a second mother to me. Why would I ever want to hurt you? Not you, of all people."

"Ramiro was my second beginning. My chance at a new life filled with love. He was so kind and gentle and understanding. When you left, it was Ramiro who comforted me and filled the void that was left. Now he's gone, and I'm empty again."

"Corella, listen to me. I sent Ramiro to the United States. I arranged for him to be transported across the border with the Sicarios. He'll have his own house in a decent neighborhood and a promising job. Once he familiarizes himself with his new surroundings and employment, we'll help him become self-employed. You and I, dear Corella, will join him in the United States. There's nothing for you here. I don't need pampering, and I can certainly prepare my own meals—or hire someone else to do that. That, my dear Corella, is your second beginning!"

Corella stood, jaw dropped, staring at Isabella. Then she took Isabella's hand, fell to her knees, and kissed it. She placed Isabella's hand on her forehead, repeating the act three times before looking up. Still kneeling, hands clasped across her chest, she whispered— what seemed like a million times to Isabella:

"Thank you, little one. Thank you! God bless you and take you in His arms. Thank you. Thank you, Bella. I always knew that you were special, revered, chosen, carefully selected, of the highest order. This day… this day shall never be forgotten."

"Oh, Corella, your age is betraying you—whispering all that mumbo jumbo. Come on, stand up," said Isabella, pulling Corella to her feet. "Punishing you? What utter nonsense. For that, I order pancakes from your kitchen."

The two women laughed and hugged again. Corella clung to Isabella, laughing through her tears, unable to stop them from flowing. She sat down again and, this time, howled like a baby. All the stress of the past two weeks—the guilt, the sight of Abby in such a near-death state—poured out of Corella, and the floodgates burst open. She sobbed uncontrollably in Isabella's arms for close to twenty minutes.

"Alright, alright, you sit, and I'll make the pancakes," said Isabella, comforting her friend.

Of course, Corella still ended up making the pancakes. When she was done, the two women ate and chatted for half the morning. Isabella was careful not to divulge her deeper intentions or strategies to Corella, to avoid any accidental revelations. Though she trusted Corella with her life—just not with *all* her life. It was better this way, for everyone involved.

After the hearty breakfast of pancakes, oats, scrambled eggs, and freshly squeezed juice that Corella had prepared, Isabella went to her room to get ready. She called the kitchen and asked Corella to move all her personal belongings to her mother's room, which, from that moment, would be her room.

Then she called Sergio and requested that he meet her in the office, instructing him to wait outside until she arrived. Sergio waited for almost an hour before Isabella finally appeared. She asked him for a detailed narrative of the previous two days' events.

Sergio went through the checklist of duties Isabella had assigned, including the demise of the two bodyguards. She asked about the follow-up on the girls' statuses and how they were adapting to their new environment. Satisfied with the results and current progress, Isabella summoned a random driver.

She instructed Sergio not to leave the house under any circumstances and to prepare a daily report, which she would request when she deemed it necessary.

She got into the car and told the driver to go.

They drove for roughly thirty minutes to the airstrip. There, they were met by four security guards and four sniffer dogs—the very ones Isabella had ordered Sergio to position around the airstrip.

Stationed on the runway was an eight-seater, ultra-comfortable Learjet. The engines were running, and the pilot was already onboard in the cockpit. Upon Isabella's arrival, the guards unleashed the dogs.

Two of the dogs ran straight toward the plane, sniffing around the wheels, the steps, and under the cockpit, noses lifted as if catching scent trails in the air. They were fast-sniffing beneath the plane. The door opened, and the dogs were allowed onboard. The other two dogs ran in and around the wooded area surrounding the airstrip—searching, sniffing as they were trained to do.

Finally, all four dogs rejoined the security team.

Isabella exited the car, which had pulled up to the bottom of the plane steps. She immediately boarded the plane, made herself comfortable, and issued the order for takeoff.

Once in the air, Isabella wrote the destination on a piece of paper, handed it to the flight attendant, and sat back. The flight attendant offered her a choice of a snack and a welcome onboard drink—either fruit juice or a soda. She chose still water. Nothing more for the moment. The flight would take three hours and ten minutes. She reclined her seat fully, closed her eyes, and fell asleep.

Twenty minutes before landing, the flight attendant gently woke Isabella and asked if she wanted anything to eat or drink. Slightly disoriented, Isabella declined and sat up in her seat. She observed her surroundings for a few seconds, and then, recollecting where she was, politely requested not to be further disturbed.

She made her way to the bathroom to freshen up. Makeup and cosmetic application on her face, at just fourteen years old, was not deemed necessary by any standard. She simply freshened up—used the bathroom, washed her face, brushed her teeth, and straightened her clothes. Even a change of clothes was not considered *de rigueur*.

The plane landed on the airstrip closest to La Hogar. Before disembarking, Isabella instructed the pilot and the flight attendant to remain available on call. No specific day or time was given, only that they were to respond promptly when summoned. This was paramount—should there be any failure to comply, the consequences for all involved would be dire. Compliance was not merely to be agreed upon—it had to be assured.

The pilot and his assistant—or mistress, as Isabella had begun to suspect—nearly took an oath of allegiance to follow her instructions without hesitation. Before exiting, she handed the pilot a note, indicating she had placed an envelope for him in the bathroom as compensation for his services.

Then she left.

Chapter Thirty-Seven
La Hogar

Miguel met her at the bottom of the steps as she descended from the plane. He looked happy to see her, but this was of no significance to Isabella.

"Isa! Wow! So happy to see you. You've grown an inch again. Come here, let me hug you, my dear, dear wife."

"Cut the crap, Miguel. Who knows I'm here?"

"Nobody. Just me and... well, the driver now. So... where to?"

Miguel brushed a kiss against Isabella's cheek as he opened the car door for her. She completely ignored the gesture, stepped in, and Miguel closed the door behind her.

"You look good, Isa, really. It seems like such a long time. You've even grown—I swear it."

"How are my babies? Has the maid taken good care of them?"

"Oh yes, of course. I made sure. Hehehe, you like that? I made sure the maid took care of the twins."

"Miguel!"

"Yes, Isa."

"Not now, okay? Not now. We'll talk at La Hogar."

They drove the rest of the way in silence.

When they arrived at La Hogar, Isabella went straight up to the twins' room. She found the maid tending to them—bathing them and putting them down for their siesta. She tiptoed out of the room, closed the door gently, and went to her office. She instructed Miguel to join her there.

When Miguel arrived, he knocked on the lounge door and waited. By this time, he knew better than to enter without an invitation. The last thing he wanted was a rebuke from Isabella for a careless act mistaken as insolence. He was determined to be on his best behavior—alert and focused—for as long as she was here.

This time, he waited only two minutes before being invited in.

They sat opposite each other in single-seater sofas.

"Miguel, I want to talk to you about this," Isabella said, handing him the invitation for the meeting in Real de Catorce.

"What is it? Where did you get this from?"

"It's an invitation to a special event that will take place two weeks from now," Isabella explained patiently.

"Where did you get it from? What does it have to do with me?"

"Never mind where I got it. It's a personal invitation to an exclusive summit to be held in Real de Catorce. It says so right here. What's significant is that the invitation is addressed to your father,

Ramon Calderon. Since Ramon is deceased, you inherit the invitation. We'll go together, and you, backward tart, will follow my lead. Got it?"

"What lead? What's a summit anyway?" asked Miguel.

"Never mind. You just do what I say when I say."

"Hmm, well, okay… if you say so."

"You learn fast. Now evaporate! I have logistical planning to take care of."

Isabella returned to Ramon's office, entered the special hidden compartment, and sat down behind the desk. She opened all the drawers, searching for any indication—any hint that could prepare her for the summit. Her father, Javier, had kept a similar invitation among his private documents.

She searched every possible hiding place—vaults, filing cabinets, beneath the floor rug—everywhere. Nothing.

She leaned back in the chair, closed her eyes, and pictured the gold-toothed Ramon with his evil smile and limited brainpower. *Where would he conceal such a document of life-threatening importance? Where?*

She pulled out the bottom drawer and turned it upside down. Taped underneath was a document in a plastic protective sleeve. Isabella took it out and read it over and over again. She memorized all the articles, paragraphs, statutes, and bylaws. Satisfied, she folded it and placed it in her pocket.

Then she summoned Gonzales.

"Get all these locks changed right now. Not *mañana*, now! Got it? Everything! You hear me? And I want to be present when the locksmith comes. Understood?"

"Sí, señora. Understood. *Prontamente!*"

An hour later, the locksmith arrived with his van. Gonzales led him to the office and explained what was required. He set about changing the latches and locks on every possible access point to the main office.

When he was done, Isabella dismissed Gonzales and led the locksmith to the underground bunker office. Concealed coded latches were installed at the main entrances, from both inside and outside.

Satisfied that no one could possibly access Ramon's private quarters from any direction, Isabella paid the locksmith. Then she showed him pictures—his children, his entire family. He looked up at her, petrified, blood draining from his face as he tried to speak.

"Look after your family… or *I* will. You were never here."

"Bueno, señora! Bueno."

The next two weeks flew by with Isabella immersed in organizing care for the twins, managing the trade route Miguel had inherited from his father, and enforcing a new system of strict rules and regulations under her sole authority. All involved were required to follow her directives—Miguel included.

383

She replaced all personnel loyal to Ramon, Angel, and the previous regime. In their place, she employed vulnerable youth and mature, reliable staff who would abide by her expectations without hesitation.

Two weeks felt like two hours; there simply wasn't enough time to put everything fully into motion. Gonzales was the only remaining employee from the previous era, and Isabella trusted—or rather, counted on—his loyalty and discretion.

Still, it was too soon to leave everything in the hands of new recruits. The twins were her priority, but she couldn't bring young children on an uncertain expedition.

Chapter Thirty-Eight
Summit

When Isabella and Miguel boarded the private jet heading to the Summit, she brought the twins along. Upon landing, she instructed the pilot and crew to fly the twins back to the Hacienda while she and Miguel continued their journey by road.

Back at the Hacienda, Isabella called Corella and instructed her to have a special nurse tend to the twins twenty-four hours a day.

"Is that the plan you were talking about? The plan on how to get into Real de Catorce?"

"Yes, it all just came together in an instant. You and the crew need to leave in two days' time. We have barely two months to prepare. I can handle things here. You go on up, but be careful; there are spies all the way along—eyes that you won't see will be watching you."

"I got that. I have a plan. A friend owes me a favor. We'll parachute onto the adjacent mountaintop and trek back through the jungle, where no one will be expecting any movement. I have two military-issue satellite communicators. They're obsolete for the

385

military but still work perfectly. One for you and one for me. I'll call when I'm in position."

The rest of the crew was already there. They boarded the helicopter that would take them to the airfield, where they would board a plane to fly over their drop point. The plane was a skydiver training aircraft owned by a friend who had served with Ryan in the Marines. His name was Scott. After leaving the Marines, Scott started a skydiving training company for private clients and enthusiasts.

Ryan and Scott had served for two years in the same unit, often going on patrol together. Ryan was a trained sharpshooter, while Scott often acted as his spotter. Each relied on the other's company for moral support, ensuring they completed their deployments with minimal mental strain. They considered themselves brothers-in-arms.

Ryan urged Scott to join them on the mission. Business was slow, and a successful operation would provide valuable cash flow for at least the next five years. Missing his "brother" and the adrenaline rush—though skydiving provided some of that—Scott agreed to join the mission to Real de Catorce.

They boarded the plane—six men plus the pilot—heading for the Mexican jungle, somewhere in the middle of nowhere, near the target village of Real de Catorce.

It took them roughly three hours to reach the jump area. Scott explained that Ryan would jump first, the others would follow, and then he would bring up the tail end. He described how they would form a circle in the air by holding hands and falling together. This way, they could control the precise drop point and avoid being dispersed upon landing.

The plan was for Ryan to be the target once they jumped. Then Scott would complete the circle, and they would hold hands, falling as one unit. When they reached the critical height, they would release each other's hands, open their parachutes, and land within twenty meters of each other. They had targeted a small clearing they had identified from the air and agreed this would be the rendezvous point.

It was time to jump. As planned, Ryan went first, followed by Scott and the four other squad members. Theory was far easier than practice. No one, except Scott, was able to reach Ryan for the mid-air circle he had described. The others failed to get close enough to grab Ryan's hand. They flew wide, panicked, and deployed their chutes almost immediately. It would have been a comic sight if not for the seriousness of their mission—a complete and utter fiasco.

But they landed within fifty meters of each other, which, all things considered, was a success in itself. They pulled in their parachutes, unhooked them from their shoulders, and folded them.

"We should bury them," said Ryan.

"Well, we can't burn 'em. Give away our position right there and then," quipped Scott.

"Pedro," called out Ryan. "You okay? I see you limping."

"It's nothing, boss. Just a slight twist when I landed," replied Pedro, one of the squad.

"Take out your shovel and bury these chutes," ordered Ryan. "Get Jimenez to help you. Far back in the trees as possible. Hurry, we need to get out of here just in case we've been spotted."

"Yes, boss," came from Pedro.

"Hey guys, what happened up there?" Scott asked the squad.

"Too dangerous, boss. Holding hands, dancing in the sky—too dangerous, boss. I had to land," Lopez said.

"Where's Freddy?" asked Ryan.

"Here, boss," came the reply from the fourth squad member. "All here, boss. We must move now. Too dangerous to stay here. This looks like a landing strip, which means it is watched."

"We'll bury the chutes first, then move out," said Ryan. Turning to Scott, he added, "Ready to roll, buddy? This is it. Action time. What you craved."

"Yep. Couldn't ask for more."

Ryan pulled out his satellite phone, called Isabella, and confirmed that they had landed safely and were on schedule. It was early afternoon, and they would find their bearings, head out, and make camp at nightfall.

They set out. Scott beamed with pride at his contribution and the successful execution of the jump by him and his buddy. Just like old times. He was happy that Ryan had asked him along. He needed the adventure more than the money. Even though—and this he had not mentioned to Ryan yet—he was soon going to be a father. They had plenty of time to chit-chat about that.

They made good progress despite the dense foliage, using machetes to cut their way through impregnable passageways. They made camp at dusk—no fires, no light. They wore their night vision goggles to see in the dark when all light had disappeared. They ate from the dry rations, drank from their canteens, and slept in secure sleeping bags.

This is the life, thought Scott to himself.

Ryan called Isabella and confirmed their progress.

"Who's Bella?" Scott asked, smiling as he shoved his buddy teasingly. "Didn't know you had a lil' missus keeping tabs on you back home. You dirty tortilla."

"She's my boss and your boss. Head of the mission. That's all I can say for now," shot back Ryan, all serious, eyes darting in all directions.

"Aw, c'mon buddy. It's me, remember? I saved your ass in Iraq a thousand times."

"More like the other way around, the way I remember things. Would do it again . . . and again! Never had a brother. You're it!"

"So . . . c'mon . . . c'mon. Bella your lil' lady!"

Ryan grabbed Scott by the upper arm and pulled him aside—all serious, no smiles.

"Listen, Scott, Bella is the head of this mission. I have to check in with her and confirm our progress every step of the way. Those guys there are my backups, but on this side of the world, backups change easily. You, my brother, you're the only one I trust to have my back. To watch me, cover me, and keep an eye on our dear companions. This right here, this mission—life or death, brother. Life or death. You'll get to meet Bella in due time. For the moment, we both need to stay focused. And I mean real focused. In the desert, we could see them or see around us for miles. Here, we can't see one foot in any direction. We don't know if we've been spotted and don't know where the danger is coming from. I need you, bro. I need you. Bella talk will come after. Okay?"

"Semper Fi, bro. Semper Fi. I got yo back, bro. I got yo back."

After that discussion, they kept chit-chat to a minimum, but the mood was still light-hearted. For the next two days, they made good progress and were within five miles of the target village by nightfall. They would camp for the night and scout around for a vantage point from which to observe the activity in the village. They would proceed with this the next day. Right now, they needed a well-earned rest. Ryan took the first watch.

The next morning, they circled Real de Catorce, keeping a five-mile radius as they searched for the ideal vantage point. They completed a full sweep around the village, rested, and then did it again—multiple times. After camping for the night, they trekked around the village a fourth time the next morning, finally settling on a high rise closer to the east side of Real de Catorce. The sun was at their backs all day, and the elevation allowed them to look down into the village.

This would be their reconnaissance point. Their camp would be further back in the thick vegetation, concealed from all angles. Ryan checked in with Isabella, confirming that they were in place. There would be radio silence on his end until she contacted him.

Chapter Thirty-Nine
Summit I

THE CHALLENGE

Isabella and Miguel flew by private jet from the Villa del Sol, where Miguel lived, directly to Charcas—a small village just north of a town called San Luis Potosí. Isabella instructed the pilot to immediately fly back to the Hacienda and await further orders. She didn't want any curious observers questioning the unusual presence in their respective domain.

Given the remoteness of the village, technological progression was unseen and unheard of. Modernization, even on the simplest scale, was beyond their realm. Witnessing the landing of a private jet in their village triggered an unprecedented curiosity. The enigma of such an event incited a gathering of all the inhabitants. It was this movement and nosiness that Isabella strove to avoid, and thus ordered the pilot and his crew to return immediately to the villa.

Isabella and Miguel took the local bus from the closest stop along the main road, heading north toward Estación de las Catorce. The bus chugged slowly along the route, reaching San Rafael Torres almost four hours later. Unaccustomed to being cramped in such horrid, sweaty conditions, Isabella requested several toilet stops along the way—simply to stretch her legs and breathe. The bus was clearly overcrowded, which was the norm, as it was the primary mode of transport in the area. People boarded whenever it stopped, yet no one got off, raising the question: where were they all going? Nevertheless, Isabella endured the discomfort, odors, and sweat-filled atmosphere of the bus.

Finally, they arrived at San Rafael Torres. Given the remoteness of the area and its inhabitants, the notion of a "taxi" was not commonly acknowledged. Isabella and Miguel had to explain to the first passerby exactly what they were looking for. Only three men in the village owned vehicles that could remotely serve as public transportation. Two of them were in San Luis Potosí on a mission—though what kind of mission was anyone's guess.

That left Isabella and Miguel with no choice but to negotiate the price for their trip. It's amazing what one hundred U.S. dollars in cash can buy—especially when Isabella offered the driver two hundred for his services. They stocked up on water and whatever junk food was available in the tiny convenience store before setting out on the final leg of their journey.

They drove along Cruz Carretas Road, which led straight to Real de Catorce. They would pass through Santa Cruz de Carretas, over the high mountain pass, and then down into the valley toward Real de Catorce. Given the condition of the vehicle, the trip would take six to seven hours.

It was just after 2 p.m. Their expected arrival time was around 9:30 p.m. By then, it would be dark—their arrival unnoticed. Ryan would break cover to meet them at the village entrance.

They arrived in Santa Cruz de Carretas at 8 p.m. They had experienced a blowout along the way, which delayed them for over an hour. Such are the encounters when one is ill-equipped for even the most basic of road incidents.

Irritated, bothered, tired, and frustrated, Isabella welcomed the sight of Santa Cruz de Carretas. They stopped at the Hotel Minería Real de Catorce, situated in the town center just off the main road. There, Isabella and Miguel were able to refresh themselves, take a toilet break, and grab a quick bite. They ate a light snack prepared by the hotel restaurant. Once they were sufficiently hydrated, they urged their driver to continue.

By the time they set off again, darkness had fallen. The town was eerily still, with only a few people walking in the shadows of the streets off the main road. They loaded up and continued their journey.

It was close to midnight when they arrived at the entrance of the village. Out of nowhere, three men sprang in front of their car, forcing the driver to slam on the brakes. The men wore full-face masks and military gear. They approached the driver, tapped on the window, and motioned for him to roll it down.

In accented Spanish, they asked who he was and what he was doing there. He explained that he was simply driving his clients, seated in the back, to Real de Catorce.

Without warning, the men yanked the driver's door open and pulled him out. They forced him face-down on the road, blindfolded him, gagged him, and tied his hands and feet before tossing him into the back of their truck. The driver thought he was going to die. Then he heard Isabella scream for help, followed by Miguel. That was the last thing he heard before a blow to the back of the head knocked him unconscious.

"Sorry we're late," said Isabella as she hugged Ryan before going to sit in the passenger seat of the truck.

"I was worried that you had some difficulties on the road," replied Ryan as he followed Isabella into the truck.

"Nothing that couldn't be repaired," she retorted.

"Okay. I've set you guys up at the Hotel Socavón de Purísima. Low key, nothing fancy, very discreet."

"Sure. I just need to rest, sleep, and hopefully get out of these clothes. Let's move," said Isabella.

They entered the hotel through the back door. Ryan had already checked them in and retrieved the room keys. He bid them good night and left to join his colleagues, who were waiting for him in the dark alleyway. When Ryan climbed into the passenger seat, they drove off to their campsite nearby.

A knock on the door roused Isabella from her sleep. She opened the door to Miguel.

"Are you awake?" he asked timidly, waiting to be invited into her room.

"What does it look like to you? I'm sleepwalking? What do you want?" she said aggressively, throwing her arms in the air as she walked to the lounge area. She didn't appreciate being rudely awakened—and least of all by Miguel.

"Have you had breakfast? I'm a little hungry. I need to eat something," he said, smiling and rubbing his belly in a playful manner.

"No, Miguel. I haven't had my breakfast yet. Go ahead, I will join you," said Isabella, turning to face him with a scowl on her face.

Secretly, Isabella admitted to herself that she had hoped it was Ryan coming to escort her to breakfast. She didn't even attempt to hide her disappointment from Miguel.

After a rather heavy breakfast of tortillas, guacamole, black beans, and scrambled eggs, Isabella summoned Miguel to her room to plot their strategy for the meeting. They discussed for hours before breaking for lunch. This time, Isabella insisted on a lighter meal with more salad and vegetables.

The Summit, as mentioned in the invitation, was being held at the Hotel Punta del Cielo at 3 p.m. Isabella coached Miguel on what was expected of him. He was like putty in her hands. He simply agreed with everything.

Finally, it was time. They left the hotel, walking side by side. Miguel attempted to loop his arm through Isabella's elbow, trying to give the impression they were a couple.

Isabella stopped, pulled him around to face her, and said, "You don't want me to slap you right here in the street in front of everybody, do you?"

"Er, no. I was just trying to show a little unity between us. That's what you've been drilling me to do all day."

"Walk! No touching. Just walk, and no talking."

Once they arrived near the venue, the atmosphere changed. Locals were sparse, shops and stalls were closed, and security personnel were everywhere. They all had earpieces, handheld radios, dark glasses, and smart suits.

Isabella's cell phone rang—just once. It was Ryan, signaling that the squad had eyes on them. Isabella and Miguel walked boldly to the entrance of the hotel, where they were met by a stern-looking security detail. They presented their invitations and waited.

Clearance was denied.

Radio contact was made with someone presumably higher in rank. There was a great deal of back-and-forth between the security detail and the higher-ups. After what seemed like an hour, they were finally allowed to proceed to the next checkpoint.

Still holding their invitations, Isabella and Miguel walked across the lobby, where they were met by a second security detail. The same questions were asked—proof of ID, more questions regarding the purpose of their visit, as their names were not on the invitations. More back-and-forth—albeit brief this time—and they were allowed to proceed.

After the second security checkpoint, they followed signs leading to the venue. They were directed to a staircase descending to a lower level. There, they encountered a huge steel door, heavily padlocked. A very discreet red arrow pointed to what appeared to be a doorbell. They rang and waited.

Two young women opened the door—no smiles, no courteous greeting, no hint of politeness, just cold blue eyes. Their features suggested they were from Eastern Europe, likely Russian. Isabella and Miguel were checked for a third time. This time, they were held up for fifteen minutes before being allowed to proceed.

They descended two more flights of stairs to a lower basement area, where they were escorted to a fourth and final security check. The same questions were asked, and this time, they were physically searched.

Isabella requested to be searched by a female staff member. She objected to being physically manhandled and proceeded to pat herself down to show she was not carrying any weapons. The guards found this highly amusing and let them through.

They arrived at a massive metal double door. It appeared to be fireproof, explosion-proof, and reinforced with every security measure imaginable. A digital keypad was mounted on the side of the door. The guards entered the code given to them by the last security detail. Once the code was entered, the massive doors swung open, revealing a large room that was already occupied.

When they entered the room, they were met with complete and utter silence. Isabella looked around as she walked toward what she assumed would be her seat.

The room was a massive ballroom carved out of solid rock, resembling a cave—except this hall was rectangular in shape with a seven-meter-high ceiling. It was beautifully sculpted and decorated with some of the rarest antiques, all painted white. Perhaps the white color was meant to brighten the space, as they were deep underground with no natural light.

Right in the middle of the conference room sat a huge oak table with six chairs on either side and one throne-like chair at the head of the table. All seats were occupied except for three—two in the middle and the ornate chair at the head. The head chair was beautifully decorated with gold, royal blue seat covers, and red and gold cushions. The other two empty seats were situated in the middle of the table, on either side, facing each other.

Isabella and Miguel assumed that the two empty seats sitting opposite each other were assigned to them. They moved silently and purposefully toward their seats and were about to pull their respective chairs out when two young girls shot out of nowhere to do the honors. On each side of the table, the girls—no more than eighteen years of age—promptly grabbed the back of a chair, pulled it out, and held it so that Isabella could be seated on one side and Miguel on the other.

Surprised by the gesture, they said nothing and took their seats.

Five minutes passed in total silence, with each member still standing and facing outward.

Then came a loud, high-pitched voice that said, "All rise, please!"

Isabella and Miguel rose and stared at the person entering the room. He was tall—around six feet—with broad shoulders, slight greying hair on the sides, but not a wrinkle on his face. He took his seat at the head of the table and said, "Please be seated."

Isabella and Miguel were the only two to sit while the other members remained standing, facing away from the table.

"Why am I being shown disrespect in such a dissentful manner?" he asked rhetorically.

Immediately, the voice that had announced his imminent entrance appeared by his side and whispered in his ear.

"Your protest, collective disagreement, rejection, dissent, and whatever you may want to call it is duly noted! Please be seated!" To which all members sat instantly.

He turned toward Miguel and said, "I am the Chairman, and you will address me as Mr. Chairman if and when granted permission to speak. You will speak only when asked to. You will not, under any circumstance, raise your voice or leave your seat unless expressly granted such clearance. Is that clear? You may speak."

"Yes," replied Miguel nervously.

"Yes, who? What did I just tell you a mere ten seconds ago?"

"Yes, Mr. Chairman!"

"Very well. Now, tell me—who are you? And what the hell are you doing here? How did you pass security?"

"My name is Isabella. That man over there is my husband Miguel, we…" Isabella's voice trailed off as two young girls—the same ones they had encountered at the third security checkpoint—suddenly yanked her up from her seat.

The Chairman turned to Miguel and said in a strong, harsh voice, "Give me one reason why I should not cut her head off! One reason—just one!"

"ARTICLE 247, paragraphs seven, eight, nine, and ten, page one hundred and fifty-five. Quote: *No weapons of any sort shall be carried into the chamber. No blood shall be spilled during the meeting. No violence will be tolerated between disputing members.*

All disputes, disagreements, and protests shall be arbitrated by the Supreme Council, and a diplomatic solution shall be the only means to settle such disputes," stated Isabella as she shrugged herself free from the hold of the two young girls.

"You do not have a voice in here. You are not welcome here, and the security that let you in will be severely dealt with!" shouted the Chairman.

"Why?" exclaimed Isabella.

"Why what?"

"Why do I not have a voice? Why am I not welcome here?" Isabella questioned. "I read the Constitution and the Code of Conduct imposed on all members, including you, Mr. Chairman. Will you now disregard your own Code of Conduct—your own rules?"

The Chairman stared unblinkingly at Isabella, frothing at the sides of his mouth, clearly angry and rattled by Isabella's regurgitation of the Constitution and the Code of Conduct by which all members were to strictly abide.

"Who are you?" he asked.

"My name is Isabella Katherine Reyes. I have come to inherit my father's seat at the table. I have inherited his invitation, as has Miguel, as our fathers are both deceased. My father was Javier Carlos Reyes Ozabel. He is dead. I am his sole heir."

"Women are not allowed as members of the Supreme Summit— members of the Order of the Brotherhood. *Brotherhood! Get it? Not Brother and Sisterhood! Order of the Brotherhood!*"

"Article 83, paragraph five. Quote: *Upon expiration, i.e., the death of a member, the membership of the defunct member shall pass to the principal heir. The subsequent seat at the table of the Supreme Summit, the Order of the Brotherhood, shall be attributed by legal decree to the surviving principal who, under these articles, is entitled to inherit designated membership.*

Under no circumstances is there a provision stating that only male members can inherit the membership. No article in the Constitution or Code of Conduct mentions any provision that excludes women. I repeat—there is no article that restricts such membership to male heirs. I am here to claim and inherit my late father's membership at the Supreme Summit Council as well as the Order of the Brotherhood."

All the other members, excluding Miguel, stood up and turned their backs to the table. Isabella expected no less from those present. She felt a little fortunate that she and Miguel had made it this far, but still, she was a little apprehensive. She had the urge to bite her nails—something she never did before—but she suppressed it. She stayed seated.

"Sit down! Any more of this silly, childish, disrespectful behavior will have consequences! No more standing bullshit! Sit!" the Chairman screamed, his face turning blue with anger.

Isabella sat down. She had been standing the entire time, restrained by the two young girls. She shrugged them off and took her seat.

The back-and-forth between Isabella and the Chairman had shaken all the members. Nobody had ever spoken out in such a manner. Nobody had ever shown such intransigence toward the Chairman before. This was uncharted territory for all members. There was a sense of insecurity among them now—stemming from the fact that Isabella had a case to be answered, and that they might now be compelled to accept and welcome the first female member.

What would be the consequences of having a female—a child, a little girl—as a full-fledged member of such an important power structure? She had the right to assume her defunct father's seat.

They all sat silently, staring down at the space of the desk immediately in front of them, hoping—just hoping—that the Chairman had a plan to save the day.

Alas, Isabella was, according to their own laws, constitutionally allowed to inherit her father's seat.

Turning toward Miguel, the Chairman asked, "Is she really your wife? I mean, how old is she? She's just a kid, right? Can't be more than ten years old, right?"

"I can speak for myself," shot back Isabella. She heard a faint rustle behind her and immediately jumped up, turning around to face any adversary.

The young girl approaching Isabella stopped dead in her tracks when she saw the swift movement and the defensive stance Isabella had adopted.

The Chairman flicked his hand backward, indicating to the girl to stand down.

"We have to take it to a vote—see the reaction of the members as to whether you will be accepted as a member and participate in the Summit meetings," said the Chairman. "How old are you, anyway?"

"Don't let my appearance influence you in any way. I am an independent, capable, adept, and guile young woman. To underestimate my determination and resourcefulness would be to the detriment of all present.

You, Mr. Chairman, have been lax in stringently defining the legal constraints of The Charter that determines membership and the legacy of such membership. Your archaic, macho, narcissistic stance—one you assumed was inherently prescribed in The Charter—is now back in your face, to haunt and intimidate you. On your own playing field.

To all of you, I am here to stay. However…"

"However what?" retorted the Chairman somewhat meekly, not accustomed to being challenged—especially not before the entire committee.

"However," continued Isabella, "I do have an escape route for you all. One that, if you should so succeed, will satisfy your narcissistic, primitive macho ideology and rid this Brotherhood of me."

"Hmm… go on. We are all listening—oh so attentively," said the Chairman, sarcastic but also clearly intrigued.

Isabella continued with her master plan.

"I propose to the committee—all of you members, as well as you, Mr. Chairman—a challenge. We'll call it *The Challenge*. I state, categorically, that I can outperform every single one of you."

"Outperform how? What? When?" the Chairman interjected, exasperated and flustered that he was no longer in control of the narrative.

"Please do not interrupt. I will elaborate—hopefully without interruption—on the goal of *The Challenge*. I challenge each and every one of you here to outperform me in productivity—that means generating higher trade revenue over a twelve-month period.

Whatever your business model, revenue base, production volume, or sales—at the end of twelve months, we will calculate the total financial value of your trade. If you outperform me based on your end-of-year financial results, you can have my seat. I will cede my position to the highest performer, and you will never see or hear from me again."

There was a rupture in the room. Everybody spoke at the same time, joy and relief in their voices as they discussed openly with everyone and yet no one in particular. There was a rumble of voices as they all appeared to approve of *The Challenge*.

"Why?" said the Chairman, rapping his judge-like wooden hammer for silence repeatedly until the rumble died down. "What's in it for you? Why this false bravado?"

"No false bravado, Mr. Chairman. There are rules that have to be respected. There are guidelines, there are counterchallenges that you should all be aware of."

She paused, letting her words sink in, then began to recite the rules with the precision of someone who had memorized them down to the last comma.

"**Rule number one**: Every member must agree, by written secret ballot, to participate.

Rule number two: The Chairman must participate and ratify the Challenge.

Rule number three: Twelve months of trade and activity, starting from the moment the Challenge is ratified.

Rule number four: There will be no collaboration between members to increase trade volume and thereby inflate financial performance.

Rule number five: My seat will be accorded to the highest performer.

Rule number six: Trade performance will be audited by an independent audit firm, specialized in such affairs. I can nominate such a firm if necessary. The selected firm must be unilaterally approved by all members.

Rule number seven: Any member who forfeits the Challenge will lose their seat to me.

Rule number eight: Any member falsifying trade data or financial performance will forfeit their seat to me.

Rule number nine: There will be no challenge to the audit results. Any member, whether expressly or otherwise contesting the results, will forfeit their participation and thereby cede their seat to me.

Rule number ten: I will accede to the seat of every member that I outperform—including the Chairman."

She looked up, meeting each member's eyes before continuing.

"The audit results will be final. I will attain not only the seat but full voting rights on the committee for every seat I win. Should I outperform everybody, then every member will vote according to my wish. Their role in the committee, their participation, their assigned seat—all of it will be determined by me. To stipulate it bluntly: I will be the committee."

The room erupted into murmurs, the members shifting uneasily in their seats. Some exchanged incredulous glances, while others leaned forward, their faces pale with shock. The Chairman, however, remained motionless, his expression unreadable as he stared at Isabella in total disbelief.

"Now," Isabella continued, her voice cutting through the growing rumble, "are there any questions? Does everybody understand the rules and regulations?" She turned to the Chairman, her gaze steady and unflinching. "Mr. Chairman? Care to summarize for the many with limited understanding capabilities—then put it to the vote?"

The rumbling started again while the Chairman stared at Isabella. He rapped his wooden hammer on the desk, bringing the committee to order. Then, he summarized her challenge, simplifying the terms and clarifying exactly what was at stake for each member.

Once all members nodded in understanding, he questioned each of them individually. After completing the interrogation, the young women standing silently against the walls stepped forward and handed a small envelope to each member to begin the voting.

Fifteen minutes later, the Chairman rapped the hammer once again, cleared his throat, and addressed Isabella directly.

"All members have understood the rules and regulations of your challenge, and I willingly inform you that your challenge has been unanimously accepted. I will proceed to ratify the Challenge and record this event in the minutes of this meeting. You are hereby dismissed. You and your flimsy husband."

"If you don't mind, I will wait for my signed, ratified hard copy of the minutes before being dismissed offhandedly by you. As a parting phrase, I say this to you all: may your uncouth, macho egos permeate your uneducated brains and misguide you into underestimating me."

Isabella stood, walked around to the Chairman, and stretched out her hand.

There was a brief shuffle of papers from the office situated immediately behind the Chairman's seat. A few seconds later, his assistant came forward with several printouts of the minutes of the meeting. The Chairman signed all copies, took out his personal seal, and stamped the bottom of every page. The assistant then prepared a special folder with all the signed and sealed pages, which he then handed to Isabella. He rounded the table and handed Miguel his copy.

The meeting had lasted a full four hours, with Isabella dominating both the discussion and the agenda. As a result, the committee members never addressed the other issues or topics originally planned.

The Chairman stood and walked out of the room without further addressing the committee. All remaining members of the committee stood in silence and turned their backs to the table.

Isabella and Miguel walked out of the room, escorted by the two young women. Just before reaching the exit, the women stopped in front of them, tears in their eyes. They shook Isabella's hand, then bent forward and kissed it.

Isabella checked her phone as it beeped twice. Then she and Miguel stepped out into the late afternoon sunshine. Daylight was fading, and the sun was setting on the horizon.

Isabella had rocked the committee and the Chairman to a degree never experienced before. The challenge she had instigated succeeded only in alienating her and Miguel further from being accepted—thereby putting both of their lives at risk. Restoring honor and saving face were of paramount importance to the committee members. Such insolence, such abominable behavior and defiance, could never be tolerated or allowed to happen again.

Isabella had to go. And Miguel with her.

There were three short flashes in the distance as they stepped into the street, and Isabella immediately recognized the sign. In an instant, a truck drove up and picked them up, heading straight out of town toward the main road leading out of the village. About a mile later, the truck rounded a curve, slowed down, and Isabella jumped out. Miguel was literally pushed out. They were ushered into an open doorway and led up a flight of stairs into an apartment overlooking the square they had just left. The truck continued, speeding out of town.

Minutes later, repeated gunfire rang out, followed by an explosion as the truck was hit by a series of mortar rounds, eventually bursting into flames. Heavily armed men in paramilitary uniforms swarmed the square. The streets were empty except for the military presence.

Somewhere in the room, a satellite phone buzzed.

The man who had led Isabella and Miguel into the building answered with a grunt. "Huh?" He then turned to Isabella and said, "It's for you!"

In a low voice, Isabella said, "Ryan? Yes, all good. Is... err... oh! Great. I'm glad he's fine."

She hung up, handed the phone back to their security agent, and sat on an old sofa in the corner of the room. By this time, Miguel had stopped crying. He looked at Isabella questioningly. He was in total shock, unable to speak.

Isabella looked at him pitifully and said, "It's okay. We just have to wait until darkness to leave."

Miguel sat on the floor, back against the wall, and closed his eyes.

It was past midnight when the satellite phone buzzed again. Same grunt. Same reaction. Isabella took the phone and listened without speaking. She handed it back to the agent, stood up, and went over to wake Miguel.

It was completely dark in the room. It was completely dark outside—no moonlight. Silently, they retraced their steps down the flight of stairs to street level.

Ryan was there when they exited the building. Isabella was relieved. He led them through a maze of alleyways until they reached an abandoned farmhouse on the outskirts of the village. They entered and waited. Still, no words were spoken.

Then the rest of the team joined them, in full military gear and wearing night goggles. They had scoured the exit route, searching for a possible ambush. There was no one on the streets. It was eerily silent.

They filed out of the farmhouse and made their way down a steep embankment. They walked for almost two hours before arriving at a small village. It appeared uninhabited, and the buildings were derelict. Ryan led the group to a building in the center of the village that resembled a bar and hotel.

He turned to Isabella and said, "We stay the rest of the night and leave in the morning. It's safe here."

Isabella nodded and walked up the stairs to find a bathroom. There were two rooms on the first floor and a third room a few stairs higher. She chose the third room and requested Ryan join her.

She woke the next morning to the sounds of voices and the creaking of wooden wheels on farm carts turning. She rubbed her eyes, disoriented and flustered from lack of sleep. Ryan was already up and fully dressed.

"Hungry?" he asked.

"Hmm, a little. More tired from lack of sleep. Where are we?"

"A little village a few miles from Real de Catorce. We have a truck here, ready to go. It should take us a little over five hours to the airfield. Let's grab some breakfast, then get out of Dodge."

The place was not a bar, but a hotel restaurant. They all met downstairs for breakfast. A teary-eyed Miguel was still shell-shocked. After breakfast, they got into the truck and left. There were actually two trucks, and they traveled in convoy.

Isabella and her group arrived at the airfield six hours later. She boarded her plane, accompanied by Ryan, Miguel, and the rest of the group. The first stop was the Hacienda, where they left Miguel. They continued on to SAN.

When they arrived at the airfield in SAN, Isabella instructed the pilot to park the plane in the hangar and to be available at short notice.

At the house, she went straight to her room, where she showered for what seemed like an hour. She washed her hair, put on all the hair products she could find, and scrubbed her body until her skin went a little off-color. Finally, when she was satisfied she was clean again, she dried herself, dried her hair, got dressed, jumped into bed, and fell asleep.

The whole series of events that took place during the summit was well-rehearsed and predictable to a certain degree. But certain details—the midnight walk, the abandoned farmhouse, and the sleeping village—were all off script, so to speak, and had an overwhelming effect on Isabella, not to mention Miguel. Planning for incidents and actually experiencing them are, needless to say, two very different things.

From the outside, it was clear that Isabella was shaken by the events of the previous night. An assassination attempt on unfamiliar terrain would perturb even the most ardent of sentinels. Isabella had provoked the tiger in its den, and the reaction was instant, fearsome, and deadly.

She had planned attacks and succeeded, but having an attack planned against her was terrifying. Perhaps it had occurred to her that sticking her hand in the lion's mouth would result in it being bitten off. That would assume the plan had been to remove the lion's teeth beforehand to eliminate the risk. Pre-planned or not, toothless lion or not, it was obvious that Isabella was now in uncharted territory, constantly looking over her shoulder.

Ryan, without a shadow of a doubt, would lay down his life to protect her. Given the new status quo, he might be called upon to do just that.

Ryan and three other crew members boarded the private jet for Colombia. There was no time to lose. Isabella needed to be proactive and set her plan in motion without hesitation. The flight to Colombia took nearly three hours. By the time they arrived at their destination, Isabella had fully regained her composure and was lucid.

Their destination was a remote airstrip deep in the Colombian jungle. For the last hour of their flight, the pilot flew just a few meters above the mountaintops in an irregular pattern. He claimed this maneuver would confuse ground radar tracking the aircraft. Whether it actually worked, no one questioned.

After circling for nearly thirty minutes, dipping and climbing several times, the jet finally landed.

They were met with an overwhelming show of force. Surrounding the aircraft were military-style jeeps and armored tanks, with heavily armed personnel spilling out to encircle the jet.

As Isabella and the crew exited in single file, a bulletproof Mercedes-Benz pulled up alongside them. In the passenger seat sat a young Colombian woman in uniform. She gestured for Isabella to climb into the backseat. Ryan sat beside her, while the rest of the crew remained with the jet.

The drive from the airstrip to the main compound took only fifteen minutes. When they arrived, a medium-built man stood in the middle of the square. He was bald with an ash-white beard and leaned heavily on a walking stick, a smile on his face.

As the car came to a stop, he stepped forward and opened the rear door for Isabella to exit.

Chapter Forty
Uncle Benny

"**U**ncle Benny! Oh, Uncle Benny, so good to see you! I missed you. How are you?" said Isabella, rushing into the old man's arms and kissing him lightly on the cheek. The two remained in a warm embrace for a full five minutes.

"Bella, oh Bella, my dear. How you have grown. You've grown into a beautiful, elegant, charming young woman! I wish my sons could see you—then they would understand why I'm at a loss for words when trying to describe you to them."

"Oh, Uncle Benny, you are such a suave charmer. You still have a way with words—and still can charm the oil out of a sunflower seed. Uncle Benny, you remember Ryan? He follows me everywhere I go and protects me."

"Ah, my dear. You don't need any protecting here. Even the mosquitoes know better than to approach you!"

Isabella kissed the old man on his cheek again, hooked her arm in his, and the two entered the main house. Ryan followed. After a hearty banter between Isabella and Benito, she excused herself and was led to her quarters. Ryan would be staying with her.

The next morning, after breakfast, Benito gave Isabella a grand tour of the property and the subsequent operation. Ryan was not welcome.

Benito presented his dwellings, his plantation, and the production process—the packaging and the transport logistics—to Isabella. She had never before witnessed the cultivation process, the harvesting, and the ensuing production phase. Isabella was completely fascinated by Benito's operation. It was so well organized, yet all so remote—deep in the inaccessible Colombian jungle, invisible from any and all government spy satellites.

Benito turned to face Isabella. Holding both her hands, he said, "I didn't just stumble upon this location, in case you're wondering. My parents—my mother and father—often came hiking in those mountains. One day, my father looked out and said, 'Let's move out here. It is so peaceful.' And so they left family and friends behind and moved here. They became farmers—coffee producers—plus the usual vegetables, until one day they stumbled upon this plant that my grandmother said had healing powers.

"When my father fell ill, my mother crushed the dried leaves of this plant and nursed him back to full health. Here I am, a few decades later, cultivating this plant for all purposes."

"Do you still produce coffee?" asked Isabella.

"I've reserved a small part of the farmland for coffee production. Helps disguise the main product when shipping."

After lunch, Benito invited Isabella to have dessert on the patio. Ryan was not included in the invitation. While comfortably seated and eating their dessert, Benito turned to Isabella and asked:

"Tell me, my dear, what is going on? Why are you here? I love you like a daughter. I'm happy to see you, have you visit, and all that. God knows I don't even get a visit from my sons. So—what is bothering you? Why the urgency?"

"Uncle Benny, I attended the annual meeting of the Black Hole—at least, that's what they call themselves. The Black Hole. They all wear long red and black robes and masks like those worn in Venice, Italy.

"The Chairman has appointed himself the Divine Symbiosis—the Supreme Divine Holy Vessel, or whatever. He claims to communicate with the deities of the past, sacrificing his body as a vessel through which they convey their desires. He alone nominates and validates candidates for a seat at the Sacred Communion Table.

"When my father died, I inherited his seat at this table. Only, women—especially young girls—are not allowed to participate. Women can never be members of this macho, sacred, secret, men-only club. Except... they forgot to explicitly mention that in the Articles of Incorporation. The Articles state that, upon a member's death, his seat is to be inherited by his eldest offspring. They forgot to specify male offspring only."

"Go on, my dear. What happened when you attended?"

"I received a very hostile reception. The members turned their backs on me and threatened to walk out and annul the meeting. The Chairman, blinded by his so-called sacred powers—and his ego, might I add—allowed the meeting to continue, determined to humiliate and eliminate me without recourse.

"He failed, of course. I challenged them all to outperform me over the next twelve months. If they succeed, I will gladly renounce my seat and any pretense of participating in this meeting."

"How can I help?"

"Uncle Benny, please—I need you to redirect all your production to me and me alone. Please do not supply any other distributor."

"Well, that is almost impossible. I have long-term commitments, long-term agreements with partners that I trust—and they trust me. Should I renege on those agreements, it will cause serious repercussions for me and my family. This is very serious, what you request from me."

"Uncle Benny, I would never come here and personally request such a tall order if it wasn't of the highest importance to me. But I understand your predicament and apologize for even contemplating such an act of commercial treason. Please forgive me. Let us discuss other matters—like, where are your sons and why don't they ever visit?"

Benito stood up and beckoned for Isabella to follow him. They walked in silence down a path leading to the farmland where the coca plants grew. The path veered off into thick brush, flanked by tall trees and dense undergrowth.

They continued in silence until they reached a steel chain tied between two small concrete pillars. Benito stepped over the chain, and Isabella followed. They walked another fifty meters before Benito stopped, parted the underbrush with his hands, and stepped into the thicket. Isabella followed.

Right in front of them stood a steel door embedded in a heavy concrete façade, leading into a cave. There were no lights inside, but Benito retrieved a powerful lamp hidden behind the door. He switched it on, revealing mountains of U.S. dollar bills—neatly bundled, wrapped in plastic for protection, and stacked on pallets. At least a hundred pallets filled the cave, with stacks of cash reaching the ceiling.

Benito turned to Isabella and said, "What will it take for you to win this challenge? See all this? Take what you need. Take it all if you want! It means nothing to me. You, my dear sweet Isabella— you mean everything to me. You saved my life. I will never forget that."

Stunned, Isabella grabbed Benito's hand, kissed it lightly, and said, "Oh, Uncle Benny. I don't know what to say. The funds have to come from business transactions, not from savings or donations. It won't work!"

"From this moment on, all shipments from here—from my farm—everything I produce, will be brokered through you. I will advise all existing clients and update all agreements. Whoever refuses will provoke a breach of our agreement, and I can safely cancel the shipment to them. In the meantime, you need a head start on the brokerage agreement between us, so I will pay you a signing-on fee."

"Uncle Benny! Thank you! The first thing I will do is nominate you to the Black Hole Committee. I promise you!"

Benito smiled with a twinkle in his eye. "Bella, my darling, my daughter—I was once the Chairman of this committee."

Isabella leaned against the wall, unsteady on her feet from the new information. *How? When? Where?* These were the immediate questions flooding her mind.

Shaking her out of her mini-trance, Benito said, "Come, let's go back. I'll tell you all about it another time. When you accede to the Chairmanship—which I'm sure is your goal—I will be an invisible member through your presence. The other side of the cave leads to the airstrip. I'll have my most trusted assistant load your jet with as much as you want."

They walked back to the main house arm in arm. They chatted about his sons, what they were doing, and why they were so obstinate about not visiting. It turned out that Benito's two sons had set up several mobile laboratories manufacturing synthetic fentanyl and cooking methamphetamines for export to the United States.

Isabella was pleased when Benito offered to request his sons to slow production or, better yet, sell it all through her. Benito promised to go one better—he would seize all production, as he was the family patriarch and still commanded authority over all concerned.

On the flight back to the hacienda, Isabella briefed Ryan on everything she had discussed with Benito. The trip was a complete success. They had stayed a little longer than planned but achieved much more than she had hoped for. Isabella had attained her objective with unimaginable success. Uncle Benny's unconditional help and understanding had set her plans in motion. She had a head start.

During the twelve months that followed, all produce out of Colombia—whether from the laboratories in Medellín or from farms in the mountainous region—was controlled and distributed by Isabella. She raised all prices significantly, thereby limiting the margins for wholesalers and subsequent retailers. She then established her own network of sellers with direct distribution contacts.

Isabella had succeeded in bypassing the previous distribution status quo, limiting their respective flow of product, and vastly reducing their revenue to a trickle. The big players retaliated by attempting to sabotage shipments and threatening newly established retail markets with extreme violence and intimidation.

Isabella had foreseen all these maneuvers and put safeguards in place to protect her subordinates. Not only did she have a favorable financial advantage due to the funds she had received from Benito, but she had also surpassed all realistic goals she had estimated necessary to outperform the members of the Black Hole. The funds from Benito served as a cushion.

Chapter Forty-One
Isabella

BACK TO SCHOOL

Commuting from the hacienda to her new school across the border in McAllen was exhausting and challenging. To counter the issue, Isabella moved in with Corella and Ramiro on a temporary basis until she could determine a more permanent solution.

A new school meant new friends. She had graduated top of her class at her previous school. Once she moved across the border, she lost contact with McAllen—her closest friend—and all her other classmates from before. She was in high school now. Her new friends were regular girls from more modest backgrounds. Isabella never let on that she came from an affluent family or who her mother was. She wanted to be accepted for who she was—not for what she represented in terms of wealth and influence. This sincerity she demanded in return from her circle of new friends.

The new school was attended by local students, mostly from the surrounding area. The majority of the student body, whether intellectually capable or not, didn't have the means to attend high school in other cities or counties. Bussing wasn't an option, so they all simply attended the closest school. Isabella loved everything about the school and its students.

On one fine day, Isabella walked the short distance between home and her friend's house. The sun was warm that bright early morning, and Isabella was delighted to see her friends and attend school again. She walked with a bounce in her step, missing the distant chirping of the birds she had grown used to when waking up at the hacienda.

Now, all she heard was the sound of cars honking impatiently at slow drivers at traffic lights, and the constant barking of dogs at anything that moved—territorial claims announced loud and clear. Cats were rare in this part of the city. People seldom had the time or patience to care for them. It was generally considered a luxury, a waste of energy better spent on a second or third job. A few litter cans were overturned, presumably by strays asserting their own territory. Whatever food-like contents spilled across the pavement had already been half-devoured by critters.

Still, school beckoned, and Isabella wanted to catch the school bus with her friend Gabriela. She whistled a tune her mother used to hum while putting her to bed. It was one of the ways she kept her mother close—constant, private reminders tucked away deep inside her. No framed pictures on her nightstand, no lockets with her mother's photo inside. Just personal moments she didn't have to share with anyone.

The day was warming quickly. Isabella was dressed in loose-fit denim jeans and a deep pink cropped top, her hair tied in a single braid down her back. She knocked on Gabriela's door and waited on the porch.

Two minutes later, Gabriela—"Gab," as Isabella affectionately called her—came out wearing short denim shorts, a mauve crop top that revealed her midriff, and white sneakers. When Isabella gave her outfit a second look, Gabriela asked defensively, "What?"

"Hmm… nothing! Just checking you out, girl."

"It's hot already—and gonna be hotter. So," she replied.

"Yeah, I completely get it, girl. You look hotter than today!"

Both girls laughed, slapped high-fives, and walked to the bus stop.

Gabriela was medium height, around five foot six, slim, with medium-sized breasts and long, dark hair that she usually let cascade over her shoulders. She had long, naturally toned legs and dark, black eyes—a real Latin beauty.

"Text Anna-Maria and see if she's already waiting for us," Isabella said, noticing Gabriela glued to her phone, checking WhatsApp, texts, and all her social media.

"Oh, she's already at school," Gabriela replied.

"Okay, I guess we'll meet her there," Isabella said.

They rode the bus to school, both preoccupied with their phones, checking social media and texting rapidly. Isabella was messaging Ryan, asking if everything was okay.

Ryan replied that he was "active," meaning he was mobilized and in position. They texted back and forth, Isabella showing emotion and confessing that she missed him.

Ryan responded with a heart emoji and a smiley face, followed by: *"I'm not more than fifty yards from you."*

"Yeah, but I can't touch you!" she wrote back, followed by a string of beating heart emojis.

The bus stop was roughly one hundred yards from the school gates. The two girls walked toward the school, still engrossed in their screens. When they finally looked up from their social media bubble, they heard shouting and saw a crowd of students gathered near the entrance.

As they approached, the shouting grew louder. Isabella pushed her way through the group to see what the commotion was—and to her horror, she saw three girls beating on her friend Stefanie.

She dropped her school bag and rushed to her friend's aid.

She pulled back one of the girls who was furiously kicking Stefanie in the back while she lay on the hard ground, shielding her face. The girl turned around, ready to strike whoever had dared to interfere. But she hadn't counted on the agility and skill of Isabella.

Isabella struck first, punching the girl as she spun and simultaneously kicking her in the stomach. The kick was so powerful that the girl flew backward, landing flat on her back, coughing and gasping for air.

Isabella lashed out at the other two. She kicked one and punched the other so hard she broke the girl's nose. The second girl, heavy-set and steady on her feet, lunged at Isabella—but she was no match for the local martial arts champion.

Isabella punched her in the throat, slammed an elbow into her temple, grabbed her outstretched arm, and drove her own elbow into the back of it. Still gripping the girl's arm, she twisted and slammed her knee into the crouching girl's face—once, twice—then brought her forearm crashing down onto her back as she collapsed forward.

The other two girls remained on the ground, not wanting to experience the same punishment. Blood was pouring from the girl with the broken nose. She stood up, bent over, holding her face, but no one in the crowd offered any assistance. The heavy-set girl lay on the ground, screaming in pain—her arm clearly broken in several places. Yet, for all their earlier goading and encouragement, the crowd fell silent and slowly moved back, not wanting to be mistakenly associated with the three girls or risk similar punishment.

Isabella helped Stefanie to her feet and put an arm around her bleeding, tearful friend. Gabriela finally made her way through the crowd, and Isabella asked, "Where were you, Gab? I needed you to have my back!"

"Hmm, I think you were doing just fine. By the time I got through this mob, you had the situation under control. What can I say except that I'm glad I'm friends with a ninja?"

"Are you okay? Need an ambulance?" Isabella asked Stefanie.

"I wanna go home. I wanna go home," Stefanie said, weeping helplessly.

"Okay, we'll get you home. I'll call an Uber. But first, what was that all about? Who were those girls, and why were they beating you up, Stef?"

Stef—short for Stefanie—was the nickname Isabella and Gabriela used for her.

"I don't know. They just jumped me. No explanation, no words. They just started punching and kicking me. They knocked me to the ground and kept kicking. One sat on top of me and started punching, calling me a bitch and saying they were going to teach me a lesson. I couldn't defend myself, so I just covered my face. I wanna go home, Bella. I just wanna go home."

"Uber is on its way. We'll wait with you," Isabella said comfortingly.

The crowd slowly dispersed into the school grounds and entered the building. Just another day at school.

By the time the Uber arrived and they loaded Stef inside, everyone else was already in class. The first period of the day was *History of Art*. Gabriela hated this class. The only art she was interested in was painting her face to look beautiful. She never tired of sitting in front of the mirror, experimenting with different foundations, eye shadows, and lip glosses. Looking good every day—that was real art and, in her mind, took real skill.

Isabella, on the other hand, loved school, learning, and art. At home in the hacienda, they had various works painted by renowned international artists. One name that always stood out to her was *Chagall*. It reminded her of *seagull*. There was no real reason for remembering seagulls, but the names just sounded alike.

Just as the girls took their respective seats in class, Isabella was summoned to the school principal's office over the loudspeaker. The art teacher paused her lecture and urged Isabella to report immediately. Gabriela stood to accompany her, but the teacher firmly insisted that she stay seated and remain in class.

Isabella made her way to the second floor, where the school administration was located. Two benches lined the hallway outside the general administration office. Above each was a sign that read:

"SILENCE."

It was not a request—it was an order.

Students summoned to the principal's office had to report to the secretary upon arrival, then wait silently on the bench until called. The principal's office was at the end of the corridor, two doors down from reception. On the door was a large gold sign that read:

"MARCO JUAREZ"

Principal.

Access to the principal was tightly controlled by the receptionist, who also doubled as his secretary. There were no connecting doors between the principal's office and any other room. A sign on the wall, mid-height and to the right of the principal's office, read:

"PLEASE TAKE OFF YOUR SHOES."

Isabella ignored the receptionist entirely. She walked past the reception area without stopping or announcing herself. She headed straight down the corridor, whistling to the tune of Taylor Swift's *"Look What You Made Me Do."*

Without knocking, and without removing her shoes, Isabella barged into the office—still whistling. The receptionist came running out after her, calling for her to sign in and sit quietly on the bench, but by the time she reached the office door, Isabella had already entered and slammed it shut behind her.

Stunned beyond comprehension, Marco—the school principal—opened his mouth, but no words came out. Slowly, the realization of what had just happened hit him, and he stood up, belligerent, rebuking Isabella for her audacity and lack of respect for his authority and personal space.

He was livid. His face flushed through a series of colors—white with rage, then pink, then red, then a deep purple, before finally settling back on a furious red. He was shouting, pointing his finger at her as he paced.

Isabella calmly sat in one of the chairs opposite his desk, feet crossed at the ankles, her white sneakers neatly touching. She smiled at him—not to calm the situation, but to provoke it further.

"What the hell do you think you're doing? Who the fucking hell do you think you are? Get the fuck out of my office! I don't want to see your sorry fucking ass in my school again!"

"Sit down, Marco. Sit down and shut up for a second," Isabella said, smiling infuriatingly.

Marco was a middle-aged, bald man with a goatee beard and a protruding belly. He stood about five feet eight inches tall, thick around the waist, and weighed roughly 180 pounds. Two gold teeth gleamed from his upper row of teeth. He had a round face, chubby cheeks, and small, dark brown eyes that reminded Isabella of a venomous snake.

Despite—or perhaps because of—Isabella's smooth, calm voice, Marco was uncontrollable. He moved around the desk and stood over her, while she remained seated, her cocky smile never wavering.

"Get out! Get out now before I lose control and have you physically thrown out! You little bitch, get out!"

The door opened, and the receptionist poked her head in to check if things were still manageable. After all, Isabella was a student—and a minor—and had to be afforded the full protection of the institution, regardless of the offense.

433

Marco turned toward the open door and screamed, "Get the fuck out! Out! Out!"

The door slammed shut, and Isabella was left alone in the office with Marco.

Still smiling, she looked up at him and said, "Marco, you called me! What do you want?"

Taken aback by Isabella's cool, calm, and collected demeanor, Marco stood speechless. He made his way back to his side of the massive office desk and sat down.

"What the fuck was that this morning? You—"

"Excuse me? Addressing students using profanity, are we?" interrupted Isabella.

"You're rude, have no respect, and a profane attitude, so why should I show you any respect? Huh? Why should I?"

"You were in a fight this morning. You broke a girl's arm and three ribs. Another girl had a broken nose and a broken arm. The third girl had a broken knee and a broken collarbone. The families of all three girls are suing the school—as well as your family. They insisted on reporting the incident to local law enforcement. You are suspended until further notice. Now get out. That's all I have to say to you."

"Why do you ask everybody to take off their shoes?" Isabella asked nonchalantly. "Nothing special in here."

"What? What are you talking about?"

"The sign, Marco. The sign. Right outside your door: 'Please take your shoes off.' Why?"

"You're dismissed. Now get out!" Marco shouted, his voice rising toward hysteria.

Isabella rose from her chair, walked to the door, opened it, and called into the reception area, "Susanah! Susanah, can you come, please!"

"What are you doing?" Marco snapped. "I said you were dismissed. Go! Get out! Go home!"

Susanah, a short, middle-aged woman with streaks of gray in her hair, emerged from the reception area and walked briskly to the principal's office. She stepped inside, and Isabella shut the door behind her. Then Isabella returned to her chair and gestured for Susanah to sit in the empty seat beside her.

Susanah was a second-generation Cuban American whose parents had fled Cuba during the first wave of exodus after Fidel Castro came to power. They initially settled in Miami before moving to New Mexico for work. Fair-skinned, Susanah could easily pass for Caucasian. She was divorced from her Cuban husband, who had left her for their divorced neighbor. Together, they had two children who were now grown and married. Susanah was a grandmother to two boys and one girl.

"Marco," Isabella said, addressing the principal directly.

Susanah's eyes widened at the lack of fear in Isabella's tone toward the school's director. To Susanah, Marco held absolute power over all aspects of the school. To disrespect him was employment suicide. She was terrified of him.

When Isabella addressed him, Marco didn't respond. He was fuming at the flagrant disrespect—especially in front of a subordinate—and yet, he seemed powerless to stop it. How could he command authority after this debacle?

"Marco," Isabella repeated, "when was the last time you attended a School District Convention?"

A deep frown creased his forehead. His eyes widened, his face twisted with confusion and fury, then went blank. He said nothing, offering no response—only a perplexed stare.

"Two years, maybe three," Isabella answered for him. "Do you know why?" She didn't wait for an answer. "Because, my dear Marco, this school was sold by the School District. It's no longer under their jurisdiction or concern. But if you'd been paying attention, you would've known that. Isn't that right, Susanah?"

Afraid to speak, Susanah simply nodded in agreement.

"That means—if you'll allow me to draw you a picture, my dear Marco—that this high school is now a private school. *Duh!* You, Mr. Asshole, work for a private institution. A private owner. If you relied on your monthly salary like everyone else, you'd have noticed.

"Susanah knows. She sees her paycheck every month. She saw the change. But you? No, no, no. Too busy with extracurricular activity—using the school and your position here to enrich yourself."

Isabella leaned forward, her voice sharp and steady.

"Well, Marco—*toute bonne chose a une bonne fin.* To translate from French, that means *all good things come to an end.* My mother bought this school from the State Board of Education for one dollar. One fucking dollar! That's how much the District of Education values this school, its students, and its staff. One dollar, Marco. One dollar—and your value is included in that price."

Marco sat in silence. No comment. No expression. Just a blank stare aimed at Isabella.

She clicked her fingers in front of his face. "Hello? Anybody home? Lights are on, but nobody's home!"

Still no reaction—only disbelief. Marco's mind had drifted elsewhere, calculating the significance of what he'd just learned. No more school board. No more oversight. No regulations. Marco envisioned a new world of absolute power. He was already forming plans—private security, expanded control—not just over the school, but the entire neighborhood. His fantasy spiraled until—

"Marco! Marco! Hello? Wake up, fool!"

Suddenly, recognition returned to his eyes, and he sat up with a slight jolt.

"What? Yeah, so? Private school and all that. So what?"

"Marco, this is *my* school. And you, nickel-and-dime drug dealer piece of *guano*, are fired."

Both Susanah and Marco stared at Isabella with puzzled expressions at the word *guano*.

Isabella turned to Susanah and said, "Guano is bat droppings. Bat shit."

Susanah laughed aloud, then quickly covered her mouth to stifle it.

Isabella turned back to Marco. "You have ten minutes to clear your desk and get the hell out of *my* school."

"Are you crazy? Are you out of your mind? You can't fire me! Do you know who I am? I am *connected*, you little pompous bitch!" He spat the last word like venom, a poison meant to sink deep.

"Nine minutes and forty-five seconds and counting, *Mister Connected.*"

Turning to Susanah, Isabella said, "Susanah, you are the new principal of this school. Go get your stuff and install yourself in this office. Oh, and take down that stupid 'Take Your Shoes Off' sign."

Marco smiled a wicked, cold smile and said with the utmost vulgarity to Isabella, "Mongrel bitch, with the click of my fingers, I can have you pleasure my boys for weeks—maybe months—before they decorate the top of their Christmas tree with your hairless and toothless head!"

"Look at your chest, Marco. Go ahead, look down at your chest."

Marco looked down. He was wearing a white shirt with no tie, and the red dot was in plain view. He jumped up and tried to move away from the window, ducking his head and covering his face with his hands.

"Marco! Marco, no use trying to duck and dodge. Here, take this." Isabella opened the palm of her hand. In it lay a bullet with *MARCO* engraved on it. "This is for you. You now have six minutes before that red dot makes a red pool on your especially bright white shirt. Start packing.

"Oh, and Marco—call me a bitch one more time, and all bets are off. My boyfriend, the one with the red dot, will just refurbish this office with whatever sewer molten your heart is pumping. Five minutes."

Marco looked down at his chest again. The red dot followed his every move. He was marked for death. The realization finally hit him. Sweat began to pour down his face. His eyes widened with fear.

"I need more time. Please, tell your friend I need more time," he begged.

"Truth be told, he ain't my *friend*. He's my husband. The man of my life. My chosen one. He doesn't like gutter trash and sewer fluid like you insulting me and calling me names. Sorry, Marco. Three minutes."

"I have to open my safe. Please turn around."

"Marco, open your fucking safe and take that shit in there with you. You think I don't know about your drug dealings here in the school? Using the students to sell drugs to other students? Using violence and intimidation? You don't deserve to be incarcerated, Marco. You have another sentence.

"Take your shit—you and your connections—and get the fuck outta my school, outta my district, outta my town, and all the fucking way outta my *state*! If I see you or hear about you... even the critters won't want to touch your body. Two minutes."

By this time, Marco had opened the safe, taken out stacks of dollar bills and a wrapped package that resembled a kilo of drugs. He threw it all into a backpack and ran out of the office. He sprinted down the hallway, clutching the backpack, trying to swing it over his shoulder. He ran out of the building and all the way to the front gates. He climbed into his car and drove off, cell phone pressed to his ear, talking hysterically to what could only be assumed were his "connections."

Susanah walked back into the office carrying a medium-sized box filled mostly with picture frames of her grandchildren, a paper punch, a stapler, and a mug half-filled with pens of various colors. Still a little apprehensive, she set the box on the big wooden desk, stood up straight, arms at her sides, and looked at Isabella, who was talking on her cell phone.

She waited patiently, motionless, still trying to comprehend and absorb the events of just moments ago. Susanah glanced down at her shoes, unsure of what to think. Finally, Isabella hung up and turned to her.

"Come with me. Let's walk."

Susanah obediently followed Isabella down the hallway, down the stairs, and out the front of the building. They walked in silence to a large open space that continued around to the back. Roughly two hundred yards out, a line of trees marked the beginning of a wooded area.

"You see all this open space? All the way past the wooded area? It belongs to the school. I bought it—I mean, my mom bought it. It's now part of the school.

"You, my dear Susanah, are going to be the principal of the biggest private school and college in the state. This building," she gestured toward the school, "will be torn down. In its place will be the biggest public library.

"Over there," she pointed to the area beside the building, "will be the new high school. And over there, right by the wooded area and beyond, will be the new college—for students who can't afford to leave the state to attend university."

"You'll be given new directives on what's expected of you and the students when the time comes. In the meantime, acquaint yourself with private school regulations and aspirations."

They walked back to the building, discussing the new project, the status of the new institution, and the proposed library. Susanah had many questions, and Isabella answered them on a need-to-know basis.

When they re-entered the school, Isabella returned to her class, and Susanah went upstairs to assume her duties as the new principal.

She entered the office just in time to hear an announcement over the loudspeaker:

"Attention all students and faculty. Principal Marco Juarez is no longer associated with this school. His role as principal has been terminated, effective immediately. As of this moment, I have been appointed principal of the school and have already assumed my duties. Ms. Maria Dolores Rodrigeuz will assume the role of faculty coordinator, effective immediately. Further changes will be announced shortly. Thank you!"

Isabella smiled to herself. Susanah wasn't that timid after all. The school was in good hands.

At lunch in the cafeteria, there was a lot of chatter and speculation about what had prompted Principal Juarez's sudden dismissal. Nobody seemed to regret his departure—except for a few. Isabella offered no insight into what had occurred. Instead, she listened attentively to the various commentaries, observing the reactions of the "runners" who had been privileged under Juarez's regime.

The day centered around talk of Marco's ousting and the immediate appointment of a new principal.

At two o'clock, the bell rang, signaling the end of the school day. Gabriela and Isabella slowly made their way out of the building toward the front gates. A crowd appeared to be gathering there.

When Isabella and Gabriela approached, just as curious as everyone else to find out what was going on, the crowd parted and let them through.

Isabella stood with her arms crossed over her chest as she took in the three cars—each with two young men inside—parked across the street. As she and Gabriela made it to the front of the crowd, the doors of all three cars opened simultaneously.

Six young men, in their late teens and early twenties, got out and walked toward them. One of the guys twitched his right eye ever so slightly, and what appeared to be the faintest of smiles was evident to the most microscopic of observers. But Isabella noticed. She turned to Gabriela, who winked back. When Isabella turned again, she pretended to rub dust from her eyes. Gabriela moved behind her and hesitated slightly as Isabella kept walking forward.

The young men approached in two rows, three in each, and stopped roughly twenty feet away. The one who appeared to be the leader clapped his hands. The others followed suit.

"Well, well, well! Live and in person—Miyagi-Do Kung Fu Panda! Jeez, sho put on a real ass show dis morning, *beeatch*!" He raised his arms to his sides and lifted one knee, imitating the famous Karate Kid stance. "Whoo-hah!"

Isabella placed her hands on her hips and said nothing. She stood, feet slightly apart, staring straight and hard at the one standing two feet in front of the others—clearly the alpha of the group.

"You broke my lil' sister's arm, you fucking deadbeat whore," said one of the guys, now standing alongside his crew. "I'm gonna enjoy peeling your skin off your whole body while I stick it in you."

"Shut the fuck up, Jimmy! You get her when I'm done with her."

"She fucked up my sister, bro. She gotta pay. She's gonna pay!"

"I said shut up, or I'll shut you up."

He turned to Isabella. "Do you know who I am?"

"Should I?" came the short reply.

"Yes, you should. My name is Kevin Antony Derulo. This is my cousin Pablo Derulo. We call him PD. Maybe now that means something?"

"Hmm, PD! In French, it's pronounced *pédé*. You know what that translates to? Well, I'll tell you—since I can see you didn't make it out of primary school. It means 'homosexual.' Or for crude scum like you, it means 'faggot.'"

"Who you calling a faggot, bitch?! Fuck it, I'll just fucking cut her fucking head off right here!"

"*Stop!*" shouted Kevin, holding his hand to Pablo's chest to keep him from advancing. "I got this."

Hands still on her hips, Isabella asked, matter-of-factly, "What do you want?"

444

"I first want to know if you know who we are," Kevin said.

"I know who your father is. You and *faggot* over there are the sons of the Sicario Brothers. Self-proclaimed Kings of the People Movement. Well, the only thrones they sit on are when they take a shit! Look what happens when you don't flush—*you're* born! I had to hold my breath when I met both your fathers. Talk about sewer waste... they were worse!"

"I'll kill you, bitch, right here!" Kevin lunged forward. As he came within striking distance, Isabella kicked the inside of his forward knee and immediately struck his groin. He crumbled to the ground, unable to stand.

Before the rest of his crew could reach for their weapons, Isabella raised her arms and shouted, "*Stop!*"

She turned, grabbed Gabriela's phone, and raised it above her head. A single shot rang out, putting a clean hole through the middle of the phone. The crowd of students dropped to the ground, covering their heads. Complete silence followed.

Pablo helped his cousin to his feet.

"Look at your chests. *All* of you. See that red dot?" Isabella said. "All I have to do is raise my hand, and you'll be on the same bus *out of state*. Get in your cars, drive away, and never look this way again. Go. *Ten seconds.*"

Pablo half-dragged his cousin to their car. Before getting in, he turned back and snarled, "I ain't gonna put no apple in your mouth like a little piglet when I serve your head to my fucking dogs. It'll be your boyfriend's dick! *Beeatch!*"

They climbed into their cars and sped away, honking loudly and persistently as they pulled off.

Isabella turned to the students still laying low on the ground and said, "Go home and do your homework."

When the crowd dispersed, Isabella and Gabriela walked silently to the bus stop, each deep in her own thoughts.

In Isabella's mind, she replayed the morning's events: the unprovoked attack on Stefanie. How could anyone accuse Stefanie of wrongdoing? She was so gentle, polite, and friendly—she wouldn't hurt a mosquito. Innocent, naïve, shy, discreet Stefanie. Who in their right mind would accuse *her* of flirting? Especially with someone involved in illegal activities.

His jealous girlfriend?

But Stefanie hadn't even set eyes on the boy. Or... had she?

Then Isabella remembered the winking incident. She wasn't quite sure of its significance. Was she imagining it? Was it a muscle twitch? Or was it deliberate?

Not wanting to confront Gabriela immediately, Isabella let the thought slip. But it bothered her. The more she tried to dismiss it, the more her mind returned to it. Still, she resisted the urge for further confrontation. Even if Gabriela was one of her best friends,

Isabella decided to investigate first—*quietly*—before opening that door.

They arrived at the bus stop, both still lost in thought. No small talk. No excitement. No adrenaline-fueled chatter. Just silence.

The sun shone relentlessly in the afternoon sky, drawing sweat from both girls as they waited for the bus. Perhaps it was the heat and humidity that stifled conversation—or perhaps the unspoken accusation from one and the hidden guilt from the other.

Gabriela tied her hair into a ponytail and fanned the front of her tank top, trying to cool herself.

Isabella, meanwhile, stood almost in a trance, unfocused on her surroundings. Her mind churned. How had things escalated so quickly and so violently that extreme security measures had to be called in?

Why? Who was to blame?

All these thoughts raced through her mind—fermenting slowly, brewing into something she knew she'd have to face soon.

Finally, the bus arrived, and both girls boarded. They sat next to each other, still in quiet contemplation. The first stop was Gabriela's. She kissed Isabella twice—once on each cheek—said goodbye, and descended.

Isabella said goodbye, wished her a pleasant afternoon, and looked straight ahead to the front of the bus. There weren't many people onboard—some students from school and a few elderly people, likely returning home from work or the mall.

It was stuffy inside, despite all the windows being pushed open. Clearly, there was no functioning air-conditioning system to combat the fierce temperatures.

Two stops later, a flustered Isabella descended the steps and walked briskly home.

During the week, Isabella lived with Corella and Ramiro. The two had been relocated from across the border and set up in a modest three-bedroom home, intended to provide accommodation for Isabella during school. All expenses were covered by Isabella.

It was a white, single-story house with a modest front garden, a white picket fence all around, and a two-car garage, which Ramiro used for his work van and personal car. Corella didn't drive, so there was no need for a third vehicle.

From the sidewalk, a small pedestrian gate opened onto a paved walkway that led to the front door. On either side, Corella had planted yellow marigolds—flowers that didn't wilt in the summer sun—and a green, well-kept lawn complemented the colorful beds.

When Isabella opened the front door and entered the house, Corella rushed to greet her, pampering her with questions: how her day went at school, whether she was hungry or thirsty, what she'd like for dinner. But Isabella was distracted and went straight to her room.

She changed into her training kit and walked back out. Corella knew better than to ask any questions.

The sun was now lower in the sky and less intense, but the day remained hot and humid. Still, Isabella broke into a light jog toward the empty lot behind the houses. At the far end was a small patch of green and a few trees. She jogged over and began her stretching routine before launching into an intense fifteen-minute fitness session.

Ryan emerged from behind the treeline, and together they began practicing Tai Chi. After flowing through the movements, they transitioned into a karate kata routine. It was a well-rehearsed sequence that needed no coordination beforehand. Like two dancers, they moved harmoniously and gracefully across the grass.

Forty-five minutes later, sweating profusely, they lay on their backs, gazing up at the clear blue sky.

"What do you think?" Isabella asked.

"They got the wrong girl," Ryan answered.

"That's what I thought. Stefanie is a sweet, homely girl—any kind of contact with the opposite sex would be dreadful and unthinkable for her."

"How is she coping?"

"Still in shock, but grateful."

Isabella rolled over so she was now lying next to Ryan. He was staring blankly upward, as if stargazing.

449

"Race you to the corner and back; loser pays for dinner," she said.

Before Ryan could respond, Isabella was on her feet and running.

When they got back to the green patch, it was hard to tell who let whom win—but Isabella arrived first. She fell into his arms as he returned, and they stood there for a few moments, cherishing the silence. She kissed him lightly on the cheek and hugged him tightly.

"They won't let this go, you know," he said.

"Yeah, I know," she replied. "But I'll take them all out before I let them intimidate me."

"I was afraid you'd say that," Ryan said, smiling.

"Walk me home, please," she said, not letting go of his hand.

They walked hand in hand across the empty lot toward the house.

"What are we doing tonight?" he asked.

"Take me home," she replied.

"I am. I'm walking you home—to your front door."

"No, *home*," she said. "To the Hacienda. Home-home."

"Does this have anything to do with today?"

"Business, mostly," she said softly. "But also... I need to go home to find my bearings." She tilted her head slightly to the side. "Come in and wait for me while I shower and get myself ready."

"You have school tomorrow."

"School can wait. But this has to do with the school too."

"How far is the car?"

"I'll get ready while you bring it around. And Ryan?" she added, pausing. "I have plans to erase the current school and build an education complex—grade school, college, and a university. I'll also build a library and a sports center."

She looked him in the eye.

"I need to go home to prepare the funding for this project."

Chapter Forty-Two
Gabby and Mathilda

Ryan drove the car around to the front entrance of the house and waited for Isabella. Half an hour later, they were driving down the highway on their way to the border when Isabella received a text message from an unknown number.

The message read:

"You beat up my cousin. Now I beat up your friend and feed her to my pigs."

"Turn the car around! Ryan! Turn the car around. Now!" Isabella shouted.

"What's wrong? Isa, what's wrong?" exclaimed Ryan as he pulled over and prepared to turn the car around.

"They got Gabby! Revenge for beating those three girls at school who attacked Stefanie this morning. Now they've gone after Gabby. They have her. We must go to her house. We'll take it from there!"

Then, a second message came through, showing a picture of Gabby lying naked on a bed. Her face was bruised, but worse, she was visibly drugged. A young man stood at the foot of the bed, smiling.

Ping! Another text message.

"Thank you for this beautiful puta! Me and my cabrones are enjoying. When we are finished, you are next!"

"Let me see. Let me see," urged Ryan.

"No. No. Not like this. Don't want you to see her like this. I got this."

When they arrived at Gabby's house, Isabella got out of the car and walked around to the driver's side. Ryan rolled down the window and told her he would wait for her, but she declined, telling him to round up the crew and assemble the heavy artillery instead. They would be going in hard—and with a bang. She told him to follow the satellite signal from her phone for the exact address.

When Gabby's mother opened the door and saw Isabella, she began howling like a baby. She clung to her, sobbing and trying to talk at the same time, but her words were incomprehensible. Gently, Isabella led her to the lounge and sat her down, reassuring her that everything would be alright and urging her to calm down.

As soon as she was able, Gabby's mother explained that a young man she had never seen before had picked Gabby up from home. Gabby had told her she was going on a date—to the movies and then dinner—and that she would be home late.

Only an hour later, the phone rang, displaying Gabby's caller ID. When she answered, a young man spoke, telling her that Gabby was with him and that if she wanted to see her daughter again, she needed to prepare one hundred thousand US dollars by tomorrow.

Gabby's mother shrieked and howled uncontrollably again, wailing that she didn't even have one hundred dollars, let alone one hundred thousand.

"It's okay. I'll bring Gabby back to you safe and sound. Don't worry. Please stop crying. I'll bring your daughter back."

"How? I don't have any money."

"Trust me, okay? Please! Just trust me. I said I'll bring Gabby home, and I will. She's my best friend. You sit by the phone and answer if it rings. If they call again, tell them you will bring them the money."

"But I don't HAVE the money. Oh, oh, oh, what am I going to do? Madre de Dios, Padre de Dios, help me!"

Isabella stood and said to Gabby's mother, "I'll be back. Stay strong, and don't answer the doorbell to anybody."

Isabella walked out of the house and called a taxi. Her next call was to Stefanie, telling her to meet her outside in ten minutes.

The taxi driver waited while the girls spoke in Stefanie's front yard. Her face was still swollen from the beating, but she had regained her composure. Upon hearing of Gabby's fate, Stefanie panicked and began to cry, blaming herself for the whole mess. She told Isabella she couldn't go with her—she was too scared to confront the gang again.

Stefanie's younger sister, Mathilda, came outside and asked what was going on. Isabella explained that Gabby had been kidnapped, but it was probably a setup to get to her. Regardless, she was going to confront them and bring Gabby home.

Mathilda adamantly insisted on going in her sister's place.

The two girls got into the waiting taxi and instructed the driver to take them across town to a rundown, dangerous suburb controlled by jobless delinquents and rival gangs. The taxi driver hesitated to go all the way to the address, offering instead to drop them off on the outskirts. Isabella offered him an extra five hundred dollars to take them the full way. After much haggling and hesitation—out of genuine fear—she ultimately paid him a total of one thousand dollars.

They were able to locate the house in question by triangulating the last ping from Gabby's phone. Ryan and his crew had provided the technical assistance that enabled them to track Gabby's last whereabouts.

The taxi driver dropped them off outside a run-down, two-story white house. A white picket fence enclosed the property, and a stone pathway led to the front door. The windows on the upper floor were boarded up, giving the house an abandoned look. Yet from inside, loud music blasted—a heavy Latino rap track, the bass so overpowering it distorted the sound.

Isabella asked the taxi driver to wait for them, but as soon as they stepped out, he sped off without a second glance.

"Stay behind me and just play along with whatever I do, okay?" Isabella instructed Mathilda.

"I'm right behind you. I'm not afraid of these cowards."

"Good. Let's go."

They walked cautiously up the stone path. When they were halfway to the door, it suddenly swung open, and a young boy— barely sixteen—stepped out. He was shirtless, nearly six feet tall, and solidly built, his muscular frame suggesting regular workouts. His two gold front teeth gleamed under the dim light.

Fortunately for them, he was heavily under the influence of alcohol and drugs. He swayed unsteadily, a dazed smile on his face as he stared at nothing in particular, clutching a bottle of rum in one hand.

"Ah! More live action! Hehehe, come here, my lovelies. All for me!" he mumbled.

"Stay close to me, Mathilda. Stay close. I got this."

As the young boy approached, arms open as if to grab and hug both girls at the same time, Isabella kicked him in the groin and simultaneously thrust her fist into his solar plexus. His knees buckled, and he went down, stunned. Isabella connected her right elbow to his temple, and he threw up. His head hit the ground first, slamming against a rock on the side of the pathway, and he lost consciousness. Isabella kicked him hard in the groin again, simply out of anger.

Without looking back at him, the two girls walked up to the open front door and strode in boldly. There, on a completely tattered red couch, were three people: two young girls, barely into their teens, and a young man almost Ryan's age, smoking a drug pipe. *Probably heroin,* thought Isabella. He was sharing his pipe with the two girls.

On a single sofa was another young man molesting a semi-conscious girl. Drug paraphernalia was strewn across the floor and all around the room. At the end of the room was a staircase leading to the upper floor. At the foot of the staircase sat a young man with an AK-47 rifle in his lap. He was clearly drugged and unaware of his surroundings, pretending to guard the rooms upstairs.

Not seeing Gabby, the girls walked to the staircase and kicked the man's foot, indicating they wanted to pass. In slurred speech, he told them that nobody was allowed upstairs—boss's orders. It took every bit of Isabella's training to stop herself from rolling her eyes. This was the least intimidating man she'd ever faced.

Isabella pointed to Mathilda and said, "Boss's orders. You want to disappoint him?"

The young man grabbed the railing and stood up, the AK rifle falling off his right shoulder and nearly hitting the ground. He was in a daze and clearly out of sorts. He stood aside and indicated they could pass.

"It's going to be real noisy up there," Isabella said to him. "Do not disturb!" she added, flashing him a smile.

At the top of the staircase was another young man with a similar rifle. He stood up, alert and ready to move into action, blocking their pathway. Isabella turned toward Mathilda and repeated what she had said to the first sentry at the bottom of the staircase. This time, however, the sentry told her he had not received such orders. He instructed them to wait and not move a muscle while he checked their story.

Two minutes later, he returned and let them through.

Isabella repeated, "Gonna be real noisy. Do not disturb."

Mathilda was nervous now. She clung to Isabella as they walked toward the room at the far end of the corridor. Isabella turned to see the sentry still watching them. She opened the door slowly and, grabbing Mathilda's hand, they entered.

Her knees wobbled, and she nearly threw up. She swallowed hard, gripped Mathilda's hand tightly, pulled her into an embrace, and stood upright.

There, lying naked on the bed, was Gabby. Her body was covered in bruises. She had cigarette burns on her inner thighs and black-and-blue marks on her ribcage from blunt force trauma. Both her eyes were swollen and bruised, with dried blood around her mouth and nose. She was completely drugged and lay motionless on the bed. Three young men were assaulting her at the same time, laughing while filming their actions on their cell phones.

When Isabella stepped further into the room, one of the young men turned his head halfway to face her without stopping his actions.

"Come in, come in. I've been waiting for you. I see you brought me a peace offering. How very thoughtful of you. Three for three. Get undressed. You're next."

By this time, Isabella had regained her composure. She whispered to Mathilda to ease her way toward the side cabinet where two guns lay. Without warning, Isabella lashed out with a kick to the head of the closest man. The impact was so violent that he crashed into one of the others.

Moving with agility and speed, Isabella drove her elbow into the face of the second man, then hooked her hand behind his neck, yanking him downward and smashing her knee into his already bloody face. She followed up with an elbow to the back of his head, knocking him out.

Before the other two could react, Isabella stomped on the groin of the first man, then kicked the side of his head, knocking him unconscious. She continued stomping on his face with both feet, completely shattering his nose and teeth.

The third man, who appeared to be the boss—the one who had orchestrated the kidnapping and assault—stood upright, still unclothed. He was smiling.

"You like it rough, I see."

Those were his last words as a shot rang out from across the street, splattering his inner skull against the wall.

Hearing the gunfire, the sentry came running into the room, weapon ready. Isabella opened the door for him, and he stumbled. As he fell toward Mathilda, she stepped aside and smashed the butt of the Glock she had picked up from the side cabinet into the back of his head. He collapsed, his eyes still open.

The two girls hugged, tears streaming down Mathilda's face.

"Did I kill him?" she sobbed.

"No, you didn't. He fell and hit his head. The drugs did the rest. Come, let's get Gabby and get out of here."

As they lifted Gabby between them, they searched for her clothing. Nothing.

Isabella opened a drawer in the side cabinet and pulled out a pair of shorts and a T-shirt. They dressed her and carried her out of the room.

Chaos, gunfire, and explosions echoed from downstairs.

Mathilda started crying again. "We'll never make it out of here. We're going to die here. Oh, Bella, what are we going to do?"

"Those are my people downstairs. We are not in any danger. Come, help me get her downstairs."

At the top of the staircase, they were met by Ryan and Isabella's three close-proximity security girls. The security detail grabbed Gabby while Mathilda fell into Isabella's arms, sobbing hard and clinging to her. She buried her face in Isabella's shoulder as they walked down the stairs.

Out on the street, two vans pulled up. Gabby and the three other female minors were loaded into one van, which sped away. Isabella, Mathilda, and Ryan climbed into the second van and drove off.

As they left, explosions erupted and a massive fire broke out. The cleanup team was doing their job. The house burned down with the bodies of the perpetrators inside. It took nearly two hours before the fire brigade arrived to contain and extinguish the flames.

Gabby and the three girls were taken to an off-grid hospital ten miles north of the city. It was a run-down farm with a broken wooden picket fence and crumbling outbuildings. The roof of the barn had caved in. Between the half-standing barn and the farmhouse was a tornado shelter. It had a steel manhole cover that opened outward, and a metal ladder fixed into the wall led down into a spacious shelter roughly ten feet below.

This room was fitted out with a large sofa bed, three single-seat sofas, a television set, a fridge, a stove, and a large freezer. Two doors led off the main room—one to a bathroom and shower, and the other down a corridor. At the end of the corridor was an even larger room with five hospital beds, each separated by curtains. Off this room was an additional space that served as an operating theater where emergency surgery could be performed. It was fully equipped with surgical lights, generators, refrigerators, and every medical instrument one could think of. To say that this "hospital" was fully equipped would be an understatement—it was over-equipped.

A doctor and two nurses were present when the van arrived with the four girls. They were immediately transported below ground. Gabby was rushed into surgery, where the doctor examined her for internal bleeding. She was placed on life support and eased into a medically induced coma.

The other three girls were treated for overdose symptoms and fitted with IV drips to counter the effects of the drugs they had ingested. Their lives were not in danger. Gabby, however, was in critical condition. The doctor asserted that the next twenty-four hours would determine whether she would survive.

The van carrying Isabella and Mathilda stopped at Gabby's mother's house. The girls got out and delivered the news. Gabby's mother screamed and collapsed to her knees, head bent forward, crying and screaming and praising the Lord all at once. Isabella dropped to her knees beside her, holding her close and whispering that Gabby was in good hands, that the Lord had already saved her. Tears streamed down Isabella's face, but she forced herself not to cry.

Stefanie, who was already there waiting, burst into tears and hugged Mathilda. It was an emotional moment, with all the girls sobbing loudly and holding one another. It took a while for Gabby's mother to process that her daughter was being treated and had a good chance of pulling through. The doctor had said that all Gabby needed was a little rest and recuperation and she would soon be home. However, it was not advisable to visit her in the hospital just yet—she needed complete rest.

Given Gabby's condition, Isabella couldn't return to the Hacienda. So she stayed and visited Gabby every day, stopping by her house after each visit to update her mother.

Two weeks later, the three other girls were back on their feet. All traces of addiction had been reduced, if not completely eradicated. They were placed in therapy, which was held in the farmhouse by a social worker. Their parents didn't seem to care where they were or who they were with. At the end of a ten-day program, they were offered the opportunity to join the Female Brigade while continuing their education. All three accepted and were sent to the camp to begin training.

A month had passed. Isabella spent her time between school, Mathilda—who had become her closest friend—and visits to Gabby. Gabby was stronger now; her facial bruises had almost disappeared, leaving only a slight cut on her lip. Her eye sockets and ribs had healed. Her internal organs were functioning normally, as was her digestive tract. There were no signs of withdrawal symptoms from addiction. Gabby missed her mom and wanted to go home.

As part of her rehabilitation therapy, she was encouraged to walk and engage in light exercise. These physical tasks, strongly recommended by the doctor, were carried out with Isabella. There were a few old horses on the farm, and sometimes the three girls— Mathilda included—would go for horseback rides around the property.

"You should rebuild the farmhouse and the barn and bring this place to life," Gabby suggested to Isabella.

"Who owns this place?" asked Mathilda.

"Hmmm, I'm not really sure," Isabella replied.

The other two girls laughed out loud and said at the same time, "Oh, come on, Bella. We know you do."

Two days later, Gabby returned home. Her mother cried, howled, shrieked, and prayed—all at once. Gabby explained that she was only home for a week or two, and then she and Mathilda would be joining Isabella at a training camp. Nothing and no one would deter her from this decision.

Mathilda's parents didn't offer any kind of objection. All they wanted to know was whether they would be paid.

Stefanie declined to join them and largely isolated herself from the trio. She had a boyfriend and was not about to sacrifice her happiness for any dream in the sky.

A week later, Mathilda and Gabby left for the Female Brigade.

Chapter Forty-Three
Back At the Hacienda

When Gabby was finally released from care, Isabella and Ryan returned to the Hacienda. At the border crossings—ones they had passed through so often—they were no longer stopped or questioned about their destination. Ryan was respected as an ex-Marine—not just a veteran, but a *Semper Fi* (short for *Semper Fidelis*, which translates from Latin as "Always Faithful"). Sometimes, with the more sociable guards, it was just "RAH" (short for "Oorah"). *Rah* was a Marine-exclusive greeting or enthusiastic expression for anything discussed.

This crossing was a warm *RAH*, and they passed into Mexico. Isabella was greeted by the guard coming to attention: heels together, arms tightly at his sides, and head bowed—no eye contact.

It was still quite warm under the early evening sun. Isabella had showered after her workout with Ryan in the park. She dressed lightly and comfortably in black slacks and a large, loose white T-shirt. She had kissed Corella on the forehead and told her not to fret, as she would be gone for a while. Isabella never gave any information about her movements or plans—this was no exception. Even Ryan was often informed only at the last minute.

They drove in silence for a while, each preoccupied with their own respective concerns. Ryan had his earbuds in, listening—eyes, mind, and thoughts on the road. There was a crackle in his earbuds, and he promptly answered.

"BAMCIS," he shouted back.

This was Marine talk for: *Begin the planning, Arrange for reconnaissance, Make the reconnaissance, Complete the planning, Issue the order, and Supervise the situation.*

"KILL," came the reply. This meant, "YES, understood, let's do this."

The route was secured, and safe passage was assured without incident.

With Ryan close by—in this instance, right by her side—Isabella was unconcerned about her security or the unpredictable behavior of rogue youth elements. She had heard the command *BAMCIS* before and knew that it meant to contain and secure the area—no questions, no prisoners. She trusted that it would be executed to the utmost detail.

The landscape was desert-like, with dried-out tumbleweeds floating across the dry, rocky ground. There were no trees and no clouds. Fortunately, the car was equipped with a robust air-conditioning system.

Isabella closed her eyes and let the calm and quiet of the vehicle relax her mind, then dozed off.

Three-quarters of an hour later, they turned off the main highway and proceeded onto a side road that led to the gates of the Hacienda. It was more than just a side road—it had a dual carriageway with a flowerbed separating the opposing lanes. There were two lanes in each direction. This was a private road; no public use was tolerated, and it was owned and maintained by the Hacienda.

It was a further five miles to the Hacienda from the turn-off. Every half-mile featured a trench crossing both lanes, covered by a metal grid. At first glance, the grids appeared to be part of a rain drainage system. In reality, they housed devastating explosive devices. The spacing between each grid was designed to destroy and isolate any hostile vehicles, whether approaching or leaving.

Along Hacienda Road, as it was commonly called, on either side and hidden from view, were camouflage tents. These positions were manned twenty-four hours a day. Under no circumstances were the personnel to reveal their presence to road users. These ambush tents were heavily armed with rocket-propelled grenades and portable anti-tank missile launchers. This section of the route was, to say the least, heavily fortified and secure. Isabella never expressed any concern to the contrary.

They arrived at the Hacienda, and Isabella proceeded straight to the kitchen to acquaint herself with the new housekeeper. When

Corella was dispatched across the border, a suitable, affable substitute had to be installed as soon as feasible.

In Isabella and Ryan's absence, the domain was managed by Pixano—nicknamed *Pickaxe*. It was alleged that he once punched a tender tree and split it in two. He was one of the most feared and respected lieutenants at the Hacienda.

When Isabella entered the kitchen—her favorite place in the house—Rosaria, Pixano's wife, stopped what she was doing, got down on her knees, bowed her head, raised both hands in prayer form to her face, and greeted Isabella.

"Your Majesty, your Highness, my Queen—please... welcome! Welcome, my Queen. I am Rosaria. Please, anything you need— Rosaria will do."

"Thank you, Rosaria. I am here with my Chief of Staff and Security. His name is Ryan. Please prepare something to eat for us both. We will dine in the main dining hall in one hour."

Head still bowed, hands still raised, Rosaria replied, "Yes, yes, I will execute your request immediately. Yes, my Queen. Promptly, promptly."

Isabella smiled and walked straight up to her room. She had taken over her mother's room, while Ryan was given the main bedroom—the master bedroom—which had once belonged to Javier.

When she was done, Isabella knocked gently on Ryan's door and waited. Ryan opened the door, and Isabella walked in without waiting to be invited. She hugged him and informed him of their dinner plans before heading to the office across the courtyard. There was an underground passage, but Isabella preferred the outdoors.

Sitting behind the large desk, she picked up the phone and called Pickaxe. She never familiarized herself with staff, never shared more than was necessary, and never joked with anyone about anything.

He entered without delay. He had watched her cross the courtyard heading to the office and anticipated the call.

"Ah, Pixano, good to see you! I trust there are no issues that need my urgent attention?"

Chapter Forty-Four
Qir Bank

When the private jet landed on the airstrip near the Hacienda, Isabella, Ryan, and the security detail boarded the three vehicles waiting for them. Out of precaution, Isabella boarded the old, rusty open-back truck parked a little off the strip, with Ryan as her driver. The two girls who were part of her inner security detail boarded the luxury vans and followed.

"Bella, Bella!" the twins yelled as they came running out of the house into her arms.

"Ahhh! My sweet heartthrobs," Isabella said, embracing them with open arms. "What have you been up to? How is preschool? Do you like your teacher? Come, tell me all about your adventures and what you've been doing while I was away."

She hugged the twins, squeezed them tightly, and then walked awkwardly into the house with them still clinging to her. She went straight to the kitchen, where they had a snack and chatted incessantly about everything they had done and learned.

Once the excitement settled, Isabella went straight to work. She summoned Sergio to her office, situated across the yard, and demanded a complete and detailed account of events during her absence. Together, they descended into the underground bunker to inspect the deliveries. With each shipment, she looked at Sergio and asked if he had verified the numbers.

"We counted it all, Your Highness—every single bundle. We noted everything in the journal," Sergio replied.

"Are we short anywhere?"

"With all due respect, Your Highness, no. We are not short. The count is good."

"You may leave, but I want everything ready for shipment out within the next few weeks. I will leave the girls with you for added security. Not a word to anyone about the move."

"Yes, My Queen. Not a word."

With that, Sergio left, and Isabella descended into the ultra-secure fourth basement. Satisfied that all security was intact and untampered with, she proceeded to the walk-in vault. She pulled open a few drawers and took out some exquisite, ultra-rare jewelry her father had locked away—pieces he hadn't even shared the existence of with his wife, Abby. Isabella had discovered them after his death, and they were now hers by inheritance.

She exited the bunker, not daring to wear any of the jewelry—not even the yellow gold ring fitted with the largest diamond she had ever seen, surrounded by rare deep-green emeralds.

Over the next three days, Isabella split her time at the Hacienda between managing daily business affairs and spending time with the twins. She had a home cinema built for them, where they spent time watching cartoons and children-oriented films. She even had a popcorn stand and ice cream vendor cart installed. The twins loved it. They were having the time of their lives.

Content with the daily operations and movements at the Hacienda, Isabella decided it was time to return to school in Texas. Disconsolate at the thought of leaving the twins after such joyous moments together, she sought to ease the transition by discussing her departure with them.

Ryan drove them into town, where they had burgers and ice cream. They went to the local cinema and watched a film about mermaids. While they sat in the diner eating their burgers and fries, Isabella attempted to broach the subject. She explained that she had to return to school and that if she stayed away too long, her teachers would punish her. She promised she wouldn't be gone for long again and that they would do more activities together the next time.

This seemed to appease the twins, but Isabella knew that when the moment of departure came, it would be filled with tears and heartbreak for everyone involved. As a gesture of reassurance, Isabella asked Ryan to assign a girl from the Brigade to act as a personal security detail for the twins. The girl arrived within twenty-four hours, and Isabella gave her firm and precise instructions regarding her role.

In the early hours of the next morning, Isabella and Ryan left for Texas. They drove in Isabella's favorite rusty old open-back truck. Their route was coordinated with the Semper Fi team, who tracked their every move. The road was secured, with no movement in either direction all the way to the border crossing.

At the crossing, Ryan was greeted with a pumped fist and a loud "Semper Fi." The border guard stood at attention as he waved them through. His colleague approached and asked what that was all about.

"Semper Fi. Marine greeting. I did one tour in Afghanistan with Sergeant Mc Sergio. Saved my life when I froze under incoming fire. We were ambushed and under attack. I froze—and he came to get me amid flying bullets and mortars. He got shot in the shoulder. Never forget that day. Total respect for him."

"You're a civilian now. That's all in the past, bro!"

"Once a Marine, always a Marine. We don't leave anybody behind in the field. Bring 'em all home!"

"Whatever."

Isabella asked Ryan to drive her straight to the town center. They parked the truck in an outdoor public lot and walked to the downtown area. Main Street was lined with buildings, businesses,

473

restaurants, and bars—but two buildings stood in juxtaposition to the rest. Directly across from one another and standing seven stories tall, one hosted an insurance company. The other—the one they entered—housed the only bank in town: Texas Rangers Thrift Bank. It occupied all seven floors, although the top two floors were empty and not available for rent.

"Good morning. How can I help you?" greeted the teller.

"Good morning," replied Ryan. "You must be new here."

"No, despite my young age, I've been at this bank for almost twenty-four months," the teller replied.

"Well, it says right here on your lapel, 'Just In'!"

"That's my name. *Justin*," said the teller, turning red, then crimson. He clearly didn't find Ryan's attempt at humor very amusing.

"I'd like to open an account here," Isabella interjected, redirecting the teller's attention and somewhat easing his embarrassment.

"You'll have to speak to the manager," Justin replied. "I'll call her for you. Please take a seat over there." He gestured toward two armchairs and a sofa in the corner of the hallway.

Ten minutes later, a bespectacled, stocky woman with greying hair approached them and introduced herself. She explained that they were the only bank in the county and that parental approval was required for minors.

"How old are you, Miss, if you don't mind me asking?"

"Almost fifteen."

"I'm afraid you'll need approval from one of your parents or legal guardians. Will that be a problem for you?"

"Who owns this bank?" asked Isabella.

"I'm afraid I can't answer that. This bank is privately owned, and that information is strictly confidential."

"Why are you so afraid?" asked Isabella.

"Excuse me?"

"Well, you keep saying, 'I'm afraid.'"

The manager stood up, looked down at Isabella and Ryan, and said, "I don't have time for adolescent games. If you want to open an account, here are the account opening forms and procedures. Good day."

"You like your job, Ms. Ramirez?" asked Isabella. "Because if you don't, then you're on the right path to separating ways with your daily occupation. However, if you like your job and need this job, then sit back down. Open your ears and close your mouth. Answer the questions I ask as concisely and directly as you possibly can. Got it?"

Ms. Ramirez turned and walked away, clearly exasperated. A subordinate came rushing over with a cell phone and handed her the call.

"Hey, new boy," Ryan called out, smiling at the teller.

Isabella squeezed Ryan's hand and said, "Oh, give him a break." Turning to Justin, she added, "What time do you break for lunch? We'd like to invite you for a caviar and lobster lunch."

"What's caviar?" asked Justin.

"Never mind. When do you break for lunch?"

"Half an hour," he said.

Ryan wrote down an address on a piece of paper and told Justin to meet them there as soon as he was free.

Over the course of lunch, both Isabella and Ryan quizzed Justin about the ownership of the bank, its structure, and its clientele.

It didn't take much prompting for Justin to reveal that one Mr. Jack Browser—who spent most of his free time on the golf course— owned the bank and the insurance company. Justin spilled everything he knew about the shenanigans of the bank and its subsidiary, Basic Insurance Company: fraud, years-long delays on even basic claims, noncompliance with federal laws—the list went on.

Isabella and Ryan spent the rest of the day researching and verifying everything Justin had said. They discovered that the bank had passed a federal compliance audit and survived an internal audit, even though it showed the bank had virtually no reserves.

The next day, early in the afternoon, Ryan and Isabella went golfing. They rented all the equipment they needed and set out to enjoy the day on the course. At the golf club reception, however, they were denied entry—it was a strictly "members-only" club.

Isabella calmly explained to the young receptionist that she knew all about her interactions with Jack Browser in exchange for financial gain. She added that Jack Browser was her father and that she would be calling her mother to come down and deal with the situation.

The receptionist flushed with embarrassment and, without another word, led them into the facility.

Ryan lingered back a bit while Isabella headed straight to the driving range. Her hunch paid off—there, hitting balls with vigor, was Jack Browser himself. Isabella sauntered over, placed a few balls on the tee, and hit them into the range.

Her research had indicated that Jack had a weakness for young, underage girls and boys—whichever was readily available. Isabella fumbled a few balls into the close range, muttering to herself until the man edged closer, pretending to offer technical advice.

"You have to stand with your feet slightly apart. Don't hit the ball—swing the club and let the club make contact with the ball."

"Let's make a bet," said Isabella nonchalantly. She raised her right forefinger to the side of her head. "I bet you," she said, smiling cunningly, "I can hit the ball farther than you can. However, if you hit it a greater distance, I'll give you fifty bucks—make that a hundred. What do you say?"

She turned to face him, finger still touching her temple. Her smile had vanished, replaced by a grim look.

"What? Are you out of your mind? What are you doing here? How old are you? Who let you in? Forget it. I'm calling security! You have to leave—right now!"

"Jack, Jack, Jack," Isabella said mockingly. "Don't get your panties in a twist. First of all, your little underage mistress let me in. I told her I'm your daughter," she added, laughing to herself. "Okay, Jack…"

"Stop calling me Jack! I don't know you! I'm not your friend! Security! Security!" he shouted, waving both arms and turning to face the clubhouse.

At that moment, Ryan appeared, dressed in a security uniform.

"Sir?" he said calmly.

"We have a trespasser here. Kick her out! Now!"

"Hundred bucks, plus if I lose, I leave!" said Isabella, pulling a ball from her bag. "Tee up, Jack," she added, turning a few steps away from him.

Isabella placed a golf ball on a tee, positioned herself with confidence, and swung her club. The ball soared past the 200-yard marker.

Jack took his turn. Using the same club—the woods—he swung with elegant precision. His ball flew past the 400-yard line.

He turned to Isabella. "Now get out of my golf club and never come back."

Ryan approached Isabella and pretended to escort her off the course.

"Oh, and by the way, you owe me one hundred dollars," Jack Browser said smugly.

Smiling, Isabella responded, "My dear Jack. Are you Jack the Ripper or Jack the Stripper? Stripping young girls and boys of their innocence and youth. Let's up the stakes a little, Jack. Nine holes. Let's have a nine-hole match between you and me."

She continued, "If you win, I will cover the fifty-million-dollar hole in your bank—no questions asked. I'll also call off the federal audit scheduled for next month, which is likely to reveal that you've misappropriated client funds. Lastly, I'll cover all the outstanding claims your insurance company is facing—roughly twenty-five million dollars. To round it off to a nice, even one hundred million, I'll even pay off your divorce proceedings and your future ex-wife's claims."

Trembling at the corners of his mouth, eyes twitching, his face flushed red—then crimson—then pale, Jack Browser rasped dryly, "Who sent you? I've never seen you before. Who are you? Who are you working for? You're too young to know so much!"

By this time, sweat was pouring down the sides of his face. Wet patches had formed under his arms. He brushed his hair back with his right hand while pacing back and forth. It was a setup. He was trapped. How could he get himself out of this mess? One moment, his life had been perfect—then came the hurricane in the form of this young girl. This baby. Now, the world as he had known it was over.

"You don't have that kind of money. Did your father send you?"

"I have the money. If you like, I'll transfer the funds before we play, but you'll have to sign over some papers, too. Then we both hand everything to your security guard here for safekeeping. Okay for you?"

"What papers?"

"If you lose, my dear Jack the Stripper, you sign over all your assets to me. Everything. Your house, two buildings, the bank, the insurance company, and the yacht moored off the Gulf of Mexico. I want it all, Jack! Everything. Make sure you don't lose! Oops! You lost already. Come see this."

Isabella took out her cell phone and opened the gallery app. She pulled up a video that had been recorded that morning.

"Recognize anybody?" she asked him.

"That's my wife and kids. What are you doing with a video of my wife and children? I'll kill you! If anything happens to them, I'll kill you!"

"Jack, Jack, Jack! Look closely. See, your wife is smiling. Happy. Look even closer. She's taking all her personal belongings.

She's leaving you, Jack! Taking the kids. Going to start a new life without you. Nobody is kidnapping your family. You see all the auxiliary staff there, as well as my security detail.

"In return for a new life in a new state, your wife has revealed all your secrets—all your shady, underhanded dealings, money laundering, wire fraud—you name it. Lucky for you, she gave me everything in exchange for a lot of dollar bills and discretion about her whereabouts. Her lawyers, paid for by 'you know who,' will contact you. Don't worry, Jack. Focus on the game now. Nine holes. You win, you keep the bank and the insurance company. You lose, and you're mine," said Isabella, her big blue eyes wide, her face straight, her voice sweet and innocent.

Unsteady on his feet, Jack sank onto the bench behind him. He hadn't seen any of this coming. His wife's maneuvers had completely blindsided him.

Isabella stood in front of him and said, "Uncle Jack, are we going to play or not?"

After a few moments, he stood up, took a deep breath, and said, "Enough of this Uncle Jack crap. Let's play."

Before they teed off, Isabella withdrew three contracts from her golf bag. Jack studied each document carefully before signing and passing them over to Ryan, who countersigned as a witness. Isabella countersigned, then opened an app on her phone and initiated a wire transfer of $100 million from an account in the Cayman Islands to

Jack's bank. The account's beneficial owner was one of Uncle Benny's sons, but Isabella had been granted power of attorney (POA) before Uncle Benny's death, giving her full control over its funds.

The transfer was successful, and the money was deposited into the Texas Rangers Bank account.

Play began.

Isabella teed up first. Before taking her shot, she handed Jack Browser a pair of field glasses.

"These are for you," she said. "You'll need them to follow the ball's trajectory and verify where it lands since we don't have independent witnesses."

The first hole was about eighty yards out. Isabella took her shot. Jack raised the field glasses to track the ball's path. Suddenly, he dropped the glasses and threw his club to the ground in frustration.

She'd just hit a hole-in-one.

Jack stood in stunned silence. Unbelievable. How? The question churned through his mind. Still reeling from what he had witnessed, he took his turn. His ball veered wide off the mark. They walked toward the first green, with Ryan following silently behind. Jack's ball had landed in the tall grass, forcing him to take three strokes to sink it.

Isabella teed off for the second hole. Same result. Hole-in-one.

Jack Browser muttered under his breath. Something had to be off. Yet he had watched it happen with his own eyes, following the ball's trajectory straight into the hole.

This repeated for two more holes. At the fifth hole, a slight gust of wind nudged Isabella's ball off course, landing it just half a meter from the hole. The putt was an easy one.

By the time they reached the ninth hole, Jack was seventeen strokes behind. Isabella had won—hands down.

"Security! Security! I need to speak with you! If you value your job, you'll come here right now!" called out Jack Browser to Ryan.

Ryan complied dutifully and approached Jack with a smile on his face.

"Hand me those contracts. Hand me those contracts, I say. Hurry up!" Jack demanded.

Isabella laughed and said, "Jack Browser, here are your conditions of release:

"One, you will never set foot in my golf club ever again.

"Two, you will sign over the title deeds of your house to the bank as compensation for your unpaid, excessive overdraft.

"Three, you will sign over ownership of your luxury and sports car collection to the bank.

"Four, you will sign over all the contents of your safety deposit box held at the bank to the bank, including all your luxury designer watches and other jewelry.

"Five, you will pay compensation to the young receptionist and her family for the abuse she has endured at your hands and never make contact with her again. I set the figure to one million dollars—non-negotiable.

"Six, you will voluntarily seek rehab and counseling for your pedophilic tendencies and behavior.

"Seven, you will fully accept without reserve the divorce terms as set out by your ex-wife.

"Eight, you will not leave this state without my explicit consent.

"Nine, you will forfeit and hand over any and all personal effects of any value not covered in the sections above.

"Ten, you will undertake community service work as determined by me—without reserve.

"Jack Browser, you are mine to do with as I please. May God be with you and spare your soul. There is a vehicle in the parking lot that will drive you to your new abode. Be off with you, you despicable excuse of a human being."

The next morning, Isabella and Ryan walked into the Texas Rangers Thrift Bank. They headed straight for Justin and told him to close his till and come around the counter. He protested at first, but upon their insistence, he did as requested and walked over to the sitting area.

After a brief recap of the previous day's events and their respective interactions with Jack Browser, Isabella and Ryan invited

Justin to accompany them to the notary office two blocks down the road.

There, Isabella was notified that she needed an appointment to meet with the notary officer—and that the earliest available date was two months away. As Justin turned to walk away, Isabella strode past the reception desk and walked directly into the notary officer's office. The receptionist ran behind her, shrieking that she was not responsible for this intrusion on Isabella's part or that of her companions.

Samuel, the notary, waved the receptionist away and welcomed Isabella, Ryan, and Justin into his office.

Isabella explained in detail the events of the previous day and the circumstances by which she had obtained the signed documents, which she handed over to Samuel. He studied them, reassured her that they were legal, and stated that he would be registering them under state and federal law.

Isabella outlined her aims and respective targets. The holding company that would oversee both the bank and the insurance company would be named **QIR Holdings**. The bank would become **QIR Bank**, and the insurance company would be rebranded as **QIR Insurance**.

"What does QIR stand for?" asked Justin.

"Queen IR!" chimed in Ryan.

"Who is Queen IR?" Justin pressed further.

"That's all you need to know for the moment," snapped Isabella. "Justin here will be the CEO of QIR Holdings. All employees of the bank and all employees of the insurance company will report to him. He will run everything."

Turning to Justin, she added, "Don't disappoint me. You are Justin; be proud of your name. Don't make me change it to 'Just OUT!' Got it?"

Turning red, Justin simply nodded while Ryan chuckled.

Before heading out, Isabella pulled an envelope from her bag and placed it on the desk in front of Samuel.

"Thanks, Sam," she said. "Say hi to the family for me."

"Will do," he replied without acknowledging or touching the envelope.

"One more thing," she added. "I want QIR subsidiaries in all the surrounding counties and towns. Can you see to that?"

"Sure. Consider it done!"

The three walked out into the warm sunshine, traffic blaring as impatient drivers honked at the slower ones. They walked silently back to the bank, each lost in their own thoughts.

In the bank hallway, Ms. Ramirez was waiting for Justin.

"Where have you been? You can't just walk off in the middle of a busy day for coffee with your friends. Never mind—you're fired. Pack your personal stuff and leave right away. Security! Security, please come over and escort Justin out of the bank."

Everyone stopped what they were doing. Customers were shocked that this was playing out in front of them. Isabella and Ryan stepped away from Justin and looked at him quizzically, waiting for his reaction.

Justin looked at them both. Isabella folded her arms across her chest. Ryan smiled broadly and motioned with his hand that the ball was in Justin's court—it was his move.

When security approached, Justin cleared his throat and said softly to the officer, "Please escort Ms. Ramirez to her desk, allow her five minutes to clear her belongings, and then kindly escort her out of the bank."

The security officer turned to Ms. Ramirez, who was now speechless, and said, "Please, ma'am, don't make a scene. Come this way."

"What's going on? What's going on?" repeated Ms. Ramirez, her eyes wide with confusion and indignation.

"Everybody back to work," Justin ordered.

Then, turning to Ms. Ramirez, he gestured toward Isabella and Ryan and said, "Allow me to introduce you to the new owners. YOU, my dear ex-boss, are fired. I am the new CEO of this bank. As of this moment, your account is frozen, and all your funds will be returned once we confirm there was no mismanagement on your part. Thank you for your service. We wish you well in your next job."

Turning to Isabella and Ryan, Justin said, "Thank you for your trust in me. I want to reassure you both, Isabella and—"

"You will never EVER address me as Isabella, whether in private or in public," she interrupted sharply. "You will bow your head when you see me and address me as 'Your Highness,' 'Your Majesty,' or, lastly, 'O' Honorable One.' Got that?"

"Yes, sure... Oh... Jeez, are you the queen in QIR?" Justin blurted out excitedly.

Both Ryan and Isabella turned to face Justin squarely, their expressions stern and unsmiling.

Ryan spoke firmly, "Justin, yours will be the shortest promotion in the history of anything if you don't take this seriously. Pay attention—I will only say this once. Never make eye contact with Her Highness, and never speak unless ordered to do so. You will bow your head at all times in her presence, and you will begin every sentence with, 'With all due respect, Your Highness.' You will NEVER—and I repeat, NEVER—answer any questions to anybody about Her Highness or your employment contract. Is this clear, Justin?"

Justin lowered his head. "With all due respect, Your Highness, please forgive my insolence. It will never occur again. I am grateful for your trust in me and my ability, Your Highness."

Isabella and Ryan walked out of the bank without another word.

Standing on the sidewalk at the bank's entrance, Isabella gazed at the building across the road that housed the insurance company. Speaking to no one in particular, she said, "This building needs to be torn down and replaced with a large mall. The basement must be at least fifteen meters deep. We need a tunnel connecting the new mall to the bank, and construction should also begin on a tunnel linking the mall to the Hacienda. Get it done, okay?"

She then turned, kissed Ryan on the cheek, and said, "I need to go to school on Monday. I'll be fine. I can manage on my own. You focus on the construction across the road."

Chapter Forty-Five
Summit II

ACCENTUATING POWER

Twelve months to the day—or almost—Isabella was heading back to Real Catorce. She sat next to Father Tomaso on the bus, disguised as a church choir singer. Her face and hands were darkened with tint and foundation. She wore brown contact lenses and dilapidated brown sandals. Father Tomaso had assembled a choir of twelve girls, all more or less Isabella's age—around fourteen.

Miguel was not with them and would not be attending this year's Black Hole Conference. Isabella had never thought to question the Chairman about the committee's name. At the time, she'd been too preoccupied with resisting expulsion—or rather, exclusion. Twelve months ago, she and Miguel had been young, naïve, and awestruck by the existence of such an event and the characters of its members.

The battle was far from over. Unseating the Chairman in his own domain was nearly impossible, to say the least. She had instigated the proceedings, and now, twelve months later, she was prepared for the outcome.

The bus journey was long and hot. The only reprieve came from short toilet stops, letting them stretch their legs for a few moments. Eventually, the other girls' excitement gave way to the exhaustion that comes with heat.

Close to the city limits, the bus was met by a roadblock manned by five guards in military gear. Isabella moved to sit with the other girls, and they all started singing hymns again. The militia ordered everyone to exit the bus. They had sniffer dogs on leashes, walking them in and around the bus before moving on to the passengers. All the while, the girls continued singing church songs. The guards found nothing.

As they were about to proceed with a third round of sniffing, Father Tomaso said to the leader in a firm tone, "My girls are tired. We are all hungry, for we haven't eaten for twenty-four hours now. We are not transporting drugs, if that is what you are looking for, my son. Please, look at the girls—they are weak, hungry, and afraid of these ferocious dogs."

The leader turned to Father Tomaso and said, with an almost toothless grin, "We are not looking for drugs, priest. We are looking for a clandestine passenger. Maybe you have stuffed this passenger in your bag. Which one is yours? Bring it here, open it, and take everything out."

491

Father Tomaso dutifully complied. Having failed in their search, the men were simply out to humiliate him. When all his clothes and possessions were laid out on the road, they burst into laughter.

"Well, she is not here!"

A few minutes later, they were all back on the bus and on their way. Isabella sat next to Father Tomaso and apologized for the humiliation.

"It is nothing, Your Highness, it is nothing," he replied. "Before becoming priests, we are subjected to the most intense humiliation in God's worship. We must be void of all ego, pride, and arrogance and submit fully and completely to the service of the Lord. The devil, the Cursed One, said, 'Pride is my greatest weapon against humanity.' Fret not, Your Highness. God is with us all."

The journey finally drew to an end as they entered the main square in Real Catorce. A few villagers came to meet the bus and reunite with their loved ones. Father Tomaso led the girls, including Isabella, to the church. Sitting in the pews were five men who appeared to be in deep prayer. Nobody paid any attention to Father Tomaso and the girls as they walked in. They went up to the altar, knelt, made the sign of the cross, and then took seats in the front row.

A priest walked out from a side door.

"Welcome to my church," he said. "I am Father Ignacio, and I am pleased to be your host. I have organized accommodation for you all amongst the villagers who will welcome you into their homes. Please come with me. They are all waiting around the back."

Father Ignacio led the way as Father Tomaso and the girls filed out through the side door. Isabella remained seated. Stealthily, the five men advanced and sat in the second-row pew behind Isabella.

"We could have taken them out at the roadblock. Had the girls in mind. Didn't want to traumatize them."

"I know," replied Isabella. "I saw you."

"We've studied the underground tunnels of the whole village. We're good. We placed a change of clothes for you in the Confession Box over there. Father Ignacio is mindful of our presence. We couldn't have sped things up without his assistance."

"Thank you," said Isabella, as she turned and kissed Ryan lightly on the cheek before heading to the Confession Box.

There was a maze of tunnels heading in all different directions. Clearly, village life centuries ago had operated underground. They navigated several twists and turns in the maze and finally followed one that led to the hotel where Isabella would be staying. When they reached the area beneath the hotel, they ascended a flight of steel steps leading into the hotel kitchen storeroom.

The kitchen was deserted when they opened the door—no one in sight. There were no elevators, so they all took the stairway up to the third floor. Before entering the room, Ryan and the crew conducted a security sweep, then beckoned Isabella inside.

Safely settled, Isabella showered and then lay down on the bed to rest. She awoke the following morning.

"Good morning! I took the liberty—breakfast in bed, kisses on me!" joked Ryan when Isabella opened her eyes. "Ah! Those eyes, those amazing turquoise laser-sharp rays of flawless beauty. Hmm… but something can be said about the brown eyes you had yesterday. Certainly fooled those fools."

Isabella, taking a pillow and arranging it against the wall, sat up, smiling at Ryan's comments.

"Kisses on you?" she queried jokingly. "Hold that thought, Don Juan!"

"Don Juan?"

They both laughed.

A distance away from the village square, where the outside crew was setting up for the Sacred Black Hole Summit, Isabella busied herself with her toiletries and personal preparations. She could hear the buzz, the shouting, helicopters flying overhead, and the militia going door to door—no doubt looking for her. She showered again, washed her hair, dried it, brushed it, then styled it.

By the time Ryan knocked on her door to escort her to the Summit, Isabella was focused, attentive, and ready to vanquish the obdurate committee and its arrogant, obstinate chairman.

With Ryan in the lead, dressed in a dark suit, they made their way through the maze of tunnels to the venue where the Summit would be held. Isabella wore a red dress with black sleeves and black lace extending from the waist down and around. She carried a cancan skirt in a bag, which she planned to wear once inside the venue.

Directly beneath the location, Ryan, Isabella, and two of the ex-Marine crew ascended a metal staircase that led into a dimly lit concrete room. They opened a door leading into a study with a large desk and bookshelves lining opposite walls. In front of the desk was a seating area with a large sofa and two armchairs.

This was the Chairman's private chamber.

Ryan and his two ex-Marine teammates waited outside in the hallway while Isabella put on her cancan skirt under her red dress. She was ready!

Isabella opened the door and walked through the hallway to the compartment, with Ryan close behind while his two buddies remained in the hallway. She thrust open the huge, heavy wooden door and entered. There were only two empty seats—Miguel's and hers. Shock and total disbelief were frozen on the faces of all the members. Disgust and utter disdain radiated from the Chairman's expression. A complete silence fell over the room as nobody moved, and all eyes locked onto the pair.

Isabella walked over to her seat and gestured for Ryan to take Miguel's seat opposite her. As she sat down—quite laboriously, given the cumbersome cancan she was wearing—the Chairman finally spoke.

"How did you…?"

"Get here? Hmm… well, surprise, surprise—I'm here. How did I pass through your security checks all along the way?" Smiling, Isabella added, "It doesn't really matter how. I did! Now, what is the first order of business for the day?"

"Where did you come from? The underground passage in my chamber? How dare you? How did you even know it existed? How to get there, how to enter?"

Isabella addressed the committee members directly. "Everybody, I would like you to meet my future husband, Ryan. Miguel will not be attending today. In fact, he will no longer be a member of this committee. Ryan will occupy this seat from now on. Thank you for your understanding. Now, Mr. Chairman, shall we proceed with the first order of business for today, please? I believe that at our last meeting, I issued a challenge to you all. Every single one of you accepted this challenge. So, I would like each of you to write down, on the piece of paper in front of you, the exact total of your business transactions over the last twelve months—including you, Mr. Chairman."

"I dictate the agenda of this meeting! I decide who does what, when, and how! You are just an insolent imposter! You have desecrated my personal space—you and your husband. God only knows how many husbands you have. Like a female canine, for politeness's sake."

"Please place your declarations in the envelope provided and pass them down to our honorable Chairman, who will then arrange them in numerical order, starting from the highest to the lowest. Don't forget to write your seat number at the top of your paper—that way, we can identify you."

The Chairman stood up and walked out of the Summit. He opened the door, saw the two ex-Marines standing in the doorway, and turned back to his seat. His face was white with shock. All blood had drained from it.

The committee members of the Sacred Black Hole Summit were astounded. The events unfolding before them far exceeded those of the previous year.

One of the Sicario Brothers spoke. "Fucking bitch! Who the fuck do you think you are? ¡Puta madre! ¡Me cago en tu madre!"

Before he could utter another word, one of the girls standing silently against the wall, dressed in black military fatigues, crept up from behind and snapped his head violently. His neck broken, his head flopped and banged onto the tabletop. The two ex-Marines stepped in, lifted the lifeless body out of his chair, and carried it out of the room. Stupor engulfed the visibly shaken members, including the Chairman. His ashen face, drained of all blood, showed genuine fear for the first time. He sat muted in his seat.

Then Isabella addressed the Black Hole Committee. "Anybody else with insults for my mother?"

Silence.

"I thought so. Now," she said, turning to the Chairman, "can we please proceed with the agenda? Pass your envelopes to the Chairman, please."

Hastily, they complied. Once he had all thirteen envelopes, including the one from the now-deceased Sicario Brother, the Chairman summoned his assistant.

"Please enter these on the spreadsheet and list them in numerical order."

Several minutes passed in silence, the air electric with tension. The assistant returned with a printed sheet. As he was about to hand it over, Isabella interposed and ordered the list to be given to her.

"I will read this in reverse order, starting from the lowest to the highest earner."

She took a few moments to study the list, then spoke.

"Okay, lowest earner with zero revenue—our dear, beloved Chairman! Really, Chairman? Nothing? Nada? Zero? What have you been doing for twelve months? Oh, I'm sorry—abusing the young girls you bus in from all around. Please stand and vacate your seat."

"I am the Chairman! I am above your silly challenge. I didn't participate and therefore cannot be held accountable for my supposed revenue. I have listed zero revenue because I will not willingly disclose my earnings under any pretense."

One of the girls assigned to stand behind the Chairman approached his seat silently from behind. She towered over him, hands folded behind her back. As all eyes focused on her movements, the Chairman turned to face her. Fear overcame him as he silently rose and vacated his seat.

Isabella stood and moved to occupy the now-empty Chairman's seat.

"Thank you, ex-Mr. Chairman," she said mockingly. "I, dear members, am your new Chairman! My word in this and all future reunions is and will be absolute—no dissension, no opposition, no protestation. ABSOLUTE! As I have outperformed all of you, with over four billion US dollars in total revenue for the past twelve months, I have complete control over all your seats! There will be no voting on any issues, as my word is final!"

Turning to address him directly, Isabella told the former Chairman that he was ex-communicado. His immunity from retribution was revoked, and he was now persona non grata in the entire region. The girl standing behind him escorted him out of the room, straight to the village square. There, he was met by a posse of village parents and inhabitants, who seized him and led him away for local justice.

Back in the Black Hole Summit, Isabella subordinated the remaining Sicario Brother, Alvaro Mendez, to report directly to Ryan. His seat was to be instantly vacated without recourse. Any future progression within the network would depend on structural organization and conduct. He was granted limited immunity from territorial aggression and retaliation. Alvaro was then escorted out to the village square.

"Welcome to the New Sacred Black Hole Committee. Your presence here is by no means guaranteed and is no longer an inheritable asset to be passed down to your heirs and offspring. Your assigned seats are dependent on my personal invitation to each individual, based on their respective contribution to the Committee. Your immunity from retribution is accorded by my grace and goodwill and can be revoked at a whim's notice.

I encourage you all to accept the new status quo and wholeheartedly embrace your prestigious new positions. The direction I have envisaged for this Supreme Council is one that will be mutually beneficial to all concerned, and one that will ensure conformity, respect, coordination, comprehension, and organization at the highest level.

You will all conform to the new Charter, which I will draft at my earliest convenience. Should any member deviate—whether willingly or otherwise—it will be at the behest of expulsion and ex-communicado. You are all well advised to comply with the directives of the new Charter. Unconditionally! Are there any questions?"

All shook their heads in response.

"I have a question. Why was this council of leaders called the Black Hole?" asked Isabella.

The assistant of the ex-Chairman raised his hand, requesting permission to answer the question.

"Yes," said Isabella, nodding in his direction.

"In space, a black hole is one of the most powerful phenomena, pulling in everything within its reach with an immensely powerful magnetic field. A black hole can absorb and swallow even the biggest and brightest stars, billions of light-years away. This council, likewise, has the power to absorb and control any activity it chooses."

"Hmm… Black Hole it is, then. Supreme Council of the Black Hole. A tad long, but that's what we will call this. I like that— sucking in and absorbing anything and everything, even a billion light-years away." Isabella smiled.

"One more thing. You will not address me as Lady Chairman, Chairwoman, or Chairperson. You will all address me as *Your Supreme Highness*—and you will never look me in the eye. Ever! This meeting is adjourned. The council is dismissed. You will receive your invitation for the next meeting in due course. Now get out!"

Outside in the courtyard, all members of the paramilitary unit ordered by the Chairman to locate, arrest, and eliminate Isabella were detained by the crew. They sat in the center of the village square, bound and gagged, bent forward awaiting their fate.

Father Tomaso and Father Ignacio emerged hurriedly from the church, walking briskly toward Isabella and Ryan. They had rosaries in their hands and were hailing Mother Mary repeatedly as they walked. They stopped in front of the group and said a prayer. When Isabella finally exited, the two priests approached her, hands clasped, pleading for forgiveness on their behalf. Isabella, looking exhausted, nodded and walked back to her hotel, Ryan by her side.

Seven days later, Isabella, Ryan, and the crew were still in Real de Catorce. A convoy of trucks transporting various goods had been ordered to the village by Isabella. One truck was filled to the brim with clothing for children of all ages. Another truck carried canned food, bottled water, hygiene products, baby food, baby formula, and a pallet of currency. The funds were given to Father Ignacio, who was tasked with overseeing their equitable distribution among the villagers.

On the seventh day, a helicopter flew into the village and landed in the main square. Four men dressed in smart suits exited and went straight to the council room. They were escorted from the helicopter by two girls from Isabella's security detail.

Two hours later, a second helicopter landed in the village square. This time, only two men exited the chopper. They, too, were escorted to the council chambers.

There, on the lower floor, the two parties were kept apart. They sat and waited. After what seemed like an eternity, they were ushered into the chamber and seated on opposite sides of the grand table.

Several minutes later, Isabella and Ryan walked in with six girls in tow, all still dressed in their paramilitary uniforms. Isabella was dressed in a long black gown with red lace sleeves and a black veil covering her face. She sat at the head of the table, with one team to her right and the other to her left. Ryan and the girls stood in the background.

Isabella turned to her right, facing the team of two men.

"Do you know why I had you brought here?" she asked.

"Yes. I was kidnapped by your goons and brought against my will," said the round-faced man sitting on her right.

"You have both been summoned here…"

"Who are you anyway? Some kid that thinks this is a game? Playing with people's lives like this," interjected the round-faced man.

"Enough!" snapped Isabella. "Anyone who speaks out of turn again will be restrained in the most unpleasant manner."

She lifted the veil, her turquoise-blue eyes staring coldly first to her right, then to her left.

"You two men and your respective political parties and activists are creating wanton violence in your country, and innocent people are paying the price. Collateral damage, you may argue, but this must stop—and it must stop now!"

Turning first to her right, then to her left, she continued.

"Do you know where you are? I will enlighten you. You have the privilege of being before the *Supreme Council of the Black Hole.* No entity in the world is higher than this congress. We mediate and recommend solutions to disputes that garner our attention. Today, we will hear your arguments. Then I will retire to my quarters to balance your dissension and declare my resolution. Mr. Medro, you may speak. You have ten minutes."

The delegation on Isabella's left, the four men led by Mr. Medro, huddled together, whispering, before the leader rose to speak.

"You may remain seated, Mr. Medro. Your allotted time has already begun."

"On Friday, Venezuela's election authority ratified my victory— *our* undisputed victory. My party won about 52% of the votes to Mr. Guzman's 43%, from 97% of the votes counted. The opposition has produced fake evidence to contest the result. We believe that third-country intervention is behind this farce and attempted coup. We will not yield. The opposition—that man sitting there opposite me— is responsible for spreading false information and encouraging violence in Venezuela."

The four men huddled together again. Then a second man spoke.

"Your Highness, my name is Machado Rodríguez. I have here a letter signed by Mr. Guzman of his own volition. I have strongly requested that Mr. Guzman take back his claim that he won the elections. I have audio evidence of our conversation debunking the opposition candidate's claims. However, Mr. Guzman claims that he was forced to sign the letter under duress. To that, I say this: if you signed under pressure, how is it that one of your daughters still lives peacefully in Venezuela with her family, just like any regular Venezuelan?

You see, Venezuelans may think one way or another, but all of them have a place in the territory of the Bolivarian Republic of Venezuela. Here, there is no place for violence or fascism."

Mr. Medro then showed photos of an alleged meeting between himself, Vice President Delacruz, Mr. Rodríguez, and Mr. Guzman at the Spanish Embassy in Caracas on the eve of the opposition candidate's departure earlier this month. Prior to his departure for Spain, a Venezuelan judge had issued an arrest warrant for Mr. Guzman, accusing him of conspiracy, forging documents, and other "serious crimes"—all of which Mr. Guzman has denied.

Further evidence handed to Isabella showed that Venezuela's National Electoral Council (CNE) claims Maduro, 61, won 52% of the vote in the July 28 elections, while González received 43%.

"Thank you," said Isabella, addressing Mr. Medro's delegation. "Your time is up. Mr. Guzman, you have ten minutes starting now. Please begin your counterclaim."

505

"Thank you, whoever you are."

A young girl approached ever so silently and swiftly behind Mr. Guzman and whispered in his ear.

"Please forgive me, Your Highness. Thank you for allowing me to speak. That letter they have produced—I was forced to sign it, forced to recognize Mr. Nicholas Medro as the winner of the election. I sought asylum in the Spanish Embassy in Caracas. In exchange for my freedom to leave the country and seek asylum in Spain, I was coerced into signing that letter, which means absolutely nothing.

The Venezuelan Electoral Council announced Mr. Medro as the winner, but I won this election by a landslide, and we have undeniable proof. My campaign aides have obtained receipts from more than 80% of polling stations, confirming my overwhelming victory. I have convincingly defeated Mr. Medro. Thank you."

Isabella looked up at Ryan and nodded discreetly. The delegations were ushered out of the main chamber into separate lounges on either side of the room. Isabella rose and retired to her personal quarters.

An hour later, the delegations were brought back, and Isabella entered. She had changed her attire and was now wearing black pants with a gold shirt, flat shoes, and a long, flowing white and gold open robe.

She took her seat, then nodded to the assistant. On a large screen fitted to the wall at the far end of the room, a video began to play. The footage showed a woman and her three children alighting from a private jet before being whisked away in a luxury van. Each family member had Hawaiian leis placed around their necks as they disembarked.

Mr. Medro jumped up from his seat, shouting, "What is the meaning of this? This is my family! My family!"

One of the girls swiftly approached Mr. Medro from behind and thrust him back in his seat. She whispered in his ear, "Sit, be quiet, or I'll make you quiet."

"You are correct, Mr. Medro. This *is* your family. Please continue to watch."

The video then showed the family arriving in an exclusive, affluent suburb, disembarking from the vehicle, and being presented with the front door keys to a magnificent house. The woman shrieked with excitement as the children ran around the garden, shouting and screaming in delight.

She then approached the camera, formed a heart shape with her fingers, kissed the lens, and mouthed, "Thank you, darling. See you soon."

Visibly shaken and traumatized, Mr. Medro whispered in a meek voice, "Please, please don't hurt my family. I'll do whatever it takes. Just spare my wife and children."

"Mr. Medro," Isabella said, "your family is safe. What you just witnessed was their arrival in Hawaii. They have been relocated at my request to a new home, where they will now settle indefinitely.

You, Mr. Medro, have a choice. You can join them in exile and live out your days in peace, or you can choose martyrdom and wither away in detention—somewhere. Your associates, however, do not have the luxury of choosing their destiny. They will be exiled to a country of my choosing—somewhere close.

So, what will it be, Mr. Medro? Martyrdom or freedom? Never again will you enter politics. But before you make a decision— perhaps an erroneous one—I want you to meet a third delegation invited to this hearing."

Isabella nodded to the girls, who opened the door and led in four men and a woman. Three of them were dressed in smart military uniforms, while the other two—a man and a woman—were dressed in formal civilian attire.

"I'm sure you are well acquainted with Army General Rodrigo, Navy Admiral Pedro, Elite Special Forces Commander Johnny Calvo, Alexandro Jiminez, head of the Venezuelan Secret Service, and Angela Machado, Chief of Police and Internal Affairs."

Sweating, Mr. Medro buried his face in his hands and sobbed silently.

"I accept, I accept!" he wept.

"Well, what exactly do you accept, Mr. Medro?" Isabella asked, her voice devoid of emotion.

"I accept to join my family and renounce all political aspirations, now and indefinitely. Please, please let me go and join my family."

"Very well. I must inform you that you will be under constant surveillance. Any deviation from what you have been assigned will result in the extermination of you and your entire family."

Isabella nodded to the girls, who led Mr. Medro out of the hearing. A helicopter flew him down to the airstrip, where a jet was waiting to take him to join his family.

Back in the large chamber, Isabella produced a set of papers and handed them to Mr. Guzman and the five new arrivals.

Elated by the outcome of the meeting, Mr. Guzman eagerly grasped the papers and began skimming through them. However, he soon paused, then resumed reading more carefully. His expression grew grim as he reread the documents, this time with greater scrutiny. Looking up, he muttered to no one in particular, "These are contracts."

"Mr. Guzman," said Isabella. "Victory has a price. Fate has a price. Life, Mr. Guzman, has a price. You have the unequivocal support of the most influential elements in the Venezuelan political spectrum. However, you do not have the mandate to govern alone. You are merely the face of the decision-making process that will govern Venezuela.

I do not need your signature on any of those documents, as they have already been approved by the delegation before you. You are duly informed."

"This is outrageous! You have literally appropriated the country's only lifeline—our only bread and butter, without which there is no country. Is this the price I have to pay? I cannot and will not connive in such an abhorrent violation and abscission of our economic lifeline."

Isabella nodded, and the girl standing behind Mr. Guzman approached and whispered in his ear, "You are dispensable. Look around you."

"My father was Spanish. My grandfather shaped the Spanish political landscape and groomed its political participants to his ideology. I have inherited my family's vast fortune in Spain, accumulated by my grandfather. My family's influence—nay, *my* influence—in all aspects of political life in Spain is immeasurable."

Your exile to Spain will be revoked should I wish it to be. You will be granted retirement in Hawaii, like your predecessor. Your retirement, Mr. Medro, will be right here in this village."

Isabella addressed the girl still standing directly behind Mr. Medro. "Please escort Mr. Medro to the church and ask Father Ignacio to find a role for him here in the village."

"Perhaps I have been too hasty in my remarks, Your Highness. Please accord me a minute to comprehend the key components of these contracts."

Having re-read the contracts put before him, Mr. Medro signed every page of each one.

The contracts granted Isabella and the Supreme Council of The Black Hole exclusive future rights to oil drilling, extraction, and production for all Venezuelan oil. Under the agreement, the Venezuelan government would receive a fixed U.S. dollar amount per barrel, with no discussion on this amount.

Furthermore, the Governor of the Venezuelan Central Bank would be appointed by Isabella. The military, police, secret service, and navy would all be funded directly by her. The entire Venezuelan economy was now in the hands of Isabella and the Supreme Council.

Before adjourning the meeting, she invited the ranking military commander, General Rodrigo, to attend the next congregation of the Supreme Council in twelve months' time. He was delighted and honored.

Mr. Medro was not invited.

Chapter Forty-Six
Uncle Benny Demise

Overjoyed at her rapid ascension, Isabella sought to share her euphoria with her close entourage. She invited six of the girls and the entire ex-Marine crew to join her on a trip to Colombia to visit Uncle Benny and share her success with him.

The jet landed on the airstrip adjacent to the farm. Strangely, they were not met by anybody. This was totally uncharacteristic of operations under Uncle Benny. Ryan led the way through the jungle path toward *La Casa Verde*, the name of Uncle Benny's farm.

The group trudged through the greenery until they came upon the green villa. The usual hustle and bustle were conspicuously lacking, and Isabella was anxious that something was amiss. Ryan, true to his instincts, ordered the group to split into three. He would head Alpha Team. Roger, one of the most trusted crew members, took three girls and headed Echo Team, while the remaining members followed Mike in Team Zee. The three teams spread out and encircled the *Casa Verde* villa.

Isabella, taking the lead from Ryan, walked straight up to the front door, pushed it open, and called out to the maid.

"Maria Dores? Hello, Maria Dores, are you here?"

There was an eerie silence in the big villa. Echo Team came up from behind the house, dragging the gardener with them.

"It's okay," said Isabella. "I know him. He's good." Addressing the gardener, she asked, "What is going on? Where is everybody?"

"Señor Benito," was all he could utter.

"Where is Señor Benito? Where? What happened to him?"

"Señor Benito—*infarto de miocardio. Ataque del corazón.*"

"Where did they take him? Come on, where? Where is he?"

"Hospital Medellín, Su Alteza. Medellín."

"Where is Maria Dores?"

"Compound, Su Alteza."

Perturbed, Isabella issued orders to the three teams. Team Alpha would accompany her to Medellín. They would fly there; she knew where there was an airstrip to land on. Team Echo and Team Zee would secure the perimeter and not allow any movement in or out until they returned. Satellite communication would be the only means of contact.

Alpha Team worked their way back to the jet. They boarded and flew to Medellín. Isabella had used the gardener's cell phone to call ahead for a pickup and direct transport to the hospital.

When she entered the hospital room, she was shocked to see all the tubes Uncle Benny was attached to. Her eyes opened wide, her face—drained of color—was ash white as she clasped both hands over her face. She sat on the chair next to his bed, and tears flowed down her cheeks. She sobbed silently at the sight of her beloved Uncle Benny connected to all these life-supporting tubes and machines.

"Oh, Uncle Benny, oh, Uncle Benny, why, why, why, why? You were so strong, so full of life. Why, oh why?"

The door to the room pushed open, and two young men walked in. Isabella paid no notice, barely glancing up to acknowledge the two intruders.

"What are you doing here? Who are you?" said one of the men.

"What the fuck… get away from my father," said the other.

"Our father," chimed in the first speaker.

Isabella stood slowly, wiped the tears from her eyes, and walked toward the two men. She stopped right before them and said, "You must be Benito Alvarez Jr., and you must be Santana Alvarez—Carlos, as you like to be called. After the musician."

She walked past the two astounded men, who stood there speechless.

As Isabella walked past them, they turned around to address her and said in unison, "And who are YOU?"

"I am Isabella. The man lying there is my Uncle Benny. Your father. No blood relation, but he is the only man I look up to like a father. Your loss is my loss too." And she walked out.

Twenty-four hours later, Benito Alvarez Dos Almeidas expired.

At the hospital, Isabella crossed paths with the two brothers again.

"The funeral is in five days. We will follow Uncle Benny's last wishes to the letter. He will be buried on the grounds of *Casa Verde*. We will have a showing at *Casa Verde* for two days for all to pay their last respects. We will not wait for latecomers." She turned around and exited the hospital. She never heard the vile and vulgar exclamations from the two brothers.

On the day of the funeral, the two brothers, Benito Jr. and (Carlos) Santana, stood near the hearse, wearing dark suits and dark glasses. They assisted in carrying the casket from the hearse to the gravesite. Once the casket was placed on the stand, they sat next to each other, somber-looking.

After the priest concluded his sermon and prayers, Isabella stood up.

"Uncle Benny, this was too sudden. You were never ill a day in your life, except for the one time when you first visited my parents' home. We bonded from that fateful day, and you became my beloved Uncle Benny. But you were more!

515

The blood of the covenant is thicker than the water of the womb. I was your blood of the covenant. You called me your daughter; you protected me like one. A piece of my heart is buried with you here today.

You are NOT in a better place. A better place is HERE! With ME! Oh, Uncle Benny!"

And she wept outwardly. Ryan stepped forward, put his arm around her, and she buried her face in his chest.

A wake was held in the main dining hall back at *Casa Verde*. Most of the attendees were employees of the villa and the plantation. No observers or acquaintances were invited for security reasons.

At one point, a man wearing a beige suit and carrying a backpack approached the two brothers. After a brief conversation, the three men silently left the room and headed for Benito's study.

Hardly a minute had passed when the man approached Isabella and explained who he was.

"Miss Isabella…"

"I know who you are. You will address me as *My Lady*, for now."

"My Lady Isabella, I am Juanito Jorge, Señor Benito's most trusted attorney and confidant. I have Mr. Benito's last testament, and I would like to seize this opportunity to read and execute his last wishes while all parties are present. Would you kindly follow me to the study, please?"

When Juanito Jorge accompanied Isabella into Benito's study, the two brothers stood up and protested.

"What is she doing here? She has no business here!" Benito Jr. barked.

Santana looked past Juanito and spoke directly to Isabella.

"This is personal. It has nothing to do with you. You have already created enough havoc and immensely embarrassed my brother and me. You have overstayed your welcome. Will you and your troops please leave my father's property—OUR property—and never come back. Now, please!"

"Everyone, calm down, please! Please be seated. I have the last testament of one Benito Alvarez Dos Almeidas Sr. I have been appointed executor. That is the purpose of this meeting. I ask you all to please be patient while I read the will. You are all involved. Thank you."

The room fell silent, though the air remained thick with tension. Benito Jr. and Santana exchanged a glance, their expressions a mix of curiosity and unease. Reluctantly, they sat down, their eyes never leaving Juanito as he unfolded the document and began to read.

"To my son, Benito Alvarez Dos Almeidas Jr., I bequeath you the following:

1. *A bank account held with Sunset Investment Bank, Antigua. The account number and details are with Mr. Jorge.*

2. *The building in Manhattan, NY. The exact address, the title deeds, and all relevant information are held with Mr. Jorge, who will assist you in managing this affair.*

3. *Two office blocks situated in the heart of London's business district.*

4. *All stocks and shares held in Pear Electronics.*

5. *All stocks and shares held in GenZee Software Development.*

6. *My yacht, The Al Meidas, moored off the coast of Aruba.*

To my son, Santana Alvarez, I bequeath you the following:

1. *A bank account held in Moonwalk Trust and Investment Bank, Barbados. Account number and details with Mr. Jorge.*

2. *The entire block of office space and apartment buildings in downtown Bogotá. Details with Mr. Jorge.*

3. *The island of Jiminez in the Caribbean Sea.*

4. *My custom-made Boeing 888.*

5. *All stocks and shares held in Belleza Extrema beauty products.*

6. *Castle Mary in Scotland, UK.*

To the daughter I never had, Isabella Katherine Reyes, I leave you the love of my life: *Casa Verde* and everything in it.

I have drawn up the transfers of ownership, title deeds, and beneficial ownership of all trusts right here. Please initial every page and sign in full on the last page."

"Who reads a will on the same day the person is buried, anyway? This is a legal process that has to pass through the courts, probate, and the will's executors. You can't just walk in here, read all this crap, distribute everything as you wish, expect us to sign, and then everything is hunky-dory!" proclaimed Benito Jr.

"Do I need to remind you all exactly how your father accumulated his wealth?" said the probate lawyer firmly. "You think he did this through the courts? Huh? No, no, no, people. This was all undisclosed. You have ownership and control. You are beneficial owners, but you cannot step in and start attempting to actually run the businesses. You are owners, and you will be compensated accordingly.

Please do not ruffle the feathers of the authorities in these various jurisdictions or cause any ripples. Lay low, please."

Juanito Jorge passed the contracts around to each person. Isabella signed hers, tears streaming down her cheeks as she stood up and left the room. She knew what "everything in it" meant—the cave Benito had taken her to, the contents he had privileged her to see. It was just too much for Isabella. She was overwhelmed with grief and emotionally overcome with gratitude.

As she was leaving, Mr. Jorge handed her a small, sealed envelope. It was marked *QIR*. She opened the letter as she walked out.

Chapter Forty-Seven
Columbia – La Casa Verda

The next morning, Isabella, Ryan, and the security staff took a short helicopter ride down to the airstrip, where the private jet was waiting. They flew directly to *La Casa Verde* in Colombia. The first order of the day was a visit to Uncle Benny's tomb. She spent an hour there—cleaning, watering, and talking to him.

Next was business. She summoned the man she had left in charge and discussed the crops and production. Everything was running smoothly, with no major issues requiring special attention. Neither of Uncle Benny's two sons had visited *La Casa Verde* since the funeral, and Isabella was fine with that. She didn't want them meddling in her affairs.

When all seemed relatively calm, Isabella invited Ryan to join her on a quad bike ride into the forest. They rode for a while until they reached the ridge that hid a cave below. They walked a few hundred yards, as the terrain was inaccessible for the quads. Isabella disappeared behind a large boulder and called for Ryan to follow.

At first, he was at a loss, trying to figure out where she had gone. She called out to him again, and he followed. Inside the huge cave, they found wooden crates filled with stacks of U.S. dollar bills, all wrapped in plastic. There was close to five hundred million dollars in total packed into the crates. Uncle Benny had left all of this to Isabella as his "thank you" for saving his life.

As Isabella and Ryan walked around the crates, they discussed transporting them by plane to the Hacienda. Isabella suggested that Ryan order a cargo plane to fly down and meet them at *La Casa Verde*. They would personally supervise the loading of the crates onto the aircraft.

When they arrived back at the main house, Isabella and Ryan were met by a convoy of Colombian military officers and subordinates. Four military trucks carried soldiers, while two luxury cars transported two generals and four other high-ranking officers.

Surprised by the unannounced visit, Isabella called over her foreman and whispered in his ear. He turned to her and shrugged. This had never happened before.

"How can I help?" said Ryan.

The first general stepped forward. "Do we look lost?" Turning to the other general, he asked, "Are we lost?"

The second general turned to the four officers and said, "Are we lost?"

The officers turned to the soldiers disembarking from the trucks, asking, "Are you lost? Are we lost?"

The soldiers snapped to attention, their voices ringing out in unison. "Sir, no, sir!"

"See, we are not lost. We do not need your help," said the first general.

"So what do you want?" said Isabella impatiently. "This is private property, not a military campsite. Either you state why you are here, or you leave!"

"Ah! She is direct! Straight to the point. No dilly-dallying, as they say! So, I go to your point as well. We came to take over. Benito is no longer alive—but we are! This is our country; you are an intruder! We came to take what is rightfully ours. We do not discuss; we do not ask. We take!"

Turning to the troops, the general gave the order to disembark and take up attacking positions.

In response, Isabella raised her hand, keeping it in the air, and said to the two generals and the four officers, "When I lower my hand, all six of you will be dead. Look at your chests, each of you."

The Colombian military officers looked down and noticed red dots on each of their chests. The first general turned to address his troops and issue a stand-down order—only to see that all the soldiers had already been overpowered, guns held to their heads.

"What's it gonna be, General? Ask, discuss, or take? Shall I lower my hand?"

"No! No, no! Please, no!" All six officers dropped to their knees, pleading for clemency and forgiveness for their gross error in judgment.

Isabella lowered her hand, and the six officers collapsed, shot by her security team. The remaining troops were ordered back onto the trucks and transported deep into the Colombian jungle, where they were put to work digging trenches.

Uncle Benny had given Isabella a number to call should any similar event take place. Apparently, he had been a target of the military for decades. Each attempt ended in a similar fashion—yet they kept coming. She called the number, and the Secretary of Internal Affairs answered. Isabella explained who she was and what had just happened.

The Secretary assured her that these were rogue elements and that this would never happen again.

"Your compensation is on its way," he reassured her.

Two days later, the cargo plane arrived. Isabella, Ryan, and the female security detail supervised the transport of the crates from the cave onto the plane. One crate was left behind, containing approximately fifty million dollars. Isabella held this back to cover all local expenses, payments, and purchases.

Before leaving for the Hacienda, Isabella instructed the foreman to increase production and speed up delivery. She had noticed too much lag and reminded the foreman that, should there be any unsatisfactory issues, he would be replaced—and would never see his family again.

Then, they all boarded the Learjet and flew to the Hacienda.

Chapter Forty-Eight
Summit III

POLITICAL POWER

At seventeen years old, Isabella presided over her third Summit. The setting was the same: the old village of Real de Catorce, the simple villagers, and the three-hundred-year-old church, which was the center of life in the community. Father Henriquez, the local priest, enjoyed a cult-like hero status among the villagers. Prosperity, respect, recognition, and economic sustenance were some of the progressions in this tiny mountainous region that he was credited with.

Father Henriquez never doubted that the true benefactor of life in Real de Catorce was Her Highness, Queen Isabella Reyes. During the Summits, security was always tight, and comings and goings in and out of the village were strictly controlled. Village preparations for the Summit were orchestrated by the Church, which assembled the entire village and set about organizing accommodation, supplies, and the logistics required of the locals.

This year, the villagers planned a parade with homemade disguises and local performers to be held in the village square. Children of all ages were encouraged to participate and offer whatever talents they possessed. From being an intimidating, fear-filled, abusive event to an annual village celebration, the Summit had become a total success and had achieved what no politician ever could in such a short time span.

The Summit was a time for togetherness, commerce, fun, and sharing, as the entire village displayed their wares for sale to the visitors. There were smiles on all faces, light-hearted banter, and an eagerness to collaborate with a successful Summit in mind. This was the setting for Isabella's third Summit. She had brought this to the village. She had given hope to the villagers, stopped the abuse of their daughters, educated them, trained them, and given them dignity rarely found in such remote dwellings.

As usual, Ryan and the crew were dispatched one month before the Summit. They set up a campsite in the mountains overlooking the village. This year, the team was equipped with custom-made satellite phones—non-hackable and non-traceable. All movements, including the hawks and larger birds flying around in search of a meal, were scrutinized to detect any deviation from their habitual patterns.

It was said that some rival gangs used birds to carry cameras, and sometimes even explosives attached to their underbellies. When the bird flew over the target area, a sharp electrical jolt would send it spiraling out of control, causing it to fall and trigger the explosive device. Fable or fact, this was no time for debate. The birds were monitored.

Isabella arrived by helicopter one day prior. Her security team consisted of two young women who were habitually assigned to her, as well as a third young woman who had recently graduated from the academy.

Once the pilot dropped off Isabella and her team, the helicopter was flown to a clearing in the mountains near the camp where Ryan was stationed. Ryan's team would secure the helicopter, prevent any interference or sabotage, and ensure a rapid evacuation for Isabella should the need arise.

Just like before, she stayed in the same hotel. She requested the suite on the top floor, with two rooms on either side of her suite. The entire kitchen staff was replaced with chefs and auxiliary staff flown in one month prior. There were no other guests in the hotel. Isabella had sequestered the entire building, from top to bottom.

Despite the fact that the entire village was indebted to Isabella for their current well-being, economic, and social welfare, no one was allowed to approach the hotel under any pretense. Room service staff, laundry staff, reception staff, and all auxiliary personnel had been flown in.

There were four guests on the top floor, while a suite was reserved for Miguel on the second floor—two floors below Isabella.

Miguel was not permitted any attendees. In the hotel dining room, Miguel ate alone. He had requested a meeting with Isabella when he arrived, but she declined. Miguel was history; he was on his own. Isabella did not need to count on his support for anything.

She didn't mean to abandon Miguel, but he had served his purpose. She owned the Haga, the domain, and all the surrounding property where Miguel lived. She was the primary carer for the twins and, most importantly, she owned his vote at the table.

To suggest that Isabella was fond of Miguel in any sentimental way was a gross misunderstanding of the situation. Miguel had been forced onto Isabella in a way that, at first, benefited her father but ultimately benefited Isabella. In a sense, given Miguel's emotional and social aspirations, Isabella bore the burden of his personal security and well-being. The death of his father and his release from the obligations regarding the upbringing of the twins freed Miguel to pursue—without pretense and without judgment—his own chosen path in life.

On the day of the Summit, Isabella woke early to prepare herself. She dressed in light jogging gear and went for a run on the outskirts of the village. Her path led her in the direction of one of the camps higher up in the mountains. Without consciously planning her route, Isabella found herself running up the trail that led even higher. She hadn't requested a security detail to follow her, but she sensed that, some ways back, someone *was* following her.

Thirty minutes later, she was hidden from view in the dense vegetation. The trail became rocky and sometimes faded, but she continued, jumping over dead logs, large rocks, and areas where the path had deteriorated. Still, she ran upward, with no particular objective or destination.

After an hour and thirty minutes, Isabella—running through thick forest—tripped over a dead, rotting log, slid on some loose rocks, and nearly fell forward, grabbing onto a tall tree to break the imminent fall. She held onto the tree, breathing heavily.

"Close call," came a voice a few feet from her.

"Yeah!" she replied. "What are you doing here?"

"Needed the exercise," replied Ryan. "Besides, I missed you."

"Was that you I saw back there?" she asked.

"Hmm, I thought I was in ghost mode. Invisible."

"Smelt you before I heard you—then saw you. Need to sharpen those skills."

Laughing, Ryan kissed Isabella lightly on the cheek and said, "Race you back down."

"Before I kick your ass back down, I need you to do something for me."

"Shoot!"

Isabella outlined a plan she needed Ryan to execute within twelve to twenty-four hours. It needed to be done urgently. Then, without warning, she took off running back down toward the village.

It was a tight finish back to the hotel, with Isabella a nose in front of Ryan. When they burst through the door, they found Miguel sitting alone in the reception area. Feeling a little empathy for him, Isabella walked up to him.

"You okay?" she asked.

"Isa! Yes, yes, I'm fine, thank you. A bit deserted here in the hotel. Nobody around. I brought someone along with me that I would like you to meet."

"Who?" Isabella asked cheekily.

"My partner. His name is Rodri. You will like him."

"You need my permission to bring anyone up here! This is not a vacation camp, not a resort! This is the Summit, Miguel. What got into you? I always have to be near you to think for you. You idiot! It's too late now, anyway. Just make sure he stays in the room, or I will have him shot! You get that?"

Isabella stormed off before Miguel could answer. She ran all the way up the stairs to her room. Breakfast was laid out for her, but she wasn't very hungry. The frustration of having to deal with Miguel's incompetence—and his inexperience of the outside world—took away her appetite.

She felt angry both at Miguel and at herself for insisting on having him present for the Summit. By this time, she didn't need to count on his support. She ate a little, drank orange juice, and then showered.

It was time to head out to the Summit. Isabella instructed one of the girls to escort Miguel down the small road across the village square to the Summit venue. One of the main reasons she retained the hotel accommodation was the tunnels. Her two female security escorts walked the ten-minute route with her to the venue.

She was still dressed in regular clothing. They walked through the maze of tunnels beneath the village until they came to the entrance to the quarters that served as the personal chambers of the Chairman. The two security guards did a quick three-hundred-and-sixty-degree check of the rooms, running electronic devices in search of possible hidden bugs. There were none.

They left Isabella alone to prepare herself for the Summit meeting.

It took approximately an hour before Isabella was satisfied with her appearance. She opened the door to walk through the corridor to the main chamber. The main room. The Summit Chamber. One girl walked in front, and one behind, as the three made their way to the chamber.

The girl in front opened the door, and the Summit clerk called out loudly across the chamber, "All rise!"

As the majority of attendees were from the previous Summit, everybody rose, looked down in front of them, and made no eye contact with Isabella.

She was stunning. She wore a long, floor-length black gown with intricate gold-leaf lacing down the front, back, and sides. The gown had long gold sleeves with black lacing at the ends and at the wrists, paired with a black and gold veil that completely covered her face. Her eye makeup was black; her lipstick was black. She wore gold and silver blush on her cheeks—just enough to bring out the color through the veil. Nobody moved until Isabella took her seat, and the girls "melted" into the background.

Isabella officially opened the Summit by welcoming everybody. Miguel was present and had obeyed Isabella's instructions regarding his partner. He looked straight down in front of him and didn't utter a single word throughout the entire session.

Isabella questioned all the participants on their respective activities: merchandising, transport, market share, and revenue. Each member was handed a leaflet with the name **QIR** on it. Isabella explained that this was her bank and ordered that, as of that moment, they were all instructed to deposit their revenue and all cash holdings with any branch of QIR Bank. There was to be no more cash hoarding, no more offshore banking.

She further advised them that QIR Bank would take a twenty percent commission on all deposits.

Total silence followed—no protests, no arguments, just silent agreement.

Finally, after a marathon four-hour session, Isabella addressed the issue of membership renewal.

"I will call out your number—your number being the seat number you are and have been occupying at this and previous Summits. When I call out your number, please stand.

"Number 3!"

Miguel stood, hands folded in front of him, not daring to look in Isabella's direction.

"Number 3, your seat will be vacated. You are no longer a member of the High Table. Your membership has been revoked by unanimous decision. Your market territory is subordinated to me. *You* are subordinated to me. Your very existence is entirely dependent on my goodwill. You may leave. Please exit silently.

"Number 5. Your territory is subordinated to me directly. You no longer have any influence in this territory. Your membership has been revoked by unanimous decision."

"What unanimous decision? Nobody voted. It says so in the Charter. A vote must be taken, and the result of the vote will stand!"

Isabella raised her hand and directed it to the girl standing behind Seat Number 5. Looking at the girl, she said, "It's okay. Let him speak."

Turning to Seat Number 5, she said, "I own all the votes at the High Table. Or have you forgotten? I can vote whenever I want. All you need to know is that I have voted! Please leave."

"Number 7, 8, 11. Number 12, 13, and 14. Your membership has been revoked and your territory placed under my direct control. Please leave.

"The rest of you—Number 4, 6, 9, 10—your respective memberships have been reduced to auxiliary status. You will maintain your territorial control, but you will submit your planning and organization to me. You will only attend the Summit on special invitation.

"Any questions?"

There were none.

Isabella rose to leave when the Summit Clerk called out, "All rise!"

Isabella retired to her chamber through the corridor. She used the bathroom, poured herself a soda, and sat back on the large, comfortable sofa. Her personal security detail entered the room. When Isabella was dressed in Summit garments, nobody was allowed to address her without permission. The girls bowed their heads and stood with their backs against the wall. Isabella said nothing.

Then the phone rang. It was Ryan.

Isabella raised her hand and dismissed the girls. As soon as the door closed behind them, she answered the call.

"Yes! Is it done? What? Now? Okay, okay, give me a few minutes. Yes, yes, I'm ready. Thirty minutes? Okay, good."

534

She hung up.

An hour later, Isabella headed back to the Summit Chamber, still dressed in her Summit garments, with the veil covering her face.

Seated at the table were the six new members that Isabella had invited to the Black Hole Committee.

Seat Number Three was occupied by Yakamoto Namurata, head of the all-powerful Yamaguchi-gumi family from Japan. The Yamaguchi-gumi is the largest family within the powerful Yakuza gang network in Japan.

Seat Number Five was occupied by Russian *pakhan* Grigori Tatinov. Tatinov was the head of the prison and street Bratva, with close ties to the Russian president. Rumor had it that this was the president's personal hit squad, eliminating all dissent and opposition.

Seat Number Seven held the newest gang element in modern Japan, the loosely organized Tokuryu. They lacked a formal hierarchical structure and mostly operated in lawless, mob-style fashion. Isabella had singled out the largest Tokuryu group to attend the Black Hole Committee as a way to instill some form of structure and quasi-discipline.

Seat Number Eight was for Liu Wun Chun of the Chinese Triad gang.

Seat Eleven was occupied by the Gangster Disciples, and Seat Twelve by the Mungiki Sect from Africa.

Seat Thirteen was occupied by the head of the Cosa Nostra from Sicily, and the final seat, Seat Fourteen, was held by the head of the MS-13 gang from California.

"All rise!"

Nobody moved. The new members stared across at each other—cold, blank, expressionless stares. Their eyes were shifty and untrusting, waiting for the slightest hint to attack whoever or whatever came their way.

"All rise!"

Still, nobody moved.

Then came the forceful electric jolt surging through each seat. Everybody jumped up, cursing in their respective languages, grabbing their backsides, and looking down at the seat they had just occupied. Shock, disbelief, and anger consumed their faces all at once. They shrieked their revulsion at having been shocked so violently when the call came.

"Please remain standing until Her Royal Highness is seated. Thank you!"

Isabella took her seat at the head of the sacred Black Hole Committee.

"Please be seated. Thank you all for coming. We have a very busy agenda to address. I trust that you have all checked your cell phones, pagers, wiretaps, earplugs, and any other electronic device you may have been carrying. I trust that you have all checked in your egos, too. This is a secure environment. Impenetrable from all perspectives."

The Summit Assistant then spoke.

"Her Royal Highness, Queen Isabella, is your host. She has gracefully extended her personal invitation to you all. Should you accept, you will be installed as a permanent member of the Sacred Black Hole Committee. Rules and regulations regarding each of your commitments and behaviors as members are defined in the leaflet in front of you. We have taken the time to translate each leaflet into your personal language. Please study these rules carefully. Any intransigence will not be tolerated. Ever."

The leaflet in question defined the rules and expected disciplinary conduct of each member, irrespective of their ranking within their own organization. Here, they were all equal and at the same level. The only person who outranked them all was Isabella. There would be zero tolerance for any aggression, hostility, violence, repudiation, or arrogance toward Isabella.

Isabella didn't need to unite the new members behind her or request their loyalty and obedience. She merely outlined that QIR Holdings and all its subsidiaries controlled the world's production and supply, as well as all transportation and distribution. Most importantly, QIR Holdings could, at any given time, replace them within their own organizations.

She detailed the operations of each gang—their primary sources of revenue, their methods of control, and, most importantly, how each of their respective activities was linked to QIR Holdings.

When Isabella concluded her presentation of the new member organizations, she showed them a live feed of the scene outside the venue and the surrounding area. There was no security. The villagers were preparing for the usual Summit feast and parade. The subordinates that each gang leader had brought with him were nowhere to be seen. There was no individual security presence outside in the village square.

Outside, the sky was a clear blue, with the occasional bird flying overhead. No gunship-toting helicopters, no agents with dark glasses and earpieces pacing back and forth in front of the building. Just the local villagers chatting and preparing their food stalls, clothing, and trinket stands.

Shock, insecurity, and—for the first time—fear engulfed each member's face.

"You are secure here. Your respective security teams have been moved to Santa Cruz de Carretas, a thirty-minute drive from here. In this village, in this room, *I* am the only security you need. Remember that. Look around you."

The new delegates rapidly looked around the room. Noticing nothing in particular, they all turned to face Isabella. She nodded her head and raised her hand, and the girls from the Female Brigade appeared.

Stunned, the men shifted uncomfortably in their seats.

"Allow me to introduce you to the Female Brigade Elite Force. The deadliest strike force living and breathing. This is no idle boast. They have been trained by Shadow Stalkers. *They* are the shadow. Cross me, cross QIR, and you will never see them coming.

"I believe that all present have a mutually beneficial reason for being here and that all supreme-level international transactions can and will be conducted within these walls, at this table. You are strongly recommended to abide by these regulations, conditions, etiquette, and honor code. There is no second chance. *Honor The Code, and The Code will honor you.*"

"All rise!" said the Chamber Chief.

Everybody stood at attention, facing forward, with no eye contact with Isabella. She left as swiftly as she had entered.

After the second Summit meeting, during which she welcomed the new international delegates, Isabella was exhausted. She sat in her chambers, readying herself to return to the hotel to rest for a moment before greeting the villagers.

Then the phone rang. It was Ryan.

Once again, she dismissed the security with a wave.

"You're kidding me. I just this minute entered my chambers. It was long, a total marathon. You won't believe the issues we had to iron out. Anyway, talk to me."

Ryan talked for a minute when Isabella exclaimed, "Oh no, no, no! Not today. This can wait!"

"They're already here. Let's get all this over with ASAP. I'll be in the meeting with you."

"Give me an hour. I'll be ready."

She hung up, undressed herself, and took a long, cool shower. It was hot outside, and she really needed to cool down, freshen up, and look lively.

When she was done showering, Isabella dressed in a loose-fitting tracksuit. She lay down on the bed in the sleeping quarters of her chamber. She dozed off for what seemed to her like five minutes—but was, in fact, an hour and a half.

One of the girls came into the room to wake her up and help prepare her for the next meeting. This time, Isabella chose a different ensemble. She wore a full black gown—no trimmings, just all black. Her veil was silver and black. Isabella sent the girls to precede her.

She walked into the room. Four men were seated around the table, with one standing up. Around the room, there were six girls, "frozen" and camouflaged within the space. Ryan was the man standing.

"All rise!" came the call from the Summit Clerk.

The four seated men were totally confused and remained seated. Noticing they had not complied, Isabella halted.

Then came the jolt—a high-voltage electrical surge activated in the seats of the four men. It was so sharp that the men were half-propelled, half-jumping into the air.

"All rise!" came the call again.

The men stood to their feet, totally perturbed, cursing and gesticulating.

Isabella halted a second time.

Then came the slaps—four open-palm whacks to the face of each individual from behind, forcing them to turn around, cowering and murmuring in pain. Realizing what was required of them, the men fell silent, remained standing, and turned to face Isabella.

Whack! Then a whisper instructed them not to make eye contact but to focus on the space directly in front of them.

Isabella took her seat.

"Please be seated."

The four men hesitated until they were thrust down into their respective seats.

After a marathon previous session, Isabella wasted no time in addressing the convened men.

"I've seen you on television. You are the opposition presidential candidate for the Mexican presidential elections," she said, addressing one of them directly. "Felipe Juanito Maria Henrique!" said Isabella, clapping her hands in applause.

"You talk too much and yet you say nothing. You open your mouth, and nothing but pig feculence pours out. I'm wondering— do you actually believe the tripe you dribble out? You write that crap out yourself?"

"I, err... I don't know what you mean..."

One of the girls stepped forward, ready to correct his demeanor. Isabella raised her hand, and the girl stepped back.

Felipe nervously turned around, both hands covering his face.

Isabella continued, "Well, I don't like what I hear. I don't like what you represent. I don't like what I see. And I don't like *you!* You have the charm and personality of an ironing board. Nobody is going to vote for you. So, here's what's going to happen:

"You, Felipe Juanito Maria Henrique, will step down. You will no longer be the opposition candidate. You will resign, abandon, quit—or whatever—from the presidential race. You are no longer the candidate. You will disappear."

The Summit Clerk handed him a large envelope.

"Here," said Isabella. "Take this. It is repayment or reimbursement for all your expenses. Take your family on vacation and don't come back until the election is over. Is that clear?"

"No, well... I have invested..."

Whack! Whack! Two sharp slaps across both cheeks.

542

He fell off his chair, howling and screaming obscenities. His mouth was forced open, a cloth shoved into it, a noose placed around his neck, and he was yanked up.

Ryan sat coolly in Seat Number Two, smiling as he watched the girl drag Felipe out of the Summit Chamber. Felipe's face was turning blue from lack of oxygen.

Turning to the second man—much younger than Felipe, early to mid-thirties, well-dressed, articulate, and very good-looking—Isabella said, "Xavi Enrico Lopez! *XL!* I have no doubt that you will excel in the elections and win the presidential election. Felipe's name will be withdrawn from the ballot and your name will replace his.

"You were Felipe's campaign manager. Now, you are the campaigner, and I will provide you with a manager. I will also provide you with personal security and whatever financing you will need. You *will* win this election. And when you do, you come back here—to this very same place—and *pledge!*"

The man, Xavi Lopez, looked directly at Isabella and replied, "Pledge what? I'm not even sure I want this role. Who said I want to be president?"

Whack, whack, whack!

"Lesson number one," said Ryan, "you will *never* make eye contact with Her Majesty.

"Lesson number two, you will *always* address Her Majesty as *Your Royal Highness, Your Majesty,* or *Your Greatness.*

"Number three, you will stand in the presence of Her Royal Highness until told to be seated.

"Number four, you will never, *ever,* question Her Majesty's decisions.

"If you forget any of these rules, you will be instantly executed, and your remains will be fed to the village pig farm.

Are these rules clear to you?"

Xavi nodded his head.

"Look at me and speak up, man," said Ryan.

"Yes, it is clear to me. Please forgive me. Thank you, Your Majesty, for choosing me to run for president. I will obey your every command. I am happy. My family will…"

"That's enough! Sit!" said Ryan.

Ryan nodded his head to the Summit Clerk, who handed Xavi an attaché case filled with U.S. dollar banknotes.

"Take that and use it well," Ryan said to Xavi. "We will issue you more financing as you go along. The two young girls standing behind you and the two young girls standing by the door will be your new personal security. Abuse them, and you abuse us. They will vet all your calls and check and verify your every movement. You are safe with them. Whatever happens, whatever the situation, you will be protected by the Summit. Do you have any questions?"

"No, sir—err, I mean, yes, sir. I have many questions."

"Figure them out yourself," replied Ryan. "We are watching your every move. You will win this election."

"All rise!" the Summit Clerk called out as Isabella rose and left the chamber.

Back at the hotel, Ryan asked Isabella if she was alright. He was worried about her change in demeanor. He had noticed a discoloration on her face; her eyes appeared glazed, and she was silent. That's why he had stepped in and managed the meeting.

"Are you okay, Isa?" he asked, rubbing her shoulders and then pulling her into his arms in a warm embrace.

"Yeah! Fine. I'm okay, thanks. I'm just a little fatigued. I was expecting this encounter tomorrow, but I'm glad it's over. I'll rest, and then we can go home tomorrow."

"Your eyes... they were glazed back there. Seemed like the blood was drained from your face. You sure you're okay?"

"I, er... yeah, something strange came over me. Felt like I was watching myself from within. I was there, but somebody else was there, too, controlling me. I was a bystander; I couldn't move, just observed. Strange feeling. Drained my energy. I need to rest. You go have fun with the village celebrations and partying."

"Are you sure you don't want me to hang around? Put you to bed, watch over you?" he smiled as he said that.

"I'm good. Now go! Let me rest."

Isabella showered after Ryan left and went straight to bed.

Chapter Forty-Nine
Santiago Arturo Hernandez

It was early afternoon when Santiago Arturo Hernandez was released from a federal prison in Central Florida. He was granted parole based on "exemplary" behavior.

Santiago Arturo had been incarcerated more than a decade ago for violent aggression, assault with a deadly weapon, carrying a concealed weapon, armed robbery, and a host of misdemeanors. The more serious charges of murder and homicide were rejected by the jury, as the prosecution failed to prove that Santiago Arturo had delivered the fatal blows that killed the two victims.

The events of that day—almost twelve years ago to the day—centered on an inconspicuous, red-bricked, run-down townhouse on the corner of a semi-abandoned area in a forgotten neighborhood. When the county decided to rehouse the inhabitants due to the imminent danger posed by the derelict houses, which threatened to collapse on their tenants, the new mayor upheld at least one of her campaign promises: to tear down the dilapidated, uninhabitable district and move the residents to more secure accommodations.

The more "secure" accommodations consisted of high-rise apartment blocks with appropriate facilities and amenities nearby. Schools were built, strip malls opened, and community parks developed within the vicinity.

The effect of this transfer of livelihood from a nearly century-old neighborhood to a new, modern community center was twofold. First, it provided fresh impetus to a desperately impoverished community that had felt abandoned by the system and entrenched in profound misery, with the hope of any form of humane integration into society feeling completely lost.

Second, the delay in tearing down these death traps—not only due to the imminent threat of collapse but also because of the dampness and mold that could cause immeasurable health complications—invited a different kind of danger. The drug industry moved into these empty buildings faster than the previous occupants were able to move out. In some instances, tenants were relocated to their new subsidized accommodations by the very drug lords commandeering their former homes.

The result was that crime moved in, and poverty moved out.

One such instance was the strategic move into a red-brick house that provided a nearly 270-degree street view. The only "blind spot" was the rear, which was attached to adjoining structures. This was easily resolved by placing cameras on the rooftop to cover the back.

One afternoon, almost twelve years ago to the day, three men approached the front door of the red-brick house, appearing to make a purchase. A fourth man—Santiago Arturo—crept along the roof toward the front entrance. Two men were guarding the entrance, though they appeared to be just two young men casually conversing. These were the runners; any potential purchase order would be conveyed through them. They would then ring the intercom and pass on the order.

The intriguing part: there was no actual door—just an intercom.

As Santiago Arturo's three accomplices approached, the two runners stopped talking and eyed them suspiciously. Suddenly and swiftly, the runners were tasered and collapsed, moaning on the ground. One of them was shot in the head at close range. The other was helped to his feet, forced to place an order via the intercom, then immediately shot in the head.

Meanwhile, Santiago Arturo lay flat on the roof, waiting. From an opening in the rooftop, a head emerged from inside the building to drop the order—tied to a rope—down to the front entrance. But he never got that far. Santiago Arturo yanked him out of the opening and threw him down. The man fell headfirst, smashing his skull on the pavement below. He was immediately shot again to ensure he was dead.

Two grenade explosions at the front entrance blew a substantial hole in the bricked-up doorway, leading to a large open-space room.

548

Inside were three more men with submachine guns who opened fire on the intruders. One of the intruders was fatally hit.

Santiago Arturo fired from his rooftop position, killing one and injuring another. The third occupant fled into a backroom, firing wildly as he ran. Santiago Arturo's accomplices chased after him, unloading hundreds of rounds as they advanced. The man was eventually struck by several armor-piercing rounds, killing him instantly.

Descending from the rooftop, Santiago Arturo approached the injured occupant and demanded to know where the product was stashed. The man explained there wasn't much product—this was just a "side-show." The main operation involved counting, stacking, registering, and preparing money for transport.

It was a money-counting operation.

There were three counting machines and huge piles of dollar bills scattered across the room. *Bingo!* thought Santiago Arturo as he glanced around and began stuffing dollar bills anywhere he could—into his clothes, pockets, wherever space allowed.

The three men finally gathered all the money they could carry and began to flee, fully aware that they had stirred up a hornet's nest.

"Get down! Get down! Hands in the air and get down on your knees!" came a voice from a megaphone. "Flat on the ground! Hands behind your head! Do not move a muscle. If you move, you will be shot right where you are!"

Santiago Arturo and his co-conspirators complied without resistance, fearing the wrath of the S.W.A.T. team that surrounded them.

The three were arrested and held without bail in a county jail. After a two-year deferment, the two accomplices were sentenced to death by lethal injection.

Santiago Arturo, however, negotiated a plea deal. He was charged with homicide with mitigating circumstances—meaning that he fired the fatal shot in self-preservation. The defense argued he fired only to protect himself, as the occupants had opened fire first. He was also charged with carrying a concealed weapon and possessing a deadly weapon without a legal permit.

Why was Santiago Arturo offered a plea deal and not the others?

The answer is hard to pin down, but the prevailing account is that Santiago Arturo had previously provided—and would continue to provide—intelligence on senior cartel personnel.

And so it was that Santiago Arturo came to be housed in a federal penitentiary in Central Florida.

After several years in the general population—working shifts as a toilet and shower cleaner, yard cleaner, and laundry worker—Santiago Arturo was nominated as librarian. The push came from above and was met with skepticism from his fellow inmates. But he prevailed, and soon he earned the nickname *Bookworm.* "Book" because he distributed books to his fellow inmates from the prison library, and "worm" because he had "wormed" his way into the position.

But he was harmless, very rarely in conflict with anyone, and eventually became tolerated—if not liked—by his peers.

Santiago Arturo didn't particularly care for the nickname *Bookworm*, which he recognized as an insult to his genius for survival. That's what he was. That's who he is:

Mike Horn, the survivor.

Chapter Fifty
Deseo De Muerte

The Death Wish

During one of his rounds distributing books in prison as the prison librarian, Santiago Arturo met El Asquerosa—The Disgusting Hyena. El Asquerosa had been in solitary confinement for almost fifteen years, exercising alone in the yard when all other inmates were in their cells and only interacting with the prison guards and the librarian.

"So, *Cabron,* you are the new librarian." It was not a question, more of a mocking statement. "Do you know what happened to the last *Cabron* librarian? His heart ceased to beat! Do you know why his heart ceased to beat, *Cabron?* Because I tore it out of his chest while he was standing right where you are standing right now! Do you know why?"

Santiago Arturo stood motionless, not uttering a sound. He had heard of The Hyena, and he had heard of hyenas in the wild. They don't kill their prey before feasting—they feast on their quarry while it is still alive. Tearing into the flesh, a mouthful at a time, incapacitating the prey, eating while the prey is alive and feeling the excruciating pain, and eventually dying from immense loss of blood and missing vital organs.

Was this why this inmate got the nickname? Was it because he fed on his victims, attacking their organs without killing them at the onset? Santiago Arturo was spellbound. He stood motionless. No eye contact, staring at the floor, listening.

"I spare your heart, but maybe I take your lungs!" El Asquerosa continued, absolutely loving the effect he had on Santiago Arturo.

"I want you to recommend a good book each week—the best you can find and one that I have not read before. If you bring me a stupid book, like science fiction, for example—I hate science fiction—if you bring me a science fiction book, I'll rip out your kidneys and give them to the hospital for organ donation. What do you recommend for today, huh, *Cabron*?"

"Harry Potter!" said Santiago Arturo.

"I see you think that you don't need your kidneys. Think you can survive without your kidneys, huh, *Cabron?* You didn't understand what I just told you! *Harry Potter* is science fiction!"

"*Harry Potter!*" repeated Santiago Arturo. "You will like it. Here is the first book. I highly recommend it for you. Please take it! If you don't like it, I will give you my lungs and my kidneys next time I come!"

"You have *cojones, Cabron.* I will call you *Cojones Cabron!*"

Santiago Arturo left the book for El Asquerosa and continued his rounds.

A week later, he returned, standing at the entrance of El Asquerosa's cell. This time, he didn't wait to be asked. Planting his feet firmly, he met the inmate's gaze without wavering.

"I recommend *Harry Potter: The Sequel* for you this week."

There was no response, just silence on the part of El Asquerosa.

Then, a loud and raucous guffaw as The Hyena applauded, clapping his hands hard and loud, laughing with his mouth but never with his eyes or his heart.

"I like him! And the girl—she's good. Yes, I like him, *Harry Cabron Potter.* Bring me all the books until I finish the story. I am *SLYTHERIN, The Snake!* Maybe in the next book, they will make *Harry Potter* a *HYENA!*"

After that incident, Santiago Arturo and El Asquerosa became friends—or as much as one could define friendship in such an environment.

In prison, to be friends with someone meant not having to defend yourself against them. The more appropriate term would be "favorable." You do me a favor, I'll repay the favor or credit your account. I owe you.

One evening, when all inmates were in their cells preparing for lockdown, a prison guard instructed Santiago Arturo to exit his cell and follow him to the yard. El Asquerosa was already there, exercising—running back and forth and doing push-ups. He beckoned Santiago Arturo over, and the two sat down on a bench.

"You attempted to rob the downtown red-brick house in Centerville, Macon, Georgia. You shot five men but got away with it. Two of your friends are in Atlanta maximum security while you are here in Central Florida. *The Librarian!* You cut a deal with the Feds, this I know. Saved your ass from death row. I know everything I want to and need to know about you. You are a *RAT! A RODENT! A WORM!* No spine, just creeping where it is warm and damp! Right here, right now, I could rip your tongue out, then stick my hand down your throat and rip out your intestines. But you humor me. I owe you for *Harry Cabron Potter.* Good call."

He said the last part, patting Santiago Arturo on the back really hard.

"Good call, my friend. Now, I will repay the favor. You see, *Cabron,* up to this point, I spared you. I know your case since day one. Since the first minute you stepped into my domain. You are the librarian here because I told the warden to make you librarian. I wanted to see you face to face. I wanted to eat you alive so that you could watch yourself die. But, you succeeded in humoring me.

"Do you know who you robbed, *Cabron?* ME! You robbed me, MY HOUSE. Killed my people. One of those *cabeza hueca* was my nephew. You killed my nephew, my sister's son. But you have no sister. Or I would rip her uterus out from her ass. But you have no sister. Maybe a nephew, but he will be of value later.

555

"You will be released soon. This is what I want from you.

"I was the biggest, most important producer, distributor, manufacturer, banker in all of Latin America. Number one! You understand me, Number one! Untouchable—until young *mofetas* sold me out. Stole from me and branched out on their own. They formed a union—today, a CARTEL—and divided the territory amongst themselves. With *my* money! *My* success!

"That is why I am here today. They took pictures, voice recordings on their *telefono móvil* and gave it to their DEA *putas*. I was kidnapped from my home while I was sleeping, with my wife next to me—taken, you hear me, taken to be tried in the U.S. My wife was shot because she fought like a tigress—scratching, pulling, and fisting until they shot her. My children are with their grandmother. Changed their names, birthdates, everything, so that they can be free of me. I accept this.

"Now, my time has come, and YOU, *Cojones Cabron,* will serve me because you owe me. You will serve as my *ángel de la venganza,* my *deseo de muerte.*"

"How?" asked Santiago Arturo. "How do you know that I will be granted parole and released?"

"The Warden, the head of the Parole Board—these are my people. After *Harry Cabron Potter,* I knew that you were the one and that you were ready. So, I told them to release you on parole."

"Okay," said Santiago hesitantly. "What do you have in mind?"

556

"Simple—take back my Empire!"

"How?"

"Follow my instructions. Screw me, and you know what I will do to you—and all the people you know. Even the bus driver—if she says 'hello,' she will fall with you. Everybody, Cabron! Everybody! You understand me?"

"Okay, I accept. Tell me what you want me to do."

It was early afternoon, one of those central Florida days with no clouds in the sky. The sun was fiery, beating down with a vengeance. Temperatures were in the hundreds, and humidity was equally high. Was this one of those NASA-observed solar flares or a geomagnetic storm? It certainly felt that way—like the storm was happening directly over Central Florida.

Dressed all in white, Santiago Arturo walked out of prison to a car stationed in the public parking lot. There were no buses, motorcycles, or any other cars around—just the one. As he approached the vehicle, a hand shot out and passed him a pair of gold-rimmed sunglasses. No words were spoken as Santiago got into the passenger seat.

"Seatbelt, Cabron!"

Santiago dutifully obliged, and the car drove off.

Before leaving prison, Santiago had one last face-to-face with El Asquerosa. He trembled as he entered the cell, which was more like an apartment, with imitation Versace sofas and a large flat-screen television. Santiago stood, waiting to be invited to sit, but was left standing as The Hyena spoke. He had his back to Santiago and didn't turn around when he began.

"Your mission, Jim Cabron, should you choose to accept it. But know this: if you don't accept it, I will eat you alive, rip out your insides while you still breathe. You must start a fucking war between the motherfucking cartels. Bring 'em all down here to this prison, where I will feast on their cojones. You hear me, Cabron?"

The Hyena turned around and faced Santiago, his mouth frothing as he repeated, "You hear me, Cabron?"

"Yes! Yes! Jefe! I hear you!"

"Now fuck off and earn the air you breathe before I take it away!"

In fact, Santiago had two missions: start a war between the cartels and infiltrate the DEA to supply El Jefe with the name of the agent who killed his wife as she fought to protect her children—El Jefe's children.

He was assigned a twenty-four-hour escort to ensure he focused solely on his mission. This was a suicide mission. A death wish.

During the ride from prison into the city, Santiago couldn't help but smile to himself. He *was* the DEA agent who had broken into The Hyena's house, looking for incriminating evidence, and had unintentionally killed his wife. It was an undercover bust gone wrong.

Still undercover, the DEA arranged for him to go to prison to infiltrate The Hyena's network. Armed with intel from the DEA, Santiago traveled to Laredo, Texas, to reassemble The Hyena Cartel. Fresh out of prison and carrying specific orders from the boss, he was confident he could muster enough support to rekindle cross-border activity.

News of El Asqueroso's wishes had preceded Santiago, and when he arrived in Laredo, The Hyena Cartel was already awaiting his arrival. THC—The Hyena Cartel—was fired up, and gang members quickly resumed their previous roles.

Santiago's escort never left him alone for a minute. He was constantly accompanied and followed wherever he went.

The establishment of QIR Bank in Laredo raised a few eyebrows among THC. Questions were asked, and investigations ensued. When THC went underground after the arrest of El Asqueroso, the local bank in Laredo filed for Chapter 11 under the protection of its creditors. THC lost whatever deposits they had with the bank.

Now that they were back in business, they demanded their funds. However, QIR Bank was not responsible for their losses. This proved to be the bone of contention that set both parties—QIR Bank and THC—on a confrontational course.

Furthermore, across the border in Coahuila and Nuevo León, THC was claiming territorial rights and exerting its influence in the area.

Back at the Hacienda, Isabella had heard of THC's emerging presence. It was she who had orchestrated the trap that led to El Asqueroso's arrest. She had prior knowledge of the DEA sting and the raid on his family residence and had assisted in having him captured.

Isabella knew exactly who Santiago was and who he worked for. Now, he was becoming a thorn in her side. He had to be eliminated. She had a plan.

Isabella and Ryan flew to Central Florida to visit the federal high-security prison that housed El Asqueroso. They sat patiently behind the thick glass that separated prisoners from their visitors.

El Asqueroso walked in, his hands chained in front of him and leg irons restricting his pace. He shuffled into the room, took one look at Isabella and Ryan, then turned around and asked the guard to take him back to his cell.

"Guard! Guard! I don't know who these people are. She's not my daughter, not my family. I want to go back. I have nothing to say to them."

Before the guard could escort him out of the visitor's room, Isabella said two words: "Harry Potter."

"What did you say?" asked El Asqueroso, turning back slowly to face Isabella and Ryan.

Isabella nodded and indicated for him to sit and take the intercom handset.

"What did you say? Who are you?"

"Do I have your attention?" mocked Isabella, an amused look on her face.

"How do you know about Harry Potter?" asked El Asqueroso.

"I know everything that goes on here in this prison. I know everything about you. It is *me* who put you behind bars and in this particular prison—far away from THC and Laredo."

"What do you want? Do you know why they call me The Hyena?"

"Are you done? You give yourself too much importance, El Mosquito. Irritating noise around my ear. One slap and you're gone. Now shut up and listen.

"Santiago Arturo—the prisoner who gave you Harry Potter books, the one recently discharged from this prison, whom you sent to Laredo to avenge your family murder? Well, he is a DEA agent. He is the one who killed your family. It was a botched raid—crossfire—and your family were collateral damage.

"You let him slip right through your fingers, right here in this prison. His role was to infiltrate your inner circle, dig up intel on you, and take over your cartel. I'm here to do you a favor. I'm here to pass on this valuable piece of information to you. Capiche?"

"What do you want in exchange?"

"Nothing. I take what I want, when I want, and where I want. You and THC are insignificant to me. Take care of Santiago Arturo.

THC will report to me directly. I own the whole region. The whole country.

"You? You get to stay alive and live well—with a new television, Netflix, a private toilet and shower, and conjugal meetings once a week. Good life, considering where you are. Cross me, and I'll crisscross you!"

"Hah ha ha! Bravo! Who's the mosquito making silly noises by my ear now? Huh? Who? You are nothing but a little whore! I, *The Hyena*, will eat you alive—*you* and your whole family! Then I will eat every single member of the DEA that attacked my family.

"You served me well—bringing me this useless information that I already knew! You see, Santiago's mission is to provide me with all the names of the DEA operating in the entire region—all the way up to the man who gave the order to strike my family home.

"When I'm done with them all, I will cut off the arms, the legs, and his dick, then leave him alive like a helpless jellyfish washed up on the shore. *Capiche?*"

Isabella smiled and hung up the handset. She stood and nodded at the guard standing behind The Hyena, ready to take him back to his cell.

The Hyena turned around, and the blood drained from his face as he realized that, all along, the prison guard had been standing right behind him in the room. Isabella's nod was the signal to eliminate The Hyena. His arrogance was his undoing.

Isabella left the visitor's room, and Ryan followed her out.

Overpowering THC in open warfare using the intel that Santiago enjoyed from the DEA would prove costly in human lives and attract too much attention. This would jeopardize the relatively smooth and hindrance-free border crossing, as it would prompt an unwanted, temporary concentration of troops in the area.

At the time, Isabella was focused on transporting excess cash reserves to the QIR banking group.

"How do you want to handle Santiago?" asked Ryan.

"We need to move discreetly. No need to attract unwanted attention. Choose two of our most trusted agents from the Female Brigade and have them infiltrate Santiago and THC. I need to know his every move. I need access to all the electronic devices he communicates with. Finally, we need to hack into the DEA server from his device and obtain a list of all the agents operating throughout the region. This will keep us a step ahead."

"I'm on it."

This was the diplomatic option that Isabella deemed viable and best for business. She had plans for QIR Bank to expand further north into San Antonio, Waco, Dallas, and Houston, and she wanted this expansion to occur as smoothly as possible.

They flew back to the Hacienda and then drove north to McAllen, Texas. Isabella was missing school and her friends.

Chapter Fifty-One
the Kidnapping

When Isabella and Ryan arrived back in McAllen, Texas, they watched as news outlets reported on the unfolding story of the recent kidnapping of Rory Hollington and his nineteen-year-old girlfriend, Tyler Muster.

Rory Hollington was the twenty-year-old son of the Speaker of the House of Representatives. He and Tyler had been hiking when they stopped overnight in Falcon Estates. The next day, the two young hikers ventured to Falcon Lake for an afternoon of water skiing.

Horsing around and unaware that they had strayed deep into Mexico, Rory and Tyler suddenly found themselves surrounded by several speedboats and jet skis. The motorboat pulling them on their water skis was boarded by two masked men armed with AK-47 assault rifles. The ropes were cut, and they fell helplessly into the water as the jet skis roared around them in circles, creating waves and turbulence. Finally, they were plucked from the water, taken aboard one of the boats, and driven to shore deep inside Mexico.

Once on shore, hoods were placed over their heads, and they were driven for two hours along dusty roads until they reached a small, rundown peasant farm. They were then transported from the windowless van into a barn. Tyler cried and screamed for help, and each time, she was met with a sadistic laugh and a rough slap across her face. Rory was kicked repeatedly from behind and violently ushered forward.

When the hoods were removed, Rory and Tyler found themselves in an underground bunker that had clearly housed hostages before. There was a single bed with no cover, chains on the wall, and a bucket that reeked of urine and excrement. There were no windows or air vents. All they could see was a metal ladder fixed into the wall, leading up into the barn.

They heard nothing. Tyler screamed for help, but to no avail. She cried until her tears dried up and she could no longer utter a sound. Exhausted, she collapsed into Rory's arms, and the two lay down on the dirty single bed.

They were tired, afraid for their lives, homesick, and hungry. Fear kept them awake most of the night, but in the end, fatigue overcame them, and they fell asleep.

Tyler and Rory's disappearance played on national networks over and over again. The Speaker of the House, Paula Hollington, appeared on television, pleading for the safe return of her son and his young girlfriend. Rewards were offered. The FBI got involved.

They swarmed the area, suffocating all movement on the U.S. side of the border.

Entry in and out of the United States—along the entire border, all the way down to the Gulf of Mexico—was restricted. This was bad for business.

Isabella took it upon herself to intervene. The two agents from the Female Brigade were already in place, but no contact had been initiated—too dangerous, too risky, and their lives were at stake.

Ryan assembled the crew, and they were dropped by stealth helicopter across the border in Nuevo León. They had assets and a safe house in the area. Communication was strictly via satellite phone.

Isabella was the communication fulcrum. She received and disseminated intel regarding Santiago Hernandez and his gang members to the crew. The rules of engagement were simple: secure the hostages and eliminate all hostiles—at whatever cost.

At extremely high risk to her own safety and security, Maria Magda, one of the agents sent to infiltrate THC, called Isabella from a public phone booth. She claimed that while out drinking and partying with the boys, she had overheard talk of a huge jackpot that would bring the American beasts to their knees. They were showing off, boasting that they would all be issued Green Cards to work legally in the United States.

One of the boys, who was completely drunk, bragged that he had been part of the team that kidnapped the two young Americans. He even joked that once he received his Green Card, he would join the Marines and come back to shoot all his friends for smuggling. They shot him dead, but not before he whispered to Maria Magda where the two Americans were being held. She passed this intel on to Isabella.

The area was vast, and searching for an old abandoned farmhouse would be like looking for water in the desert. Jacinta, the other agent from the Female Brigade, had cozied up to the gang leader. He appeared to be in direct contact with a superior.

The two women only pretended to drink the large amounts of alcohol offered, secretly spilling it on the floor or into plastic bottles they emptied when "going to the ladies." As a result, while everyone else was staggering and intoxicated, Jacinta and Maria Magda remained lucid. They planted a tracking app on the leader's phone while he was passed out and immediately activated it.

The next morning, the leader received orders to regroup at the farmhouse. Ryan and the crew received the first ping at 10 a.m.

Hungover, the gang—including Jacinta and Maria Magda—drove off in a convoy of three all-terrain vehicles. Jacinta, faking a hangover, rested her head on the leader's shoulder as he drove. After hours of driving on dusty backroads, they came upon a rusty, half-hanging metal gate. There was no fence, just the two sides of the gate attached to poles on either side. Jacinta was literally pushed out of the vehicle to open the gate.

They drove up to the farmhouse, which appeared totally deserted. There was no movement, no sign of life, no animals—just the sound of the dry wind rustling up dust as they approached. They waited for almost ten minutes in the vehicle, not moving, when men appeared from the rooftops of the barn and the main house and indicated for them to disembark.

Ryan and the crew decided to wait a couple of hours before following. They tracked the zigzagging of the convoy from a distance, always maintaining a time gap—never approaching closer than two hours behind.

When the convoy arrived at the farmhouse, Ryan and the crew were almost four hours away. Ryan assumed that the movements of the convoy would be monitored and verified for pursuit.

Two hours from the target, Ryan and the crew set up base. Before leaving Nuevo León, Ryan had passed a list of necessities to their local asset. Those supplies were now being delivered as they set up the base.

From the base, Ryan sent out a three-man unit to observe all movements, assess numbers, and, if possible, locate where the targets were being held. Backup was arranged two hours from the base. The backup team included medical support, air evacuation, and heavy artillery.

Back in McAllen, Isabella instructed the school to organize a field trip to Washington, D.C., for the tenth graders. The trip included a visit to the White House and Capitol Hill, where she insisted the school schedule a meeting with lawmakers.

From McAllen, the students flew to Washington, D.C., by private jet—arranged by Isabella—to Dulles International Airport. It was a three-hour flight, and the students were excited to visit the nation's capital and explore its historical buildings and institutions.

They were immediately bused to the White House from the airport for an exclusive visit. After a two-hour tour, Isabella and her fellow tenth graders were driven to Capitol Hill. This was the focal point, the centerpiece of the nation's legislative branch. The students were taken through all the public areas but were not allowed to take any pictures.

Once inside the building, Isabella instructed the teacher accompanying them to show them the office of the Speaker of the House of Representatives. However, they were informed that this area was highly restricted and that public visits were not allowed. Isabella insisted that the students only wanted to offer their support and encouragement to Ms. Harrington regarding the kidnapping of her son. The Secret Service duty officer promised to pass on their sentiments to Ms. Harrington.

At the door, as Isabella and the students were about to leave, Ms. Harrington appeared and approached the group.

"Thank you for your kind support. This is a truly trying time for me and my family, and I just wanted to thank you all, personally, for your kind words and well wishes."

One by one, the students turned and hugged Ms. Harrington before leaving. When it was Isabella's turn, she hugged the Speaker. As she released her, she dropped a burner phone into her side pocket without the Speaker even noticing. Isabella held the Speaker's hands, looked at her, and said, "My sincere regard is with you and your family. It will all work out. He'll come back to you safe and sound. Trust in God."

"Thank you so much," said Ms. Harrington, with tears in her eyes.

Isabella and her fellow students spent two days in Washington before heading back to McAllen, Texas.

Three men climbed down the metal ladder fixed to the wall of the bunker. When they descended, they chained Rory to the wall. The hoods and blindfolds had been removed from both of them. This was a bad sign.

One of the men punched Rory repeatedly in the abdomen, ribs, and kidneys. He collapsed, crying and curling himself into a fetal position. They then chained him to the wall.

The men then focused on Tyler. They ripped her clothes off and took turns raping and beating her. They slapped her across the face violently and punched her in the belly and rib cage to break her resistance. She lay on the dirty bed, unable to move, unable to scream, or even cry. She blanked out, staring unblinkingly at the ceiling.

The rape and beatings had been going on for three days straight. Rory had repeatedly soiled himself, as had Tyler. The men simply threw buckets of cold water on her to wash off the urine and excrement and continued to violate her.

Ms. Harrington heard a phone ring, but she didn't recognize the ringtone and dismissed the call. However, the call was persistent, and the ringtone was disturbing, so Ms. Harrington searched around her office for the source. It was coming from her blazer pocket. She removed the phone and answered the call.

"Hello," she said nervously. "Did you lose your phone or forget it here in the building?" she asked, assuming it may belong to one of the students.

"Shut up and listen!" came the distorted voice.

"We have located the whereabouts of your son. A rescue operation is underway. We will bring him home to you. You must not inform anyone—not even your husband—of this conversation. You must not make any televised announcements. You must not inform any of the agencies. This is a secure line. You, and only YOU, must answer this phone when it rings. It will ring three times. I will hang up and then ring again. Answer on the third ring. Is this clear to you?"

"Who are you? What have you done with my son? What do you want? Money, I can get—"

"Shut up! You have not paid attention to anything I've just said. Do you want to see your son again? Answer yes or no!"

"Yes! Yes, please, yes!"

"Shut up! Answer yes or no. No commentary. You must listen to the instructions and follow them if you want to see your son again. Understood?"

"Yes!"

"Good. Now go home and wait for my call. No comment, no discussion, no explanation to anybody. Is that clear?"

"Yes!"

"Good. Your son will be home within twenty-four hours. When he is delivered home, you will NOT make any televised appearances. No comments! No explanations! Clear?"

"Yes!"

The phone clicked off before Ms. Harrington could say her last "yes."

Isabella called Ryan next. "Hey! ETA extraction?" she asked.

"We have eyes on Casino. No eyes on Jackpot. We're good to go."

"Secure the girls, please. Come back safe!"

"Hoo-Rah!"

The entire crew was in place, completely surrounding the farmhouse. Advanced recon had established that there were twenty-five gang members holed up at the farmhouse. Some were in the surrounding brush, with the majority in the farmhouse and barn.

Ryan took Brandon with him while Scott and Dave approached the back of the barn stealthily. Camouflaged like the mesquite terrain, Ryan and Brandon, armed with sniper rifles fitted with silencers, eliminated the perimeter security. They counted seven down. Brandon waited, scouring the area in case they had missed one or two.

Ryan joined Scott and Dave behind the barn. There, sitting on a stool, was a sentry smoking what looked like marijuana. He was history. The wood constituting the barn walls was so decayed that Scott was able to peer inside. There, sitting at a table playing amateur poker, were five sentries.

Ryan, Scott, and Dave lined up three sentries in their respective sights. Splat—three down. Before the other two realized what had happened, they were down.

Carefully cracking open a hole in the barn's back wall, the three crew members entered. They located a metal manhole on the floor. Silently, Ryan and Scott descended while Dave kept cover.

Not even the worst atrocities they had witnessed and experienced in Afghanistan had prepared them for what they encountered below. Scott threw up; Ryan had to gag his mouth with his shirt and turn away for a second before proceeding.

Lying naked on the dirty single bed was Tyler. She was covered in blood and excrement. Her two front teeth were missing. Her hair was matted with dirt and dried blood. Dried excrement covered her entire body. There were black marks all over her rib cage, back, kidney area, and inside her thighs. There were cuts all over her hands, legs, abdomen, and backside. She had two black eyes, swollen shut.

Ryan tore off his shirt and covered her. He lifted her over his shoulder and climbed the metal ladder.

Rory was in a similar condition. Both eyes were swollen shut, with cuts on his head that had been shaved bald by something not very sharp. Both his legs were broken, and he had bruises all over his body. His baby toes had both been cut off. Scott picked him up and carried him over his shoulder.

In the barn, Ryan and Scott found two blankets and covered Rory and Tyler. Rory regained consciousness and asked for Tyler.

"You're safe, buddy. You're safe. We're taking you home. Tyler is right here. Hang in there, buddy. Hang in there," said Scott.

Tyler remained unconscious. They held their position in the barn, calling for backup from Dave and the other crew members.

"Pie, come in. Pie in the Sky, ears to the wind?" Ryan called on his satellite phone.

"Pie in the Sky? That's a new one! Yes, I'm all ears," called back Isabella from McAllen.

"Casino isolated, not secured. Slot machine one secured, three sevens and Jackpot. Slot machine two secured, one seven. Touch and go!"

"EVAC initiated. Stand by! Did you locate the roulette tables?"

"No stand by—immediate EVAC. Air support requested. Repeat: air support requested. Casino not yet secured. No eyes on roulette tables. Will secure."

"Eagles on their way. Secure roulette tables. Vital! Out!" said Isabella.

She called the base and instructed the team to launch an all-out heavy assault on the farmhouse. The rules of engagement were simple: no prisoners. Extraction of the two targets and the two undercover female agents was indispensable.

Having secured the two young Americans, Ryan, Scott, and the crew returned to the main house to eliminate the remainder of the gang.

Jacinda walked out, wanting fresh air, when Ryan grabbed her and spun her around so she could recognize him. He then thrust an automatic pistol into her hand and sent her back in. He followed closely behind. She indicated where the leader lay still asleep while she sought out Maria Magda.

The whole operation lasted only a few minutes. The majority of the gang were still asleep in their beds and were blindsided by Jacinda and Maria Magda's actions.

Back at the base, two doctors intervened on Rory and Tyler simultaneously. Tyler was placed in a deep coma, with her chances of recovery very slim. Rory was cleaned up, treated, and placed under observation. His condition was not life-threatening, but it was critical. His body needed rest, nutrition, and healing. He could not be moved.

The next day, a specially transformed mobile ambulance picked Rory up from the base medical unit and transported him to the Hacienda. There, he was cared for by the field medical staff assembled by Isabella and Rosella.

Once Rory was safely settled in his new surroundings, Isabella picked up the phone to deliver the news to his mother.

After the third ring, Ms. Harrington answered meekly, "Hello!"

"Hi, Mom," Rory replied, his voice weak.

There was a loud shriek, then a crash as Ms. Harrington screamed in shock and passed out. Isabella hung up and told Rory they would call back in thirty minutes.

True to her word, thirty minutes later, Isabella dialed Ms. Harrington's number once more. This time, the call was answered almost immediately.

"Hello, Rory? It's Mom. Are you okay?"

"Hi, Mom. Yeah, it's me. I'm so sorry, Mom. I'm so sorry . . ." said Rory as he wept loudly and uncontrollably over the phone.

Isabella gently took the satellite phone from his hand and spoke to Ms. Harrington.

"Ms. Speaker?"

"Yes?"

"Your boy is safe. He was in bad condition. We couldn't bring him home to you in that state. We'll bring him home tomorrow. Remember my instructions: no interviews, no information, no discussion. Thank the Mexican policemen if you must. That's all. Here, talk to your boy—and be brief."

"Mom, I'm really, really sorry about everything. It all happened so fast. Mom, please, Dad, I'm sorry. I want to come home. I want to come home," Rory wept again. Tears poured down his face, wetting the bedsheets.

"You have nothing to be sorry about. Just come home, and we'll talk about everything. I love you, Rory, oh so much. Just come home."

"Mom, I'm sorry about Tyler. She didn't make it."

At that point, Isabella grabbed the phone and hung up. She told him to get some rest, as he would need it for the journey home the next day.

Tyler, for her part, was airlifted to a special off-grid hospital deep in the Arizona Mountains, near the San Carlos Reservation. There was a monastery close by. Tyler was placed in an induced coma to allow her body to heal. There was far too much internal damage.

Rory was told that Tyler had not made it out of the farmhouse to prevent constant questions and family intervention. It was Ms. Harrington who was tasked with informing Tyler's family that she had not survived. However, Isabella left the door open by telling Ms. Harrington that Tyler's body had not been found, and that it could have been moved prior to the rescue assault. If it was any comfort to the family, there was no proof of life—but there was no proof of death, either. The family lived in hope.

Six months later, the doctors awakened Tyler from her coma. Her internal organs had healed steadily, she was breathing on her own, and her body fluids were flowing correctly. Tyler's recovery was a miracle. The intensive care provided by the doctors and their staff, twenty-four-seven, no doubt played a huge part in her healing.

Here she was—eyes open for the first time. From that moment, her physical progress was rapid. She was able to eat and begin physical therapy.

Three months later, Tyler was transferred to the monastery. It was built of stone—big, heavy stones placed one on top of the other. There were nuns everywhere in blue and white habits, doing everything from cooking to cleaning to laundry to endlessly praying. One woman, however, didn't wear a habit but was always praying alongside the nuns.

Tyler could walk unassisted, so when they arrived at the monastery, she immediately stepped out of the vehicle and admired the setting and the buildings.

A tall blonde woman appeared and walked straight up to her, offering her hand.

"Allow me to introduce myself. My name is Abigail Jenkins. Please, call me Abby. I own and run this institution. Come, let me look at you. Well, I must say—you're not much older than my own daughter. Her name is Isabella. I call her Bella. You must be starving after that long drive. Come, let's get you something to nibble on."

This was Abby's calling. She had shunned city life, shunned her family, and even shunned her beloved daughter to hide out in this monastery—offering help and rehabilitation to broken women. Just like she had once been.

Chapter Fifty-Two
Summit IV

When Isabella and Ryan returned from the Hacienda, they Isabella moved into the mansion she had appropriated from Jack Browser following their golf challenge.

It was a huge estate, situated in the wealthy, exclusive suburbs of McAllen, Texas. The mansion was too spacious for two people alone, so Isabella invited Corella and Raul to move in with them. With Gabby and Mathilda still in camp and Stefanie moving in with her boyfriend, Isabella saw no need to remain in the old neighborhood.

The mansion had a two-floor basement. On the second floor, Jack Browser had parked his luxury car collection. Isabella and Ryan chose a 1952 Dodge pickup and a 1967 Mustang for their personal use. Corella and Raul chose a 1968 Cadillac DeVille. The car collection was impressive.

Once settled in their new abode, Isabella and Ryan crisscrossed Mexico, Colombia, and the United States—managing, controlling, and directing trade, production, delivery, and transportation. Supply routes were never repeated due to the high risk of sabotage.

Married at sixteen—at least spiritually and emotionally—Isabella was still visibly on a honeymoon high one year later. At seventeen, the only change in their intimate relationship was that they officially shared the same bed. Ryan still revered Isabella, bowing his head when entering a room or when others were present.

For her part, Isabella was still enrolled in school. Her academic participation was conducted virtually; she carried her laptop everywhere, always finding time to complete coursework and submit assignments electronically. Whenever she was stateside, she attended classes in person.

Isabella's business ventures were growing tenfold. The entire Mexican peninsula was owned or controlled by QIR interests. All production came from Colombia, Bolivia, Peru, Ecuador, and Venezuela—where Isabella and QIR directly owned and managed operations. In addition to cultivating coca plantations, Isabella also controlled crude oil production in Venezuela and Mexico. In Mexico, oil operations were handed to her by the newly elected president, Xavi Lopez.

As part of a broader strategy, she authorized the remaining Sicario brothers to increase illegal border crossings from Mexico to the United States tenfold. She subsidized the costs for families wanting to cross into the U.S.

In the Gulf of Mexico, twenty miles off Matamoros, QIR Holdings retained exclusive oil drilling rights. Oil rigs were being moved into place, and drilling would begin as soon as setup was complete. Plans were underway to expand the city of Matamoros to more than three times its current size. Labor and technical expertise would be drawn from both the U.S. and Mexico. Xavi was dispatched to Washington to negotiate the convention in good faith. The town was projected to grow into a medium-to-large city.

QIR Bank was the sole institution financing the oil exploration, as well as the construction in and around the expanding city. Plans included new schools, accommodations, libraries, widened streets, malls, sports centers, and factories.

With attention fixed on Matamoros' expansion, Isabella and Ryan discreetly began tunnel construction under McAllen. At any given time, deep in the underground basement, QIR Bank vaults held close to two billion U.S. dollars in banknotes—a figure that continued to rise exponentially year after year.

Along the border in northern Mexico—in Coahuila, Chihuahua, and all the way up to Sonora—Isabella established pharmaceutical companies. Their mission was to mass-produce opioids under strict medical regulations, effectively suffocating small, uncontrolled producers. Isabella oversaw all aspects: production, preparation, transportation, routes, and distribution. She also maintained complete control over the financial side. Nothing escaped her watchful eye. In her entourage, there were no second-time offenders—first-time offenders were dealt with swiftly. No exceptions.

On the educational front, Isabella and QIR Holdings owned roughly ten thousand hectares of land northwest of Edinburg, where she planned to build three schools. Closest to the town would be a preschool for over one hundred children. Next, she planned a primary school attached to a junior high school. A little farther away would be a senior high school and a college.

Surrounding what she called *Education City* would be a museum, a vast library, a complete sports center, and outdoor sports fields. *Education City* would be the first of its kind in the world. The current high school she attended would be demolished, and apartment blocks for single parents would be built in its place.

While Isabella and Ryan were en route to North Korea, she contacted the Korean leader and requested a sit-down. All he wanted to know was how many delegates to prepare for. Two: Isabella and Ryan.

When they arrived, they were met at Pyongyang International Airport by his sister and daughter. Back at the presidential palace, Kim DeYoung On welcomed them in the stateroom, where formal discussions with heads of state typically occurred.

A formal state dinner followed, with the room filled with generals and high-ranking military officials. The discussions were polite and vague, carefully avoiding anything that might disconcert their host.

When formalities concluded, Kim DeYoung On, his sister, and his second daughter gathered in the family room for informal talks. It was during these exchanges that Isabella raised her concerns about escalating tensions between North and South Korea.

President Kim laid out his demands plainly. Isabella, in turn, allayed his fears, promising nothing but vowing to return if her requests were ignored. President Kim laughed at her suggestions, then invited her to return whenever she pleased.

In a firm but cheerful tone, Isabella requested that he stop threatening the South with military rhetoric. She also demanded an end to long-range missile testing in the sea. She encouraged dialogue between the two nations and offered to sponsor any détente between President Kim and the Western world.

She handed him a flyer with the date, time, and location of the next summit. His seat was assured, and he would be welcomed under Isabella's full protection. President Kim showed the flyer to his sister, and the two laughed out loud before walking out of the room.

The next day, Isabella and Ryan were on their way back to the Hacienda.

The couple stayed at the Hacienda for a week. Rosaria was instructed to prepare the twins and Josefina for travel. They were leaving indefinitely to live in the big mansion with Isabella, Ryan, Corella, and Raul. Rosaria would be joining them, too, with her primary responsibilities being the care and welfare of Josefina and the twins.

While she was at the Hacienda, Rosaria supervised the loading and transportation of ten pallets of U.S. dollar bills. They were to be transported to QIR Bank in San Antonio, the newly designated headquarters of QIR Bank. QIR Holdings would remain in McAllen.

Three months before the summit, Gabby and Mathilda graduated from the academy. Mathilda excelled in almost every discipline and was commissioned as a sergeant upon graduation. Gabby was commissioned as a corporal. Isabella ordered them to be integrated into her personal security detail immediately.

There were now four girls from the Female Brigade, as well as Ryan. Isabella didn't need such a substantial security presence, but she wanted her friends with her at all times. Not only did she trust them with her life, but she also wanted to have fun and enjoy a little girl talk. She missed that.

The mansion was so spacious, with a multitude of rooms and facilities, that the two extra girls were no imposition. Meals were full and noisy, and Isabella loved it. Her life was almost complete. She was surrounded by her husband, her twins, and her best friends—Josefina, Corella, and Raul. She longed for her mother to be present among them, but that was impossible for the moment.

The Sacred Black Hole Summit was fast approaching. Isabella had sent Mexican President Xavi Lopez to New York for a United Nations Emergency General Assembly conference. The conference had been called by the rotating speaker of the General Assembly to discuss the Middle East conflict.

President Lopez assembled all the leading Mexican journalists and held a press conference. He strongly reiterated that Mexico was attending the conference as a powerful, influential nation and would make bold recommendations to the UN Assembly. Mexico was now an equal partner in world affairs and no longer a bystander. He hailed Mexico and its people as the leaders of what he called the New Populist Front for World Peace. As he put it, Mexico did not need a sword to neutralize the bull—only strong arms to wrestle it into submission without fear. He invited the press to accompany him to New York and report on his proactive mission.

The fact of the matter was that Isabella had dispatched Xavi Lopez to New York to deliver invitations to certain nations she had chosen to attend the summit. It was Isabella's idea to create the fanfare and press buzz. She wanted this young, good-looking, articulate man to garner all the international attention he could muster. With the entire international press focusing on President Lopez, other prominent world leaders would seek him out to share the limelight.

The plan worked. At first, there was a joint interview with the Chinese leader, Chairman Hu Wan. Then came an invitation to participate in a group interview with several leaders, including Europeans—most notably French President Marie Pennaté. During this group debate, the center of attention was President Xavi Lopez, who conducted himself admirably.

Then, the floodgates opened. Every leader, major or minor, wanted to be seen talking to or photographed with him. This "New Kid on the Block" phenomenon didn't go unnoticed by the host nation's president. U.S. President Camilla Harold sought out President Lopez for a face-to-face debate on border issues and bilateral economic trade agreements.

The expedition to New York was a total success. Xavi Lopez was the card up Isabella's sleeve, and she played it well. Xavi was able to distribute the invitations and then publicly declare that she had invited several leaders from the world's principal economies to attend a new format: G11.

Having sought his publicity and wanting to share in his limelight—as they did—all invited leaders publicly praised the initiative and boldly accepted the invitation.

With the invitations issued and the acceptances secured, Isabella instructed Ryan to dispatch the Female Brigade graduates, the crew, and auxiliaries to Real de Catorce under Scott's command. Ryan and Scott divided all personnel into squads of five, with each squad nominating a team leader who reported directly to them.

New, specially designed, unhackable satellite phones were issued to each team, with strict instructions on their use. The teams were stationed across San Luis Potosí: Estación Catorce, Santa Cruz Carretas, Los Catorce, El Potrero, Las Es, La Pila, and in and around Real de Catorce. The entire area was secured by the presence of the QIR Elite Forces. They established bases and patrolled the skies using highly sophisticated radar devices.

Seven months later, the Sacred Black Hole Summit was convened under the pretense of the new G11 economic summit. Since there was no aircraft landing strip in Real de Catorce, every leader arrived by helicopter. Scheduling landing times was a logistical nightmare. By this time, Ryan was present and had assumed command of all troops. Each leader arrived with their own heavily armed security detail.

The worst logistical challenge came with the arrival of the President of the United States. President Camilla Harold was preceded by a team of Secret Service agents seven days in advance. Scott and the team had to remain invisible and undetectable. Movement was strictly limited and only allowed under urgent circumstances.

To remain undetected during these conditions, Ryan ordered the villagers to create a small distraction—just enough to provoke a response from the Secret Service. President Harold was accompanied by several business leaders seeking to negotiate lucrative trade deals with the attending nations, along with a team of economic negotiators.

These auxiliary attendants were informed that all private bilateral negotiations would be carried out within the walls of the church. Only the leaders would be allowed access to the Summit Chamber—no one else. No security agents, Secret Service, or private bodyguards were allowed in. However, each security team was permitted to occupy a strategic area of their choosing, both in and around the village, including the village square.

Xavi Lopez was the first to arrive, smiling and waving—though to no one in particular. There was no press. The press was banned from entering the restricted area, which was monitored and controlled by the QIR Elite Force. These elite agents were highly trained for all situations, ranging from kidnapping and airplane hijacking to bomb disposal, rapid intervention, search and rescue, and close protection.

During the summit, they were required to operate in stealth or shadow mode. There were no villagers to wave to, as they had been instructed to remain inside their homes. Nonetheless, Xavi walked boldly to the Summit Headquarters, accompanied only by his personal secretary. Perhaps he hadn't noticed the empty streets or the absence of media coverage—yet he smiled and waved. As the host nation's representative, he wanted to be the first to welcome all the other delegates.

It took nearly an hour for the U.S. President to arrive. She had waited for the Russian President to arrive first, while he, in turn, had waited for her to arrive before him. The cat-and-mouse game was finally resolved when word reached both presidents that the Summit would begin without them. Still, the "game of checkers" was won by U.S. President Camilla Harold, who arrived ten minutes after Russian President Boris Karpov.

When each president entered the Summit Headquarters, Mathilda and Gabby met them at the entrance. They were then escorted to their respective seats. The seating was assigned as follows:

Seat 3. United States – President Camilla Harold

Seat 4. United Kingdom – Prime Minister Harry Mounthampton

Seat 5. Germany – Chancellor Wilfried Gunther

Seat 6. France – President Marie Pennaté

Seat 7. People's Republic of China – Chairman Hu Wan

Seat 8. Brazil – President Rodrigo Philippe Dos Sciementos

Seat 9. Japan – Prime Minister Sakamoto Hashimoto

Seat 10. Russia – President Boris Karpov

Seat 11. People's Republic of South Korea – Yo-chan Park

Seat 12. Canada – Prime Minister Justin Mulrooney

Seat 13. Mexico – El Presidenté Jefe Xavi Enrico Lopez

Seat Two was unavailable, as it was occupied by Ryan when he was present.

Once everyone was seated and cordial introductions were exchanged, discussions began. A loud murmur of voices filled the room—conversations directed across the table at adversaries, side discussions between neighboring delegates. Accusations were made, fingers pointed, and voices raised.

President Camilla Harold of the United States was in a heated dispute with Russian President Boris Karpov. She accused him of energy blackmail and went as far as to call him the architect of the Russian mob. Karpov responded by accusing the United States of state-sponsored terrorism and global interference.

South Korea pointed fingers at China, accusing it of proxy state terrorism through its heavy influence on North Korea. The North had attempted to intimidate the South by floating garbage across the border and testing long-range warheads capable of reaching Seoul within minutes. In response, Seoul floated balloons with loud pop music and dropped CDs containing South Korean TV shows and movies.

The hum of rising tension was abruptly cut short when the Summit Clerk called, "All rise."

Suddenly, the noise ceased, and all eyes turned as Isabella entered the Summit Chamber. She wore a white, full-length gown adorned with delicate gold embroidery—the most beautiful of all her gowns. Her head and face were covered by a thin gold lace veil. Gold heels added to her height.

At seventeen, Isabella appeared every bit a grown woman. The aura she exuded upon entering the room was enough to silence the squabbling and debates that had filled the chamber. The Clerk didn't need to call for order. Isabella was simply splendid—magnificent beyond comparison, truly sublime. Everyone in the room stood to welcome her.

She took her seat gracefully. Only then did the Summit Clerk say, "Please be seated." All eyes remained fixed on Isabella as she spoke.

"Welcome," she said. "Thank you for accepting my invitation to this Summit. You are all first-time attendees, with the exception of Xavi Lopez. It is my great pleasure to welcome you all. Look around; each of you has been chosen for a specific reason. This is the most important of all meetings and the foremost decision-making Summit. It is the most significant of all debates—the ultimate diplomatic solution to any situation, grievance, or dispute. All will be resolved here. The recommendations made by this committee will be binding. They will be the laws by which each and every one of you and your respective nations will abide. This is the Supreme Black Hole Council, and you are all members! Once again, welcome."

The first to speak was Russian President Boris Karpov.

"Who are you again? How old are you anyway? Shouldn't you be in school somewhere?"

Whack!

It came from behind—a sharp, open-palm smack to the side of his head, right over the ear. The force and sound of the slap rang through President Karpov's head, leaving him dazed and unstable. His head fell forward. It took a couple of minutes for him to regain his composure and process what had just happened.

Shadow Stalker Mathilda had delivered the slap. None of the leaders seated around the table witnessed the motion or follow-through. Silence fell upon the Chamber.

The Summit Clerk stepped forward and spoke.

"Please respect the rules and regulations of the Chamber. These rules are set out in the leaflet in front of you. Please take the next few minutes to review these regulations to avoid a similar incident."

He then stepped back into the shadows of the Chamber.

Isabella continued.

"There is a serious crisis in Africa. Migrants are fleeing poverty and persecution in their nations, seeking economic refuge in Europe. We must address this now. This is the first topic on our agenda. I will pass the debate to the French, German, and UK delegates to share their concerns and possible solutions."

The discussion came alive. There was constructive debate, proposals, and back-and-forth exchanges. Even nations not directly affected by the issue offered their opinions.

Next on the agenda was the East China Sea dispute over the Senkaku/Diaoyu Islands. Though tensions were slightly reduced, no compromises were reached by either side.

Many issues centered on global security. Economic matters, such as energy production and distribution, were also a major focus. Mexico accused the United States of undermining its oil production and sales in order to block exports to China—Mexico's largest oil trading partner. Mexican oil production was, of course, Isabella's oil production and distribution.

Trade routes, tariffs, quotas, and illegal immigration were among the most heated and vocal debates. Isabella allowed the delegates to break into smaller discussion groups before calling the Summit back to order.

After a marathon five-hour session, Isabella raised her hand. The Summit Clerk stepped forward from the shadows and spoke.

"Silence! Please be silent. Her Majesty Queen Isabella will speak."

Murmurs echoed across the room:

"What? Queen who? Queen of what? Queen from where?"

"Silence!"

Isabella lifted her veil, revealing her milk-complexioned face. She wore black eyeliner and blue eyeshadow that enhanced her deep, sparkling blue eyes. A dusting of red blush made her appear mature beyond her tender sixteen years of age.

What happened next stunned all the delegates. Mathilda and Gabby stepped from the shadows of the Chamber to stand immediately behind Isabella. Her right arm twitched, and then her fingers curled into a fist. She shivered. Mathilda stepped forward and covered her face with the veil.

Isabella's face contorted. Her eyes glazed over, shifting from blue to green, and she froze. Her arms stretched out in front of her, trembling. She began making strange noises, repeatedly clearing her throat. Then, she laughed—an eerie, mocking sound that unsettled everyone in the room.

Abruptly, she stood and pointed a finger at each delegate individually. Then, she threw off her veil, slammed her fist on the table, and jerked her head backward, staring up at the ceiling. Her head snapped forward again, as though yanked by an invisible force.

Isabella was not afraid. She was experiencing the most aggressive out-of-body event to date, and she welcomed it. She watched from within, fully aware of the possession taking place. Father Tomaso had coached her on what to expect and how to remain composed. And she did.

This time, Isabella relinquished only partial control of her body, allowing Coatlicue to take over. She stood willingly, amused, confident that she could return and reclaim control at any moment. She wanted this—welcomed it—and embraced the power it brought.

When they were one like this, Isabella was elated. Between her and Coatlicue, they were unstoppable. She wasn't necessarily a thrill-seeker, but she reveled in the exhilaration of channeling the celestial power of the deities.

Coatlicue spoke.

"The Senkaku/Diaoyu Islands will become independent from the disputing states. In North Africa, the nations will unite to build economic infrastructures within the migrant nations. You will contribute to the development of these countries—creating employment and well-being to prevent the population from seeking livelihoods elsewhere.

"In Haiti, the United States, Canada, and Mexico will join forces and send troops to combat the wanton violence controlled by street gangs. You will restore law and order under the current leadership."

U.S. President Camilla Harold objected.

"We are not sending our troops to a country that fosters and promotes murder, torture, drug trafficking, and lawlessness. We have no vested interest in developing that economy. It's beyond restoration."

Coatlicue responded.

"The United States has fought many wars away from its shores without any direct threat to its own national security. Wars fought purely for economic and financial benefit. You have intervened directly and used proxy nations to fight your battles. You've sold your intelligence-gathering capabilities to favorable nations in exchange for boots on the ground.

"Haitians need help. Outside intervention. You will provide this help—or we will thwart your every move on the global front. The United States will lead the ground intervention to eliminate the thugs and street gangs in Haiti."

When President Harold attempted to interrupt, she was gently tapped on the shoulder from behind and firmly instructed to be silent.

Coatlicue continued:

"All nations will be granted statehood. No nation will depend on an invasive power for economic, political, social, or security livelihood—unless specifically requested by that nation. There will be no surrogate nation-states."

For every topic discussed at the Summit—whether by bilateral concern or geographical influence—Coatlicue addressed the issues and issued directives. There was no room for discussion or interpretation. Her instructions were direct, final, and unambiguous.

After the slap to his head, the Russian President offered no further objections. On the contrary, Hu Wan objected vigorously to the self-determination order issued for the Diaoyu Islands, as did the Japanese for the Senkaku Islands in the East China Sea.

Isabella—now Coatlicue—had been seated while delivering the directives. Suddenly, she stood.

She pointed at Hu Wan, then at Sakamoto Hashimoto, and spoke in a hoarse, raspy voice:

"I am Coatlicue. Wife of Teteoh Innan."

As she said the name *Teteoh Innan*, she pointed at Seat Number Two—Ryan's seat.

She continued:

"I am the goddess of life and childbirth. I am the mother of all gods and goddesses. I gave birth to the moon and the stars—and to Huitzilopochtli, the god of the sun and of war!

You will respect me. You will follow me."

She cleared her throat and said in a firm, commanding voice:

"Cross me, and I will cancel you. Remember this forever. I am your Goddess."

www.ingramcontent.com/pod-product-compliance
Lightning Source LLC
Chambersburg PA
CBHW061129120626
46546CB00005B/1712